AYER

The Arguments of
the Philosophers

EDITOR: TED HONDERICH

Professor of Philosophy, University College, London

The purpose of this series is to provide a contemporary assessment and history of the entire course of philosophical thought. Each book constitutes a detailed, critical introduction to the work of a philosopher of major influence and significance.

Already published in the series

AYER

John Foster

Fellow of Brasenose College, Oxford

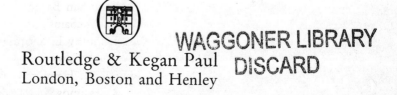

Routledge & Kegan Paul
London, Boston and Henley

First published in 1985
by Routledge & Kegan Paul plc

14 Leicester Square, London WC2H 7PH, England

9 Park Street, Boston, Mass. 02108, USA

Broadway House, Newtown Road,
Henley on Thames, Oxon RG9 1EN, England

Set in Garamond, 10 on 12pt
by Input Typesetting, London
and printed in Great Britain
by Thetford Press

Library of Congress Cataloging in Publication Data

Foster, John, 1941–

Ayer.
(The Arguments of the philosophers)
Bibliography: p.
Includes index.
1. Ayer, A. J. (Alfred Jules), 1910–
I. Title. II. Series.
B1618.A94F67   1985   192   85–1829

ISBN 0–7102–0602–X

To my mother

Contents

CONTENTS

Preface

Alfred Jules Ayer was born on 29 October 1910 and still flourishes. From 1946 to 1959 he was Grote Professor of Mind and Logic in the University of London and from 1959 to 1978 Wykeham Professor of Logic in the University of Oxford. Among his many honours, he is a Fellow of the British Academy, an honorary member of the American Academy of Arts and Sciences, and Chevalier of the Légion d'Honneur. And in 1970, in recognition of his enormous contribution to philosophy, he was knighted. About his life and academic career I shall say no more. I would only mention that his own autobiography (*Part of My Life*) provides a delightfully revealing account of the first thirty-five years, and I gather that this will shortly have a sequel covering the period 1946–63.

Ayer's philosophical writings to date include fourteen books (not to mention those he has edited) and a host of essays, articles, and reviews more numerous than I should care to count. The quality of this work is beyond dispute. The breadth of vision, the clarity of thought, the ease and elegance of style, the bold, incisive arguments, the searching appraisal of fashionable doctrine, and, above all, his peculiar genius for getting to the core of a problem and setting the issues in the right perspective – all these characteristics make his writings the model of how philosophy should be done. This mastery of philosophical technique and the sheer extent of his contribution to such a wide range of topics assure Ayer a place among the major philosophers of the century. He is widely acknowledged to be the most distinguished British philosopher of his generation; and, among twentieth-century British philosophers, he would arguably rank second only to Russell.

A high regard for Ayer's philosophical achievements does not, of course, commit one to endorsing his philosophical views. And I do not myself share the radically empiricist outlook which he inherited from

Russell and the members of the Vienna Circle, and which from the beginning has dominated his whole philosophy. In certain respects, admittedly, I am as empiricist as Ayer. I share his fondness for a sense-datum account of perception (indeed, without his reservations about its status as an objectively true theory); and, with certain qualifications, I think he is right to accord sense-data, and their organization at the phenomenal level, a foundational role in our knowledge and understanding of the physical world. But I have considerably less sympathy than he with the view that all our concepts are derived from experience; and I am hostile to the doctrine, which pervades so much of his work, that a statement must be (in principle) empirically verifiable if it is to have factual significance. In these respects, I am in fundamental disagreement with Ayer; and, as a result, there are a number of important issues on which I incline to a more rationalist or more 'metaphysical' position than he would countenance. Although my aims are not primarily polemical, these points of disagreement will inevitably surface in the course of my discussion.

The discussion divides into three parts, each of which can be read (more or less) independently of the others. The first part, entitled 'Meaning and Verification', deals with Ayer's earliest work – mainly his book *Language, Truth and Logic* – in which he first sets out the fundamentals of his empiricist approach. This is only a small fragment of Ayer's total output and I think it falls short of the stature of his later writings. But in view of the great interest it aroused and the influence it exerted, and because his subsequent philosophy can be seen as a development from this early position, it seemed appropriate to examine it in some detail. The second part, entitled 'Knowledge and Scepticism', focuses on that field of inquiry – the theory of knowledge – which has, over the greater part of his philosophical life, formed Ayer's predominant concern and in which he has, in my view, produced his most valuable and creative work. The central topic, in this area, is our (supposed) knowledge of the physical world, and Ayer's main objective is to show how this knowledge, together with the distinctive concepts it employs, is founded on and secured by the character of our sensory experience. The pursuit of this objective, especially in relation to what he terms the 'construction of the physical world', reveals Ayer at the height of his powers, and displaying an artistry and virtuosity which it would be hard to surpass. The third part, entitled 'Man and Nature', is more diverse than the other two, ranging from topics in the philosophy of science (e.g. induction, causation, and the character of natural law) to topics in the philosophy of mind (e.g. the relationship between mind and body, personal identity, and free will). Despite this diversity, the topics in the different areas are closely connected, and I have organized my discussion in such a way that the examination of one topic always leads naturally into the examination of the next. A further common factor to emerge is that, in each case, we find Ayer defending a broadly Humean position, in conformity with his general empiricist outlook. As in the second part, my discussion of these topics is not restricted to any particular period in Ayer's philosophical development, though, in most cases, his later work (especially that in the late nineteen-sixties and early seventies) is given more prominence.

With such a quantity of material to consider, I have had to be selective, and I am all too conscious of the valuable work which I have passed over and the important issues which I have not pursued. Whether I have made the best selection will be for others to judge. But I have tried to bring out the general character of Ayer's philosophy, while providing a fairly detailed study of most of his major concerns.

If I have had to be selective, it is also true that there is more material available now than when I was writing my book. In particular, Ayer has just brought out a new volume, *Freedom and Morality and Other Essays* (Oxford, 1984), and both the title essay and the one on causal priority have not been published before. These two essays are relevant to some of the issues I discuss (notably in the section on ethics in Part I and in the sections on causation and free will in Part III), and, while their influence on my discussion would have been no more than marginal, I think that, given the opportunity, I would probably have made some reference to them.

For all I know, there may be other important works in preparation. Certainly there is no indication that Ayer is about to retire from the philosophical arena, and given his temperament and current vigour, I think he is more likely to look to his laurels than to rest on them. There is some risk, then, that in (say) ten years time, my book will need to be retitled *Ayer: the Early and Middle Periods*, or, echoing his autobiography, *Ayer: Part of his Philosophical Life*. But if this is the only respect in which his future work will prove my discussion of him to be deficient, I shall be more than content.

July, 1984

John Foster
Brasenose College
Oxford

Acknowledgments

In Part III I have included, with only minor changes, a large portion of my paper 'Induction, Explanation and Natural Necessity', which appeared in the *Proceedings of the Aristotelian Society* 1982–3, and I am grateful to the Editor of the Society for allowing me to reproduce this material here. I am also grateful to Brasenose College for granting me leave of absence in Michaelmas term 1983 and Hilary term 1984; it was during this sabbatical period that the bulk of the book was written. On a more personal level, I would like to thank Ted Honderich, the Editor of the Series, for his helpful comments on an earlier draft, and Howard Robinson for valuable discussions on a number of issues. Finally, I would like to offer special thanks to my wife for her help and encouragement throughout.

Bibliographical Note

In citing passages from Ayer's books, I have used the following editions and abbreviations (the date when the book was originally published is given in brackets at the end of each entry).

Language, Truth and Logic (LTL), 2nd edition (with additional introduction), Victor Gollancz, 1946 (1936).
The Foundations of Empirical Knowledge (FEK), St Martin's Library, 1964 (1940).
Philosophical Essays (PE), Macmillan, 1954 (1954).
The Problem of Knowledge (PK), Pelican, 1956 (1956).
Logical Positivism (LP), ed. Ayer, The Free Press of Glencoe, 1959 (1959).
The Concept of a Person and Other Essays (CP), Macmillan, 1963 (1963).
The Origins of Pragmatism (OP), Macmillan, 1968 (1968).
Metaphysics and Common Sense (MCS), Macmillan, 1969 (1969).
Probability and Evidence (PAE), Macmillan, 1972 (1972).
The Central Questions of Philosophy (CQ), Pelican, 1976 (1973).
Hume (H), Oxford, 1980 (1980).
Philosophy in the Twentieth Century (PTC), Weidenfeld & Nicolson, 1982 (1982).

This is not a complete list of Ayer's books up to 1982. It does not include *British Empirical Philosophers* (ed. with R. Winch, Routledge & Kegan Paul, 1952) or *Russell* (Fontana, 1972), neither of which I mention in my text. Nor does it include *Russell and Moore: The Analytical Heritage* (Macmillan, 1971), which I mention, but without citing any passages.

In 1979, Macmillan published a Festschrift for Ayer entitled *Perception and Identity*, edited by G. F. Macdonald. The final section of this book, headed *Replies*, contains Ayer's comments on the essays presented to him, and it is under this title that I shall make references to it in my text.

Part I

Meaning and Verification

1 *The criterion of significance*

Even if Ayer had written nothing except *Language, Truth and Logic* (*LTL*), he would have achieved an enduring place in the history of philosophy. The book was finished by the summer of 1935 and published in January of the following year. Ayer was only twenty-four when he completed it and it had taken him just eighteen months to write. It was, as Ayer himself put it some ten years later,[1] 'in every sense a young man's book', radical in approach, bold and uncompromising in tone, and displaying an astonishing assurance that the issues which had taxed the minds of philosophers for centuries could be resolved at a stroke. The views it espouses are of a strongly empiricist kind, in the tradition of Hume and Russell, and reflect the positivist outlook of the Vienna Circle, whose meetings Ayer attended in the winter of 1932–3. With hindsight, it is easy to detect faults in the arguments; and, in my view, the central thesis itself is misconceived. But I cannot think of a philosophical work which is more stimulating and challenging, or in which a systematic position is expounded with greater clarity and vigour. Whatever its failings, the book is the very paradigm of a *tour de force*. It is not surprising that it became an international best-seller and exerted so strong an influence both on the subsequent development of analytical philosophy and on the intellectual climate of our age.

Its central thesis is that any genuine proposition must be either a tautology or empirically verifiable. In Ayer's terminology, a proposition is said to be a tautology if and only if it is 'analytic', and it is said to be analytic if and only if 'its validity depends solely on the definitions of the symbols it contains' (*LTL*, 78). Ayer's wording here is a bit loose; for, strictly speaking, it is sentences, not the propositions they express, which contain symbols. But I shall leave the discussion of this point till the next section. Because their validity (i.e. their truth) depends only on

1

their meaning, and not on how things are 'in the world', Ayer holds that analytic propositions are devoid of factual content: they make no claim about matters of fact. Consequently, he sometimes abbreviates the central thesis to the bare assertion that any factual proposition must be empirically verifiable.

Where a sentence (or, to allow for cases of context-dependence, an utterance of a sentence by a person at a time) is genuinely assertoric, but fails to express a genuine proposition, it is said by Ayer to be 'nonsensical' or to be 'devoid of literal significance'. So yet another way in which he formulates the central thesis is as a criterion of sentential significance: a sentence has literal significance if and only if it expresses something which is either tautologous (analytic) or empirically verifiable. Of course, Ayer recognizes that an assertoric sentence which is denied literal significance by this criterion may still have meaning in some broader sense, in contrast with specimens of total gibberish, such as 'fannish please virtue an', which are wholly unintelligible. Indeed, if this were not so, the criterion would have no interesting application. For its application is only interesting when we can understand the sentence in question sufficiently to identify, as Ayer puts it, a 'putative' proposition which it expresses and can then consider whether this putative proposition qualifies as genuine in either of the ways (i.e. its being tautologous or its being empirically verifiable) which Ayer allows. The whole point of the criterion is to expose forms of nonsense which, unlike the gibberish, are not explicit – forms which might pass unnoticed but for the criterion. The distinctive feature of sentences which lack literal significance in Ayer's sense is not that they are wholly unintelligible (though some of them will be), but that, while assertoric, they are not semantically equipped to say anything true or false; and it is in this sense that they fail to express genuine propositions. This point is more clearly expressed in his later *Introduction*, which appeared with the second edition of the book in 1946.[2]

It should be noted that in speaking of the 'putative' proposition which a sentence expresses, or, as he alternatively puts it, the proposition which a sentence 'purports to express', Ayer is speaking figuratively. For where a sentence fails to express a genuine proposition, there is not really something which could be described as the proposition it purports to express or the spurious proposition it succeeds in expressing. On this point, as we shall see, Ayer tries to tighten up his terminology when he re-expresses his position in the *Introduction*. Nor is this the only respect in which, in the original text, Ayer's terminology is loose. We have already mentioned his speaking of propositions as containing symbols. In line with this, he also sometimes speaks as if not only sentences and sentence-utterances, but also propositions, or putative propositions, are to be classified as either significant or nonsensical. This does not, I think, reflect any confusion in his thought or leave his meaning unclear.

Ayer uses his criterion of significance to dispose, in the most summary fashion, of much of what passes (or at the time of his writing passed) as genuine philosophy. He claims that many of the assertions made by philosophers are shown to be nonsensical, being neither tautologies nor empirically verifiable, and that many of the questions which have formed the traditional subject-matter of philosophy are shown to be pseudo-questions, since they demand nonsensical answers. He is particularly concerned to expose as nonsensical the suggestion that there is, or may be, a reality transcending the empirical world of ordinary observation and scientific theory. Thus the assertion that the empirical world is really an illusion concealing an underlying reality of some quite different character, the assertion that the core of a material object is an in-itself-featureless substance in which the object's empirical properties inhere, the assertion that a person's experiences are the acts or states of an immaterial substantival ego, and the assertion that there is a realm of objective values, to be discerned by some faculty of moral intuition, are all dismissed as nonsensical (devoid of literal significance) – as assertions which purport to say something factual, about the nature of reality, but fail to achieve factual significance because they are unverifiable. In claiming that such assertions are nonsensical, Ayer is claiming that they do not express genuine propositions and, consequently, are neither true nor false. Thus in Ayer's view it would be a mistake to reject these assertions by asserting their negations; for if the assertions are neither true nor false, so are their negations. In this way, the very questions which these assertions are attempting to answer, such as whether the empirical world is real or illusory and whether material objects contain a featureless substance, are dismissed as spurious. It is not the business of philosophy to look into these questions, since there are no significant answers to be found.

Ayer describes the philosophical assertions and questions which his criterion eliminates as 'metaphysical'. Indeed, he explicitly defines a 'metaphysical sentence' as one which 'purports to express a genuine proposition, but does, in fact, express neither a tautology nor an empirical hypothesis' (LTL, 41), so that a sentence only qualifies as metaphysical if it fails to satisfy the criterion. Whether or not this definition accords with ordinary usage is a question of no importance. What matters is that, in Ayer's view, the criterion condemns as nonsensical much of what has traditionally gone under the title of 'metaphysics' and that, in Ayer's view, the criterion is correct. Thus the only important issues are whether the criterion really is correct and whether it really does condemn what Ayer thinks it condemns.

Although Ayer intends his criterion to serve as a corrective for philosophy, he does not intend it, at least to the same degree, to serve as a corrective for common sense. Indeed, as we shall see, one of the arguments he offers in defence of the criterion is that it yields intuitively acceptable results in cases where there is no philosophical issue at stake. The trouble, however, as Ayer himself recognizes, is that many of our non-philosophical assertions, made in the context of ordinary discourse or scientific theory, appear, on the surface, to involve metaphysical commitments of the kind he is seeking to eliminate. Thus ethical and arithmetical assertions seem, in their different ways, to make factual claims of a radically non-empirical kind; and assertions about the remote past or about the mental states of other persons, while they concern the character of the empirical world, seem to be beyond the reach of adequate verification. Even assertions about the current state of one's physical environment, such as 'there is a table in this room', are problematic. For if, as Ayer accepts, the immediate data of sense-perception are purely phenomenal entities, whose *esse* is *percipi*, it seems that, in trying to characterize what lies beyond the perceptual data, such assertions are unverifiable. Ayer's response is to try to save the threatened assertions by philosophical analysis – by arguing that once we have understood what the assertions really mean, we can see that they are not condemned by the criterion. How this result is achieved varies considerably from case to case. When he deals with ostensibly empirical assertions, such as those about the physical world, the past, and other minds, Ayer's analysis takes the form of a reduction: the problematic sentences are shown to be empirically verifiable by their equivalence to sentences about the (potentially) available sensory evidence. His treatment of arithmetical assertions is quite different; these he reconciles with the criterion, not by giving them empirical content, but by construing them (when true) as mere tautologies, which make no claims about matters of fact. His approach to ethical assertions is different again. For (at least in respect of their ethical content) these turn out, on Ayer's analysis, to be not genuine assertions, but expressions of feeling; and, as such, they fall outside the scope of the criterion. We shall consider these analyses in more detail later.

As Ayer sees it, the analysis or, more broadly, the clarification of our concepts is the only legitimate business for philosophy. This, indeed, is a direct consequence of his criterion of significance. For the only other task which philosophy might hope to undertake would be to uncover certain fundamental synthetic (non-analytic) truths about the nature of reality. But, according to the criterion, any synthetic truth would have to be empirically verifiable, and this means that their discovery falls within the province of empirical science, not of *a priori* philosophy. The only truths which a philosopher can legitimately hope to establish, by *a priori* reasoning, are those which are already implicit in our concepts –

4

truths which he can make explicit by conceptual analysis and clarification. And this is just another way of saying, what Ayer explicitly claims in the Preface, that philosophical truths are analytic. Since Ayer regards analytic truths as devoid of factual content, this seems to have the unpalatable consequence that philosophers can only avoid nonsense at the cost of vacuity. However, even from Ayer's standpoint, the description of philosophical truths as 'vacuous' would be misleading. For even if they are, in some technical sense, devoid of factual content, this does not mean that they are obvious or easy to establish. Quite the reverse: their discovery often involves considerable ingenuity and the truths which emerge are sometimes quite surprising. Similar remarks apply, of course, to discoveries in mathematics and formal logic.

That analytic truths can be surprising, even counterintuitive, is something which must be borne in mind when considering the status of Ayer's central thesis. Ayer is claiming that any genuine proposition (any proposition capable of being true or false) must be either analytic or empirically verifiable. Opponents of positivism commonly object that this claim is self-refuting, since even its defenders cannot classify it under either of the categories it permits. But this objection is misconceived. Certainly the claim is not an empirical hypothesis; but, unless there are other objections to it, there is nothing to prevent its classification as analytic. If there seems to be, it is only because, like many other philosophical claims, it is neither self-evident nor easy to establish. But this is compatible with its being something whose truth depends solely on its meaning.

In insisting that philosophical truths are themselves analytic, there can be little doubt that Ayer intended this to cover his central thesis. And this interpretation is borne out by a passage in his later *Introduction*.[3] In his subsequent writings his position is more guarded. He comes to view the thesis more as the enunciation of a sound policy than as something objectively true. His point seems to be that our ordinary linguistic practices are not sufficiently sensitive to the demands of philosophical propriety to make the thesis true by definition. As he puts it in *Logical Positivism* (*LP*), of which he was the editor, 'it is not contrary to ordinary usage to say that metaphysical utterances are meaningful' (*LP*, 15). Nor is he merely acknowledging here, what he acknowledges in both the text and the *Introduction* of *LTL*, that the word 'meaning' is ambiguous and that it is only in one and a rather special sense that he holds metaphysical utterances to be meaningless.[4] For it is precisely with respect to this special sense that he takes the thesis to be recommendatory: thus what he takes to be prescriptive is 'the suggestion that only statements of these two kinds should be regarded as either true or false' (*LP*, 15), and it is precisely the capacity to be true or false which defines his notion of literal significance and his notion of a genuine proposition. I think Ayer is guilty of some confusion here and that he would have done better to retain his original position. His reason for abandoning this position is that the denial of his thesis is, as he puts it, 'not contrary to ordinary usage'. But what exactly does this mean? If it means merely that very many perfectly competent English speakers would reject the thesis and be happy to accord truth-value to propositions which fall into neither of Ayer's categories, this is certainly the case. But its being so does not preclude the analyticity of the thesis, since, even on conceptual questions, the judgments of ordinary speakers are not infallible. On the other hand, if it means that, given the ordinary sense of the terms in which it is formulated – in particular, the ordinary sense of the terms 'true' and 'false' – the meaning of the thesis does not guarantee its validity, then this indeed would preclude its analyticity. But, unless the thesis can be discredited on other grounds, there seems to be no reason why Ayer should concede that this is so. And if he does think that the thesis can be discredited on other grounds – that it gets things wrong philosophically – then he cannot restore its credit by stipulation.

2 *The a priori and the analytic*

Ayer intends his central thesis, which divides genuine propositions into the analytic and the empirically verifiable, to imply that all *a priori* truths are analytic. Strictly speaking, the thesis as such does not have this implication. For to say that a proposition is an *a priori* truth is to say that it can be established by *a priori* reasoning on its own, without appeal to empirical evidence; and the fact that something can be established by *a priori* reasoning does not entail that it cannot also be verified empirically. Thus the proposition that $97 \times 85 = 8{,}245$ can be established *a priori*; but it can also, in a perfectly good sense, be verified empirically by means of a calculator. Whether or not Ayer overlooked this point is of no great concern. In dividing genuine propositions into his two groups, he clearly intends to restrict membership of the second group to propositions which are not only empirically verifiable, but cannot be verified in any other way – to propositions which are contingent and *a posteriori*, and not establishable by *a priori* reasoning alone. Given this restriction, the central thesis does entail, quite trivially, that all *a priori* truths are analytic.

The claim that all *a priori* truths are analytic is one which Ayer is at great pains to defend. He is well aware that philosophers of a more rationalist persuasion would oppose his central thesis by denying this claim – by arguing that there are truths which are both *a priori* and synthetic, truths which can be established by pure reason, but which are factual in a way that analytic truths are not. This indeed was the position of Kant, and Ayer devotes almost the whole of one chapter (*LTL* Ch.4) to the task of refuting it. Of course, even if Ayer were forced to give way on this issue, he could retain his positivist thesis in other, and arguably the most important, respects. For, while conceding that some *a priori* truths are synthetic, he could still insist that all genuine propositions are either *a priori* truths or empirically verifiable. And this would still impose a very severe test of significance on assertoric sentences: it would mean that outside the rather narrow domain of *a priori* truth, the verification principle remained in force. But while this would be a severe test of significance, it is not sufficiently severe for all Ayer's purposes. As we have seen, part of what Ayer wants to achieve by his criterion is a restriction on the *a priori* methods of philosophy. The elimination of metaphysics involves, amongst other things, denying the existence of any intellectual faculty by which philosophers could acquire *a priori* knowledge of the nature of reality. As Ayer sees it, one of the main reasons why so many philosophers end up making nonsensical assertions or discussing spurious questions is that they fail to appreciate the limits on what *a priori* reasoning can achieve. They fondly suppose that there is some realm of supra-empirical facts which their intellectual faculties equip them to discern and fail to see that the only truths which can be established *a priori* stem from nothing deeper than linguistic convention. Thus it is only by vindicating his claim that all *a priori* truths are analytic that Ayer can hope to restrict philosophy to what he regards as its sole legitimate business – that of conceptual clarification and analysis.

It is at this point that we encounter our first major problem. For, given the way in which analyticity has been defined, it is far from clear how the claim is to have any restrictive force at all. Ayer defines an 'analytic' proposition as one whose 'validity depends solely on the definitions of the symbols it contains' (*LTL*, 78). As we noted at the beginning, his wording here is loose, since strictly it is sentences, not propositions, which contain symbols. But presumably what he means is that an analytic proposition is one which is expressed by an analytic sentence and that an analytic sentence is one whose meaning (determined by the definitions of its symbols and their syntactical arrangement) ensures that it expresses a truth. Now suppose that proposition P is an *a priori* truth and that S is a sentence which expresses P. Being *a priori*, P is also (we may assume) a necessary truth (certainly, if there are any *a priori* contingent truths, they are not relevant to the present issue). So it is impossible for a sentence to express P without expressing a truth. But in supposing that S expresses P, we are supposing that it does so irrespective of the context of utterance – otherwise we should have said not that the sentence as such, but that a certain utterance of it, expresses P. In other words, we are supposing that S expresses P solely in virtue of its meaning. So not only is it impossible for a sentence to express P without expressing a truth, but also it is impossible for S to mean what it does without expressing *P*. It follows that *P* is analytic in the sense defined. For it is expressed by a sentence, *S*, whose meaning ensures that it expresses a truth.

Now all this may seem very satisfactory for Ayer. After all, he wants to be able to establish that all *a priori* truths are analytic in his sense, and this we have just done. Moreover, we have done it in a way which, I think, more or less reflects his own reasoning. The trouble is, however, that if the claim can be established in this way, it does not amount to very much. In particular, it does not impose any controversial restrictions on the scope of *a priori* reasoning or imply that *a priori* truths are, in any interesting sense, non-factual. Thus, to take one example, suppose a certain philosopher claims that we possess a faculty of moral intuition which, when properly exercised, enables us to discern *a priori* the objective truth of certain moral principles. Such a claim is undoubtedly one which Ayer rejects and which he would regard as at variance with his own claim that all *a priori* truths are analytic. But if we construe analyticity in the way proposed – apparently in accordance with Ayer's own definition – the two claims are perfectly compatible. Thus if the intuitionist regards it as an *a priori* truth that, say, torture is always morally wrong, he will also, presumably, regard it as a necessary truth and thus accept that the sentence we have just used to express it is guaranteed by its meaning to be truth-expressing. In this way, he can happily acknowledge that the proposition is analytic in Ayer's sense without compromising his intuitionist position. And, of course, we get the same result in every case where Ayer and the rationalist are supposedly in conflict: the rationalist can retain the substance of his position, with respect to both the scope of *a priori* reasoning and the factual status of the truths it reveals, while acknowledging the correctness of Ayer's claim as we have interpreted it. In short, Ayer's claim, thus interpreted, is wholly uncontroversial and contributes nothing to his attack on metaphysics.

The correct conclusion to draw from this is not that there is no real dispute between Ayer and the rationalist, but that, as we have so far interpreted it, Ayer's claim that all *a priori* truths are analytic understates his true position. What Ayer intends this claim to mean, as is clear from the whole drift of his discussion, is that *a priori* truths are not merely ones where the sentences expressing them are guaranteed by their meaning to be truth-expressing, but ones which are themselves the product of linguistic meaning – truths which are created by the linguistic conventions governing the usage of the symbols we employ. It might seem that, in taking *a priori* truths to be the product of linguistic meaning, Ayer is committed to denying their necessity – that he is committed to saying, for example, that if the meanings of our arithmetical symbols had been suitably different, 7 + 5 would not have equalled 12. But this is not so. Like the rationalist, Ayer accepts the impossibility of a world in which

7 + 5 is not equal to 12 (though, of course, like anyone else, he accepts the possibility of a world in which the expression '7 + 5', having a different meaning, does not designate the number 12). His claim is only that this impossibility is sustained by the contingent facts of linguistic meaning in the actual world. If this still seems incoherent, it is because we are crediting *a priori* propositions with a factual content which Ayer would reject. We are supposing that there is some realm of arithmetical facts outside the framework of language and that linguistic conventions are only relevant in furnishing the symbolic materials by which these facts can be expressed. But Ayer will insist that there are no such facts. As he sees it, its being a necessary truth that 7 + 5 = 12 amounts to no more (nor less) than the fact that our arithmetical symbols have certain conventional meanings and that these meanings ensure the correctness of asserting the relevant arithmetical sentence. It is for this reason that he rejects the view that *a priori* knowledge involves some special faculty of intuition. Because *a priori* truths are the product of linguistic meaning, our recognition of them is wholly explained by our understanding of language. My *a priori* knowledge that 7 + 5 = 12 is wholly explained by my understanding of the sentence '7 + 5 = 12' and my knowledge, implicit in this understanding, that (given its meaning) I can correctly assert this sentence irrespective of my empirical evidence.

The claim that all *a priori* truths are the product of linguistic meaning certainly has the restrictive force Ayer wants: it is incompatible with the view that *a priori* propositions have factual content and it reduces *a priori* knowledge to a form of linguistic competence. The only difficulty is in seeing how such a claim could be defended. And here the problem is not just that the claim is intuitively implausible, but that, without some modification, it seems to be self-defeating. Thus suppose we try to account for the *a priori* truth that 7 + 5 = 12 by citing the fact that the meanings of the symbols '7', '+', '5', '=', and '12' ensure the correctness of asserting the sentence '7 + 5 = 12'. Even if this were satisfactory (and I do not think it is), we would be left with the question: *How* is the correctness of such an assertion ensured by the meanings of these symbols? The answer must be that it is *logically* ensured – that is, that it is a logical, and hence an *a priori*, truth that if the symbols have these meanings, then the assertion of '7 + 5 = 12' is correct. So in trying to account for the *a priori* arithmetical truth in terms of linguistic meaning, we have had to invoke a further *a priori* truth connecting the assertability of the relevant arithmetical sentence with the meanings of the symbols it contains. But if *all a priori* truths are the product of linguistic meaning, then this further *a priori* truth must, presumably, be explained in a similar way – that is, by invoking still further *a priori* truths connecting the assertability of the sentences expressing this truth with the meanings of the symbols they contain. If this is so, then the process will be

9

viciously regressive: it could only terminate if at least some *a priori* truths were not the product of linguistic meaning – indeed, were wholly independent of it – and this is just what the theory excludes. It might be objected that, at some stage in the process, residual *a priori* truths could be replaced by rules of deductive inference, so that we could invoke these rules, rather than the truths, to show how meaning ensured assertability. But this does not meet the problem. Assuming their validity, the rules of deductive inference on their own generate a range of *a priori* truths. If the rules are independent of linguistic meaning, so are these truths. If they are not, we are back with the regress. Either way, the claim that all *a priori* truths are the product of linguistic meaning (or even that all are to some extent dependent on linguistic meaning) collapses.

The collapse of this claim seriously weakens Ayer's case against the rationalist. If some *a priori* truths are independent of linguistic meaning, then to that extent *a priori* knowledge depends on some faculty of intuition, or rational insight, by which such truths can be discerned. Nor does there seem to be any interesting (i.e. potentially controversial) sense in which such truths could be denied a factual status. One might say, I suppose, that they are the product of human rationality rather than part of the fabric of the universe. But I cannot see any way of interpreting this claim which would not leave it either incoherent or trivial. If what is meant is that *a priori* truths have no 'absolute' validity, but only one which is relative to some mode of rationality, and that, in consequence, if we are trying to be objective, we should acknowledge that the proposition that $7 + 5 = 12$ is not true (and necessarily true) *as such*, but only true (and necessarily true) *from our viewpoint*, then the claim is surely incoherent. For our own mode of rationality simply does not allow us to entertain this relativist thesis: it obliges us to accept as absolute the truths which it reveals and to discount as spurious any rival system of thought in which they are rejected. If, on the other hand, all that is meant is that *a priori* truths are of an abstract character and that the facts which they record are not part of the concrete universe of space and time, then the claim is correct. At the same time, it is hardly something which the rationalist will want to dispute.

It does not follow, of course, that Ayer has to abandon his anti-rationalist position altogether. Even if he must acknowledge a faculty of *a priori* intuition and accord a factual status to the truths which it reveals, he could still set severe limitations on its scope. He could insist that it is only the most basic logical truths (e.g. the truths of classical predicate logic) which we can intuit in this way and that all other *a priori* truths must be reducible to these truths by conceptual/semantic analysis. With a suitably austere logic, such a position would have the restrictive force Ayer wants. It would impose the requisite constraints on the *a priori* methods of philosophy and would explicitly exclude theories, like that of moral intuitionism, which credit us with *a priori* faculties of a more far-reaching kind. Whether such restrictions could be justified and whether they would allow for the *a priori* status of mathematics, which Ayer acknowledges, are further questions. Unfortunately, they never properly surface in Ayer's discussion, since he thinks that the whole issue of *a priori* truth is settled by the analyticity-claim as originally interpreted. He supposes that because *a priori* truths are expressed by sentences whose meaning guarantees that they are truth-expressing, linguistic meaning is the sole and sufficient source of *a priori* truth. Admittedly, he takes note of Russell's attempt to reduce mathematics to logic and thinks that, if successful, it would be of value in making the analyticity of mathematical truths transparent. But what he stresses is that the logicist programme is irrelevant to the main debate:

> For even if . . . it is not possible to reduce mathematical notions to purely logical notions, it will still remain true that the propositions of mathematics are analytic propositions . . . For the criterion of an analytic proposition is that its validity should follow simply from the definition of the terms contained in it, and this condition is fulfilled by the propositions of pure mathematics. (*LTL*, 82)

The irony is that he criticizes Russell (if only mildly) for either missing this point or not making it sufficiently clear. But really it is Ayer who has missed the point. The proof that mathematical propositions are analytic in Ayer's sense leaves the rationalist with a free hand; a successful and sufficiently austere logicism would keep the rationalist in check.

3 *The principle of verification*

If we ignore the issue over the status of *a priori* truth, Ayer's central thesis can be reformulated as the claim that any genuine proposition must be either an *a priori* truth or empirically verifiable. As we have already noted, even in this weaker form the thesis imposes a very stringent criterion of significance on assertoric discourse. It means that, apart from those whose truth can be established *a priori*, the only significant assertions we can make – the only assertions which can properly be said to be true or false – are ones which are open to empirical verification. Even to raise the question of how things might be (contingently) in some verification-transcendent reality is to lapse into nonsense. For if the alternative answers cannot be tested empirically, they cannot be significantly formulated and the question cannot be significantly raised. Obviously, we need to look very carefully into how Ayer interprets this principle of verification, why he accepts it, and how he employs it in philosophical argument. It is the first of these questions that we shall now consider.

Ayer begins by formulating the principle as follows:

> We say that a sentence is factually significant to any given person, if, and only if, he knows how to verify the proposition which it purports to express – that is, if he knows what observations would lead him, under certain conditions, to accept the proposition as being true, or reject it as being false. (*LTL*, 35)

It might seem curious that Ayer should count as a way of *verifying* a proposition evidence which would lead one to *reject* it. But in fact he often uses the term 'verify' as short for 'verify or falsify' and this is one such occasion. The important point is not his terminology, but the fact that he is prepared to count both empirical verifiability and empirical falsifiability as sufficing for factual, and hence literal, significance. And in this respect, at least, he is surely right. For sentences which are devoid of literal significance do not express propositions at all and hence do not express anything true or false. All one needs to add is that Ayer should, in a similar way, allow significance to sentences whose negations are analytic (or can be established *a priori*), though there is no indication that he is willing to do this and at least one passage where he explicitly takes the contrary view.[5]

One obvious defect in the formulation, as it stands, is that it assumes that a person's evaluation of his observational evidence is always rational. It assumes that someone has actually verified (or falsified) a proposition if his observations lead him to accept (reject) it. And this assumption is clearly false. As Ayer himself points out in his much later *The Central Questions of Philosophy* (*CQ*):

> Someone may be disposed to accept a proposition on the basis of observations which do not genuinely support it. For example, someone who prays for rain and sees it subsequently fall may treat his observation of the rainfall as a reason for accepting the proposition that God exists. (*CQ*, 26)

This defect is, of course, easily corrected. Instead of speaking of the observations which would *induce* acceptance (or rejection), we have to speak of those which would *justify* it. And, in fact, the defect, though apparently unnoticed by Ayer at the time, gets corrected in his subsequent elaboration.

As the first step in this elaboration, Ayer draws two distinctions: between verifiability *in practice* and verifiability *in principle*; and between *strong* (conclusive) verification and *weak* (probabilistic) verification. In each case Ayer chooses the more liberal alternative, which makes the requirements of significance easier to meet. Thus, in respect of the first distinction, he acknowledges the significance (i.e. genuineness) of the proposition that there are mountains on the further side of the moon:

> No rocket has yet been invented which would enable me to go and look at the farther side of the moon, so that I am unable to decide the matter by actual observation. But I do know what observations would decide it for me, if, as is theoretically conceivable, I were once in a position to make them. And therefore I say that the proposition is verifiable in principle, if not in practice, and is accordingly significant. (*LTL*, 36)

Likewise, in respect of the second distinction, he argues that 'if we adopt conclusive verifiability as our criterion of significance . . . our argument will prove too much' (*LTL*, 37), since many significant empirical statements cannot, even in principle, be conclusively validated or confuted. He focuses on the example of generalizations of law such as 'arsenic is poisonous' and 'a body tends to expand when it is heated'. Such statements cannot be conclusively validated, since we can never check through the potentially infinite number of cases to which they apply. Nor, as he sees it, can they be conclusively confuted, since, although their falsification only requires the discovery of one negative instance (e.g. an instance of non-poisonous arsenic), there is always a logical gap between our ultimate sensory evidence and the conclusion that this negative instance obtains. Ayer, indeed, thinks that this point applies to empirical statements quite generally – that no empirical statement can be conclusively validated or confuted – though in his later *Introduction* he made an exception of statements recording the content of a single experience ('what may be said to verify them conclusively is the occurrence of the experience to which they uniquely refer' (*LTL*, 10)). His response is to make factual significance depend, not on *conclusive* verifiability, but merely on the possibility of favourable or unfavourable evidence:

> Accordingly, we fall back on the weaker sense of verification. We say that the question that must be asked about any putative statement of fact is not, Would any observations make its truth or falsehood logically certain? but simply, Would any observations be relevant to the determination of its truth or falsehood? And it is only if a negative answer is given to this second question that we conclude that the statement under consideration is nonsensical. (*LTL*, 38)

It is at this point that Ayer starts to run into difficulties. For some reason, which he does not reveal in the book itself, he regards this formulation of the verification principle as insufficiently clear. In his later *Introduction* the reason he gives is that the word 'relevant', as it occurs in the phrase 'relevant to the determination of truth or falsehood', is 'uncomfortably vague' (*LTL*, 11) – a remark which is itself uncomfortably vague. Perhaps the point is that, without some further restriction, the notion of relevant evidence is too broad to serve Ayer's purposes. For example, a student beginning philosophy could acquire evidence for the truth of some metaphysical doctrine simply because his tutor – an acknowledged expert – claimed that it was demonstrably correct. And the possibility of this kind of evidence would not show that the doctrine was significant. At any rate, for whatever reason, Ayer thinks that his position needs to be re-expressed as follows:

> Let us call a proposition which records an actual or possible observation an experiential proposition. Then we may say that it is the mark of a genuine factual proposition, not that it should be equivalent to an experiential proposition, or any finite number of experiential propositions, but simply that some experiential propositions can be deduced from it in conjunction with certain other premises without being deducible from those other premises alone. (*LTL*, 38–9)

The trouble with this, as Ayer later came to see, is that it excludes nothing. For, given any indicative sentence '*P*', and any sentence '*Q*' expressing an experiential proposition, we can deduce '*Q*' from '*P*' in conjunction with the additional premise 'If *P* then *Q*'. And so according to the criterion, every indicative sentence will count as expressing a genuine factual proposition, even if it is manifestly nonsensical. The source of the trouble is that Ayer has set no restriction on the kind of additional premises which can be employed. Perhaps it was an implicit recognition of this which led him, in a subsequent passage, to speak as if the additional premises had to be empirical. Thus, in the course of arguing for the metaphysical status of theism, he remarks:

> . . . if the existence of such a god were probable, then the proposition that he existed would be an empirical hypothesis. And in that case it would be possible to deduce from it, and other *empirical* hypotheses, certain experiential propositions which were not deducible from those other hypotheses alone. (*LTL*, 115; my italics)

Whether or not this indicates his recognition of the problem, it certainly cannot provide Ayer with the solution. For he would then need a further criterion of what counts as an empirical hypothesis, which was what the verification principle was intended to supply.

In his *Introduction*, Ayer tries to solve the problem by providing a recursive definition of verifiability. As a preliminary measure, he slightly alters his terminology. He has become aware of the awkwardness of speaking of 'putative propositions' or of the propositions which sentences 'purport to express', and he now adopts the word 'statement' as a technical term, to signify the quasi-propositional entity which a grammatically well-formed indicative sentence expresses, whether or not it is literally meaningful.[6] (How this relates to his use of the term 'statement' in the original text is unclear.[7]) Following on from this, he introduces the term 'observation-statement', in place of 'experiential proposition', to signify a statement which records an actual or possible observation. The recursive definition is then formulated as follows:

> I propose to say that a statement is directly verifiable if it is either itself an observation-statement, or is such that in conjunction with one or more observation-statements it entails at least one observation-statement which is not deducible from these other premises alone; and I propose to say that a statement is indirectly verifiable if it satisfies the following conditions: first, that in conjunction with certain other premises it entails one or more directly verifiable statements which are not deducible from these other premises alone; and secondly, that these other premises do not include any statement that is not either analytic, or directly verifiable, or capable of being independently established as indirectly verifiable. And I can now reformulate the principle of verification as requiring of a literally meaningful statement, which is not analytic, that it should be either directly or indirectly verifiable, in the foregoing sense. (*LTL*, 13)

This is an ingenious proposal and elegantly expressed. But unfortunately it does not work. Its failure was first demonstrated by Alonzo Church, who considered the complex formula 'Either (not-O_1 and O_2) or (O_3 and not-S)', where 'O_1', 'O_2', and 'O_3' are (or strictly, express) observation-statements which are logically independent of one another and 'S' is (expresses) any statement you care to choose. Since in conjunction with 'O_1' it entails 'O_3', and since *ex hypothesi* 'O_1' alone does not entail 'O_3', this formula qualifies as directly verifiable in Ayer's sense. But this means that 'S' qualifies as indirectly verifiable, since in conjunction with the formula it entails 'O_2', which is not deducible from the formula alone. Since 'S' can be any statement you please, it turns out that any statement whatsoever counts as significant on Ayer's new criterion, as on the old. The same point can be proved even more simply. Let 'S' be any statement you please and 'O' any observation-statement which does not entail 'S'. Then obviously 'S and O' is directly verifiable; for, since 'S and O' entails 'O', it also does so in conjunction with any other observation-statement which does not entail O. But then 'S' qualifies as indirectly verifiable since, in conjunction with 'O', which is directly verifiable, it entails 'S and O', which is also directly verifiable and which is not deducible from 'O' alone.

At this point, it seems to me, a verificationist of Ayer's general persuasion has a choice between two possible courses. One possibility would be to return to the original definition of verifiability, whereby a

15

statement or proposition is (weakly and in principle) verifiable (i.e. verifiable or falsifiable) if and only if there could be observational evidence for or against it, and then try to impose on the notion of evidence-for-or-against whatever restrictions are needed for a suitable criterion of significance. At the very least it would be necessary to exclude cases, such as testimony, in which the evidence bears on the truth or falsity of the statement independently of what the statement purports to say – in other words, to confine ourselves to cases in which the evidence for the truth (falsity) of 'P' is, quite directly, evidence that P (that not-P). Otherwise, we would have to count *any* statement as significant through its potential endorsement by a reputable authority.

However, the notion of evidence is not the only complication. Ayer wants to restrict the title 'significant' to those assertoric sentences which express genuine propositions, and presumably he does not want a sentence to count as expressing a genuine proposition if one of its components is nonsensical. But now suppose 'N' is some nonsensical sentence and that we have (or could have) observational evidence (of the relevant kind) for the truth of 'P' and for the falsity of 'Q'. By applying the standard deductive rules for disjunction and conjunction, it seems that we then have observational evidence for the truth of 'N or P' and for the falsity of 'N and Q' (since a disjunction is entailed by each of its disjuncts and a conjunction entails each of its conjuncts). And this would allow these complex sentences to qualify as significant, if verifiability (i.e. verifiability or falsifiability) were the only requirement. One may be tempted to reply that, since they are nonsensical, the complexes are already excluded from the domain of sentences to which the deductive rules apply, so that we cannot treat the evidence for 'P' as evidence for 'N or P' or the evidence against 'Q' as evidence against 'N and Q'. But this would be beside the point. If verifiability is to serve as a *criterion* of significance, we must be able to decide its application without prejudging the questions it is intended to settle. We would not be employing it as a criterion if we counted the complexes as unverifiable in virtue of their nonsensical status.

The right response, presumably, is to strengthen the criterion by requiring of a factually significant sentence not only that it be verifiable in the relevant sense, but also that its component sentences, or those that show up on analysis, be either analytic or verifiable. Admittedly, this does not deal with the whole problem. It allows us to classify as nonsensical any sentence which contains, as a component, a nonsensical *sentence*. But the problem also extends to cases where the offending component is a predicate or predicative expression. Thus consider the sentences (a) 'every cat on the mat is either slithy or black' and (b) 'some cat on the mat is both slithy and black', in which the predicate 'slithy' is nonsensical. There could be observational evidence for 'every cat on the mat is black', which formally entails (a) and observational evidence against 'some cat on the mat is black' which is formally entailed by (b). Since they contain no grammatically complete sentences as (proper) components, and since no such sentential components would emerge through analysis, (a) and (b) would qualify as factually significant under the suggested criterion. But presumably they should count as nonsensical, in the same way as 'N or P' and 'N and Q'. The solution is to add the further requirement that if S is to be a factually significant sentence, then, for each of S's component predicates and predicative expressions (or those that show up on analysis), there must be a sentence S', containing just one occurrence of that component and containing no other predicative expression, such that S' is either analytic or verifiable. (Of course, it will only be in rare cases that there is an analytic S'.) This would have the required effect, since in the case of a nonsensical predicate or predicative expression there is no such S'. And, as far as I can see, it would not make the conditions for significance more stringent than Ayer wants them to be.

This, then, is one of the possible courses open to the verificationist – to return to Ayer's initial definition of verifiability and try to extract a criterion of significance from it along the lines just suggested. The other possibility would be to continue with the idea which underlies Ayer's abortive attempts to provide what he regards as a clearer and more precise formulation of his position and take this idea to its logical conclusion. The idea is, I assume, that the factual significance of a statement lies in its observational content – that is, in its contribution to the deduction of observation-statements. The reason why his formulations have failed is that they are not sufficiently stringent to exclude superfluous content – content which is irrelevant to such deduction or only relevant in the context of a totality of statements whose content exceeds the needs of such deduction. Thus Ayer's final formulation, in the *Introduction*, allows the conjunction of a nonsensical statement 'N' and an observation-statement 'O' to qualify as directly verifiable, since we can deduce 'O' from 'N and O' (and hence from 'N and O' in conjunction with any other observation-statement). And accordingly, it allows 'N' to qualify as indirectly verifiable, since from 'N', in conjunction with 'O', we can deduce the directly verifiable conjunction. What has gone wrong here is that the conjunction has qualified as directly verifiable simply in virtue of the observational content of its second conjunct ('O'), and this makes 'N' indirectly verifiable even though it is devoid of observational content.

In a short but perceptive article,[8] Jonathan Cohen has suggested a way of emending Ayer's formulation so as to exclude such cases. His basic idea is that where a statement contains superfluous (i.e. non-observational) content, this shows up in the fact that there is an equivalent conjunction of statements such that each of the conjuncts is needed to maintain equivalence with the original statement, but at least one of the conjuncts is redundant with respect to the deduction of observation-statements. Thus the superfluous content in 'N and O' shows up in the fact that any observation-statement which is deducible from it, with the help of any additional premises which are free of superfluous content, is also deducible from 'O' alone, with the help of the same additional premises. Likewise, if 'S' is nonsensical, the superfluous content in Church's formula 'Either (not-O_1 and O_2) or (O_3 and not-S)' shows up in the fact that there is an equivalent conjunction '(O_2 or O_3) and (not-O_1 or O_3) and (not-O_1 or not-S) and (O_2 or not-S)' such that any observation-statement which is deducible from the formula, with the help of any additional premises which are free of superfluous content, is also deducible from the smaller conjunction '(O_2 or O_3) and (not-O_1 or O_3)' alone, with the help of the same additional premises.

Cohen now turns this idea into a recursive definition of 'observational verifiability'. Taking observation-statements and their negations to be 'observationally verifiable at level 0', he stipulates that

a . . . statement S, and its negation, are . . . observationally verifiable at level 1 if and only if the following three conditions are jointly satisfied:

i. S is not analytically true or analytically false.
ii. At least one observation-statement E is formal-logically deducible from the conjunction of S with zero or more observation-statements that do not themselves suffice to entail E.
iii. For any class C of statements, if
   (a) the conjunction of members of C but of no proper subclass of C is formal-logically equivalent to S, and
   (b) no non-logical term occurs more often in any one member of C than it occurs in S,
then there is no C', such that C' is a proper subclass of C and any observation-statement E, that is formal-logically deducible from the conjunction of S with zero or more observation-statements that do not themselves formal-logically entail E, is deducible from the conjunction of the members of C' with the same observation-statements.[9]

He then goes on to stipulate that a statement S, and its negation, are 'observationally verifiable at level $n + 1$' if and only if S satisfies, in respect of statements which are observationally verifiable at level n, the same three conditions whose satisfaction in respect of observation-statements defines observational verifiability at level 1.[10] He concludes by defining a statement as 'observationally verifiable *tout court* if and only if there is some level at which it or its analytic equivalent is observationally verifiable'.[11] This definition is intended to make observational verifiability cover Ayer's cases of direct and indirect verifiability, but without the admission of observationally superfluous content – content irrelevant to the deduction of observation-statements. The only qualification is that Cohen does not intend to exclude superfluous content in cases where it is irrelevant to the deduction of *anything*. 'I am assuming . . . that we do not have to exclude a conjunctive statement from being observationally verifiable merely because one of its conjuncts is a tautology formulated in terms of non-observational predicates.'[12]

Even with this qualification, I doubt if the definition is entirely successful. Let us assume, with Cohen, that each observation-statement takes the form of an 'atomic' sentence, comprising just one n-place predicate, signifying an observable property (in Ayer's system, a phenomenal property), and an ordered n-tuple of proper names or demonstrative phrases, designating observable objects (in Ayer's system, sense-contents). If 'a' and 'b' are names of observable objects, '$a = b$' clearly qualifies as observationally verifiable at level 1 (perhaps also at level 0); in particular, we can conjoin it with an observation-statement about a to deduce an observation-statement about b, and *vice versa*, and I assume that such deductions qualify as 'formal-logical' in Cohen's sense. Consequently, the negation of this statement, '$a \neq b$', also qualifies as observationally verifiable at level 1. Now suppose that 'F' is the non-observational predicate 'is created by a god'. Cohen wants to exclude 'F' from his observationally verifiable statements (with the qualification noted above). Thus, in particular, he does not want the statement 'Fa and not-Fb' to satisfy his three conditions at any level. But how does it fail to satisfy them at level 2? Obviously, it satisfies conditions i and ii – it is not analytically true or analytically false; and it formal-logically entails the statement '$a \neq b$' which is observationally verifiable at level 1. So, to exclude it, Cohen must show that it fails to satisfy condition iii, and, as far as I can see, he cannot do this. It is true that we can find a formal-logically equivalent conjunction which separates the observational from the superfluous content. One example would be '$a = b$ and Fa and ($a = b$ or not-Fb)'. This statement gives Cohen almost all that he needs: it is formal-logically equivalent to 'Fa and not-Fb'; no conjunct can be eliminated without destroying the equivalence; and its first conjunct exhausts its observational content, in that any statement S which is observationally verifiable at level 1 and which is formal-logically deducible from 'Fa and not-Fb', together with zero or more additional premises which are observationally verifiable at level 1 and do not themselves formal-logically entail S, is formal-logically deducible from '$a \neq b$', together with the same additional premises. Where it fails is in not meeting the requirement expressed by clause (b). For the non-logical term '*b*' occurs twice in the third conjunct but only once in '*Fa* and not-*Fb*'. Of course, we could replace this conjunct by '(not-*Fa* or not-*Fb*)' and this would preserve the equivalence of the whole conjunction with '*Fa* and not-*Fb*'. But then we would fail to meet the requirement expressed in clause (a), since the first conjunct, '*a* ≠ *b*' would become logically redundant. I cannot see any way of avoiding this dilemma – any way of constructing a conjunction which meets both of the requirements expressed in the antecedent of iii and, by gathering all the observational content into some proper subset of the conjuncts, fails to meet the requirement expressed in the consequent. And unless there is such a conjunction, '*Fa* and not-*Fb*' will turn out to be observationally verifiable.

No doubt Cohen's definition can be emended to avoid this objection. Perhaps we could do this by simply omitting clause iii(b). For I cannot see what purpose it serves. Cohen must think that there are some statements which do not contain observationally superfluous content but which would fail to qualify as observationally verifiable if clause (b) were omitted. But suppose *S* is such a statement. Since *S* would fail to be observationally verifiable if clause (b) were omitted, there must be an equivalent conjunction, of the relevant sort, which shows this. But *ex hypothesi* this conjunction would fail to be observationally verifiable even if clause (b) were retained, since it is bound to satisfy this clause *with respect to itself*. It follows that if the definition is satisfactory in other respects, clause (b) should be omitted. For either it makes no difference or it makes the unwanted difference of assigning a different status to two statements which are formally equivalent. And if the definition is otherwise satisfactory, this difference could only take the form of allowing one of the statements to qualify as observationally verifiable when both should be disqualified – as in the example of '*Fa* and not-*Fb*' and '*a* ≠ *b* and *Fa* and (*a* = *b* or not-*Fb*)' considered above. The only reason Cohen gives for including clause (b) is that, without it, his definition 'would exclude any generalization (x)(Rx → Sx) from observational verifiability because of its formal-logical equivalence to the conjunction $((x)(Rx \rightarrow Sx) \lor ((\exists y)Ry \rightarrow (y)Sy)) \ \& \ ((x)(Rx \rightarrow Sx) \lor - ((\exists y)Ry \rightarrow (y)Sy))$'.[13] But here he is mistaken. For, since the first conjunct on its own is formal-logically equivalent to the generalization, the conjunction does not satisfy the requirements of clause (a) and hence does nothing to impugn the observational status of the generalization.

Whether Cohen's definition is satisfactory in other respects is a question I shall not pursue. For it seems to me that what he was trying to achieve can be achieved more simply in a quite different way – by following (more or less) the strategy of Carl Hempel in his article 'The Empiricist Criterion of Meaning'.[14] Let us say that a language *L* is an *observational language* if and only if it satisfies the following four conditions:

(1) The vocabulary of *L* consists of (no more than) names, predicates, individual variables, truth-functional operators (e.g. 'it is not the case that', 'and', and 'or'), and the standard quantifiers (i.e. 'for every . . .' and 'for some . . .').
(2) The syntax of *L* (i.e. its rules of sentence-formation) is that of ordinary predicate logic.
(3) The universe of discourse of *L* (i.e. the values for its variables and the referents of its names) is restricted to observable entities (i.e. the kind of entities referred to in observation-statements) and to classes all of whose atomic constituents are observable entities (i.e. classes of observables, classes of such classes, and so on).
(4) Apart from predicates for identity and class-membership, the names and predicates in *L* are observation-terms (i.e. the kind of terms suitable for use in observation-statements).

Further, let us say that a statement *S* falls within the scope of a language *L* if and only if, for some sentence *S'* which formulates *S*, one of the following three conditions obtains:

(1) *S'* is an *L*-sentence.
(2) *S'* is analytically equivalent to an *L*-sentence (i.e. turns out, on semantic analysis, to be logically equivalent to an *L*-sentence).
(3) *S'* is analytically equivalent to an infinite truth-functional complex (e.g. an infinite conjunction or disjunction) of *L*-sentences.

(The reason for including the third condition will emerge in due course.) Finally, let us say that a statement is *purely observational* if and only if it falls within the scope of some observational language. Then the class of statements which Cohen was trying to demarcate (relative to a prior notion of observation-statement) by his recursive definition of observational verifiability is, I think, precisely the class of. statements which are purely observational in this sense. And if this is not the class he was trying to demarcate, then, it seems to me, it should have been. For it is surely just these statements which are devoid of superfluous content in the *relevant* sense.

Let us now pick up the threads of the argument. We saw how Ayer's two attempts to formulate his verification principle in terms of the deducibility of experiential propositions or observation-statements failed, since in neither case does the criterion of significance exclude anything. I then suggested that there were two possible courses open to a verificationist of Ayer's general persuasion. The first was to return to the original conception of weak verifiability, claim that a statement has factual significance (or a proposition has factual content) only if there could be observational evidence, in some suitably restricted sense, for or against it, and then strengthen this requirement (in the ways we envisaged) so as to ensure that no complex statement qualifies as factually significant if it contains a nonsensical constituent. Let us call this the *evidence-principle*. The second possibility was to continue with the idea which seems to underlie Ayer's two reformulations – the idea that factual significance lies in observational content – and press this to its logical conclusion. This conclusion, whether or not it can be re-expressed along the lines that Cohen suggests, is that a statement has factual significance if and only if it (or its content) is, in the sense I have defined, purely observational, i.e. if and only if the statement falls within the scope of an observational language. Let us call this the *content-principle*. It is clear that these alternative principles are not even extensionally equivalent. Admittedly, we may reasonably expect that any statement which qualifies as factually significant under the content-principle will also qualify as factually significant under the evidence-principle, given that the latter principle does not require the evidence to be available in practice or to reach any particular strength.[15] But what we certainly cannot expect, unless we adopt some quite radical form of scepticism, is that the same will hold in reverse – that the only statements which are open to observational evidence are ones with a purely observational content. To illustrate this point we need only consider the example of scientific theory. Many scientific hypotheses postulate entities and states of affairs which are not directly observable: hypotheses concerning atomic and subatomic structure are a case in point. 'Realistically' construed, these hypotheses do not fall within the scope of an observational language, but they are still held to be subject to observational tests, according to how well or badly they explain our observational data. So under the content-principle they count as nonsensical, but under the evidence-principle they qualify as factually significant – at least they do so unless, on the lines of the radical sceptic, we reject the epistemological methods of science altogether. And quite generally, we can see that given ordinary (non-sceptical) standards of what counts as evidence, the content-principle yields a much more stringent criterion of factual significance than its rival.

The question now arises as to which of these principles represents, or comes closer to representing, Ayer's intentions. On our present information there is no obvious answer. Ayer's initial formulation of his position seems to indicate an acceptance of the evidence-principle, while his subsequent formulations, especially that in the *Introduction*, suggest an acceptance of the content-principle. Nor does he show any awareness of the discrepancy. He regards the subsequent formulations merely as clarifications of a position already, if less explicitly, stated: the point of defining verifiability in terms of the deduction of observation-statements (or experiential propositions) seems to be to show exactly how his initial evidence-principle is to be interpreted – in effect, to show how the notion of evidence-for-or-against must be understood if the evidence-principle is to be a suitable criterion of significance.

I think Ayer's intentions become clearer when we consider some of the ways in which he employs the verification principle in his subsequent arguments. In the first place, we have his insistence on a thorough-going phenomenalism with respect to statements about the physical world. We shall examine his phenomenalist position in more detail later. What needs to be stressed at this point is that his adoption of it was motivated not by a dispassionate consideration of what physical statements mean – a consideration undertaken without any prior philosophical commitments – but rather by his acceptance of the verification principle itself, combined with the natural assumption that such statements are significant. As he puts it:

> . . . we know that it must be possible to define material things in terms of sense-contents, because it is only by the occurrence of certain sense-contents that the existence of any material thing can ever be in the least degree verified. And thus we see that we have not to enquire whether a phenomenalist "theory of perception" or some other sort of theory is correct, but only what form of phenomenalist theory is correct. For the fact that all causal and representative theories of perception treat material things as if they were unobservable entities entitles us, as Berkeley saw, to rule them out *a priori*. (*LTL*, 53)

Ayer is presumably aware that a representative theorist, such as Locke, would not automatically have to concede that, because material objects are not directly perceptible, there can be no observational evidence for or against the truth of any physical statement – though this may be the consequence which the radical sceptic tries to derive from his position. The fact that Ayer feels able to rule out the representative theory without even mentioning the sceptical arguments shows, I think, that he was relying on a verification principle of a very strong form – a form which requires all factual content to be observational.

His espousal of phenomenalism is one (and the most important) of a number of cases in which Ayer feels obliged by his verification principle to adopt a reductionist position – that is, to claim that a certain class of statements, which are nominally about something unobservable, can be translated into another class of statements, which are explicitly about the observable. And in each case, it seems to me, it is his implicit acceptance of the content-principle which accounts for the reductionist approach. Perhaps the clearest illustration of this comes in his discussion of the problem of other minds. Many philosophers, Ayer notes, claim that one can justify a belief in the existence of other persons by an argument from analogy:

> They would maintain . . . that, although one cannot in any sense observe the existence of other people, one can nevertheless infer their existence with a high degree of probability from one's own experiences. They would say that my observation of a body whose behaviour resembled the behaviour of my own body entitled me to think it probable that that body was related to a self which I could not observe, in the same way as my body was related to my own observable self. (*LTL*, 128–9)

It is Ayer's reply to this which is particularly revealing:

> The correct way to refute this view . . . is to point out that no argument can render probable a completely unverifiable hypothesis. I can legitimately use an argument from analogy to establish the probable existence of an object which has never in fact manifested itself in my experience, provided that the object is such that it could conceivably be manifested in my experience. If this condition is not fulfilled, then, as far as I am concerned, the object is a metaphysical object, and the assertion that it exists and has certain properties is a metaphysical assertion. And, since a metaphysical assertion is senseless, no argument can possibly render it probable. But, on the view which we are discussing, I must regard other people as metaphysical objects; for it is assumed that their experiences are completely inaccessible to my observation. (*LTL*, 129)

If Ayer was here relying on the evidence-principle, which only requires that factually significant assertions be open to favourable or unfavourable evidence, this dismissal of the argument from analogy would be blatantly question-begging: in claiming that the hypothesis which it purports to render probable is completely unverifiable, he would be assuming in advance that the argument fails. The only way we can make sense of the passage is to assume that Ayer is endorsing the content-principle, which requires factually significant assertions to be (in the sense defined) purely observational. As the analogical argument construes it, the assertion that other human organisms have minds is not purely observational. For, from the standpoint of the assertor, such minds, unlike (at least on a phenomenalist view) the bodies to which they are supposedly attached, would be unobservable, and thus their existence would transcend the facts expressible in an observational language.[16] It is for this reason that Ayer sees the argument as trying to justify a metaphysical (i.e. nonsensical) assertion and as consequently worthless. And it is also for this reason that he is led to take a further step of reduction. For, being unwilling to reject as nonsensical all our ordinary assertions about the mental states of others, he finds himself obliged to analyse them behaviouristically – an analysis which, combined with his phenomenalistic analysis of physical statements, secures their observational status in the requisite way.

This interpretation of Ayer's position is borne out by a passage in the *Introduction*, shortly after his definitions of direct and indirect verifiability. Since it is the nearest Ayer comes to an explicit endorsement of the content-principle, I shall quote the passage in full:

> It has sometimes been assumed by my critics that I take the principle of verification to imply that no statement can be evidence for another unless it is part of its meaning; but this is not the case. Thus, to make use of a simple illustration, the statement that I have blood on my coat may, in certain circumstances, confirm the hypothesis that I have committed a murder, but it is not part of the meaning of the statement that I have committed a murder that I should have blood upon my coat, nor, as I understand it, does the principle of verification imply that it is. For one statement may be evidence for another, and still neither itself express a necessary condition of the truth of this other statement, nor belong to any set of statements which determines a range within which such a necessary condition falls; and it is only in these cases that the principle of verification yields the conclusion that the one statement is part of the meaning of the other. Thus, from the fact that it is only by the making of some observation that any statement about a material thing can be directly verified it follows, according to the principle of verification, that every such statement contains some observation-statement or other as part of its meaning, and it follows also that, although its generality may prevent any finite set of observation-statements from exhausting its meaning, it does not contain anything as part of its meaning that cannot be represented as an observation-statement; but there may still be many observation-statements that are relevant to its truth or falsehood without being part of its meaning at all. Again, a person who affirms the existence of a deity may try to support his contention by appealing to the facts of religious experience; but it does not follow from this that the factual meaning of his statement is wholly contained in the propositions by which these religious experiences are described. For there may be other empirical facts that he would also consider to be relevant; and it is possible that the descriptions of these other empirical facts can more properly be regarded as containing the factual meaning of his statement than the descriptions of the religious experiences. At the same time, if one accepts the principle of verification, one must hold that his statement does not have any other factual meaning than what is contained in at least

some of the relevant empirical propositions; and that if it is so interpreted that no possible experience could go to verify it, it does not have any factual meaning at all. (*LTL*, 14–15)

Ayer's main concern in this passage is to stress that, even though a factually significant statement must be open to observational evidence, there can be forms of observational evidence which are extraneous to its factual meaning. In other words, I can envisage making certain observations (having certain experiences) which would be evidentially relevant to the truth or falsity of a certain statement, but in a way which neither contributes to nor is implicit in the factual meaning I assign to it. But what is especially interesting for us is not this point, but the other points he makes, almost concessively, in elaborating it. For while he wishes to stress that the possibilities of observational evidence transcend factual meaning, this is set against the background of the claim that factual meaning does not transcend, in their totality, the possibilities of observational evidence. Thus he sees it as a consequence of his principle of verification that, 'although its generality may prevent any finite set of observation-statements from exhausting its meaning', a statement about a material thing 'does not contain anything as part of its meaning that cannot be represented as an observation-statement'. Likewise, he sees it as a consequence that a theological statement 'does not have any other factual meaning than what is contained in at least some of the relevant empirical propositions' and it is clear from the context that these latter propositions are either observation-statements, such as introspective reports of religious experience or propositions, such as those about material things, with (on Ayer's view) a purely observational content. These remarks, particularly the one about the meaning of physical statements, are virtually an explicit endorsement of the content-principle. And though they are made in the *Introduction*, and follow on from the revised formulation of the verification principle, it is clear that Ayer intends them to apply to his original position. Indeed, it is primarily to clear up a misunderstanding of this position (by his 'critics') that he makes them.

Finally, we should note how this passage reveals the close relationship between Ayer's verificationist position and the positivist slogan, enunciated by Moritz Schlick,[17] that the meaning of a statement consists in its method of verification. This slogan, of course, is open to several interpretations. 'Method of verification' could mean either the way or ways in which the statement *has been* verified or the range of ways in which it *could be* verified. Again, 'verification' could mean either *strong* (conclusive) verification or *weak* (evidential) verification; and it could be used either in an *exclusive* sense, concerned only with the establishing of *truth*, or in an *inclusive* sense, concerned with the establishing of *truth or falsity*. The version which comes closest to Ayer's position is the one which takes the second option in each case, yielding the thesis that the meaning of a statement (i.e. the factual meaning) consists in the range of ways in which there could (in principle) be observational evidence relevant to the determination of its truth or falsity. Ayer, in effect, is endorsing this thesis, though with one qualification: the meaning of the statement does not *consist in* this range, but, rather, is wholly *contained in* it.[18] The reason for the qualification is that there can be forms of observational evidence, as in the blood-on-the-coat example, which are extraneous to meaning – and this is the point which, in response to the misunderstanding of his critics, Ayer is stressing in the passage. But it is his acceptance of the thesis in other respects which needs to be stressed in the context of our present discussion. For it is this which constitutes the core of his verificationist position and explains his acceptance of the verification principle in its content-restricting form. In short, it is because he holds that factual meaning is wholly contained within the possibilities of observational evidence that he holds that factual content must be purely observational. And it is because he holds that factual content must be purely observational, that he holds that a statement is factually significant (expresses a genuinely factual proposition) if and only if it falls within the scope of an observational language. Whether Ayer was justified in holding these views is, of course, another matter. And it is this which we must consider next.

4 *Is there a rationale for the verification principle?*

If I am right, Ayer is accepting a very stringent criterion of factual significance – considerably more stringent than his initial formulation suggests. Not only does he require, of any factually significant statement, that it be open to observational evidence – that there could be 'observations relevant to the determination of its truth or falsehood' (*LTL*, 38) – but he also requires that its content be purely observational – the kind of content which can be wholly covered by some sentence or infinite complex of sentences in an observational language. As we have seen, this leads him into accepting a reductive analysis of much of our ordinary and scientific discourse, the phenomenalist analysis of physical statements being the prime example. Considered on their own merits, these analyses are intuitively implausible; and they are implausible not only in detail, but in their whole reductionist approach. Thus any attempt to translate statements about the physical world into statements about sense-contents, or statements about other minds into statements about behaviour, seems to involve a radical distortion of what the original statements mean. Ayer himself, of course, must feel the *prima facie* force of these intuitions. The reason he overrules them and offers a reductionist account is that his allegiance to the content-principle leaves him, in effect, with no alternative. At least it leaves him with no alternative other than rejecting the relevant statements as nonsensical, and this, not surprisingly, he is unwilling to do.

In view of the implausibility of the reductionist approach, it might seem that, if he was to be a verificationist at all, Ayer should have settled for the evidence-principle. For, barring certain forms of radical scepticism, this would allow statements about unobservable entities to qualify (without reduction) as significant, through their actual or possible role in explaining observations. We have already noted this point in connection with scientific hypotheses, but obviously its application is much wider. Thus, quite generally, statements about the physical world would be open to observational evidence through their role in explaining sense-experience, and, given this, statements about other minds would then be open to observational evidence through their role in explaining behaviour. Thus, by adopting the evidence-principle, Ayer could acknowledge the significance of these statements without recourse to reductionism. Admittedly, he would run the risk of having to allow significance to certain statements which he would prefer to classify as nonsensical – e.g. theological statements might be legitimized by their explanatory role. But presumably, even for Ayer, this would be preferable to a principle which either denied the significance of most of our ordinary assertions or required an interpretation of them which was a radical distortion of their ordinary sense.

However, even though the evidence-principle is, in a sense, safer than the content-principle, in that it is less likely to yield counterintuitive results, it would be a mistake to suppose that Ayer would have done better to adopt it. Quite the reverse: if there is any reason for adopting a verification principle at all, it is a reason for adopting it in its strong, content-restricting form. For, once we allow factual content to exceed observational content, we no longer confine meaning to the possibilities of observational evidence. And once meaning is thus released, there is no way of excluding, on purely semantic grounds, the possibility of factually significant statements which are not open to observational evidence at all. Put another way, unless the scope of meaning is confined by the content-principle, we automatically generate cases in which the factual significance of a statement has to be acknowledged irrespective of whether we think it is open to observational evidence or not.

Perhaps we can best illustrate this point by considering the case of statements about the physical world. Let us assume, with Ayer, that sense-contents are our only immediate perceptual data, so that, unless they are constructs out of sense-contents, physical objects are not directly observable. And let us suppose that, contrary to the content-principle, we take physical statements to be factually significant and construe them, 'realistically', as irreducibly about some mind-independent reality. This semantic position is permissible under the evidence-principle. For we could claim that, although physical objects are not directly observable, physical statements are open to observational evidence through their explanatory role with respect to sense-experience. Thus we might regard certain physical statements as observationally verified by the fact that, in conjunction with certain statements of psychophysical law (assigning experiential effects to physical conditions), they best explain our experiential data. However, given our realistic construal of physical statements, we could hardly regard their openness to this kind of observational evidence as a prerequisite of their having the significance we attach to them. If someone were to press the viewpoint of the radical sceptic, denying that such statements were open to evidence in this way, we would not see this as a challenge to our semantic position. We would not see it as something which, if we accepted it, would oblige us to abandon the claim that physical statements are both factually significant and concerned with a mind-independent reality. Rather, we would see it as raising a separate and purely epistemological issue, to be decided in the framework of, but without prejudice to, our prior semantic convictions. We may reject the scepticism; but both we and the sceptic would accept that the epistemological issue only arises because the significance of physical statements, construed realistically, is already secure. In short, in adopting our initial semantic position, in defiance of the content-principle, we have already decided that the factual significance of physical statements does not depend on how this epistemological issue is resolved.

The conclusion to be drawn from this is that, unless we accept the content-principle, there is no rationale for making openness to observational evidence a requirement of factual significance. This is not to deny, of course, that, even if we permit non-observational content, there may be some other way of establishing that all factually significant statements are open to such evidence. For there may be some way of showing that the possibilities of evidence are so rich as to encompass any significant statement we could devise. But this would be to establish an epistemological position, not a semantic principle: it would show not that openness to evidence was a criterial requirement of significance, but rather that, given the criterial requirements, the evidential possibilities were so pervasive as to cover any statement which meets them. For this reason, it seems to me that, given his commitment to verificationism, Ayer was right to develop it in the way he (on my interpretation) did – requiring factual content to be purely observational. It is true that the application of this requirement to ordinary discourse has implausible results – so implausible as to constitute a major objection to Ayer's position. But if there are any grounds for accepting the verification principle, they are grounds for accepting it in its content-restricting form.

The less stringent evidence-principle may give more plausible results, but, by its very liberality, it becomes devoid of rationale.

This brings us to a cluster of crucial questions. Why did Ayer adopt a verificationist position at all? Was he justified in doing so? Does even the content-principle have any rationale? Perhaps the most surprising feature of *LTL* is that Ayer seems to assume the correctness of his position without argument. Not that this is what he takes himself to be doing.

> As to the validity of the verification principle, in the form in which we have stated it, a demonstration will be given in the course of this book. For it will be shown that all propositions which have factual content are empirical hypotheses; and that the function of an empirical hypothesis is to provide a rule for the anticipation of experience. (*LTL*, 41)

But the trouble is that what Ayer claims will be shown in the subsequent course of the book is only shown by appeal to the principle. At all crucial points, in the elimination of metaphysical philosophy and in the legitimization of ordinary discourse, the correctness of the principle is the guiding assumption.[19] The most that Ayer can really claim to have shown in favour of the principle is that it is possible to develop a systematic and internally coherent philosophy on its basis.

In a slightly earlier article,[20] entitled 'A Demonstration of the Impossibility of Metaphysics' (*DIM*), Ayer does at least attempt some explicit defence of the principle, though not, in my view, successfully. One part of the defence, indeed, rests on a confusion between *truth*-conditions and *verification*-conditions (a confusion perhaps partly engendered by the etymology of the word 'verify'). This enables him to pass, without apparently discerning the logical gap, from the comparatively uncontroversial claim[21] that 'to give the meaning of a proposition is to give the conditions under which it would be true and those under which it would be false' to the controversial verificationist claim that 'I understand a proposition if I know what observations I must make in order to establish its truth or falsity' – and I take the 'if' here to imply, in addition, 'only if'.[22] Leaving this confusion aside, the only defence of the principle is that it yields intuitively acceptable results in the case of those putative propositions whose status is uncontroversial, and that, as far as he can see, no rival criterion can do as well:

> There are some *prima facie* propositions which by universal agreement are given as significant and some expressions which are agreed to be meaningless. Trusting our criterion if it accepts the former class and rejects the latter, we apply it to such doubtful cases as that of the propositions of metaphysics, and if they fail to

satisfy it we pronounce them nonsensical. . . . If therefore a philosopher maintains that our criterion is too narrow and that metaphysical propositions are significant, it is for him to put forward a more liberal criterion: one that allows the significance of metaphysical propositions yet is not so liberal as to allow the significance of expressions such as "jealousy pronoun live" or "siffle hip brim" which are agreed by all parties to be meaningless.[23]

In Ayer's view, this challenge cannot be met.

There are two reasons why I find this argument unconvincing. In the first place, there seems to be no reason why the metaphysician needs to meet the challenge, as Ayer conceives it. In demanding that the metaphysician should provide an alternative criterion, Ayer is assuming that there must be some way of specifying the conditions under which a sentence is significant which is both general, in that it covers all sentences, and non-trivial, in that it does not appeal to other semantic properties, like that of *expressing a genuine proposition* or of *saying something true or false*. In effect, he is assuming that either the verification principle is correct or there is some other criterion of significance of a similarly general and radical kind. But in making this assumption, Ayer is already, to a large extent, begging the question. For why should it not turn out that there is no criterion of the kind Ayer envisages? Why should it not turn out that we can only specify the general conditions for significance in *semantic* terms and that any more far-reaching considerations only arise piecemeal in applying these conditions to particular cases or types of case? Of course, if Ayer had some independent reason for accepting the verification principle, he would, *a fortiori*, have a reason for claiming that there was a criterion of the relevant kind. But he cannot just assume that there is such a criterion and then claim a victory for the verification principle in default of other candidates.

Secondly, even if Ayer were right to insist on a radical criterion, he is too optimistic about the success of his own criterion in relation to the non-controversial cases. At least he is so if the criterion he is here defending is of the strong, content-restricting kind which (as I interpret him) he employs in *LTL*. For, as we have noted, the results of this strong criterion are clearly counterintuitive: prior to philosophical reflection, there is universal agreement that statements about the physical world and other minds are significant when realistically construed, while according to the content-principle they are nonsensical unless amenable to reductive analysis. So in relation to these cases, Ayer would be using his criterion to correct our ordinary intuitions rather than in deference to them. It may be, of course, that in this earlier article it is only the evidence-principle which Ayer is advocating. Since we are primarily concerned with his position in *LTL*, this would make his argument less interesting for our purposes. But, in any case, we have already shown that the evidence-principle is untenable. It is true that if the epistemological issues are resolved in the right way, its results are intuitively acceptable. But the very fact that its success depends on how these issues are resolved shows that it cannot serve as the fundamental criterion. Once we have assigned a realistic meaning to physical and other-minds statements, we have already implicitly accepted that their factual significance does not depend on their openness to observational evidence.

The fact that Ayer himself fails to provide an adequate argument for the verification principle does not, of course, mean that the principle is indefensible. Since, in one form or another, the principle formed the corner stone of the positivist philosophy of the Vienna Circle, from whom, in effect, Ayer inherited it, we may expect to find further support for it from other and more established members of the group. I think the nearest we come to an argument of this sort is in an article by Schlick entitled 'Positivismus und Realismus' and whose English translation ('Positivism and Realism') is reprinted in *LP*.[24] There is no doubt that Ayer was considerably influenced by Schlick's writings. And since at the beginning of *DIM* he acknowledges this article, in particular, as one of the main sources of his views, it is quite likely that he was relying on Schlick's argument, or something very like it, as the rationale for his own verificationist position. At any rate, I think we would do well to examine the argument in some detail.

Like Ayer in *DIM*, Schlick begins with the relatively innocent assumption that the meaning of a statement consists in its truth-conditions. But, unlike Ayer, he does not just treat this as an implicit version of the verification principle. He detects a logical gap which needs to be bridged by argument. This argument turns on the question of how the meaning (the truth-conditions) of a statement is to be grasped. In order to grasp the meaning of a statement, we have to grasp the meanings of its constituent words. One way of grasping the meaning of a word is by a verbal definition, e.g. 'bachelor' means 'unmarried man'. But to grasp the meaning of a word in this way, we would first have to grasp the meanings of the words used to define it. So, to avoid an infinite regress, these verbal definitions must eventually terminate in words whose meanings we can grasp in some other way. According to Schlick, the meanings of these primitive words are grasped *ostensively*:

The meaning of a word must in the end be *shown*, it must be *given*. This is done by an act of indication, of pointing; and what is pointed at must be given, otherwise I cannot be referred to it. Accordingly, in order to find the meaning of a proposition, we must transform it by successive definitions until finally only such words occur in it as can no longer be defined, but whose meanings can only be directly pointed out. (*LP*, 87)

In other words, Schlick is claiming that every significant sentence must be wholly composed, or be transformable by verbal definitions into a sentence which is wholly composed, of words which are ostensively definable – words whose meanings 'can . . . be directly pointed out', or are, as I shall term it, 'ostendible'. And he is claiming that, once the verbal transformations are complete, it is by reference to these ostensive definitions that we finally reveal what the sentence means and how its meaning can be grasped. These claims make up what I shall call Schlick's *ostension thesis*.

It is from this ostension thesis that Schlick now derives his verificationist conclusion. If our understanding of a sentence finally rests on our ostensive grasp of the meanings of its constituent words, or those words which emerge through verbal definitions, then, concludes Schlick, our understanding of the sentence finally rests on our knowledge of its method of verification. For, as he sees it, to trace the meaning (i.e. the truth-conditions) of a statement back to the types of experience in terms of which its constituents are to be ostensively defined is precisely to specify the experiential procedures by which the truth-value of the statement can be established.

> The criterion of the truth or falsity of the proposition then lies in the fact that under definite conditions (given in the definition) certain data are present, or not present. If this is determined then everything asserted by the proposition is determined, and I know its meaning. If I am *unable*, in principle, to verify a proposition, that is, if I am absolutely ignorant . . . of what I must do in order to ascertain its truth or falsity, then obviously I do not know what the proposition actually states, and I should then be unable to interpret the proposition by passing from the words, with the aid of the definitions, to possible experiences. For in so far as I am able to do this I am also able in the same way to state at least in principle the method of verification . . . (*LP*, 87)

In this way, Schlick arrives at his principle that the meaning of a statement lies in its method of verification – or as he expresses it in this article, 'the meaning of every proposition is completely contained within its verification in the given' (*LP*, 106). This is a strong principle which, like Ayer's, confines factual content to observational content. And it leads him, as Ayer is led, to adopt a reductive (phenomenalistic) account of propositions about the physical world: ' . . . propositions concerning bodies are transformable into equivalent propositions concerning the occurrence of sensations in accordance with laws.' (*LP*, 107)

This then is Schlick's argument, and the question we must now consider is whether it is successful. On the face of it, the answer seems clear. Even if his ostension thesis is correct, Schlick's inference from it to his verificationist conclusion is illegitimate. For the fact that the meaning of a sentence is built out of the ostendible meanings of its parts does not entail that its meaning is wholly contained within its method of verification, i.e. 'its verification in the given'. Nor, it seems, does it even ensure that the sentence is verifiable, whether in the strong sense (conclusive verifiability) which I think Schlick has in mind, or in the weak sense (openness to observational evidence) which Ayer employs in *LTL*. For, given some group of words, each of which individually signifies something which can be directly experienced (or 'given'), why should it not be possible to arrange them into a sentence which is significant, but signifies a type of state-of-affairs whose obtaining cannot itself be directly experienced and, on certain epistemological assumptions, is not even open to observational evidence? Indeed, in a moment I shall provide what amount to some examples of this. (I say 'amount to', because, as we shall see, we have slightly to alter our conception of what it is for the words in a sentence to meet the requirements of the ostension thesis.)

In effect, Schlick seems to have confused two quite different empiricist approaches to meaning. On the one hand, there is the approach of the *empirical atomist*, who takes the basic units of meaning to be primitive (not-further-analysable) concepts, restricts genuine primitive concepts to ones which are, in some paradigmatic sense, empirical (e.g. ones which can be grasped ostensively), acknowledges other genuine concepts only if they can be analysed into such primitive concepts, and thus restricts genuine propositions to ones which are composed exclusively of concepts whose genuineness is empirically certified in this way. On the other hand, there is the approach of the *logical positivist*, who takes the basic units of meaning to be propositions, restricts genuine propositions, or at least genuinely factual propositions, to ones which are, in some sense, empirically verifiable – sometimes, to ones whose content is purely observational – and assigns content to concepts in so far as they can feature in, and contribute to the factual content of, such verifiable propositions. These two approaches, while both empiricist, are clearly different and yield quite different criteria of sentential significance. The positivist, in requiring that a factually significant sentence be empirically verifiable, is not thereby requiring that all its constituent words (or those that emerge through verbal definitions) be empirically definable in isolation, since he is taking the sentence and not the word to carry the unit of empirical meaning. Conversely, the atomist, in requiring primitive words to be empirically definable, is not thereby requiring that every significant sentence composed of such words be empirically verifiable, since he is taking the word and not the sentence to carry the unit of empirical meaning. Schlick seems to be unaware of the distinction. In particular, he seems to think that his ostension thesis, which is a version of empirical atomism, automatically validates his verificationist thesis, which is a version of logical positivism. And in this he is clearly mistaken.

It might be objected that the difference between the two empiricist accounts of meaning is not as sharp as I am suggesting, and, in particular, that, once we have a proper understanding of the requirements of ostensive definition, we can see that Schlick's atomistic premise does, after all, provide a basis for his verificationist conclusion. Prior to reflection, we are likely to assume that, for a subject to acquire an understanding of a word ostensively, he must mentally select some component or aspect of what is, for him currently, experientially given, and correctly judge that the word signifies (or, if he is imparting meaning, stipulate that the word is to signify) that selected item. But if it is this kind of ostensive procedure which Schlick has in mind, he can hardly think that the ostension thesis is to be accepted without qualification: he can hardly think that *all* significant primitive words (all the significant words which remain when the process of verbal definition is complete) are ostensively definable. For some of the primitive words will be terms drawn from the apparatus of formal logic – terms such as 'and', 'not', 'some', and 'any', as well as the auxiliary devices of variables and brackets. Obviously, in these cases, he cannot think of the word or symbol as signifying, on its own, something which could be a component or aspect of the given. Now it is possible that Schlick does not intend his ostension thesis to apply to terms of this sort – that he is taking the logical apparatus for granted and only insisting that the 'lexical' primitives, which provide, so to speak, the factual ingredients for this apparatus to structure, are ostensively definable. But this would be an uncomfortable position for an empiricist to adopt, not only because the distinction between logical and lexical items is not a sharp one, but also because, once he has conceded the possibility of primitive non-ostendible meaning, it will be hard to justify its confinement to the logical apparatus. A better, because more consistently empiricist, response would be to retain the principle that all significant primitive terms are ostensively definable, but broaden our conception of the ostensive procedure by which their meanings are fixed or revealed. Thus while a logical term such as 'and' does not, on its own, signify something which could be an element of the given, there are sentences containing it which do – sentences, such as 'this is red and round', which can be used to report some state of affairs which is directly experienced. So Schlick should say (and presumably would say) that the word 'and' does have indirectly an ostendible meaning, via the ostendible meanings of such sentences – that we can ostensively define the word by indicating the types of experience which conclusively verify its use

35

in certain sentential contexts. Moreover, it becomes clear, on further reflection, that a similar procedure is required for the ostensive definition of *any* word. Even if we choose an explicitly phenomenal word, such as 'blue', we cannot fully specify its meaning by associating it, in isolation, with some element of the given. For the full meaning of 'blue', just because it embodies the contribution of that word to the meaning of any sentence containing it, includes its grammatical category, and this is not something which we can indicate ostensively except via its use in sentential contexts. Thus I may focus my attention on the colour of some visually presented item and pronounce that 'blue' signifies that selected element. But this does not determine whether the word is a colour-predicate, to be used in such sentences as 'this region is blue', or the name of a colour-quale, to be used in such sentences as 'this region is pervaded by blue', or even the name of a colour-property (the property of being blue), to be used in such sentences as 'this region instantiates blue'. If we are to fix its grammatical category ostensively, we must resort to the ostendible meanings, or ostendible truth-conditions, of certain sentences containing it. That is, we must, as with the logical terms, indicate the types of experience which would conclusively verify its use in the context of certain complete assertions such as (if we take it as a predicate) 'this (phenomenal) region is blue'.

If we adopt this more sophisticated account of ostensive definition, Schlick's ostension thesis appears to come much closer to his verificationist thesis than we had originally supposed. For in claiming that a sentence draws its meaning from the ostendible meanings of its constituents (or those that emerge through verbal definition) he would already be making a claim of a quasi-verificationist kind, in as much as the meanings of these constituents would be determined by the methods of conclusively verifying their use in certain sentential contexts. It might seem to be only a short step from this to the full verificationist position, in which the meaning of a word consists in its contribution to the meanings of the sentences which contain it and the meaning of a sentence consists in, or is contained within, its method of verification. In short, it might seem that the new account of ostensive definition forms a bridge between Schlick's atomistic premise and his verificationist conclusion.

In fact, however, the gulf remains. For even if the meanings of the primitive words are determined by the methods of verifying certain sentences containing them, it does not follow that *all* significant sentences are verifiable, much less that the meaning of a sentence is contained within its method of verification. We can bring out this point by focusing on two examples. Consider the two sentences:

S_1: For some x, x is triangular and x is not a sense-content.

S_2: For some x, x is a pain and x is occurring now and x is not sensibly compresent with (i.e. not part of the same total experience as) this (i.e. my current) pain.

The constituent words of both these sentences are, we may reasonably assume, ostensively definable in the relevant sense; that is, each word or symbol is one whose meaning we can grasp in terms of its conclusively verifiable use in sentences recording the content of experience. Since the sentences are also syntactically well-formed, they meet all the atomistic requirements of significance. But their meeting these requirements does not ensure that they, or the propositions they express, are verifiable (i.e. verifiable or falsifiable) even in the weak sense. For in asserting the existence of a triangular object which is *not a sense-content*, S_1 is making a claim about how things are in some realm external to sense-experience (presumably, about how things are in the physical world), and in asserting the existence of a current pain which is *not sensibly compresent with my current pain*, S_2 is making a claim about what is taking place in someone else's mind. These claims about an external reality and about another mind are ones which, from the standpoint of a radical sceptic, are not open to observational evidence. So the question of whether S_1 and S_2 are verifiable is left as a separate epistemological issue, not settled by their satisfaction of the atomist's requirements. It follows, of course, that even if, contrary to the sceptic, we take them to be verifiable (perhaps by appealing to explanatory considerations), we cannot say that their meaning is contained within their methods of verification. For their meaning has to transcend, indeed be wholly independent of, their methods of verification in order for the epistemological issue to arise.

In all this, of course, we are assuming that S_1 and S_2 are to be construed realistically, as expressing the propositions which at face value they seem to express. If we subjected them to some kind of reductive analysis, we could hope to confine their meanings to their methods of verification. But this is beside the point. For it is as realistically construed that the sentences meet the atomistic requirements. It is precisely by drawing their meaning from the ostendible meanings of their constituents, and the way these constituents are syntactically arranged, that S_1 comes to make a claim about an external reality and S_2 comes to make a claim about another mind. It may be contended that such claims are meaningless. But no support for this contention can be derived from the ostension thesis.

It is clear, therefore, that even if we allow the ostension thesis to assume this quasi-verificationist form, it provides no basis for the verificationist conclusion which Schlick derives from it. This leaves open the possibility that verificationism can be defended in some other way. But, as far as I can see, it cannot. It is only in its content-restricting form that it has any chance of a rational defence, and even in this form there is, as far as I can see, nothing to be said in its favour. There is also, of course, much to be said against it. For the restrictions it imposes are clearly counterintuitive. And here the point is not just that it has implausible consequences for ordinary discourse – forcing us to choose between rejecting most of our assertions as nonsensical and analysing them in a way which distorts their apparent meaning. It is also that, by appealing to the way in which the meaning of a sentence is built out of the meanings of its constituents and their syntactical arrangement, we have no difficulty in understanding how non-observational content can be generated. And, as the cases of S_1 and S_2 reveal, this holds true even if we impose a severely empiricist restriction on the possible meanings of the constituents – or of the constituents which emerge when the processes of verbal definition are complete.

5 Empirical atomism

Our rejection of the verification principle does not oblige us to reject an empiricist theory of meaning altogether. For there is still the approach of the empirical atomist, who takes the meaning of a sentence to be built out of the empirical meanings of its constituent terms, or those which emerge through verbal definition. At the risk of digressing slightly from our main theme, it is worth considering whether, in some form, this approach can be defended. Nor will this be entirely a digression if, as seems likely, it is empirical atomism, or something akin to it, which (via the influence of Schlick) underlies Ayer's stated position.

Perhaps the earliest version of empirical atomism is found in Hume's principle that every simple idea is a copy of (is causally derived from and exactly resembles) an earlier impression. Hume formulated this principle within the framework of an austere psychology which treated all ideas and concepts as perceptual images. He divided ideas into the *simple*, 'such as admit of no distinction nor separation' and the *complex*, which 'may be distinguished into parts'.[25] So in claiming that every simple idea is a copy of an impression, he was claiming that every idea either is itself a copy of an impression or is divisible into ideas which are copies of impressions. In his subsequent arguments, Hume used this principle as if it were an *a priori* truth – as if it set a logically necessary limit on the genuine ideas we can possess and, thereby, on the meanings of the terms we can employ. Thus he argued that we cannot have a genuine idea of objective causal necessity since there is no impression of which such an idea is a copy, nor can it be resolved into simpler ideas which are copies of impressions. The trouble is, however, that, as a claim about the causal origins of our ideas, the principle is at best an empirical truth. Hume himself admits as much, at the outset, when he allows, as a 'singular' exception, the case of the missing shade.[26] What he fails to see is that if it is only advanced as an empirical truth, though with this singular exception, then those who claim to possess the ideas which he is seeking to eliminate can plead that these are exceptions too. The principle which he should have adopted, as Ayer points out in his recent short book on Hume,[27] is that for every simple idea there could be an exactly resembling impression. This could at least be offered as an *a priori* truth (I am not saying that it is one), since it concerns only the intrinsic nature of ideas, not their causal origins. Moreover, it would accommodate cases, like the missing shade, which Hume wants to admit as exceptions to his original principle, while still allowing him to exclude the ideas, like that of objective causal necessity, which he believes to be impossible. If we also correct Hume's exclusively imagist psychology, what emerges is the principle that, for every primitive concept, there is a type of impression in terms of which it could be ostensively grasped. Re-expressed as a criterion of linguistic significance, this becomes, in effect, Schlick's atomistic principle that every significant primitive term must be ostensively definable. The only important difference in this new formulation is that, by dropping the reference to a certain type of impression, we leave room for a more liberal interpretation of the ostensive procedure, whereby it is not in isolation, but via its conclusively verifiable use in certain sentences, that the meaning of the term is ostensively explained. This, for reasons already specified, is an advantage.

Before we consider this position any further, we may pause to note, *en passant*, an interesting point about Ayer's interpretation of Hume in *LTL*. As I have already said, it may well be some form of empirical atomism which underlies Ayer's acceptance of the verification principle. But what is certainly true is that Ayer saw Hume as an implicit advocate of this principle. The passage he cites as evidence occurs at the end of Hume's *Enquiry*:

> If we take in our hand any volume; of divinity or school metaphysics, for instance; let us ask, *Does it contain any abstract reasoning concerning quantity or number?* No. *Does it contain any experimental reasoning concerning matter of fact and existence?* No. Commit it then to the flames: for it can contain nothing but sophistry and illusion.[28]

'What is this' asks Ayer 'but a rhetorical version of our own thesis that a sentence which does not express either a formally true proposition or an empirical hypothesis is devoid of literal significance?' (*LTL*, 54). The same interpretation is offered in his introduction to *LP*, where the passage is said to be 'an excellent statement of the positivist's position' (*LP*, 10). Even as late as *CQ*, where the passage is again quoted, it is said that 'the assumptions on which Hume was relying were taken up by the Logical Positivists and embodied in what came to be known as the principle of verifiability' (*CQ*, 23). In fact, however, Ayer's interpretation of the passage is mistaken. All that Hume is claiming is that the assertions of the theologians and metaphysicians are worthless, since they are not substantiated either by sound *a priori* reasoning (of the sort found in mathematics) or by sound empirical reasoning (of the sort found in natural science). He is not claiming that, because they are neither tautologies nor empirically verifiable, such assertions are meaningless. Nor, as far as I can tell, is there any other passage in Hume which endorses, explicitly or implicitly, the principle of verification. Of course, Hume did consider many of the assertions of theologians and metaphysicians to be meaningless, since they employed terms to which, in his view, no genuine ideas could be attached. But what led him to this position was not an acceptance of the verification principle, but his conviction that, with the singular exception, simple ideas must be copies of previous impressions. I have no doubt that Hume would have allowed an unverifiable factual sentence to be significant so long as it was properly constructed out of elements which themselves, or whose ultimate *definientia*, express impression-copying ideas.

As we have seen, Hume's principle, corrected and made explicitly linguistic, turns into Schlick's principle (which formed the core of his ostension thesis) that every significant primitive term must be ostensively definable. But this, on its own, does not yield a complete criterion of linguistic significance. We still have to set restrictions on the ways in which significant terms can be syntactically combined to form significant sentences, if only because not all combinations are grammatical. The principles of grammar are, of course, already implicit in the meanings of the terms, since the meaning of a term includes its grammatical classification. This, as we have seen, is one reason why we have to think of ostensive definition as fixing the meanings of the primitive terms by reference to their use in sentences, i.e. by indicating the types of experience which conclusively verify their employment in certain sentential contexts.

Let us suppose that we have supplemented Schlick's principle with some explicit statement of the rules of grammar for a particular language, so that such ungrammatical strings as 'Quickly an in and' are categorized as meaningless. It might still be argued that the resulting criterion of significance is too liberal. For consider the English sentence 'Jealousy is an orange square root of London'. This is composed of significant words grammatically arranged. But surely it is nonsensical. Moreover, there are infinitely many sentences of this kind. Perhaps the existence of such sentences was one factor which led positivists to replace the atomist test of significance by a verificational one – for, obviously, they do not express propositions which are empirically verifiable. Certainly Ayer saw it as a virtue of the verification principle that, as well as exposing nonsensical words, it exposed nonsensical combinations of meaningful words.[29]

40

But, as far as I know, he did not specifically consider the case of combinations which are grammatical but (allegedly) nonsensical.

There are two ways in which the atomist can respond to this challenge. On the one hand, he may decide to incorporate further restrictions into the principles of grammar, so as to exclude sentences of the problematic sort. In effect, words would be assigned to much narrower grammatical categories, ensuring that those in the same category can be exchanged, in any context, without changing sense into nonsense; and the rules of syntax would then be constructed on this new basis, specifying the ways in which items from these categories can be significantly combined. On the other hand, he may simply deny that the sentences are problematic. He may claim that, while they are certainly nonsensical in *some* sense, they do express genuine propositions – they say things which are either true or false – and so are not nonsensical in the *relevant* sense. This, it seems to me, is the correct response, as I shall now explain.

Consider again the sentence 'Jealousy is an orange square root of London'. Surely we can argue like this: *only numbers can be square roots; jealousy is not a number; ergo, jealousy is not a square root; ergo, jealousy is not an orange square root of London.* Or again, we can surely argue like this: *square roots are numbers; numbers are not among the sorts of thing which can be coloured; ergo, no square root is orange; ergo, nothing can be an orange square root of something; ergo, jealousy is not an orange square root of London.* If, as I would claim, such arguments are correct (though, outside the present context, it is hard to imagine circumstances in which we would have a use for them), then the sentence, and others of the same kind, turn out to be significant (i.e. proposition-expressing) but analytically false. This is not to deny that these analytical falsehoods are of a more radical kind than ones like 'Jones is an unmarried husband' and '2 + 2 = 5'; for they stem from an inappropriate combining of semantic categories. Doubtless it is this which makes them in some sense nonsensical. But if I am right, we classify them as nonsensical precisely because we discern, and discern the absurdity of, the propositions they express.

Assuming, then, that our atomistic criterion of significance is not too liberal, let us now turn to the crucial question of whether it is still, like the verificationist criterion, too restrictive. Is there any reason to accept that all significant primitive terms must be, in the relevantly broad sense, ostensively definable – that all primitive concepts must be ones whose content could, in principle, be fully specified (if only by specifying the content of certain propositions containing them) in terms of what is experientially given? Or should we allow for the possibility of primitive terms with non-ostendible meanings – allow for the possibility of primitive concepts of an experience-transcendent kind?

We should begin by conceding two points to the empirical atomist.

In the first place, we must concede that, however free-wheeling his private formation of concepts, it is only by some kind of ostensive procedure that a subject gains his initial access to the meanings of terms in a public language. Of course, once he has acquired an understanding of certain terms, he can learn the meanings of new terms by verbal definition or verbal explanation. But if there is to be any understanding at all, there must be some terms whose meanings he comes to grasp by observing the kinds of situation in which others employ them. This point is so uncontroversial as to be hardly a concession at all. It does not, as such, set any restriction on the kinds of meaning which terms can possess, save only that if they are to function as elements of a public language, there must be some way in which members of the community can discern their meaning by observing their use. Such discernment may be easier if the terms have, or are definable by means of terms which have, a purely ostendible meaning; but it certainly does not follow that discernment is impossible if this is not the case. For we have set no limit on the kinds of concept which the learning subject can bring to bear on the situations of usage he observes. Nor, of course, have we set any restriction on the sorts of language which the subject can invent for his own private use.

The second concession is more far-reaching. We must acknowledge, I think, that at least most of our concepts are ones which we could not possess unless we knew what it was like to have certain kinds of experience or to be directly presented with certain kinds of sensible item. Obviously, this will be so for concepts, like that of pain or visual awareness, which exclusively concern the character of experience. But it also applies to concepts employed in characterizing the physical world. Thus I could have no conception of physical shape without some conception of sensible shape, and I could have no conception of sensible shape without knowing what it is like, either visually or in some other sense-modality, to be sensually aware of shape. This is not to say that the shape-qualities we assign to physical objects are the very same as those which feature in the content of sense-experience – much less that the latter qualities are ones which physical objects actually possess. The point is only that without reference to sensible shape, and thereby to the character of sense-experience, we cannot form any conception of physical shape, however similar or different we take physical and sensible shape to be. Nor is this point limited to the concept of physical shape. It applies quite generally to physical concepts. Indeed, if it applies to physical shape, it has to apply quite generally. For without a concept of physical shape, we could have no concept of physical space, and without a concept of physical space, we could have no physical concepts at all.

I have said that this second concession is more far-reaching. But, of course, it still falls short of what the empirical atomist requires. For the fact that most of our concepts are ones which we could not possess without knowing what it was like to have certain kinds of experience does not entail that all are; nor does it even entail that those which are have, either directly or through analysis, an experientially definable content – one which is fully revealed by the character of the relevant experiences. This means that the atomist still needs some further argument if he is to be vindicated in those areas where, traditionally, his position has been most in dispute. This is so, for example, in what is perhaps the most important area of all – that concerned with our concept of causation. The atomist will say that, because we are not, and cannot even imagine ourselves being, sensibly aware of anything which might be termed 'agency' or 'necessitation', the relation of cause to effect, if it is to be genuinely conceivable, must be defined in a way which dispenses with such notions – e.g. in the way suggested by Hume. But we would ordinarily claim that we do possess genuine concepts of agency and necessitation, and that any attempt to define causation in a way which dispenses with these concepts fails to do justice to our understanding of the *definiendum*. Assuming the atomist cannot accommodate these concepts, the onus is on him to show that we are mistaken. He cannot do this by pointing out that the concepts transcend what could be manifested by experience, and are not reducible to experiential concepts by analysis, since it is precisely the possibility of such experience-transcendent concepts which is at issue.

Can the atomist provide a satisfactory argument for his position? Not that I can see. That is, he cannot, as far as I can see, show that experience-transcendent concepts are, in principle, impossible. What, perhaps, he can show is how *prima facie* cases of actual transcendent concepts could be explained away. But here we need to be careful. There is a crucial difference between devising a theory which, *on the assumption that we do not possess a certain concept*, plausibly explains why we ordinarily believe that we do, and devising a theory which offers such an explanation and which is sufficiently plausible *independently* to make it irrational to retain this ordinary belief. Thus consider the case of agency. The Humean argues that our intuition that we possess a concept of agency is an illusion, explained by the fact that we tend to view the world in the perspective of our own inductive attitudes: our exposure to the constant conjunction of two types of event leads us to feel justified in inferring the occurrence of one type from the occurrence of the other, and we then, as it were, project the 'therefore' which is internal to the inference onto the events themselves. Now it is a moot point whether such an explanation of our intuition is successful even in its own terms. In particular, it is not clear how the projection-theory can account for the asymmetry of the agency-relation which we suppose ourselves to understand. (This is something which I shall discuss in detail in Part III, when I examine Ayer's account of causation.) But even if the explanation is, in its own terms, successful, we still need to be given a reason for accepting it. Perhaps the Humean will say that it is the most plausible explanation available. But how can this be so? Unless the intuition has been independently discredited, the most plausible explanation for it is that it is true – that we think we have a concept of agency because we do. This has to be the most plausible explanation, from our point of view, simply because, as well as being the simplest, it is the only one which accords with our actual intuitions (assuming that the intuition to be explained has not already been discarded). Thus the Humean cannot appeal to the projection-theory as a way of undermining our intuition; rather, he would have to produce some independent argument against the intuition in order to substantiate the theory. And it is just such an argument which, as far as I can see, he cannot provide. The only objection which can be brought against the intuition is that it credits us with a concept of an experience-transcendent kind. And what the Humean needs, but lacks, is some reasoned case for denying the possibility of such concepts.

It seems to me, therefore, that, as an absolute principle, empirical atomism, like verificationism, is an unwarranted dogma, and that, to the extent that they clash with non-discredited intuitions, its restrictions on the range of possible concepts and possible forms of linguistic meaning should be rejected. This is not to say that there are no aspects of atomism which can be defended. The atomist is surely right to stress that the significance of a sentence depends only on the significance of its constituents and the way they are syntactically combined, and, in this respect, he avoids the errors of the verificationist. He is also surely right to stress the extent to which our concepts draw their content from what is experientially given and, correspondingly, right to seek a predominantly empiricist account of our conceptual scheme. Where he is wrong, and crucially wrong, is in insisting, as an *a priori* principle, that experience is the only source of conceptual content, or, more precisely, that every genuine concept must be one, or be analysable into ones, whose content can be completely manifested in experience.

6 Ayer's reductionism

Both empirical atomism and the content-principle require primitive concepts to be experientially definable. Where they differ is that the former, unlike the latter, allows these primitive concepts, and the concepts analysable in terms of them, to feature in propositions with a non-experiential (non-observational) ontology – propositions which refer to, or claim the existence of, entities that are not directly observable. Thus consider again the sentence S_1, 'For some x, x is triangular and x is not a sense-content', which we discussed above in section 4. By the standards of empirical atomism, S_1 qualifies as factually significant (as expressing a genuine factual proposition), since its constituent terms are, in the relevantly broad sense, ostensively definable – their meaning can be grasped in terms of their conclusively verifiable use in sentences recording the content of experience (sentences such as 'this is a sense-content', 'this sense-content is triangular' and 'this sense-content is not triangular'). But if we assume, with Ayer, that only sense-contents are directly observable, then S_1 does not qualify as factually significant under the content-principle – at least it does not if it is realistically construed. For, thus construed, it claims the existence of something (a triangular object) beyond the realm of sense-experience and such a claim falls outside the scope of any observational language in the relevant sense. It falls outside the scope of any observational language, since one of the requirements of such a language is that its ontology should be purely observational; that is, apart from classes, its universe of discourse (the values for its variables and the referents of its names) must be restricted to entities which are directly observable – to entities which form the ontological subject matter of observation-statements.

It is because of this ontological restriction that the content-principle generates such an acute problem over the status of our ordinary and scientific assertions. (In comparison, the problems generated by empirical atomism, e.g. over the status of causal assertions, are only minor.) Thus if, like Ayer, we limit the observational ontology to sense-contents – that is, as he uses the term 'sense-content', to 'the immediate data not merely of "outer" but also of "introspective" sensation' (*LTL*, 53) – and if we accept that sense-contents are internal to the mind, then it seems that all our assertions about the physical world count, under the content-principle, as nonsensical. Moreover if, like Ayer, we further insist that the observational ontology available to each subject, in the making and understanding of assertions, is not merely confined to sense-contents, but confined to the sense-contents of his own present and future biography,[30] then it seems that all our assertions about the minds of others and about our own past experiences are also nonsensical – at least nonsensical from our current viewpoint. Although Ayer accepts the content-principle, these are conclusions which, understandably, he is unwilling to accept. Common sense tells him, as it tells the rest of us, that such assertions (about the physical world, the minds of others, and the past) are significant. It is his determination to reconcile their significance with the requirements of the principle which leads him down the path of reductive analysis. The most important case to be considered is his phenomenalistic analysis of statements about the physical world. But before we turn to this, we should say something about his general conception of philosophical analysis, and of reductive analysis in particular.

45

In *LTL*, Ayer takes philosophical analysis to consist mainly, if not exclusively, in the provision of what he calls 'definitions *in use*'. Such definitions are contrasted with what he calls '*explicit* definitions', such as one might find in a dictionary.

> We define a symbol *explicitly* when we put forward another symbol, or symbolic expression which is synonymous with it. And the word "synonymous" is here used in such a way that two symbols belonging to the same language can be said to be synonymous if, and only if, the simple substitution of one symbol for the other, in any sentence in which either can significantly occur, always yields a new sentence which is equivalent to the old. (*LTL*, 59–60)

In contrast:

> We define a symbol *in use*, not by saying that it is synonymous with some other symbol, but by showing how the sentences in which it significantly occurs can be translated into equivalent sentences, which contain neither the *definiendum* itself, nor any of its synonyms. (*LTL*, 60)

In both cases, when Ayer speaks of two sentences as 'equivalent' he means, in effect, 'inter-deducible', though he expresses this in a more complicated (and surely needlessly complicated) way:

> . . . we say that two sentences of the same language are equivalent if, and only if, every sentence which is entailed by any given group of sentences in conjunction with one of them is entailed by the same group in conjunction with the other. And, in this usage of the word "entail", a sentence s is said to entail a sentence t when the proposition expressed by t is deducible from the proposition expressed by s. (*LTL*, 60)

As an example of an explicit definition, Ayer gives the definition of 'oculist' as 'eye-doctor'. And as an example of a definition in use, he gives Russell's theory of definite descriptions, which purports to show how sentences containing referring phrases of the form 'the so-and-so' can be translated into sentences which do not employ such phrases or anything synonymous.

As I have already said, Ayer thinks that philosophy is primarily concerned with the provision not of explicit definitions, but of definitions in use. One reason for this is that he takes a somewhat narrow, and surely a too narrow, view of what explicit definition can be expected to achieve. Thus, in considering such definition, he focuses his attention exclusively on the sort of example we find in dictionaries, like that of 'oculist' meaning 'eye-doctor', and obviously it is not this sort of definition which it is the concern of philosophy to provide. He seems to forget that explicit definitions can also be of a deep and, so to speak, philosophically pregnant kind – ones which express or reflect the resolution of philosophical issues. And, in the case of terms expressing philosophically crucial concepts, the quest for such definitions surely does constitute a major concern of analytical philosophy. (His own analysis of factual knowledge in his later book *The Problem of Knowledge* furnishes an example; for the analysis, in effect, yields an explicit definition of 'knows that' as 'has the true and justified conviction that'.[31]) But probably the main reason why Ayer downgrades the importance of explicit definition is that it is definitions in use which he particularly needs in the kind of analyses which most concern him – that is, in the reductive analyses which bring ordinary and scientific assertions in line with the requirements of the content-principle. For in all these analyses the move from *analysandum* to *analysans* involves a change in ontological perspective: sentences which are nominally about one class of objects (objects which are not directly observable) are translated into sentences about some other class of objects (objects which *are* directly observable). Thus what leads Ayer to seek an analysis of our physical terminology is that, because, on the face of it, the entities which form the ontological subject matter of physical discourse are external to, and logically independent of, the realm of sense-experience, it seems that the factual content of physical statements is not purely observational and that, consequently, such statements would not be factually significant under the strong version of the verification principle which he accepts. Clearly, this problem could not be met by providing synonymous expressions for each physical term, since, by being synonymous, such expressions would preserve the original ontology. What is needed is an analysis in which all references to, and quantifications over, physical entities are eliminated, i.e. an analysis which shows how sentences about physical entities are equivalent to sentences (or perhaps infinite truth-functional complexes of sentences) about something else. It is because such an analysis involves this change in ontological perspective that we think of it as, in a distinctive sense, 'reductive' (though an analysis which preserves the original ontology, but involves a sufficiently radical change in 'ideological' perspective, will also count as reductive[32]).

In this connection, however, there is an important point which Ayer does not mention, but which no doubt he would accept. In order to decide whether a certain analysis should count as a genuine case of ontological reduction, we must take account not only of the ontology which is *explicit* in the referential apparatus (e.g. in the use of names and bound variables), but also of what may be *implicit* in the use of certain predicates. Suppose, for example, we have a physical language L_1 whose syntax is that of the predicate calculus, whose universe of discourse is the set of points of space-time, and whose 'lexical' vocabulary consists of certain physical predicates, of varying place-numbers, applicable to such points (i.e. an n-place predicate is applicable to ordered n-tuples of points). It is a simple matter to define a co-ordinate system in which space-time points are 1–1 correlated with ordered quadruples of real numbers. And, given such a system, we can then, for each L_1-predicate P, introduce a new predicate P' which is true of a quadruple of numbers (or of an ordered n-tuple of such quadruples) just in case P is true of the correlated point (or ordered n-tuple of correlated points). This procedure yields a new language L_2 in which whatever can be said in L_1, by quantifying over points, can be re-expressed by quantifying over quadruples of numbers. But clearly the replacement of L_1 by L_2 would not involve a genuine change in ontological perspective. For although L_2-sentences are not explicitly about physical entities (no physical entities need be included in the range of values of the variables), they are so implicitly. The quadruples of numbers stand proxy for the space-time points, given the special sense of the L_2-predicates applied to them. Consequently, we cannot regard the translation of L_1-sentences into L_2-sentences as a genuine case of ontological reduction.

It may be said that we cannot even regard this translation as a genuine case of *analysis*, since we could only grasp the meanings of the L_2-predicates by first understanding the predicates of L_1, or at least possessing the concepts which the L_1-predicates express. This is presumably true, and indeed part and parcel of what makes the ontology of L_1 implicit in the sense of the L_2-predicates. But the point is that the translation meets the only requirements of analysis (of the definition-in-use type) which Ayer specifies, since L_2-sentences are equivalent to the L_1-sentences they translate, while not containing synonyms of the L_1-predicates. This is not to say, of course, that the translation fulfils the aim for which Ayer seeks an analysis of physical discourse, namely of reconciling such discourse with the content-principle. Obviously, just because there is no ontological reduction, the factual content of the propositions expressed by L_2-sentences is not purely observational.

This is not the only respect in which Ayer's requirements for analysis seem too weak. Thus suppose we are seeking a set-theoretical analysis of arithmetical concepts and, to this end, formulate rules for translating arithmetical sentences into equivalent sentences about sets – yielding the translation-manual T. Let us further suppose, for the sake of argument, that T meets all the intuitive requirements for analysis, whatever these may be. Now consider the alternative manual T' which is exactly like T except that it reverses the translations of '$2 + 2 = 4$' and '$9 \times 7 = 63$'. Since these two arithmetical sentences are analytically true (at least in the sense of expressing *a priori* truths), they are also equivalent to each other in Ayer's sense and thus equivalent to their new translations, given their equivalence to the old. Consequently, if equivalence were all that was required for a successful analysis, T' would serve as well as T. But obviously it does not. For given the difference in meaning between the two arithmetical sentences, it cannot be the case that the original translations and the reverse translations serve the purposes of analysis equally well. And since we have assumed the adequacy of T, we must infer the defectiveness of T'.

Ayer is well aware, and in fact explicitly notes, that equivalence, as he has defined it, does not guarantee sameness of meaning in the ordinary sense. But he seems to think that if two equivalent sentences do differ in meaning, the difference is merely one of psychological effect and something which the philosopher can afford to ignore.

> . . . I think that although a complex sign of the form "the sentences
> s and t have the same meaning" is sometimes used, or taken, to
> express what we express by saying "the sentences s and t are
> equivalent", this is not the way in which such a sign is most
> commonly used or interpreted. I think that if we are to use the sign
> "meaning" in the way in which it is most commonly used, we must
> not say that two sentences have the same meaning for anyone, unless
> the occurrence of one always has the same effect on his thoughts
> and actions as the occurrence of the other. And, clearly, it is possible
> for two sentences to be equivalent, by our criterion, without having
> the same effect on anyone who employs the language. . . .
> Accordingly, one should avoid saying that philosophy is concerned
> with the meaning of symbols, because the ambiguity of "meaning"
> leads the undiscerning critic to judge the result of a philosophical
> enquiry by a criterion which is not applicable to it, but only to an
> empirical enquiry concerning . . . psychological effect . . . Such
> empirical enquiries . . . are quite distinct from the logical enquiries
> which constitute philosophy. (*LTL*, 68–9)

Now Ayer is clearly right in claiming that philosophical analysis need not preserve *meaning* in that psychological sense – the sense in which he believes that the term is most commonly used. (Indeed, I doubt whether any two expressions would have the same meaning in that sense, though, partly for that reason, I also doubt whether *that* sense is the one in which the term is most commonly used.) Where he goes wrong is in supposing that equivalence is enough. For, as the arithmetical example shows, it certainly is not enough in cases where the sentences to be translated are analytically true or analytically false. Nor, in fact, is the point restricted to analytic sentences. The three synthetic sentences 'There is a table in this room', 'If $2 + 2 = 4$, there is a table in this room' and 'If there is not a table in this room, $1 + 1 = 3$' are equivalent. But we can hardly say that, for the purposes of analysis, a good translation of one would be an equally good translation of all.

Still, for the purposes for which Ayer needs an analysis of ordinary and scientific discourse, this point is of no great concern. What Ayer has to show is that, contrary to initial appearances, certain sentences have factual significance under the content-principle. To show this, it suffices to show that these sentences are equivalent to sentences whose factual significance under that principle is already established. For, since equivalence is transitive and since a sentence is purely observational (i.e. expresses a purely observational statement) if and only if it is equivalent to a sentence, or to an infinite truth-functional complex of sentences, in an observational language, then obviously if two sentences are equivalent and one is purely observational, the other is purely observational too. So, even though Ayer's requirements for analysis are, in general terms, too weak, they are sufficient for his particular purposes.

They are also sufficient for the purposes of those philosophers whose concern with the analysis of ordinary and scientific discourse stems from a concern about the metaphysical status of its subject matter. Thus in the case of the physical world, which is the most important example, the traditional metaphysical issue has been the dispute between realists and idealists. Realists take physical entities and states of affairs to have an ultimate and irreducible reality, logically independent of their perceptual and cognitive apprehension by minds. Idealists take them to be the logical product of, and hence nothing over and above, the organization of human sense-experience and the way we interpret it. This metaphysical issue is not, as such, an issue of linguistic analysis. But questions of analysis may be relevant to it. Thus one way of trying to establish the idealist position would be to argue for some form of linguistic phenomenalism, whereby statements about the physical world are translatable, and in an ontologically reductive way, into statements about experience. But, clearly, such translation need not achieve anything stronger than equivalence. For if each physical statement is equivalent to an experiential statement, then physical facts cannot be anything over and above experiential facts. Even if, in some philosophically important sense, the meaning of the physical statements cannot be fully captured in the phenomenal language, the fact that equivalent statements can be formulated in such a language is enough to settle the metaphysical issue in favour of the idealist. So here again Ayer's requirements for analysis serve well enough.

Ayer, of course, although he accepts linguistic phenomenalism, would not classify himself as an idealist. For, in line with his general position, he regards the metaphysical dispute (i.e. the metaphysical aspect of the dispute) between realists and idealists as wholly spurious.[33] The only legitimate questions, as Ayer sees it, are either empirical or analytical. If realism were construed as the merely empirical claim that certain physical facts obtain, then it could be accepted as true and verified by the evidence

50

of our senses. If idealism were construed as the merely analytical claim that statements about the physical world are equivalent to statements about actual and possible sense-experience, then idealism could be accepted as true and demonstrable by philosophical analysis. It is when the dispute takes on a distinctively metaphysical character, when it turns on the question of how things are in themselves, when it presupposes the existence of some transcendental viewpoint behind the veil of ordinary perception and from which, if only we could reach it, the ultimate nature of reality could be discerned – it is then that the dispute becomes, to Ayer's way of thinking, spurious. And it becomes spurious because it tries to pose a question which is both factual, but not empirical, and philosophical, but not analytical. Even if the idealist defends his position by arguing for linguistic phenomenalism, he is, in Ayer's view, wrong to think that there is, apart from such phenomenalism, a significant position to be defended. The whole question of whether the physical world has a reality independent of human experience is only meaningful as the analytical question of whether statements about the physical world can be re-expressed, preserving equivalence, in experiential terms. Here, once again, I find myself in disagreement with Ayer. I think there is a genuine metaphysical issue over and above the analytical issue.[34] This is hardly surprising, since I have rejected the criterion of significance on which Ayer's view is founded.

I think we have said enough about Ayer's general conception of analysis and of its reductive role with respect to ordinary and scientific discourse. We must now consider, in more detail, how this works out in a particular case – that of statements about the physical world. I have chosen this case because it is, for two reasons, the most important. In the first place, it is the case which Ayer himself develops in most detail, though even here his account is exceedingly sketchy. Secondly, it is strategically the most crucial. For, unless he can preserve the significance of physical statements, he will have to reckon almost all ordinary and scientific assertions to be nonsensical.

As I have already said, Ayer's position with respect to physical state-ments is that of linguistic phenomenalism – the view that such statements are equivalent to experiential statements – and the point of his analysis is to elaborate that position. But it must be stressed, at the outset, that the analysis is not intended to be exhaustive. He does not offer a definit-ion-in-use for every physical term or formulate rules of translation covering every type of physical statement. Rather, he contents himself with offering what he describes as an 'analysis of the notion of a material thing' (*LTL*, 66). What this amounts to we shall see presently. But clearly Ayer regards this limited analysis as sufficing to vindicate his phenomenalist position and as indicating the general lines which an exhaustive analysis would take.

Ayer begins his account with four preliminary definitions which are stipulative rather than analytical and are intended to provide a convenient terminology for the subsequent analysis. The relations defined are those of *direct* and *indirect resemblance* and of *direct* and *indirect continuity*. Two sense-contents are said to *directly resemble* each other 'when there is either no difference, or only an infinitesimal difference, of quality between them' and to *indirectly resemble* each other 'when they are linked by a series of direct resemblances, but are not themselves directly resemblant' (*LTL*, 65). Likewise, two visual, or two tactual, sense-contents are said to be *directly continuous* 'when they belong to successive members of a series of actual, or possible, sense-fields, and there is no difference, or only an infinitesimal difference, between them, with respect to the position of each in its own sense-field' and to be *indirectly continuous* 'when they are related by an actual, or possible, series of such direct continuities' (*LTL*, 65–6). By way of explanation, he adds:

> . . . to say of a sense-experience, or a sense-field which is a part of a sense-experience, or a sense-content which is a part of a sense-field, that it is possible, as opposed to actual, is to say . . . that it would occur if certain specifiable conditions were fulfilled. So when it is said that a material thing is constituted by both actual and possible sense-contents, all that is being asserted is that the sentences referring to sense-contents, which are the translations of the sentences referring to any material thing, are both categorical and hypothetical. And thus the notion of a possible sense-content, or sense-experience, is as unobjectionable as the familiar notion of a hypothetical statement. (*LTL*, 66)

I find this last remark a little surprising. Since the relevant hypothetical statements are counterfactuals, surely they *are* problematic from Ayer's standpoint, even if they do not involve an illicit ontology. Certainly counterfactual sentences are excluded from an observational language as I have defined it, and I would have thought that, in this respect, my definition was no more stringent that Ayer's radical empiricism requires. Perhaps Ayer thinks that the counterfactual idiom will be subject to further analysis and thus disappear in the final translation of physical statements. But this is not what the passage suggests. Moreover, it is far from clear how such an analysis could be provided.

Having defined his terms, Ayer now takes the first and most crucial step of his phenomenalistic analysis:

> . . . one may assert with regard to any two of one's visual sense-contents, or with regard to any two of one's tactual sense-contents, that they are elements of the same material thing if, and only if, they are related to one another by a relation of direct, or indirect,

resemblance in certain respects, and by a relation of direct, or indirect, continuity. (*LTL*, 66)

In connection with this he notes that since the two relations of direct-or-indirect resemblance and direct-or-indirect continuity are both symmetric and transitive, the definition ensures that 'no visual, or tactual, sense-content can be an element of more than one material thing' (*LTL*, 66) – a consequence which he clearly regards as desirable. Whether the definition is satisfactory in other respects is something we shall examine presently, after we have recorded the remaining steps of the analysis.

So far, the relation of being elements of the same material thing has only been defined for visual and tactual sense-contents taken separately. The definition divides visual sense-contents into same-thing groups and tactual sense-contents into same-thing groups, but it does not tell us what it is for two groups, drawn from different modalities, to belong to the same material thing. Ayer's next step supplies the answer:

. . . any two of one's visual and tactual groups belong to the same material thing when every element of the visual group which is of minimal visual depth forms part of the same sense-experience as an element of the tactual group which is of minimal tactual depth. (*LTL*, 66)

By the way of explanation, he adds:

We cannot here define visual or tactual depth otherwise than ostensively. The depth of a visual or tactual sense-content is as much a sensible property of it as its length or breadth. But we may describe it by saying that one visual or tactual sense-content has a greater depth than another when it is farther from the observer's body, provided that we make it clear that this is not intended to be a definition. (*LTL*, 66–7)

It cannot be a definition, since, obviously, the concepts of physical distance and body cannot be primitive in the phenomenalist analysis.

There is still, of course, no provision for the assignment of sense-contents from other sense-modalities to material things. But this can be done, Ayer thinks, 'by reference to their association with tactual sense-contents' (*LTL*, 67).

Thus, we assign sense-contents of taste to the same material things as the simultaneously occurring sense-contents of touch which are experienced by the palate, or the tongue. And in assigning an auditory or olfactory sense-content to a material thing, we remark that it is a member of a possible series of temporarily [*sic*] continuous sounds, or smells, of uniform quality but gradually increasing intensity; the series, namely, which one would ordinarily be said to experience in the course of moving towards the place from which the sound, or the smell, came; and we assign it to the same material thing as the tactual sense-content which is experienced at the same time as the sound, or the smell, of maximum intensity in the series. (*LTL*, 67)

I assume that, with respect to the assignment of auditory and olfactory sense-contents, this procedure is not intended to be fool-proof. For, obviously, it would fail in certain cases, e.g. when one is moving towards some physical sound-source of constantly diminishing intensity and where the diminishing of the intensity more than counterbalances the increasing proximity.

Ayer's final step is 'the provision of a rule for translating sentences which refer to the "real" qualities of material things' (*LTL*, 67). The need for such a rule arises from the fact that the sensible appearance of a material object varies with the conditions of observation and this variation is not thought to involve any change in the object's intrinsic character. Thus the same coin, with presumably constant intrinsic shape, looks round when observed from certain viewpoints and elliptical when observed from others; and the same flower, with presumably constant intrinsic colour, looks white when observed at midday but pink when observed at sunset. Given such variation in sensible appearance, how is the notion of the 'real' (intrinsic) qualities of an object to be analysed in phenomenal terms? Ayer's answer is that

> . . . to say of a certain quality that it is the real quality of a given material thing is to say that it characterises those elements of the thing which are the most conveniently measured of all the elements which possess qualities of the kind in question. Thus, when I look at a coin and assert that it is really round in shape, I am not asserting that the shape of the sense-content, which is the element of the coin that I am actually observing, is round, still less that the shape of all the visual, or tactual, elements of the coin is round; what I am asserting is that roundness of shape characterises those elements of the coin which are experienced from the point of view from which measurements of shape are most conveniently carried out. (*LTL*, 67–8)

In conclusion, he notes that 'we define relations of quality, or position, between material things in terms of the relations of quality, or position, which obtain between such "privileged" elements' (*LTL*, 68), i.e. elements which reveal the 'real' qualities of material things according to the specified criterion.

This then is, more or less in full, Ayer's 'analysis of the notion of a material thing'. And in order to evaluate it, we need to keep two issues clearly distinct. On the one hand, there is the issue of whether the analysis is successful *in its own terms* – that is, whether it achieves what it is intended to achieve, *granted the phenomenalist standpoint*. On the other hand, there is the issue of whether the phenomenalist standpoint is itself correct – that is, whether any phenomenalistic analysis could really do justice to our concept of a material thing and to our other physical concepts. That these are quite different issues is clear. We may decide that Ayer's analysis is very successful in fulfilling the phenomenalist's aims, but at the same time regard these aims as misconceived. Conversely, we may decide that the phenomenalist's aims are sound, but that Ayer's analysis fails to achieve them. I shall begin by considering the first issue: how far is Ayer's analysis successful in its own (phenomenalistic) terms?

As I have already stressed, the analysis is not intended to be an exhaustive elaboration of the phenomenalist position. For, obviously, Ayer cannot suppose that he has provided, in any explicit form, a general procedure for translating physical statements into phenomenal statements. He has not even provided any examples of phenomenalist translation, apart from certain special cases (such as the definitional expansion of 'this visual sense-content and that visual sense-content are elements of the same material thing') in which the physical statement (assuming one can call it 'physical') is already, quite explicitly, a statement about the properties of, or relations between, sensory items. In effect, all Ayer has attempted to do is to specify some of the basic ways in which sense-experience can be organized in a physically significant fashion (e.g. how a series of appropriately related sense-contents counts as the successive presentations of the same material object), in the hope that a translation-procedure, or specific procedures for specific types of physical statement, could be worked out on this basis. This should not be taken as a criticism of him. He could hardly be expected to attempt more, given the complexity of the topic and the wide-ranging character of his book. Indeed, if there is a criticism of Ayer's general approach, it is that he has failed to appreciate the full complexity of his own, albeit limited, project. He seems to think that, in its basic aspects, the physical organization of sense-experience can be phenomenally specified in very simple terms. This is not so, as Ayer himself came to recognize in his later writings. Unfortunately, one consequence is that the analysis he offers here, as well as being only rudimentary, is, even from the phenomenalist standpoint, seriously defective. Indeed, even if we ignore the problem of counterfactuals (which is more a problem about the consistency of his analysis with his overall position than about the merits of the analysis as such), it is seriously flawed at almost every point.

The most crucial part of the analysis is, as I have said, the initial step, in which Ayer defines what it is for two sense-contents, which are either both visual or both tactual, to be elements of the same material thing. It is the most crucial part because it provides the initial bridge between the phenomenal and the physical realms over which, as it were, all the subsequent traffic has to pass. The rest of the analysis has a chance of succeeding only if this bridge holds firm. So let us look carefully at what the definition states, namely: that two visual, or tactual, sense-contents are elements of the same material thing if and only if they directly or indirectly resemble each other in certain respects and are directly or indirectly continuous. Now even from a phenomenalist standpoint this is clearly defective. Indeed, it is defective in at least two ways, each relating to the insufficiency of the (phenomenal) *definiens* for the (physical) *definiendum*.

The first defect is that it takes no account of hallucination. Even a phenomenalist has to accept the possibility of hallucination – the possibility of sense-experiences which are not perceptions (not even non-veridical perceptions) of items in the physical world. Of course, the phenomenalist's conception of a hallucination will be distinctively phenomenalistic: he will say that what makes an experience hallucinatory is not its failing to stand in a certain relation to some external reality, but its failing to stand in a certain relation to other experiences. Roughly, he will say that a hallucination is an experience which is radically anomalous with respect to the overall theme in the experiences of the individual or the community. But that hallucinations are possible, however they are construed, is not in dispute. Indeed, the phenomenalist will presumably, like the rest of us, allow that they actually occur. Now if an experience is hallucinatory, its sense-contents are not, in Ayer's sense, elements of any material thing. For, obviously, a sense-content will only form an element of a material thing in the phenomenalist's sense if there is some material thing which, as we would ordinarily put it, the subject is (*qua* recipient of that sense-content) perceiving. A fortiori, two hallucinatory sense-contents (or two sense-contents one of which is hallucinatory) cannot be elements of the same material thing. But there is nothing to prevent their standing in relations of direct (or indirect) resemblance and direct (or indirect) continuity. Indeed in typical cases of hallucination, like that of the drunkard's 'seeing' pink rats, the successive sense-contents will directly resemble each other and be directly continuous in the required way (it is partly this which allows the sequence of experiences to simulate a sequence of veridical perceptions). But if two hallucinatory sense-contents stand in these relations, without being elements of any material thing, then they satisfy Ayer's *definiens* without satisfying the *definiendum*.

The second defect is that, even within the domain of veridical experience, two sense-contents which are elements of different material things may stand in the requisite relations. Indeed, if the definition is taken literally, we can show this quite trivially. For suppose R is some region of my visual field and S is the series of visual sense-contents (phenomenal colour-arrays) which have occurred in R (each sense-content exactly covering R) since I woke up this morning. All the members of S have the same (R-type) shape and size, and successive members are directly continuous. So any two sense-contents in S satisfy Ayer's requirements for being elements of the same material thing, namely that they directly or indirectly resemble each other *in certain respects* and be directly or indirectly continuous. But in fact, since my visual scene has varied considerably over the relevant period, such sense-contents have often (indeed in the vast majority of cases) been elements of different material things, contrary to Ayer's analysis.

This problem, of course, stems from Ayer's use of the phrase 'in certain respects' to qualify the requirement of direct or indirect resemblance. But perhaps what Ayer means is that the resemblance must hold in *all* respects applicable to sense-contents of the relevant type. This would mean that, in the case of visual sense-contents, the resemblance would have to hold not only in respect of shape and size, but also in respect of colour and internal colour-arrangement. However, even if we interpret Ayer in this way, we can find plenty of examples in which two sense-contents stand in the requisite relations but are elements of different material things. This is especially clear in the case of the visual realm. For when a subject undergoes a series of visual experiences, which take him from the observation of one material item to the observation of another, the alteration in the character of his experiences throughout the series is usually so gradual as to allow the successive sense-contents which occur in the same portion of the visual field to be almost qualitatively identical. Thus suppose I am seated at a brown table on which there are two billiard balls, a red ball to my left and a white ball to my right. I start by looking at the red ball, so that there is a red circular sense-content covering some central portion of my visual field. If I then turn my eyes very slightly to the right, this central portion will acquire a new sense-content which is only slightly different from the first – a sense-content which is circular and *almost* completely red (it is completely red apart from a thin crescent of brown at its right hand edge. Obviously, by supposing the movement of my eyes to be sufficiently slight, we can make the qualitative difference between the two sense-contents sufficiently slight to count as 'infinitesimal' – whatever Ayer means by that – so that the sense-contents directly resemble each other in all relevant respects. But then, by continuing the series of eye-movements, I can, in this same central portion, pass through a series of sense-contents, the successive members of which directly resemble each other in all relevant respects, and which terminates in a perception of the white ball. The first and last sense-contents of this series will then be elements of different material things (the red ball and the white ball), but they will stand in the relations of indirect continuity and indirect resemblance. Nor could Ayer meet this problem by requiring same-thing sense-contents to be related by *direct* resemblance. For not only would this requirement fail to remove the problem entirely – since, in a homo-geneous perceptual environment, the switch from observing one material thing to observing another need not involve *any* change in the character of the successive experiences – but it would also be too strong. The sense-content I have when I look at a penny from a frontal angle close-to is more than infinitesimally different in shape and size from that which I have when I look at the same penny from a very oblique angle and at a distance. Indeed, the whole point of Ayer's introducing indirect resemblance was to allow for this sort of case.

Ayer's analysis, then, is seriously flawed in its initial and most crucial step. And it is also flawed in its subsequent steps, as we shall now see.

In order to construct material objects with both visual and tactual properties, Ayer asserts that a same-thing group of visual sense-contents and a same-thing group of tactual sense-contents belong to the same material thing when every element of the former group which is of minimal visual depth forms part of the same sense-experience as an element of the latter group which is of minimal tactual depth. My first difficulty is in even understanding what Ayer means by 'tactual depth'. His only explanation is that while visual and tactual depth are, as sensible qualities, only ostensively definable, we can say, as it were off the analytical record, that a sense-content has greater sensible depth when it is further from the observer's body. In the case of tactual depth I find this unhelpful. Presumably, if we are to make sense of it at all, we shall have to take 'the body' here as referring not to the *whole* body, but some main portion of it, probably the head or trunk, since otherwise every tactual sense-content will turn out to be of minimal depth. Thus presumably Ayer means that when I stretch out my arm to touch some-thing three feet away, the tactual sense-content has greater tactual depth than when I hold the same object close to my face or chest. But is he right? No doubt there is some difference in muscular sensation in the two cases, given the difference in the shape of my arm. No doubt also, given my familiarity with such situations, the muscular sensations would serve to tell me, even without visual cues, the physical distance and direction of the object from (the main portion of) my body. But I cannot detect any phenomenal feature of the tactual sense-contents themselves which I should want to describe as 'depth'. I am not even sure that I can detect such a feature in the case of visual sense-contents, but here, I think, the issue is less clear-cut and I am willing, for the sake of argument, to accept Ayer's position.

However, my main objection to Ayer's assertion is that, even if we allow him the notion of tactual depth, his account of how visual and tactual groups are to be correlated is clearly erroneous. Thus suppose I am looking at a leaf just in front of my eyes, so that the resulting sense-contents are of minimal visual depth, but I am not touching it with any part of my body. Suppose over the same period I am holding a small camera against my chest (or against whatever constitutes the relevant main portion of my body), but I do not see it. Then the two groups of sense-contents – the one comprising the series of visual sense-contents which are elements of the leaf, the other comprising the series of tactual sense-contents which are elements of the camera – meet the conditions Ayer specifies for belonging to the same material thing; that is, every element of the one which is of minimal visual depth forms part of the same total sense-experience as an element of the other which is of minimal tactual depth. But, *ex hypothesi*, the two groups belong to different material things. It is even more obvious that two groups may belong to the same material thing without satisfying the specified conditions. Thus I may first look at an object without touching it and then, closing my eyes, touch it without seeing it. In such a case the two groups would belong to the same material thing without any element in one being part of the same experience as any element in the other. However, I am not sure whether this counts as a further objection to Ayer's thesis. For it is possible that Ayer only intends his specified conditions to be sufficient but not necessary; after all, he only says that two groups belong to the same material thing *when* – he does not say 'when and *only when*' – these conditions obtain. Against this, it should be noted that unless he intends the conditions to be both sufficient and necessary, this phase in his analysis of the notion of a material thing will be crucially incomplete.

In the final step of his analysis, Ayer turns to the question of how we determine the 'real' qualities of a material thing, given that its sensible appearance varies with the conditions of observation. His answer, as we have seen, is that, with respect to each category of qualities (e.g. shape or colour), the member of this category which 'really' characterizes the material object is the one which the object manifests in those conditions in which qualities of that category are most conveniently measured. Thus a coin is really circular, despite looking elliptical from certain (i.e. the oblique) viewpoints, because it looks circular from that (the frontal) viewpoint from which measurements of shape are most conveniently carried out. Again, I have difficulty in even understanding Ayer's position here. In what sense is it more convenient to measure shape from one viewpoint (or one set of viewpoints) unless we already know, independently of the convenience-criterion, that this is the viewpoint (or set of viewpoints) from which, uniquely, real and apparent shape coincide? Perhaps what Ayer has in mind is that from a frontal viewpoint we can make more shape-discriminations, since the apparent shapes cover a larger portion of the visual field. This is in line with how he interprets his criterion in the case of colour:

> . . . I assert that the real colour of the paper on which I am writing is white, even though it may not always appear to be white, because whiteness of colour characterises those visual elements of the paper which are experienced in the conditions in which the greatest discrimination of colours is possible. (*LTL*, 68)

But it is hardly a matter of 'convenience of measurement' in any ordinary sense: presumably, the reason we prefer to base our colour-judgments on how things appear in conditions of greatest colour-discrimination is that, if we adopt the standpoint of the physical realist, we find it easier to explain how real differences could be masked by poor conditions of observation than how systematic differences in appearance could be wholly illusory. Nor would the discrimination-factor be of more than marginal relevance to the case of shape. The reason we regard the real shape of the penny as circular is that this is a consequence of a much larger physical and psychophysical theory which best explains (or would do so if realistically construed) the course of our experience – a theory which, in particular, explains apparent visual shape in terms of physical shape, the viewpoint of the observer, and the laws of visual perspective. This, indeed, affords the criterion of what is physically real quite gener- ally: the real qualities are those which take their place in the best overall explanation of experience. Other factors, such as discrimination, are only relevant as corollaries. And, as far as I can see, convenience of measurement, as ordinarily understood, has no relevance at all.

I am forced to conclude, then, that, even from its own phenomenalist standpoint, Ayer's analysis is far from successful. No doubt this was partly because, with so much ground to cover, he had little time to devote to this particular topic. But it has to be said that he writes as if he has provided, in its essentials, the definitive account. And I am inclined to think, as I mentioned earlier, that he failed to appreciate the full complexity of the task he set himself. To some extent this criticism applies to the whole book, as Ayer himself would now be the first to admit, though with a more complex or more tentative approach the book would probably have lost some of its impact.

We must now turn to the second and more fundamental issue as to whether the phenomenalist standpoint itself is correct. Has Ayer merely failed tactically to execute a basically sound strategy, or is the strategy itself misconceived?

We must begin by considering what is meant by the 'phenomenalist standpoint'. As Ayer uses the term, phenomenalism is the thesis that statements about the physical world are equivalent to statements about actual and possible sense-experience. It might seem, then, that, to evaluate the phenomenalist standpoint, it is this thesis which we should consider. And certainly it is this thesis which Ayer is seeking to defend. However, it is also true that this version of phenomenalism is stronger than Ayer requires for his verificationist purposes – the purposes of reconciling physical discourse with the content-principle. He could have settled for the weaker thesis that each physical statement is equivalent *either* to a phenomenal statement *or* to an infinite truth-functional complex of phenomenal statements. For, assuming the phenomenal language is observational, the truth of this thesis would ensure that physical statements fall within the scope of an observational language, in the sense defined, and thus ensure that physical statements qualify as factually significant under the content-principle. Admittedly, even this weaker thesis is stronger than is required to express the phenomenalist standpoint in its broadest sense. For, in its broadest sense, the term 'phenomenalism' applies to any position which claims that physical facts are nothing over and above phenomenal facts; and while this latter claim is entailed by the thesis that physical statements fall within the scope of a phenomenal language, it does not entail it.[35] But since our current concern is with Ayer's purposes in *LTL*, this is a point which, in the present context, we can largely ignore.

Not only does the weaker thesis suffice for Ayer's purposes, but there are positive reasons why the phenomenalist would be ill-advised to commit himself to the stronger position. To take a simple example, consider the physical statement that there is a table in this room. The phenomenalist will claim that if the statement is true, it is so solely in virtue of some phenomenal state of affairs from whose description it is deducible. But he must surely also accept that there is an infinite range of different possible phenomenal states of affairs which suffice for its truth – an infinite range of ways (involving different types of table, different numbers of observers, different sense-realms, different conditions of observation) in which the presence of a table in this room could be constituted by actual and possible sense-experience. Now let us assume, for the sake of argument, that each of these possible states of affairs can be finitely specified in the phenomenal language, so that (according to the phenomenalist) the physical statement is equivalent to an infinite disjunction of phenomenal statements. The question is: can this infinite disjunction itself be finitely re-expressed in the phenomenal language? Is there a finite sentence of this language, however complex, that specifies some generic state of affairs which both suffices for the truth of the physical statement and is common to each specific state of affairs in the infinite range? I think we should expect a negative answer. For, given the enormous diversity of the different specific states of affairs, there is unlikely to be any finite expression of their disjunction in purely phenomenal terms. In other words, it is likely that the only finite expression of the disjunction would be by reference to the physical state of affairs itself, e.g. 'things are phenomenally such as to suffice for there being a table in this room', and this, of course, would not provide an equivalent for the physical statement in the *phenomenal* language.

In all respects, then, it would be appropriate for Ayer to confine himself to the weaker thesis – a point which he concedes in his later writings.[36] However, even in this weaker form, phenomenalism is a difficult position to defend. The main problem is that, like the stronger form, it seems to distort the actual meaning of our physical statements. Our physical concepts seem to be, as it were, inherently realist – inherently resistant to a phenomenalist interpretation. Thus it seems to be a conceptual truth (analytic, as Ayer would say) that if there is a physical world at all, it is something external to, and logically independent of, the realm of human experience. If this is so, then no physical statement can be equivalent to a phenomenal statement or infinite complex of phenomenal statements, so that even the weaker version of phenomenalism is untenable. The same objection, of course, can be raised against any position which takes physical facts to be nothing over and·above phenomenal facts, and thus threatens phenomenalism in what I earlier described as its broadest sense.

It is perhaps surprising that Ayer does not consider this fundamental objection. For, in his subsequent chapter on ethics and theology, he makes an analogous point against the ethical naturalist:

> We reject the subjectivist view that to call an action right, or a thing good, is to say that it is generally approved of, because it is not self-contradictory to assert that some actions which are generally approved of are not right, or that some things which are generally approved of are not good. And we reject the alternative subjectivist view that a man who asserts that a certain action is right, or that a certain thing is good, is saying that he himself approves of it, on the ground that a man who confessed that he sometimes approved of what was bad or wrong would not be contradicting himself. And a similar argument is fatal to utilitarianism. (*LTL*, 104)

Ayer recognizes that such naturalistic definitions of 'good' and 'right' would be convenient from the standpoint of the verification principle, since they would reveal ethical judgments to be empirical hypotheses and ethical principles to be tautologies. But he rejects them on the simple grounds that they do not match up to the actual meaning of our ethical assertions. And, of course, he is right to do so. But then it would seem equally right to reject phenomenalistic accounts for the same reason. For, on the face of it, it is not self-contradictory, given our actual concept of the physical, to say that there is a physical world, but one which is not reflected in actual and potential sense-experience, or to say that there is no physical world, but that our sense-experience is organized as if there were.

It might be said that even if the objection is valid, it does not wholly undermine the phenomenalist's position. For it could still be claimed that, to the extent that they are inherently realist, our *actual* physical concepts need to be revised – that they need to be replaced by new physical concepts which are amenable to a phenomenalist treatment. Of course, to justify such a revision, we would have to show that our actual concepts (or putative concepts) were rendered defective by their realist character. And this may not prove possible, if, as I have argued, there is no rationale for the content-principle. But if it could be done, the crucial importance of our physical concepts, both practically and theoretically, might seem to provide a sufficient reason for revising them to fit the phenomenalist account, rather than just rejecting phenomenalism outright. However, even if such a revision were desirable, it is difficult to see how it could be achieved. The problem is that, on the face of it, the realist commitment of our physical concepts is so entrenched, so central to their content, that its elimination would not leave a residue with a recognizably physical character – if, indeed, it would leave a residue at all. Unless our physical statements end up implying the existence of an external and mind-independent world, they cannot, it seems, qualify as physical in any recognizable sense. This does not, of course, preclude our abandoning the physical language altogether, if we think that its realist character undermines its factual significance. But what we cannot do, it seems, is to abandon the realist frame but salvage the physical contents. Or, to change the metaphor, we cannot, it seems, hope to bring out an expurgated edition of the language with all the realist elements deleted, but with the essentials of the physical subject-matter intact.

However, the phenomenalist has another and more promising reply. He can claim that the apparent realism of our actual physical concepts is an illusion created by the 'surface grammar' of the physical language. He can say that the physical language is a *façon de parler*, within which we draw a sharp distinction between the phenomenal and the physical realms, but that the ultimate truth-conditions of physical statements are, as revealed by philosophical analysis, phenomenalistic. Thus, on the one hand, he will concede that, within the framework of the physical language, we have to speak of physical objects as external and mind-independent – which is what makes phenomenalism seem intuitively implausible. On the other hand, he will insist that the physical language itself is just a convenient medium for expressing concisely, and in an ostensibly realist fashion, the distinctive ways in which our sense-experiences are phenomenally organized – so that, from the standpoint of philosophical analysis, phenomenalism is true. This means that the question 'Is the physical world external and mind-independent?' is ambiguous, according to whether it is taken as a 'first order' physical question or as a 'second order' philosophical question. And, according to the phenomenalist, it is because this ambiguity is not initially detected that phenomenalism *appears* to distort the meaning of our physical statements: in answering the question in the negative, it appears to deny something which our actual physical concepts oblige us to assert. But this is not really so if the negative and affirmative answers are addressed to different questions. There is no contradiction in conceding that tables and chairs exist outside the mind, in a way which contrasts with sensations and thoughts, while maintaining that, in speaking of these external objects, we are ultimately describing aspects of the organization of sense-experience itself.

This is an ingenious reply. The only problem is to find some grounds for accepting it, other than a dogmatic adherence to the phenomenalist position. Clearly, if the physical language is just a *façon de parler*, it is one which is well-concealed. We do not, on ordinary reflection, recognize that physical statements are just a convenient replacement for phenomenal statements, in the way we recognize, for example, that to say that the average man dies at seventy is just a convenient way of saying that the average of the ages at which different men die is seventy. If we did, there would be no temptation, as there is, to construe the physical language as genuinely committed to realism, any more than we are tempted to think of the average man as a real entity. Obviously, then, if we were to accept the phenomenalist account, it would have to be through some deep philosophical argument. But the question is: what argument? All Ayer has offered us is the verification principle in its content-restricting form, combined with the seemingly uncontroversial assumption that physical statements are significant. But, as we have seen, this principle itself is wholly unwarranted.

My question 'What argument?' is not intended to be rhetorical. I do not, at this stage, exclude the possibility of showing that the physical language is, in some deep sense, a *façon de parler* and that the commitment to realism is only a feature of the *façon*, not of the propositions which physical sentences turn out, on analysis, to express. Indeed, I have argued elsewhere for a position not unlike this, though the sort of 'phenomenalism' I there defend is of a more metaphysical kind and would not meet Ayer's objectives in *LTL*.[37] My point is only that, given the apparent commitment to realism, the onus is very much on the phenomenalist to show that it *is* illusory. The mere fact that it might be is not enough to justify a neutral stance on the issue, any more than, in the case we considered earlier, the fact that our apparent concept of causal agency might be illusory justifies a neutral stance on the issue of empirical atomism. For we cannot avoid giving weight to our intuitive understanding of the physical language until our intuitions have been discredited. And a genuine commitment to realism is certainly part of what that intuitive understanding purports to reveal.

For the time being, I shall not explore the issue of phenomenalism any further. It will come up again in due course when we consider Ayer's subsequent writings. Indeed, the issue of phenomenalism, and the related issues of the nature of perception and our knowledge of the physical world, were to form the main preoccupation of Ayer's philosophy over the next three decades. His assertions and arguments in *LTL* were decidedly not his last word on the subject.

7 *The relativity-factor*

There is one important aspect of Ayer's verification principle which we have mentioned but not yet discussed. When Ayer speaks of a sentence as having, or failing to have, factual significance, he means this to apply to the sentence as used, or usable, by a particular person at a particular time. This, in itself, is hardly surprising, given that, in cases of context-dependence, the same sentence may be used to express different propositions, with different truth-conditions, according to the circumstances of its utterance. Thus the sentence 'I am tired', referring, as it does, to the current condition of the speaker, is used to express different propositions when uttered by different people or by the same person on different occasions. But, for Ayer, the point goes deeper than this. As he sees it, the factual meaning of a sentence for a person at a time is determined by the possibilities of observational evidence (for or against it) which are open to that person at that time. It is not just that the sentence 'I am tired' is used to express different propositions when uttered by me and when uttered by you; according to Ayer, my utterance of this sentence expresses for me a different proposition from that which your utterance of the sentence 'he is tired' (referring to me) expresses for you, since the possibilities of evidence from my viewpoint and from your viewpoint are relevantly different. Likewise, it is not just that the sentence 'I am tired' is used to express different proposition when uttered by me today and by me yesterday; according to Ayer, my previous utterance of this sentence expressed for me then a different proposition from that which my present utterance of the sentence 'I was tired' (referring to yesterday) expresses for me now, since, again, the possibilities of evidence from my present and previous viewpoints are relevantly different. (I say, in both these cases, '*relevantly* different', because, as we have seen, Ayer allows that some forms of observational evidence may be extraneous to factual meaning.) This involves a context-dependence of a much more radical kind. A sentence such as 'Margaret Thatcher is tired at midday on 6 October 1982' would normally be regarded as context-free – as expressing the same proposition whatever the circumstances of its utterance. But, on Ayer's account, the proposition will vary according to the verificational viewpoint of the interpreter. And the same will be true of all sentences which are used to make empirical claims. This is reflected in Ayer's initial formulation of his verification principle:

> We say that a sentence is factually significant to *any given person*, if, and only if, he knows how to verify the proposition which it purports to express – that is, if he knows what observations would lead *him*, under certain conditions, to accept the proposition as being true, or reject it as being false. If, on the other hand, the putative proposition is of such a character that the assumption of its truth, or falsehood, is consistent with any assumption whatsoever concerning the nature of *his future* experience, then, as far as *he* is concerned, it is, if not a tautology, a mere pseudo-proposition. The sentence expressing it may be emotionally significant *to him*; but it is not literally significant. (*LTL*, 35; my italics)

I shall call this aspect of the verification principle, whereby factual significance is relative to the verificational viewpoint of a person at a time, the *relativity-factor*.

As we have seen, Ayer accepts the verification principle in its strong, content-restricting form, whereby a statement is factually significant if and only if its content is purely observational – i.e. the statement falls within the scope of an observational language. And he accepts this principle as a direct consequence of his view that the factual meaning of a statement is wholly contained within the possibilities of observational evidence. The effect of the relativity-factor is to make the content-restriction even more restrictive, by relativizing significance to potential interpreters at particular times and confining each interpreter to an observational ontology selected to match his current viewpoint. Thus, in its new form, the content-principle asserts that a statement is factually significant for a person P at a time t if and only if it falls within the scope of an observational language for P at t, and that a language L is observational for P at t if and only if, in addition to the conditions specified earlier,[38] the universe of discourse of L is (apart from classes) confined to the sense-contents of P at or after t. Admittedly, the requirements for an observational language may have to be slightly relaxed if Ayer wants to allow counterfactual conditionals to feature in the ultimate phenomenal translations of physical sentences. But the relativity-factor will still apply, in that the subject-matter of the counterfactuals will be restricted to the possible sensory biographies of the relevant person from the relevant time.

To the extent that the relativity-factor makes the content-principle more restrictive, it also, or so it seems, demands a more thorough-going reductionism to preserve the significance of ordinary and scientific assertions. One area where this becomes particularly conspicuous is the case of statements about other minds. We would normally assume that, for a given person, the word 'pain' has the same sense whether he uses it in the context of self-ascription or in the context of other-ascription. In particular, we would assume that when Smith says 'Jones is in pain' he means to ascribe to Jones the kind of state of which he himself is sometimes introspectively aware and which he ascribes to himself by saying 'I am in pain'. This assumption would be compatible with the content-principle if the relativity-factor were eliminated. For, without this factor, different subjects would have access to the same observational language – a language whose ontology combined the items which were separately observable by each. And, consequently, each subject could interpret 'pain' as signifying a certain kind of introspective sense-content whether he was thinking of its application to his own experience or to that of others. But with the addition of the relativity-factor, the situation is quite different. If a statement is factually significant for a given person only if it falls within the scope of a language which is observational *for him*, and if a language is observational for him only if its (atomic) ontology is confined to *his* current and future sense-contents, then a person's ascriptions of pain to others would only make sense, for that person, if they were reducible to statements (or infinite complexes of statements) about his own actual or possible sense-contents. In other words, to make sense of such ascriptions, he would have to interpret them in terms of the possibilities of observational evidence available to *him*. This would mean, it seems, that, while in the context of self-ascription 'pain' signifies, for the ascriber, a certain kind of introspective sense-content, in the context of other-ascription it signifies the bodily behaviour and behavioural dispositions which are normally thought to be symptomatic of pain – and ultimately, via the phenomenalistic analysis of physical statements, signifies the possibilities of sensory evidence by which such behaviour and behavioural dispositions would be phenomenally manifested. And quite generally, it seems, it would require us to say that while a person can interpret his self-ascriptive psychological assertions 'mentalistically', he has to interpret his other-ascriptive psychological assertions 'behaviouristically', if they are to qualify as factually significant from his standpoint. (The reason for the qualification 'it seems' in my last two sentences will emerge presently.)

On the face of it, this would be a very implausible position, partly because of the implausibility of behaviourism itself, and partly because the proposed distinction between the meanings of self-ascriptive and other-ascriptive statements seems unacceptable. None the less, it is the position which Ayer adopts in *LTL*. Later, as we shall see, he came to reject it. Indeed, in a recent comment he describes his former position as actually inconsistent:

> What *was* inconsistent, I now think, was my attempt to combine a behaviouristic analysis of my attribution of experiences to others with a mentalistic analysis of my attribution of them to myself. For here I was not using the word 'my' as a constant: I was not making a factual claim to be the only creature to whom mental predicates could be attributed. The distinction was intended to hold good for anyone who referred to his own and to other persons' experiences. But, if I was bound to construe any reference to the experiences of another person behaviouristically, this would still remain true when the reference was made by him. The suggestion that he interpreted such propositions mentalistically should not have been intelligible to me, unless I violated my theory by interpreting these propositions also as referring to his behaviour. (*Replies*, 326)

However, I think that this criticism is too severe. The combining of the other-ascriptive behaviourism with the self-ascriptive mentalism is certainly implausible; but it is not, I think, inconsistent. Thus suppose Jones says to me 'I am in pain'. On Ayer's original account, the proposition which this expresses for Jones will be a mentalistic one and the proposition which it expresses for me will be the same as the proposition which 'Jones is in pain' expresses for me, i.e. a behaviouristic one. The suggestion that Jones interprets his utterance mentalistically is not unintelligible to me, though obviously, if the account is correct, I shall have to interpret the suggestion itself behaviouristically, i.e. equate Jones's mental state of interpretation with certain aspects of the behaviour and behavioural dispositions of Jones's body. And there are no special difficulties for behaviourism at this point which are not difficulties for behaviourism in general. There is no inconsistency in maintaining both that Jones's utterance of 'I am in pain' expresses a mentalistic proposition for Jones and that 'Jones interprets his utterance of "I am in pain" mentalistically', like 'Jones is in pain', expresses a behaviouristic proposition for me. Ayer's combining of other-ascriptive behaviourism with self-ascriptive mentalism would only be inconsistent if he also conceded that a person's self-ascriptive utterances express the same propositions for himself and for his audience. But it is just this which, if I have understood it, Ayer's original account denies. This, indeed, is part of what makes it implausible, but, as far as I can see, there is no internal incoherence.

Just as the relativity-factor led Ayer to adopt a reductive analysis of statements about other minds, so also it led him to adopt a reductive analysis of statements about the past – an analysis which transforms such statements into ones about the present and future. Once again, the issue is one of verificational viewpoint. The only way in which someone can obtain observational evidence for the truth or falsity of some statement about the past is by his present and future experiences – memory-experiences, of course, included. So if the factual meaning of a statement for a person at a time is wholly contained within the possibilities of observational evidence open to him at that time (in other words, if the statement must fall within the scope of a language which is observational for him then), it seems that a statement about the past, if it is to be factually significant, must turn out, on analysis, to be ultimately concerned with the present and future, rather than with the time to which it nominally refers. And this, indeed, was the conclusion which Ayer reached in the original text of *LTL*.

This reductive analysis of statements about the past is, if anything, even more implausible than the behaviourist analysis of statements about other minds. And in his later *Introduction*, Ayer came to abandon it:

> Statements about the past may be verifiable in the sense that when they are conjoined with other premises of a suitable kind they may entail observation-statements which do not follow from these other premises alone; but I do not think that the truth of any observation-statements which refer to the present or the future is a necessary condition of the truth of any statement about the past. (*LTL*, 19)

This does not lead Ayer to abandon his phenomenalism, nor even to abandon the relativity-factor, though he does radically revise his conception of how this factor operates. Thus he continues:

> This does not mean, however, that propositions referring to the past cannot be analysed in phenomenal terms; for they can be taken as implying that certain observations would have occurred if certain conditions had been fulfilled. But the trouble is that these conditions never can be fulfilled; for they require of the observer that he should occupy a temporal position that *ex hypothesi* he does not. This difficulty, however, is not a peculiarity of propositions about the past; for it is true also of unfulfilled conditionals about the present that their protases cannot in fact be satisfied, since they require of the observer that he should be occupying a different spatial position from that which he actually does. But . . . just as it is a contingent fact that a person happens at a given moment to be occupying a particular position in space, so it is a contingent fact that he happens to be living at a particular time. And from this I conclude that if one is justified in saying that events which are remote in space are observable, in principle, the same may be said of events which are situated in the past. (*LTL*, 19)

The idea is that, given a proposition about what occurs at some past time t, the verification-procedures which were *in practice* available to observers living at t are still *in principle* available to us now, since it is only contingent (i.e. not an *a priori* truth) that now (conceived demonstratively) is not t. And, as we have already noted (in section 3), it is verifiability in principle, not verifiability in practice, on which, according to Ayer's principle, factual significance depends.

It might be objected that this new approach does not work for statements which are *explicitly* about the past – statements which, because they employ the past tense, or such past-indicating expressions as 'once upon a time' and 'some years ago', indicate that the time referred to is earlier than the time at which the statement is made. For in such cases it seems that any method of verification would have to take account of the pastness of the time referred to relative to the verifier. Ayer's answer to this, developed in his essay 'Statements about the Past', which was published a few years after the *Introduction*, is that these 'token-reflexive' time-indicators are not part of the factual content of the statements (propositions) themselves:

> . . . there is no such thing as a class of statements about the past, in the way that there are classes of statements about numbers, or about people, or about physical events. There are ways of indicating, as by the use of tenses or other temporal demonstratives, that the point of view in time from which a statement is made is later than the event which it describes, but no statement says of itself that it is made from any particular point of view. When such indications are made explicit, what is stated is just that certain events stand to one another in certain temporal relations, all of which are definable in terms of the relation of precedence: and these statements are unaffected by the temporal position of those who make, interpret, or try to verify them. (*Philosophical Essays* (*PE*) 188)

Thus if I say 'Jones died three years ago', the statement I make (the proposition I assert) is simply that Jones died three years before time t (or before event e), where t is the present moment (e is some current event). The fact that t is the present moment (e is a current event) is indicated by my choice of words, but is not part of what is actually stated. And for that reason the factual significance I attach to my utterance in verificational terms is not affected by the contingent limitations on the kinds of observational evidence I can acquire in my current circumstances.

In the same essay, and in more detail in his subsequent essay 'One's Knowledge of Other Minds',[39] Ayer extends this account to cover statements about other minds.

> Just as no statement is, as such, about the past, so, I suggest, no

statement is, as such, about another's mind. What is stated is that someone who satisfies a certain description has certain thoughts or feelings: and from this it does not follow, with respect to any person who may make or understand the statement, either that he satisfies the description or that he does not. It may be indicated by the context, or by the use of demonstratives such as 'you' or 'he', that the speaker is not himself the person whom he is describing, and it may be then inferred that he is in a relatively disadvantageous position for verifying the statement that he makes. But no more in this case than in the case of statements about the past does it enter into the analysis of the statement that this or that person is in a better or worse position to pronounce upon its truth. (*PE*, 189)

In this way Ayer hopes to avoid the implausibilities of his original account in *LTL* – an account about which he had already expressed certain misgivings in his *Introduction*. Psychological predicates have the same sense in both self-ascriptive and other-ascriptive contexts, since the ascriptive viewpoint disappears in the statements made. Moreover, other-ascriptions can be construed mentalistically, since, if what they state is not essentially other-ascriptive, we can allow their factual meaning (or the factual content of the propositions they express) to be wholly determined by the possibilities of *introspective* evidence.

As we have noted, this new approach does not eliminate the relativity-factor, but revises its mode of operation. If I make some assertion about the past or about another mind, I may be, in practice, in a relatively bad position to verify the proposition in question; and certainly I am not, in practice, able to employ those methods of verification (and falsification) by which the content of the proposition is determined. But, as Ayer now sees it, the fact that I am in this less than ideal position, verificationally, is only contingent relative to the content of the proposition and my demonstrative identification of myself and my current viewpoint. Even though I know that my position is less than ideal, I can at least conceive of its being ideal and thus conceive of my verifying or falsifying the proposition in the relevant ways. In this sense, the relativity-factor is preserved. Nor, indeed, has it become entirely redundant. For although, in interpreting a given statement, I am permitted, as it were, to think of myself as occupying the (verificationally) most advantageous position (whether or not it happens to be my actual position), I still have to confine myself to a single position – a position which could be occupied by a single subject at a single time. I can imagine myself as the ideally placed observer; but I still have to make sense of the statement solely in terms of the possibilities of observational evidence (in the form of his current and future sense-contents) open to that one observer at the relevant time. I cannot, as it were, adopt different observational viewpoints simultaneously or blend them into some neutral God's-eye view.

This last point is more important than it seems; and its consequences are, I think, ones which Ayer has overlooked. Ayer believes that his revised account of the relativity-factor enables him to avoid the implausible reductions which he felt obliged, by this factor, to adopt in *LTL*. He thinks that statements about the past need not be reduced to statements about the present and future, since an interpreter can conceive of the current time (identified demonstratively) as being the earlier time (identified descriptively). Likewise, he thinks that statements about other minds need not be reduced to statements about behaviour, since an interpreter can conceive of himself (identified demonstratively) as being the other subject (identified descriptively). But, at least in the second case, he is only partially correct. It is true, of course, that an assertion such as 'Jones is in pain' can now be construed mentalistically by any subject, since any subject can conceive of himself as being Jones; more fully, any subject can envisage making observations which establish that he (identified demonstratively as 'I') satisfies the relevant identifying description of Jones and, within that framework, establishing introspectively whether Jones is in pain. The difficulties arise when we consider assertions which concern the mental condition of more than one subject – assertions such as 'Two subjects are currently in pain' and 'Jones's current pain is more intense than Smith's'. For where an assertion concerns more than one subject, there is no single viewpoint from which it could be verified introspectively – or at least, no single viewpoint from which the possibilities of introspective evidence would suffice to determine its meaning. It follows that if the factual meaning of a statement is determined by the possibilities of observational evidence open, in principle, to a single subject, such assertions would have to be analysed, at least in part, behaviouristically. This is an embarrassing result for Ayer, not only because of the implausibility of behaviourism, but also because it requires him to give quite different accounts of the meanings of other-minds assertions according to whether there is one or more than one other mind involved.

To avoid this result, Ayer would have to alter his position more substantially. He would have to allow that, in the sense in which it is relevant to factual meaning, a method of verification may combine and collate the separate stocks of evidence available to different subjects. Thus he would have to allow that 'Two subjects are currently in pain' can be verified by one subject introspectively establishing that a subject of one description is in pain at t and another subject introspectively establishing that a subject of a different and incompatible description is in pain at t, where t is the time of the assertion. And likewise, he would have to allow that 'Jones's current pain is more intense than Smith's' can be verified by Jones introspectively establishing that he has at t a pain of intensity n and Smith introspectively establishing that he has at t a pain of an intensity less than n. Consistency would then require making a similar alteration with respect to time – that is, allowing a method of verification to combine and collate the separate stocks of evidence available from different temporal viewpoints. The result, of course, would be to abandon the relativity-factor altogether. Whether Ayer could afford to do this, without destroying the core of his verificationist position, is hard to decide. For since he has provided no rationale for the position in its original form, it is hard to say which aspects of it are negotiable and which entrenched.

8 Ayer's critique of ethics

Our study of Ayer's verificationism, as found in *LTL*, is now almost complete. We have examined in detail the substance of his central thesis that any genuine proposition (or significant statement) must be either analytic or empirically verifiable and we have considered the consequences of this thesis for both philosophical and non-philosophical discourse. We have focused, in particular, on Ayer's content-restricting conception of empirical verifiability and on how this conception leads him to give a reductive account of most of our ordinary and scientific assertions. Obviously, there are a number of specific topics which we have not discussed – specific ways in which Ayer applies his verificationist outlook to a particular area of thought. But, in the main, these topics would merely provide further illustration of points which we have already made clear. There is, however, one final topic which I think we would do well to consider, both for its intrinsic interest and for the light which it sheds on Ayer's methodology. I have in mind his account of ethics.

In contrast with his productivity in the fields of epistemology, philosophical logic, and the philosophy of mind, Ayer has published very little in the field of moral philosophy. No doubt part of the reason for this is that he finds the other areas more interesting. But this, I think, is not the whole reason. Ayer's account of ethics in *LTL* is one which, if it were correct, would leave hardly anything left for moral philosophy, as traditionally conceived, to investigate. And since Ayer has found no reason to revise that account in any substantial way, it is hardly surprising that he has concentrated his efforts in other fields. The fact that the *LTL* account is, in effect, Ayer's last word on the topic and that, if it were correct, it would be, in effect, *the* last word, makes it all the more important to say something about it now.

Ayer's starting point here, as in so much else, is the problem that the verification principle seems to preclude the literal significance of a certain class of ordinary assertions.

> There is still one objection to be met before we can claim to have justified our view that all synthetic propositions are empirical hypotheses. This objection is based on the common supposition that our speculative knowledge is of two distinct kinds – that which relates to questions of empirical fact, and that which relates to questions of value. It will be said that "statements of value" are genuine synthetic propositions, but that they cannot with any show of justice be represented as hypotheses, which are used to predict the course of our sensations; and, accordingly, that the existence of ethics and aesthetics as branches of speculative knowledge presents an insuperable objection to our radical empiricist thesis. (*LTL*, 102)

Thus if I say 'Hitler was wicked' or 'Hitler's actions were morally wrong', how are the propositions expressed to be classified in Ayer's system? Clearly they are not analytic (true solely in virtue of their meaning, or, more precisely, the meanings of the sentences which express them): to deny these propositions may reveal historical ignorance or moral insensitivity, but it is not, even implicitly, self-contradictory. On the other hand, given their evaluative character, the propositions do not seem to be purely empirical: even if observational evidence may be relevant to determining their truth or falsity, it does not seem that the possibilities of such evidence exhaust their content. So it seems that, if Ayer's verification principle is correct, these ethical sentences do not express genuine propositions at all – that they are devoid of literal significance. And, on the face of it, this is a difficult conclusion to accept.

As we have seen, a similar problem arises for statements about the physical world, about the past, and about other minds. But whereas in these cases Ayer's strategy is to try to reconcile the significance of the statements with the verification principle through reductive analysis, his strategy in the case of ethical statements, and evaluative statements in general, is quite different. He is willing to accept that in so far as these statements are evaluative they are not empirical, and that in so far as they are not empirical they are not, in the literal sense, significant. His strategy is to try to show that this conclusion is not, as it initially appears to be, at variance with common sense – in particular, that it does not require the elimination of ethics, along with the elimination of metaphysics, or undermine the ordinary role of ethical utterances. And here his central claim is that, in so far as they are evaluative, such utterances are not really assertions at all, but merely expressions of emotion, which do not purport to say anything true or false. The utterer is not making a statement, but evincing his feelings.

Before we consider this emotivist theory in more detail, we ought to examine how Ayer is led to adopt it through a rejection of what he sees as the only alternatives. These alternatives are *naturalism* and, to use Ayer's term, *absolutism*. Like Ayer, I shall consider them in this order.

Naturalism is ethical reductionism. It claims that statements containing ethical terms can be translated into statements containing no ethical or evaluative terms – into statements wholly formulated in the empirical vocabulary (both ordinary and scientific) employed in descriptions of the physical world and the human mind. In other words, it claims that ethical terms can be eliminated by reductive analysis. As we have already remarked, in section 6, such a position would be very convenient from Ayer's standpoint, since, if it were true, every ethical statement would turn out, on analysis, to be either a tautology (where its truth was ensured by the analysis itself) or an empirical hypothesis. Ayer even goes so far as to concede that it may be desirable to invent a language for which the naturalist thesis would be true and 'adopt it in place of our own' (*LTL*, 105). But he also insists that this thesis is not 'consistent with the conventions of our actual language' (*LTL*, 105) – that it does not do justice to the actual meanings of our ethical terms. To illustrate the point, Ayer focuses on cases in which the naturalistic analysis takes the form of an explicit definition of an ethical predicate, such as the definition of 'is good' as 'is generally approved of' or the definition of 'is right' as 'maximizes happiness'. He thinks it is obvious that all such definitions fail, since, in each case, it is not self-contradictory to assert that something satisfies the *definiens* without satisfying the *definiendum*. (Again, this is something which we noted in section 6.) The reason why all such definitions are bound to fail, Ayer thinks, is that ethical concepts are, at least in part, normative – concerned with how one *ought* to act or how things *ought* to be – and that this normative element cannot be captured by the vocabulary of bare empirical description. This, of course, would exclude, and Ayer intends it to exclude, naturalistic analyses of any kind, whether they employ explicit definitions or definitions in use.

In all this, I am sure that Ayer is correct. His only error, perhaps, is in concluding that this point 'is fatal to utilitarianism' (*LTL*, 104). No doubt it is fatal to *naturalistic* utilitarianism, which *defines* 'right' as 'maximizing happiness'. But Ayer seems to think that it is fatal to utilitarianism altogether: 'to every other variant of utilitarianism with which I am acquainted the same objection can be made' (*LTL*, 105). However, a utilitarian may (and typically does) merely claim that the maximization of happiness, or of the balance of pleasure over pain, is what makes a right action right, without claiming that 'right' and 'maximizing happiness' are synonymous; that is, he may offer his utilitarian thesis (that an action is right if and only if it maximizes happiness) as a fundamental moral principle rather than as a specimen of semantic analysis. This is something which Ayer seems to have overlooked.

If utilitarianism is construed in this way, i.e. as a moral rather than an analytical doctrine, it could fall under the second of the alternatives which Ayer rejects – that which he calls 'absolutism'. Ayer describes absolutism as 'the view that statements of value are not controlled by observation, as ordinary empirical propositions are, but only by a mysterious "intellectual intuition" ' (*LTL*, 106). I think this description is misleading. Presumably, the view which Ayer has in mind is one which makes three claims: first, that ethical predicates, such as 'good' and 'right', signify genuine properties (this ensures that, like naturalism, absolutism is a form of objectivism); second, that these ethical properties are non-empirical (this excludes naturalism); and third, that there are certain *a priori* moral principles, whose truth is discernible by moral intuition, and which specify the empirical conditions which are (morally) necessary or sufficient for the instantiation of these ethical properties. For example, a utilitarian absolutist will insist that rightness is a genuine property, that it is not to be equated with any empirical property, such as the property of maximizing happiness, and that we can know *a priori*, through the exercise of moral intuition, i.e. moral insight, that it is all and only actions which maximize happiness which possess this ethical property. Given this, we can see why Ayer's characterization of absolutism is misleading. The point is not that he describes moral intuition as 'intellectual' – this, I take it, is only to stress its *a priori*, non-empirical character. Rather, the point is that, according to the absolutist, it is only a special class of ethical truths, i.e. those which constitute fundamental moral principles or deductive consequences of such principles, which can be established by *a priori* methods alone. The remaining ethical truths can only be established by the application of these *a priori* truths to the empirical facts, and this will require the gathering of observational evidence. Thus no absolutist, whatever his persuasion, will claim that statements such as 'Hitler was wicked' and 'Hitler's actions were wrong' can be verified by moral intuition and logical reasoning alone. For obviously, before he can bring his *a priori* principles to bear on such a case, he needs empirical information about Hitler's character and actions – information relevant to the empirical concepts employed in the principles. Nor is this point restricted to moral judgments about *particulars*. Even a general moral judgment, such as 'Stealing is always wrong' may be one which, in the absolutist's system, can only be tested empirically. This, of course, will depend on the nature of the principles which moral intuition delivers. A utilitarian absolutist would claim that 'Stealing is always wrong' could only be tested empirically, by discovering whether stealing always fails to maximize happiness. But an absolutist of another moral persuasion might claim that this sentence expresses an *a priori* truth which is either morally self-evident or deducible from truths which are morally self-evident.

It is not surprising that Ayer rejects absolutism since, as we have seen (in section 2), he denies that there is any form of *a priori* knowledge other than what is derived from an understanding of language or any form of *a priori* truth other than what linguistic meaning creates. I have already argued that this is an untenable position and that some faculty of *a priori* intuition, i.e. *a priori* insight, must be taken as basic. It does not follow, however, that there is a faculty of *a priori moral* intuition. The argument only establishes that we must credit ourselves with a capacity for *rational* intuition sufficient to reveal as self-evident the fundamental principles of logic. Whether we have a capacity for moral intuition is another question and one which must be decided on its own merits (it must be decided on its own merits, even if moral intuition is considered to be a special kind of rational intuition). And here it must be stressed that by 'intuition' we mean something genuinely epistemic – not just the non-inferential holding of certain convictions, but the direct and *a priori* recognition of certain truths. In short we mean *insight*, as I have explicitly indicated at certain points in the preceding discussion.

Even when we reject Ayer's general position on the character of *a priori* knowledge, there are, it seems, special reasons for being sceptical about the claims of intuitionism in *ethics*. The main reason is that, unlike the case of logic,[40] there is, or appears to be, considerable disagreement between different societies, and even between different members of the same society, as to what the correct principles of morality are. As Ayer himself puts it:

> . . . it is notorious that what seems intuitively certain to one person may seem doubtful, or even false, to another. So that unless it is possible to provide some criterion by which one may decide between conflicting intuitions, a mere appeal to intuition is worthless as a test of a proposition's validity. (*LTL*, 106)

(When Ayer here speaks of 'conflicting intuitions' he is, of course, using 'intuition' in a non-epistemic sense, i.e. to mean *putative* intuition.) He goes on to remark, with some plausibility, that 'in the case of moral judgements, no such criterion can be given' (*LTL*, 106), and from this he concludes that on the absolutist's theory 'ethical statements are held to be unverifiable' (*LTL*, 106). This is a slightly odd way of putting it. What Ayer means is that if the absolutist were correct in claiming that ethical predicates signify genuine but non-empirical properties, ethical statements would be unverifiable, since the remaining component of the absolutist's theory, that ethical principles can be established by intuition, is untenable. It is untenable because, given the conflict between the putative intuitions of different people and the lack of any objective criterion for deciding between them, we have no reason to credit ourselves with a capacity for (genuinely epistemic) moral intuition at all.

It must be stressed that this argument against absolutism does not depend on a prior acceptance of the verification principle. It was obvious in advance that absolutism would not be compatible with this principle in the strong form in which Ayer adopts it. Only naturalism would permit moral principles to be analytic, in the sense Ayer intends, and specific moral judgments to be purely empirical hypotheses. The point of the argument above is to show that absolutism is independently flawed and that it cannot be accepted even from the non-verificationist stand-point which the absolutist adopts. The reason why Ayer feels called upon to show this, rather than just to apply his principle, is that he is looking on ethics as an area in which his general position is, *prima facie*, vulnerable to attack. Thus at the very outset, as we have seen, he is concerned to rebut the challenge that ' "statements of value" are genuine synthetic propositions, but that they cannot with any show of justice be represented as hypotheses, which are used to predict the course of our sensations; and, accordingly, that the existence of ethics . . . presents an insuperable objection to our radical empiricist thesis' (*LTL*, 102). Absolutism needs to be independently undermined since it is something to which an objector to Ayer's empiricism is likely to appeal.

The question we must now consider is whether the absolutist has any effective reply to Ayer's argument. One possibility, of course, would be for him to retain the metaphysical aspects of his position, but discard the epistemological. That is, he could continue to insist that ethical predicates signify genuine but non-empirical properties, but concede that there are no *a priori* moral principles – no faculty of *a priori* moral intuition. Thus, in this weakened form, absolutism would become mere non-naturalist objectivism, without intuitionism. To the charge that this makes ethical truth inaccessible, the response would be: 'That's true; but, unfortunately, that's how things are.' No other response is available, since if ethical properties are non-empirical and if there is no faculty of *a priori* moral intuition, there is simply no way of discovering in what empirical conditions such properties are instantiated. Without intuitionism, the absolutist would simply have to admit that, while there is an objective answer, the question of whether Hitler's extermination policy was morally right or morally wrong is wholly undecidable, however much empirical information one possesses.

Although (as I am sure I have made clear) I have little sympathy with verificationism, I find this conclusion manifestly absurd. For there are special reasons for insisting that, in the case of morality, the facts (assuming there are moral facts) be, in principle, accessible to us. The point is simply this. Morality is centrally and essentially concerned with *obligation* – with the specification of how a person ought or ought not to act in certain types of situation. But it would make no sense to suppose that we could be obliged to act or refrain from acting in certain ways if such obligations were in principle undiscoverable by the agents whom they bind. Perhaps there are some value-facts which are in principle undiscoverable by us – facts which could only be discerned from a God's-eye view. But facts of human obligation cannot be among them and it is with such facts that ethics is concerned. It follows that the absolutist cannot afford to abandon his intuitionism in response to Ayer's objection: without the intuitionism, his position becomes incoherent.

However, the absolutist has another and more plausible line of defence. He could argue that what appears to be a conflict between different (putative) moral intuitions is really a conflict over the nature of the non-moral facts, and that, once we have controlled for this latter conflict, a consensus of moral evaluation emerges. To take a concrete example, consider the conflict in our own society over the rightness or wrongness of abortion. Within our society there is a whole spectrum of different views about the circumstances, if any, in which abortion is morally acceptable. Let us, for simplicity, focus on two extreme views – that of the extreme anti-abortionist (Person A), who holds that abortion is morally wrong in all circumstances, and that of the extreme pro-abortionist (Person B), who holds that abortion is morally right whenever the pregnant woman requests it. Now there is no doubt that A and B hold different moral views. But it could still turn out that this difference reflects a difference in their non-moral beliefs rather than a difference in their fundamental moral principles. Thus it might be that while A and B both accept the moral principle that the deliberate killing of a human being is morally wrong, A believes that the human embryo qualifies as a human being and B believes that it does not. Or again, it might be that while A and B both accept the moral principle that the deliberate killing of a creature which is made in God's image is morally wrong and both accept that the human embryo is a human being, A believes that human beings are made in God's image and B (perhaps because he is an atheist) believes that they are not. These are just two of several possible ways in which the difference in A's and B's moral views about abortion might turn out, in the final analysis, to be a difference in their non-moral beliefs within the framework of the same fundamental moral principles. Thus the absolutist could argue that, although people differ in their moral views over a wide range of issues (of which abortion is just one example), there is an underlying consensus of fundamental moral belief – sufficient, at least, to sustain the intuitionist doctrine.

I think the absolutist has a point here: certainly, there is more consensus of fundamental moral belief than is often apparent in the derivative moral judgments we make about specific issues. At the same time, I doubt if it entirely eliminates the force of Ayer's objection. It seems likely that, even when we take non-moral beliefs into account, there are going to be a large number of cases of *ultimate* moral conflict –

cases where the fundamental moral outlook of one person is substantially different from that of someone else. Thus, in the dispute over abortion, it would not surprise us to find two people who had opposing moral convictions, but agreed on all the non-moral facts in so far as they were morally relevant for either party. For it might well happen that, when all the relevant non-moral facts are known, one person puts more moral weight on the *prima facie* right of the embryo (or foetus) not to be killed and the other person puts more moral weight on the *prima facie* right of the woman to decide whether another organism should live inside her body. How could there be such cases of apparently irresolvable and irreducibly *moral* conflict, if the fundamental truths of morality were, like the fundamental truths of logic, self-evident?

The absolutist might reply that, just as people vary in their capacity for logical insight, so also they vary in their capacity for moral insight, so that someone with a less well-developed capacity may fail to perceive some moral truth which is in principle self-evident or may think he perceives the truth of some moral proposition which is actually false. This is a fair point, but, again, I doubt if it will suffice to dispose of Ayer's objection. In the first place, it does not seem plausible to suppose that the full extent of the variation in fundamental moral beliefs could be explained in this way. And secondly, if there is no objective test of whether one person's moral faculty is superior or inferior to someone else's, it is hard to see how, except, perhaps, in the area of consensus, an appeal to intuition (i.e. apparent intuition) could retain its epistemic value.

Perhaps a more effective reply would be that while we have a *capacity* for moral insight – and, among people of similar intelligence, more or less the same capacity – there are special reasons why it is very often not efficiently exercised. One obvious reason would be that, since morality tends to impose obligations which are at variance with our selfish inclinations, and since we find it uncomfortable to know that we are acting contrary to the dictates of our conscience, we have a definite motive for not allowing ourselves to think through certain moral issues in a wholly dispassionate way – a motive for only looking at the moral truth through the distorting spectacles of self-interest. The suggestion is not, of course, that we do this consciously and deliberately – presumably that would be self-defeating – but that, by some unconscious defence-mechanism, self-interest to some extent protects itself from moral exposure by disturbing the natural functioning of our moral faculties. A further way in which this natural functioning might be disturbed would be through the influence of moral 'education'. It goes without saying that, in the case of any *a priori* faculty, its efficient use partly depends on there being an efficient programme of education. No doubt we have an innate capacity for logical insight, but to some extent we have to be trained in the use of that capacity if our logical perceptiveness is to achieve its proper scope and reliability. Now the point is that, while, in the case of our logical faculty, all the factors favour the emergence of a system of education which promotes the efficiency of its exercise, this need not be so in the case of our moral faculty, if indeed we possess one. This is because, in any society, the system of education, like most other institutions, will be designed to promote the interests of its members. In general, of course, the promotion of these interests will involve, amongst other things, cultivating the efficient exercise of our truth-discovering capacities, since true beliefs are usually more advantageous than false ones. But in the case of morality the situation is more complicated. It would not be surprising if the requirements of social expediency and the demands of moral duty were to some degree in conflict; and, if this is so, there are likely to be social pressures towards the acceptance of a moral code which is, in certain crucial respects, out of line with the moral truth, and thus pressures against the proper exercise of our capacity for moral insight. In short, and putting both points together, it might well be that our acceptance of certain moral principles is often the product of a compromise between our capacity for genuine moral insight and the pressures of expediency – both the pressures of personal expediency in the form of selfish inclinations and the pressures of social expediency transmitted through moral education. If this is so, the absolutist has an easy way of explaining why there is a lack of consensus in our fundamental moral beliefs. For there is no reason to expect that the same compromise will be achieved in each person – partly because the pressures of expediency would take different forms in different people, and partly because different people would yield to them to different degrees and at different points. At the same time, the absolutist can insist that by cultivating a dispassionate attitude, and by conducting a critical examination of conventional morality, it is possible to combat the pressures of expediency and eventually reach a state of mind in which the moral truth is self-evident. And, of course, the closer different people come to that state, the closer they come to a consensus of moral outlook.

I think this reply is sufficient to rebut Ayer's objection. It does not follow, of course, that absolutism is correct. And whether it is, is not something which I shall further pursue, though I take this to be the central question of moral philosophy. Instead, I want to conclude by briefly considering the positive theory which, in opposition to both naturalism and absolutism, Ayer comes to advance.

Both naturalism and absolutism share two assumptions: first that indicative ethical sentences are, and are in respect of their ethical content, genuinely assertive – they purport to say how things are; second, that such sentences are, and are in respect of their ethical content, literally significant – they express genuine propositions, which are either true or false. Ayer is obliged to reject the second assumption by his verification principle (now reinforced, in the context of ethics, by his supposed refutation of absolutism) and his rejection of naturalism. And this leaves him with a choice between eliminating ethics altogether, in the way he eliminates metaphysics, and rejecting the first assumption. He does the latter:

> . . . if I say to someone, "You acted wrongly in stealing that money", I am not stating anything more than if I had simply said, "You stole that money." In adding that this action is wrong I am not making any further statement about it. I am simply evincing my moral disapproval of it. It is as if I had said, "You stole that money" in a peculiar tone of horror, or written it with the addition of some special exclamation marks. The tone, or the exclamation marks, adds nothing to the literal meaning of the sentence. It merely serves to show that the expression of it is attended by certain feelings in the speaker. If I now generalise my previous statement and say, "Stealing money is wrong", I produce a sentence which has no factual meaning – that is, expresses no proposition which can be either true or false. It is as if I had written "Stealing money!!" – where the shape and thickness of the exclamation marks show, by a suitable convention, that a special sort of moral disapproval is the feeling which is being expressed. It is clear that there is nothing said here which can be true or false. (*LTL*, 107)

A little later Ayer introduces an additional factor:

> It is worth mentioning that ethical terms do not serve only to express feeling. They are calculated also to arouse feeling, and so to stimulate action. Indeed some of them are used in such a way as to give the sentences in which they occur the effect of commands. (*LTL*, 108)

Thus he takes the sentence 'It is your duty to tell the truth' both as an expression of a certain sort of feeling about truthfulness and as an expression of a command to tell the truth. His overall conclusion is that 'we may define the meaning of the various ethical words in terms both of the different feelings they are ordinarily taken to express, and also the different responses which they are calculated to provoke' (*LTL*, 108).

This emotivist analysis of ethical terms is certainly ingenious. But it is also, to my mind, very implausible. To claim that when I say 'Stealing is wrong' I do not even purport to say how things objectively are – that I merely express my disapproval of stealing and/or issue a command against it – just seems to misrepresent the actual meaning of the sentence. It may be that, contrary to the views of the naturalist and the absolutist, there are no objective moral facts and that, consequently, there is nothing to make ethical sentences true or false. But one could hardly reach this result by discovering, through a dispassionate analysis of our actual ethical concepts, that ethical sentences do not even claim to be saying how things ethically are.[41] Indeed, this objection to emotivism, as an analysis of ethical concepts, is parallel to Ayer's own objection to naturalism. Ayer rejected naturalism on the grounds that ethical concepts have a normative character which cannot be captured by the vocabulary of bare empirical description – and he was right to do so. But it is equally true that ethical concepts are inherently objectivist (or realist). Moral rightness as we conceive it, i.e. as our concept of moral rightness represents it, is an objective property. Certainly it is *normative*, concerned with how we are *required* to act; but it is also, as we conceive it, a genuine *property*, not just the projection of our own emotional and prescriptive attitudes onto certain types of action. Indeed, it is not even the case, I think, that a person's emotional and prescriptive attitudes have to be in line with his moral beliefs. It seems to make sense to suppose that Satan, or a human satanist, believes that stealing is morally wrong and, for that very reason, approves of it and encourages its practice. Nor does this seem to be merely a case of the so-called inverted-commas use of ethical terms, in which what Satan really believes is only that stealing is regarded as morally wrong by those who accept divine or conventional standards. We surely want to represent Satan as someone who is consciously hostile to morality as such, rather than as someone with deviant moral views.

Since Ayer wants to deny that there are objective moral facts, and since our ethical concepts are inherently objectivist, the conclusion he should have reached is that these concepts are defective. In other words, instead of trying to salvage ethics by an emotivist analysis, he should have eliminated ethics altogether, in the way he eliminates metaphysics. He should have classified ethical sentences as assertoric nonsense rather than as expressions of feeling. Admittedly, from the standpoint of our ordinary intuitions, the difference between these positions is of no great significance. When we pronounce that an action is right or that a motive is good, we ordinarily take ourselves to be making significant assertions about the objective moral character of the items to which we refer. If this ordinary belief is erroneous, it is only a technical question as to whether the error, as well as involving a misconception of the nature of reality, also reflects a misunderstanding of our own linguistic activities. The important point is that, either way, objective morality is forfeit.

I said at the beginning that, if correct, Ayer's account of ethics would leave hardly anything left for moral philosophy, as traditionally conceived, to investigate. It should now be clear why this is so. The reason lies not so much in the emotivist analysis, as in the negative thesis which underlies it – the denial of objective moral truth. For if there is no objective moral truth, then, by and large, the traditional questions of moral philosophy, from the most general questions, like 'What makes an action morally right?' and 'What states of affairs are intrinsically good?', to the more specific questions, like 'Is abortion morally permissible?' and 'Is there such a thing as a just war?', become spurious: no genuine questions have been posed, because there are no moral facts to furnish the answers. In short, whether we construe ethical sentences as assertoric nonsense or as expressions of feeling, moral philosophy has lost the greater part of its traditional subject-matter.

No doubt as philosophers we could bear this loss with equanimity: there is plenty to think about in other areas. It is at the level of ordinary life that we would find the demise of objective morality disturbing, notwithstanding the superficial attractions of moral autonomy. As things stand, however, neither Ayer nor, in my view, anyone else has shown that the belief in objective morality is mistaken.

Part II

Knowledge and Scepticism

1 *Introduction*

Ayer's philosophical output has been as wide-ranging as it has been prolific. But his largest and most important contribution has been in epistemology, that is, the theory of knowledge. Since the verification principle is, in effect, an epistemological criterion of significance, this concern with the theory of knowledge is already implicit in his original position. But what we find in the subsequent development of his philosophy is an increasing interest in the theory of knowledge *for its own sake* – that is, irrespective of its bearing on the issues of meaning. This does not mean that the verification principle has been abandoned[1] nor that it does not continue to exert an influence on Ayer's treatment of the epistemological issues.

There are two main questions which the theory of knowledge is designed to answer, namely 'What is knowledge?' and 'How, if at all, can our ordinary claims to knowledge be justified?' Ayer's predominant concern is with the second of these questions. Or rather, he is concerned with this second question as part of his predominant concern with the more general question of how, if at all, our ordinary beliefs can be justified. His concern with this question is prompted by the challenge of the philosophical sceptic, who claims that most of our ordinary beliefs cannot be rationally defended.

Although Ayer is mainly concerned with the issue of scepticism – that is, with the question of whether our ordinary knowledge-claims and beliefs can be defended against the sceptic's challenge – it will be convenient to start with the question of what knowledge is. This, indeed, is where Ayer himself starts in his most celebrated epistemological work, *The Problem of Knowledge* (*PK*), published in 1956.

85

2 *Ayer's definition of knowledge*

In the opening chapter of *PK*, Ayer defines knowledge (i.e. factual knowledge) as the conjunction of three conditions: a subject S knows that p if and only if

(1) it is true that p,
(2) S is sure that p,

and (3) S has the right to be sure that p.

Thus Ayer is claiming that each of these conditions is logically necessary for knowledge and that jointly they are logically sufficient. Our discussion in this section will be divided into four parts: the first three parts will focus on the three conditions separately and concern the question of their necessity; the fourth part will concern the question of their joint sufficiency. I should add that this discussion, particularly as it relates to Ayer's third condition, is largely preliminary; the most important issues will have to be discussed in later sections.

(i) The necessity of Ayer's first condition is beyond dispute. It is part of the meaning of the verb 'to know' that only true propositions can be known. As Ayer himself stresses, this does not mean that knowledge is a state of mind whose intrinsic character logically guarantees the truth of the proposition onto which it is directed. It does not mean that whenever a proposition is known, its truth is deducible from an intrinsic description of the knower's mental condition. It means only that the subject's state of mind does not qualify for the title 'knowledge' unless the relevant proposition is true. It is only in certain special cases, namely where the proposition is exclusively concerned with the subject's state of mind or where it is an *a priori* truth and thus (trivially) deducible from anything, that the truth of the proposition is deducible from an intrinsic description of the subject's mental condition.

(ii) Ayer's second condition is more controversial. For S to be sure that p, or, as Ayer sometimes puts it, completely sure, S must not only believe that p, but must believe it with full conviction. He must not harbour residual doubts; he must be, as one might say, subjectively certain. It might be argued that, as a requirement for knowledge, this is too strong. Think of the case of the neurotic who, when he has established that the fire is off and now believes that it is off, feels the need to keep on checking that this is so. Can we not say that he really knows that the fire is off, despite his uncertainty? Ayer himself acknowledges that we can speak in this way. But, at least in *PK*, he regards this as just an idiomatic way of saying that the subject's doubts are unjustified, rather than as furnishing a genuine counter-example to his definition.[2]

The question of whether knowledge entails subjective certainty or merely belief is, I think, of no real importance. If need be, Ayer could weaken his requirement without undermining the essentials of his position (note that such a weakening would not necessitate a similar weakening of condition (3)). Alternatively, if he retains the stronger requirement, he risks, at worst, only a slight and theoretically harmless deviation from ordinary usage. A more important challenge comes from those who maintain that knowledge does not even entail belief, and it is this which we must consider next.

In a subsequent essay 'Knowledge, Belief and Evidence', which is reprinted in his collection *Metaphysics and Common Sense* (*MCS*), Ayer himself cites two cases in which we might suppose that there is knowledge without belief. The first is the case of self-deception, in which, because he finds the truth unpalatable, the subject refuses to accept consciously what, it is alleged, he really knows. The other is the case of someone who is temporarily unable to bring to mind information which he previously learned and which, after suitable prompting or sufficient recollective effort, he will eventually recall. These two cases are very different. But in both it is natural to think of the subject as possessing, in some form, knowledge of the proposition in question. How could someone be, as we often allege, guilty of self-deception unless he really knows the fact which he does not consciously acknowledge? And how will the subject be able eventually to recall the information which he has at the conscious level temporarily forgotten, unless he has at some deeper level retained it? At the same time, focusing on the subject's own judgments and judgmental dispositions at the time in question, it seems difficult to credit him with belief. For how can a subject be said to believe something unless he is thereby disposed to make the corresponding judgment? And he is not, at the time, disposed to make this judgment if the fact in question is one which he is either unwilling or unable to bring to consciousness.

Ayer does not regard this argument as conclusive, and rightly so. Each of the cases cited is one in which, allegedly, the subject unconsciously knows what he does not consciously believe. But, as Ayer points out, this does not oblige us to describe them as cases of knowledge without belief, since, if we take the knowledge to be unconscious, we could take the belief to be unconscious too. Still, he is willing to concede that such a description is not contrary to the rules of ordinary usage. His overall conclusion is that 'what emerges from these examples is that to insist that knowledge must entail belief is to put a slight but by no means unbearable strain upon ordinary usage' and that 'whether it is worth paying this small price for the sake of greater neatness and uniformity is a matter for decision' (*MCS*, 117). Ayer's own decision, of course, is that it is.

Why does Ayer think that the belief-requirement achieves 'greater neatness and uniformity'? His point, I assume, is that, in the standard

87

cases, knowledge is not only accompanied but partly *constituted* by the subject's belief. Consequently, if we rejected the belief-requirement, we should have to recognize two radically different kinds of knowledge, whose grouping under a single concept would lack a theoretical rationale. Even if ordinary usage allows for cases of knowledge without belief, we can improve our concept of knowledge by excluding such cases from its scope.

However, I suspect that many of those who reject the belief-requirement are trying to establish a more far-reaching conclusion than Ayer supposes. They are trying to establish, I think, that, although belief is a normal accompaniment of knowledge, it is never even part of what constitutes it. And, for this reason, they would deny that the adoption of the belief-requirement would bring a gain in 'neatness and uniformity'. Their point is not that we should stick to ordinary usage at all costs, but that the non-standard cases (like those of self-deception and temporary forgetting) help us to see that even in the standard cases the traditional account of knowledge, as justified true belief, has gone badly astray. In this respect, Ayer's reply to the objection is too complacent. There is a genuine issue here and not just one which is, as Ayer puts it, 'a matter for decision'.

None the less, I am confident that the issue should be settled in favour of the belief-requirement. For I cannot see how, if we extract belief from the knower's state of mind, what remains could qualify as knowledge in any decent sense. Obviously, for someone to have knowledge, he must be in some mental state (whether conscious or unconscious) which is directed onto the proposition in question. This state need not, and typically will not, qualify as knowledge solely in virtue of its *intrinsic* character; but at least it must be something whose intrinsic character equips it to be a state of knowledge when all the other requirements are met. But what could this state be if belief is excluded? Clearly, it must be more than just a mental representation of a proposition. But what could the additional factor be if not some kind of mental commitment to the proposition's truth?

The only answer I can think of would be that knowledge is the intellectual perception of a fact. Such a perception, it might be claimed, does not, as such, involve a belief that the fact obtains (even if it normally induces such a belief), any more than the sensory perception of a physical object involves the belief that the object exists. The perception would be, as it were, something more passive than belief, something which happens to the subject prior to his attitudinal response – the reception and storing of a factual datum, rather than a commitment to the proposition's truth.

I have no objection to calling knowledge (or perhaps the acquisition of knowledge) 'intellectual perception'. But I do not see how such perception could fail to be partly constituted by the subject's (acquisition of) belief. One thing we need to emphasize here is that, in describing knowledge as intellectual perception, we have not yet isolated the intrinsic character of the subject's mental state. Obviously, we cannot suppose, naive-realistically, that such perception is a wholly unmediated awareness of a fact, such that without the obtaining of this fact there could be no mental state of that intrinsic character. Just as we leave room for cases of sensory hallucination, so we must leave room for cases of epistemic illusion, in which things are with the subject, mentally, exactly as if he perceives some fact, when no such fact obtains. And this means that, to isolate the intrinsic character of the knower's mental state, we must describe it in a way which does not entail that it is genuinely fact-perceptive. But I cannot think of any appropriate description which does not entail belief. We might, to preserve the perceptual model, speak of its intellectually seeming to the subject that something is the case. But this is only an alternative way of saying what he believes. To speak of *intellectual seeming* is just to speak of the subject's belief, though thinking of the subject in an especially passive role.

I conclude, therefore, that whether or not it requires complete conviction, knowledge does require belief and, indeed, is always in part constituted by it. How we should describe the cases of self-deception and temporary forgetting is a further question and one which I am content to leave open. It is far from clear that they are cases of knowledge at all. It is at least arguable that, in the case of self-deception, it is not that the subject knows what he refuses to consciously accept, but only that he knows, but chooses to discount, the evidence. (If this makes the term 'self-deception' inappropriate, so much the worse for the term.) Equally, it is arguable that when a subject is temporarily unable to recall something, he has temporarily lost his knowledge. The fact that he subsequently regains his ability could be explained by the continuance of some physiological record – a record which only endows the subject with knowledge when it enables him to make the appropriate conscious judgments. But even if these cases do count as cases of (unconscious) knowledge, they also count as cases of (unconscious) belief. For there is no other way of making sense of the intrinsic character of the knower's mental state.

(iii) Ayer's third requirement for knowledge is that the subject should have the right to be sure. In my view, this requirement is clearly correct. Perhaps, contrary to Ayer's second condition, it is permissible to ascribe knowledge to someone (e.g. the neurotic) who believes something, but with less than full conviction. But, for such an ascription to be correct, the subject must at least have the *right* to be sure: the doubts he harbours must be unjustified. Likewise, if someone is convinced of something, but is not entitled to his conviction, he cannot be said to *know* the proposition in question, even if he is justified in believing it. All this strikes me as uncontroversial, at least when the term 'knowledge' is used in its standard sense.

None the less, there is one respect in which Ayer's requirement might be thought problematic. For when we come to examine typical cases in which we credit ourselves or others with knowledge, it seems that in most of these cases Ayer's requirement is not satisfied. Thus I would normally claim to know, on the basis of my memory, that I was married in Tunbridge Wells, and this knowledge-claim would normally be accepted by other people. But my memory is not infallible, and it is at least conceivable, however unlikely, that it is, in this instance, deceiving me. So how can I have the right to be sure? Again, in my present circumstances, I would normally claim to know, on the basis of my present sense-perceptions, that I am sitting at my desk in college, and this claim would not normally be challenged by others who observed my situation. But here too there is the logical possibility that I am being deceived. Perhaps I have been kidnapped by a team of physiologists and am now, at their contrivance, the victim of an unusually coherent hallucination. So, again, how can I have the right to be sure? Putting the point more generally, in almost all the cases where I would normally claim to know something and where this claim would normally be accepted by others, I can think up a story which leaves the grounds for my belief intact, but renders the proposition in question false. And if the grounds for my belief are compatible with the falsity of the proposition, how can they give me the right to be sure (i.e. completely sure) that the proposition is true?

Such considerations might lead someone to conclude that Ayer's requirement is too strong – that Ayer has provided a 'high redefinition' of knowledge, rather than an analysis of our actual concept. The argument would run: 'By the standards of our actual concept, the sorts of case we are considering qualify, paradigmatically, as cases of knowledge. But they are not cases in which the subject has the right to be sure. So the right to be sure is not, after all, a requirement for knowledge as we actually conceive it.' In line with Ayer, I regard this conclusion as false. But there is no denying that it follows from the premises; and each of the premises, taken on its own, has a certain plausibility. How, then, is the argument to be resisted?

Well let us, for the moment, assume that the second premise is true – that in the sorts of case we are considering (like my putative knowledge of where I was married and my putative knowledge of my present location) the subject does not have the right to be sure. The question now is: what reason do we have for accepting the first premise, which claims that such cases are paradigm cases of knowledge as we actually conceive it? The only reason is that these cases are ones which we *ordinarily* take to be clear-cut cases of knowledge – ones which we have no hesitation in classifying as cases of knowledge *prior to philosophical reflection*. But now we can see that to accept the premise on this basis just begs the question. For, granted the truth of the second premise, the defender of Ayer's requirement will say that, even by the standards of our actual concept of knowledge, these ordinary ascriptions of knowledge are mistaken – that we are crediting people (both ourselves and others) with a right to certainty which they do not possess. Such a conclusion, of course, is unpalatable: we want it to turn out that these ordinary ascriptions are correct. But the fact that a conclusion is unpleasant is not a reason for rejecting it. We cannot assume that a definition of knowledge is erroneous simply because it supports a sceptical position. And, as I see it, the sceptical position is unavoidable once we have accepted the second premise.

This is enough to refute the argument. But it is not the only way in which the argument can be challenged. For it is far from clear that the second premise is true. And, as we shall see, Ayer would certainly reject it. He would claim that, in the sorts of case we are considering, the subject does, typically, have the right to be sure, and, on this basis, he would deny that our ordinary ascriptions of knowledge are condemned by his requirement. In short, he would reject the second premise and thereby deny that the problem which prompted the argument even arises.

The only consideration which has been offered in support of the second premise is that, in the relevant sorts of case, the subject's grounds for belief are compatible with the falsity of the proposition believed. Thus it is claimed that I do not have the right to be sure that I was married in Tunbridge Wells because it is logically possible that my memory is deceiving me. And it is claimed that I do not have the right to be sure that I am now sitting at my college desk because it is logically possible that my current sense-experiences are hallucinatory. But such claims depend on two crucial assumptions: first that the right to be sure, where it obtains, is wholly derived from the subject's grounds for belief; second, that the possession of such a right, however it is sustained, logically guarantees the truth of the proposition in question. Neither of these assumptions is uncontroversial, and indeed Ayer denies both.

Ayer's denial of the first assumption will be explained in section 3, when we come to examine his account of what gives a subject the right to be sure. At this stage, it is his denial of the second assumption which needs to be stressed. Obviously, someone who has the right to be sure that *p* has the right to discount the possibility that not-*p*. This is why such a right could never be sustained merely by the possession of evidence of an explicitly probabilistic kind, however high the probability. (Thus, given the number of tickets sold, I may know that my chances of winning first prize in a lottery are very small; but however small my chances, I do not have the right to be sure that I will not win, though I do have reason to believe this.) But it does not follow from this that possessing the right to be sure logically excludes the possibility of error – that it is logically impossible for someone to have the right to be sure of a proposition which is actually false. And Ayer is at pains to stress that it is not. Thus in response to the question as to what gives him the right to be sure that he is looking at a sheet of paper, he remarks:

> It is enough that I am having the experience that I am and that I
> have acquired the necessary skill in identifying what I see. Of course
> I may go astray. I may on this basis come to hold a false belief. In
> that case my claim to knowledge fails . . . but it does not necessarily
> follow that I did not have the right to be sure. We are not demanding
> infallibility. (*MCS*, 121–2)

Likewise, concerning his reliance on memory, he says:

> Again, this does not exclude the possibility that I am mistaken: what
> I think that I remember may not in fact have happened. Even so,
> in normal circumstances, my seeming to remember that something
> happened does give me the right to be sure that it did happen.
> (*MCS*, 122)

Thus Ayer would deny that his third condition is in conflict with our ordinary ascriptions of knowledge. The fact that, in most of these cases, the subject's grounds for belief are not logically conclusive, or, more generally, that his method of reaching the belief is not infallible, does not, in Ayer's view, show that the subject lacks the right to be sure. And Ayer is willing to say that, in normal circumstances, the right obtains. What enables him to say this will emerge presently, when his requirements for the possession of the right are revealed.

(iv) We have looked, in turn, at each of Ayer's three requirements for knowledge and, with a slight reservation about the second (perhaps certainty should be weakened to belief), endorsed them. We must now consider whether they are, in combination, *sufficient*. Do the three statements, (1) that it is true that *p*, (2) that *S* is sure that *p*, and (3) that *S* has the right to be sure that *p*, jointly entail that *S* knows that *p*? Ayer's definition, of course, requires that they should.

There are, I think, just two respects in which Ayer's conditions fall short of sufficiency, though one of them, which I shall deal with first, is no more than a defect in formulation.

Suppose that Smith belongs to a religious sect, one of whose doctrines is that its leader is infallible. Smith, who is a recent convert, wrongly believes that the leader has pronounced that the earth is flat. On this basis, he accepts that the earth is flat. Jones, who is not a member of the sect, draws Smith's attention to the scientific evidence which establishes that the earth is spherical. Being aware of this evidence, and fully understanding it, Smith now has the right to be sure that the earth is spherical: if, on the basis of this evidence, he became convinced of the earth's sphericity, his conviction would be justified. As it is, he irrationally allows his religious beliefs to overrule the scientific evidence and remains convinced that the earth is flat. But later he discovers that he was mistaken about the content of his leader's pronouncement. What the leader really said, he learns, was that, although all the other planets are flat, the earth is spherical. He also learns that the leader's reason for believing the earth to be spherical is not that this is what the scientific evidence establishes (the leader rejects such evidence as worthless), but that this was what was disclosed to him during a session of transcendental meditation. On the basis of his new information, Smith continues to discount the scientific evidence, of which he remains aware, but comes to believe, with full conviction, the proposition which he previously denied. We have now reached a situation in which all three of Ayer's conditions for knowledge are satisfied: it is true that the earth is spherical; Smith is sure that it is; and, knowing the scientific evidence, he has the right to be sure that it is. But, at the same time, the basis of his certainty (i.e. his knowledge of the leader's pronouncement) is not the same as that which gives him the right to be certain (i.e. his knowledge of the scientific evidence). For this reason, although he is sure and has the right to be sure, he is not justified in being sure. Put another way, although he is entitled to be sure, he is not entitled to the certainty which he actually possesses. And, consequently, it is clear that Smith does not *know* that the earth is spherical. Or at least, it is clear that he does not possess such knowledge in virtue of satisfying Ayer's three conditions in that way. If he does know, it will be a case of self-deception, in which he has, deep down, known all along that the scientific evidence was conclusive, but has managed to keep this knowledge below the threshold of consciousness.

The remedy, of course, is simple. We have to reformulate the third condition as 'S is justified in being sure that p'. This enables us to withhold the title of knowledge from a case in which someone has the right to be sure but is not entitled to the certainty which he actually possesses. And, despite his actual formulation, it is no doubt this that Ayer intends. Admittedly, this new formulation does not allow us to retain the possibility of knowledge without certainty, since 'S is justified in being sure' entails 'S *is* sure'. But here again there is a simple remedy: if we weaken the second condition to 'S believes that p' we must formulate the third as 'S is justified in believing that p and what justifies his believing gives him the right to be sure'. For the present, however, I shall assume that Ayer's second condition stands and that his third condition is to be reformulated in the way initially suggested.

93

As I have indicated, there is a second and more substantial respect in which Ayer's conditions are inadequate. To be precise, they are inadequate given an assumption which Ayer himself accepts, namely that the right to be sure does not logically exclude the possibility of error. That Ayer accepts this assumption, and indeed puts weight on it, is something we have already noted. What we must now investigate are the implications of this for the adequacy of his definition.

At this moment I am sure that I am sitting at my desk. Let us call this proposition, of which I am sure, *A*, and let us assume, for the sake of argument, that I am justified in being sure of *A*. Now I recently bought a lottery ticket. I have no reason to think that my ticket will win; nor do I expect it to. But (let us suppose) for some reason I turn my attention to the proposition (*B*) that either I am sitting at my desk or my ticket will win. Being sure of *A*, and seeing that *A* entails *B*, I find myself sure of *B*. And since I am justified in being sure of *A* and my certainty of *B* is based on my perception of the entailment, I am justified in being sure of *B*. Now, according to Ayer, the right to be sure does not logically exclude the possibility of error: someone may be justified in being sure of a proposition which is actually false. So let us suppose that, as it happens, *A* is false: I am, for whatever reason, the victim of a remarkably coherent hallucination. But let us also suppose that, despite this, *B* is true: my ticket, as it happens, is going to win. We then have a situation in which, with respect to *B*, all Ayer's conditions (including the emendation to the third) are satisfied: *B* is true, I am sure of *B*, and I am justified in being sure of *B*. But clearly I do not *know B*. For since my acceptance of *B* is based on my acceptance of *A*, I do not know *B* unless I know *A*. And I do not know *A* if, as we have supposed, *A* is false.

This problem for Ayer's definition, and for others like it, was pointed out by Edmund Gettier in a brief but influential paper,[3] and it is now usually referred to as the 'Gettier problem', though the essential point was noted by Russell in his *Problems of Philosophy* as early as 1912. Ayer too, perhaps from his familiarity with Russell's writings, seems to have been aware of it at one stage. For in his earlier book *The Foundations of Empirical Knowledge* (*FEK*) he remarks:

> In the ordinary way, I think that all that is required for an empirical proposition to be known is that it should in fact be true, that no doubt should be felt about its truth, and that the belief in it should not have been reached by way of a belief in any false proposition, and should have good inductive grounds. (*FEK*, 80)

Here Ayer concedes that a true belief, though held with full conviction and adequately supported by the evidence, will not count as knowledge if it has been reached by way of a false belief. Presumably, it is the Gettier problem (not of course by that name) which Ayer has in mind, though he seems to have forgotten about it by the time he formulates his definition of knowledge in *PK*.

Assuming we accept, as he does, the possibility of justified false conviction, it is clear that Ayer's conditions for knowledge, as formulated in *PK*, need to be further strengthened. The obvious suggestion, following, in effect, Ayer's own proposal in his earlier book, would be to add a fourth condition which explicitly excludes any case in which the subject's belief is reached by inference from a false belief or from a set of beliefs which include a false belief. However, if by 'inference' we mean some actual process of reasoning, this additional requirement does not go far enough. Thus suppose I am in Westminster and, not knowing the time, I consult Big Ben. The hands indicate that it is 3 o'clock. In fact it is 3 o'clock, but, unbeknown to me, Big Ben stopped twelve hours ago and the hands have been stationary ever since. So it is 3 o'clock, I am sure that it is, and (let us assume) I am justified in being sure. Our intuitions are that this is not a case of knowledge, because my justification, in a sense, rests on a mistake: my right to be sure that it is 3 o'clock depends on my right to be sure that Big Ben is working normally – which is not the case. But it would be wrong to insist that, in acquiring my belief about the time, I have moved from the false proposition to the true proposition by a process of inference in the relevant sense. The question of whether Big Ben is working normally may never have occurred to me.

For this reason, I prefer to strengthen Ayer's conditions in the following way: *S* knows that *p* if and only if (1) it is true that *p*, (2) *S* is sure that *p*, (3) *S* is justified in being sure that *p*, and (4) there is no false proposition, that *q*, such that *S*'s being justified in being sure that *p* logically depends on his right to be sure that *q*.[4] Whether we have now reached a correct definition of knowledge could still be a matter of dispute. But it is the best we can hope for at this stage. If there is a need for further refinement, it will only show up when we have a better understanding of the notion of the right to be sure. It is to the examination of this crucial concept that we must now turn.

3 *The truth-reliability thesis*

Ayer introduces his third condition in the following way:

> . . . it is possible to be completely sure of something which is in fact true, but yet not to know it. The circumstances may be such that one is not entitled to be sure. For instance, a superstitious person who had inadvertently walked under a ladder might be convinced as a result that he was about to suffer some misfortune; and he might in fact be right. But it would not be correct to say that he knew that

this was going to be so. He arrived at his belief by a process of reasoning which would not be generally reliable; so, although his prediction came true, it was not a case of knowledge. Again, if someone were fully persuaded of a mathematical proposition by a proof which could be shown to be invalid, he would not, without further evidence, be said to know the proposition, even though it was true. (*PK*, 31)

Here, Ayer gives two examples in which someone who is completely sure of some true proposition fails to know it, because his certainty is unjustified. In the first example, the subject's certainty is unjustified because, as Ayer sees it, 'he has arrived at his belief by a process of reasoning which would not be generally reliable' – reliable, that is, as a process for reaching the *truth*. Knowing that he has just walked under a ladder, the subject infers that he will suffer some misfortune. The inference happens to be successful, but only by chance; the method of inference is unsound, since it cannot be relied on to be successful in general. The second example should be interpreted in a similar way. The subject becomes convinced of the truth of some mathematical proposition by reading what purports to be a proof of it. The proposition is in fact true, but the subject's conviction is unjustified because the 'proof' is invalid. And this is just another way of saying that the processes of reasoning involved cannot be relied on, in other cases, to yield the truth. Maybe there is a false premise; or maybe there is a step of inference which is not, in all other cases, truth-preserving.

Ayer does not explicitly say in this passage what it is for a believing subject to have the right to be sure. But the suggestion seems to be that he has such a right if and only if he has arrived at his belief in a way which is, as I shall put it, *truth-reliable* – a way which can be relied on, at least in general, to reach the truth. Sometimes, as in the examples just considered, the way of arriving at the belief involves a process of reasoning, where the subject consciously infers some proposition from others which he is taking for granted. But this aspect is only incidental from the standpoint of the thesis we are considering. A subject may come to believe some logical or mathematical proposition by simply focusing on its content; or he may come to believe something about his own current state of mind by introspection; or, again, his current sense-experience may cause him to acquire, non-inferentially, a belief about his physical environment. Each of these counts, in terms of the proposed thesis, as a way of arrival. And, according to the thesis, it yields a right to be sure just in case it is, in the relevant sense, truth-reliable. Let us call the proposed thesis the *truth-reliability thesis*.

The truth-reliability thesis asserts that the believing subject has the right to be sure if and only if he has arrived at his belief in a truth-reliable way. But I must stress here that when I speak of the subject's arriving at his belief, I mean his arriving at his *current* state of belief – that is, his state of belief at the time when his having or not having the right to be sure is at issue. This is important because, typically, many (indeed most) of the subject's beliefs at any given time are ones which he acquired at, and has retained from, earlier times. In such cases, I am taking the truth-reliability thesis to claim that, for the subject to have the right to be sure, it is necessary not merely that he should have acquired them in a truth-reliable way, but that both the mode of acquisition and the mode of retention should be truth-reliable – or more precisely, that the mode of acquisition should be truth-reliable and the mode of retention should be reliably belief-retentive. Thus, as I interpret it, the thesis allows for cases in which, while possessing a belief which he truth-reliably acquired, the subject forfeits his right to be sure because his retention-system is, or has been over the relevant period, significantly defective. To make this clear, we could reformulate the thesis thus: someone who has a belief at time *t* has the right to be sure at *t* if and only if he has arrived at his state of *t*-believing in a truth-reliable way.

Further evidence that Ayer endorses the truth-reliability thesis, or something akin to it, comes in his next paragraph.

> Claims to know empirical statements may be upheld by a reference to perception, or to memory, or to testimony, or to historical records, or to scientific laws. But such backing is not always strong enough for knowledge. Whether it is so or not depends upon the circumstances of the particular case. If I were asked how I knew that a physical object of a certain sort was in such and such a place, it would, in general, be a sufficient answer for me to say that I could see it; but if my eyesight were bad and the light were dim, this answer might not be sufficient. Even though I was right, it might still be said that I did not really know that the object was there. If I have a poor memory and the event which I claim to remember is remote, my memory of it may still not amount to knowledge, even though in this instance it does not fail me. If a witness is unreliable, his unsupported evidence may not enable us to know that what he says is true, even in a case where we completely trust him and he is not in fact deceiving us. (*PK*, 31–2)

In each case, it seems, Ayer makes the question of knowledge turn on the question of whether the subject has arrived at his belief in a truth-reliable way. Defective eyesight, a poor memory and an unreliable witness can all undermine the claim to knowledge, even in cases where they lead one to the truth. For, though they provide correct information on this occasion, they cannot be relied on to provide correct information in general. As Ayer sums things up:

In a given instance it is possible to decide whether the backing is strong enough to justify a claim to knowledge. But to say in general how strong it has to be would require our drawing up a list of the conditions under which perception, or memory, or testimony, or other forms of evidence are reliable. And this would be a very complicated matter, if indeed it could be done at all. (*PK*, 32)

This last passage might seem to be an explicit endorsement of the truth-reliability thesis. However, there is still an area of uncertainty. The uncertainty arises from Ayer's use of the phrase 'other forms of evidence'. According to the truth-reliability thesis, this phrase could be replaced by 'other ways of arriving at beliefs'. For, even in the case of empirical knowledge (i.e. knowledge of empirical statements), the thesis does not require that the subject arrive at his belief through the possession of evidence. Nor, for any type of knowledge, does it require that the subject arrive at his belief by having grounds for accepting the proposition in question. What is unclear, at this stage, is whether Ayer accepts the thesis in this austere form. Does he accept that, so long as it is truth-reliable, *any* way of reaching a belief yields a right to be sure? Or does he hold that, as well as being truth-reliable, the way of arrival must also be, to some degree, rational – a way which provides a rational basis for believing the proposition in question? And if he does accept this additional requirement, how exactly does it operate? Must the subject have grounds for accepting the proposition at all times at which he has the right to be sure? Or is it enough that the subject had and made use of such grounds at the time when he first acquired the belief, so long as both these grounds and the subsequent process of retention are reliable?

Ayer does not deal with these questions explicitly, but the next phase of his discussion makes the answers clear. He begins by remarking that 'there may very well be cases in which one knows that something is so without its being possible to say how one knows it' (*PK*, 32). Having explained that what he has in mind are cases in which the how-question clearly arises (unlike, arguably, the case of introspective knowledge), he goes on to give two examples:

Suppose that someone were consistently successful in predicting events of a certain kind, events, let us say, which are not ordinarily thought to be predictable, like the results of a lottery. If his run of successes were sufficiently impressive, we might very well come to say that he knew which number would win, even though he did not reach this conclusion by any rational method, or indeed by any method at all. We might say that he knew it by intuition, but this would be to assert no more than that he did know it but that we could not say how. In the same way, if someone were consistently successful in reading the minds of others without having any of the

usual sort of evidence, we might say that he knew these things
telepathically. But in default of any further explanation this would
come down to saying merely that he did know them, but not by any
ordinary means . . . Normally we do not say that people know
things unless they have followed one of the accredited routes to
knowledge. If someone reaches a true conclusion without appearing
to have any adequate basis for it, we are likely to say that he does
not really know it. But if he were repeatedly successful in a given
domain, we might very well come to say that he knew the facts in
question, even though we could not explain how he knew them.
We should grant him the right to be sure, simply on the basis of his
success. (*PK*, 32–3)

This passage clearly shows that it is the truth-reliability thesis in its
austere form which Ayer accepts. Neither the lottery-predictor nor the
mind-reader has any rational basis for reaching his conclusions. The
former has no grounds for expecting a particular number to win; the
latter has no evidence of what the other person is thinking. In each case,
the subject just finds himself acquiring a belief without having, or even
supposing himself to have, any reason for acquiring it. Yet Ayer is
sympathetic to the view that, if the predictions or readings were consistently successful, we could count them as cases of knowledge. This
sympathy can only be explained by supposing that Ayer accepts the
truth-reliability thesis. His thought must be that, if it is sufficiently
sustained, the subject's success is *prima facie* evidence of a reliable
capacity to reach the truth, and that if his judgments are the output of
such a capacity, then the subject has the right to be sure. In other words,
the repeated success is evidence that the subject has arrived at his beliefs
in a truth-reliable way; and if he has, then the fact that he has sustains
a right to be sure, despite the lack of a rational basis.

As I have indicated, Ayer presents these examples as an illustration of
the way in which we might credit a person with knowing something,
without being able to say how he knows it. This is why the examples
are so constructed that, while there is, or seems to be, evidence of
truth-reliability, the mechanism of truth-reliability (if it obtains) remains
mysterious. And this, in turn, explains why the subject is represented
as having no rational basis for arriving at his beliefs. For if he had such
a basis, it would account for his reliable capacity to reach the truth in
the relevant area. However, it is important to realize that cases in which
someone arrives at a belief truth-reliably, but on no rational basis, are
not bound to be ones in which the mechanism of reliability is unknown.
For example, it might be possible to construct a device which, when
suitably inserted into a person's brain, can be used to induce empirical
beliefs without the mediation of sensory evidence. If the output of this

device were suitably controlled by some external monitor, such as a camera, so as to ensure that only correct beliefs were induced, the conditions for truth-reliability would be met and the mechanism would be clear. Indeed, on certain philosophical views, the point could be illustrated without reference to artificial devices at all. Thus according to D.M. Armstrong, even ordinary sense-perception is just the acquisition of beliefs (or potential beliefs) about one's current environment – beliefs which are truth-reliably induced by the stimulation of the sense-organs, but acquired by the subject without the benefit of sense-data or anything else which might be thought to provide a rational basis.[5] The question of whether Armstrong's account is correct is, of course, another matter. It is one which we shall consider in due course when we come to discuss Ayer's theory of perception.

I have been arguing that Ayer accepts the truth-reliability thesis in its austere form. But there is one respect in which this needs to be qualified. Or at least there is one respect in which our notion of truth-reliability will need to be strengthened if the thesis is to serve Ayer's purposes.

As we have seen, Ayer accepts the possibility of someone being justifiably sure of something, but mistaken: the right to be sure does not, on his view, exclude the possibility of error. Put in the framework of the truth-reliability thesis, this means that, to have such a right, the subject must have arrived at his belief by a process which is highly truth-reliable but not necessarily infallible. The process must minimize the risk of error, but need not exclude it altogether. How high we should set the requisite reliability-degree, marking the boundary between justified certainty and 'probable opinion', Ayer sees as a matter for decision, and one of no theoretical importance.

> The main problem is . . . to settle, as it were, the candidate's marks.
> It is a relatively unimportant question what titles we then bestow
> upon them. So long as we agree about the marking, it is of no great
> consequence where we draw the line between pass and failure, or
> between the different levels of distinction. If we choose to set a very
> high standard, we may find ourselves committed to saying that some
> of what ordinarily passes for knowledge ought rather to be described
> as probable opinion. And some critics will then take us to task for
> flouting ordinary usage. But the question is purely one of
> terminology. It is to be decided, if at all, on grounds of practical
> convenience. (PK, 34)

Given Ayer's initial assumption, that the right to be sure does not exclude the possibility of error, and given his acceptance of the truth-reliability thesis, these remarks are eminently reasonable. If 'we are not demanding infallibility' (MCS, 122), then the selection of a particular reliability-degree, as the standard for knowledge, must be, to some extent, arbitrary. However, there is a problem here which Ayer has overlooked. For, once we have rejected the demand for infallibility, it is not clear how we can, purely in terms of reliability-degrees, draw a distinction between justified certainty and probable opinion at all. Thus suppose that I have bought a ticket in a lottery and the draw is about to take place. Knowing that a million tickets have been sold and that the draw will be random, I believe that I will not win first prize. The way I arrive at this believe, through a correct assessment of the probabilities, is highly truth-reliable: the risk of error is only $1/1,000,000$. But clearly I do not have the right to be completely sure, the right to discount my chance of winning altogether. Nor, if (irrationally) I am sure and, as it happens, am correct, does it count as knowledge. But, on Ayer's view, why not? It is no good his requiring an even higher degree of reliability before a right to be sure is sustained. For by increasing the number of tickets sold we can make the risk of error as small as we like, short of zero, without affecting the point of the example. If I am not to be credited with the right to be sure, it seems that the requisite reliability-degree must be set at 1 – i.e. reliability, if it is to justify complete conviction, must be infallibility. But this, of course, would be contrary to Ayer's position. It would also presumably mean that, with the possible exception of introspective knowledge, empirical knowledge was unattainable.

As I have said, Ayer fails to notice this problem. But his response, I think, would be to invoke a stronger notion of truth-reliability (though stronger in respect of type, not degree). As we have so far interpreted this notion, a way of arriving at a belief is truth-reliable if and only if it can be relied on, in general, to yield beliefs which are true. Put more briefly, W is truth-reliable if and only if W-arrival minimizes the risk of error. A way of arrival which is reliable in this sense may be said to be *reliably truth-productive*. Now I think what Ayer would say, in response to the problem, is that the sort of truth-reliability he has in mind involves an additional factor. Thus let us say that a way of arrival is *reliably truth-sensitive* if and only if, in general, given that a proposition is false, there is much less chance of one's arriving at a belief in it in that way than there would have been if the proposition had been true. Or put more briefly, W is reliably truth-sensitive if and only if, in general, the falsity of a proposition substantially reduces the risk of W-arrival. Ayer would then insist, I think, that to be truth-reliable in the epistemically relevant sense – the sense which suffices for a right to be sure – the way of arrival must be not only reliably truth-productive, but also reliably truth-sensitive. This additional requirement would not undermine our ordinary claims to knowledge: the commonly accepted routes to knowledge, through such things as perception, memory, and testimony, will be, in normal circumstances, reliable in both respects. But it does avoid the problem of the lottery. The way I reach my belief that I will not win first prize is by following the rule: 'If there is a very large number of incompatible but equiprobable possible outcomes and if x is one such possible outcome, believe that x will not occur.' Trivially, the following of this rule is reliably truth-productive: it minimizes the risk of erroneous belief. But it is not reliably truth-sensitive. For, in the improbable case where x *will* occur, I am no less likely to apply the rule and reach the conclusion that it will not. My present probabilistic assessment is in no way influenced by the actual future outcome or by anything in the current state of the universe by which that outcome is determined. Consequently, by insisting on the twofold reliability (in respect of both truth-productivity and truth-sensitivity), Ayer could deny me the right to be sure, however low the chance of my winning is set.

To do justice to Ayer's intentions, therefore, I think we should revise our formulation of the truth-reliability thesis so as to include the additional requirement: someone who has a belief at t has the right to be sure at t if and only if he has arrived at his state of t-believing in a way which is both reliably truth-productive and reliably truth-sensitive. Having seen this point, we can, in what follows, more or less ignore it. For the additional requirement, while important in itself, has no special relevance to the issues we shall discuss. Indeed, for convenience, I shall normally omit the requirement from my formulation of the truth-reliability thesis in future sections – though it is still intended to hold.

4 *Specifying the mode of arrival*

The question we must now consider is whether the truth-reliability thesis is correct. Clearly, the central issue here is concerned with the question of the rational basis. Must someone who has a right to be sure of something have a rational basis for accepting it – or at least have had such a basis at the time when he first acquired his belief? Or is it enough, as the thesis asserts, that he should have reached his current state of belief in a truth-reliable way? But before we turn to this central issue, there is a preliminary question which needs to be considered. This preliminary question too concerns the correctness of the truth-reliability thesis, but it concerns it at a more radical level. It turns on a problem which, unless it can be resolved, threatens to deprive the thesis of any definite content.

The truth-reliability thesis asserts that, where a subject believes something at a certain time t, he has at t the right to be sure of that proposition if and only if he has arrived at his t-state of belief in a truth-reliable way. But the question of whether the mode of arrival was truth-reliable often depends crucially on how that mode is described. A mode of arrival which is represented as reliable when described in one way may be represented as unreliable when described in another. The question then is: given that both descriptions are correct, how are we to decide which is the epistemologically relevant one, the one which determines, on the truth-reliability thesis, whether or not the subject has the right to be sure? Until he has answered this question, the would-be defender of the thesis does not have a definite thesis to defend.

To illustrate the problem, we may look again at a passage from *PK* which we quoted in the previous section. Having noted that claims to possess empirical knowledge may be upheld by reference to perception, memory, or testimony, Ayer points out that whether or not such backing is sufficient depends on the circumstances of the particular case:

> If I were asked how I knew that a physical object of a certain sort was in such and such a place, it would, in general, be a sufficient answer for me to say that I could see it; but if my eyesight were bad and the light were dim, this answer might not be sufficient. Even though I was right, it might still be said that I did not really know that the object was there. If I have a poor memory and the event which I claim to remember is remote, my memory of it may still not amount to knowledge, even though in this instance it does not fail me. If a witness is unreliable, his unsupported evidence may not enable us to know that what he says is true, even in a case where we completely trust him and he is not in fact deceiving us. (*PK*, 32)

Here Ayer has tried to give three examples of someone arriving at the truth, but in a way which is, arguably, not truth-reliable. And one can certainly take the point: defective vision, a poor memory and an unreliable witness are all liable to lead one into error. If, despite their failings, the subject arrives at the truth (as he does in the cases envisaged), it is, in the ordinary sense, partly by good fortune. Yet the fact that it is partly by good fortune does not mean that it has no explanation, nor, indeed, that it cannot be explained in terms of the specific way in which, on this occasion, the subject arrives at his belief. We can plausibly suppose that there are certain factors in the situation, which would be included in a more detailed description of the mode of arrival, and which ensure that, thus reached, the belief is true. Thus we can suppose that the subject's visual capacities, while not generally reliable, were working well enough on this occasion (in these specific circumstances) to ensure the reception of correct information; and their efficient working on this occasion would be included in a detailed description of the physical and psychophysical processes which led to the acquisition of the belief. And, of course, we can make similar suppositions in the cases of the erratic memory and the unreliable witness. But if there are certain factors which ensure that the subject arrives at the truth and which can be included in a sufficiently detailed description of his mode of arrival, then, by selecting this description, we can represent the mode of arrival as truth-reliable.

So the claim that it is not truth-reliable, and that, consequently, the subject's conviction does not amount to knowledge, can only be sustained if we can show that such a description is too specific – that it gives too much weight to details of the situation which are epistemologically irrelevant. And it is far from clear how this can be done.

A similar problem arises when we consider the reverse situation, in which someone arrives at a false belief in a way which Ayer would regard as truth-reliable. Thus, just as the person with defective eyesight and operating in dim light will sometimes come to make a correct visual judgment, so a person with excellent eyesight and operating in favourable conditions of illumination will sometimes be led astray. As we have seen, Ayer wants to treat this latter case (or at least certain versions of it) as one in which the subject has the right to be sure. The subject has reached his belief in a way which is generally truth-reliable (not, of course, infallible), even though, through some mishap, it has led him into error on this occasion (see *MCS*, 121–2). Again we can take Ayer's point, but only by confining ourselves to a fairly generic description of the mode of arrival. For if we allow the description to be too specific, it will take account of the particular factors which caused the mishap; and once these factors are thought of as essential to the mode, its truth-reliability is undermined. For example, if the visual experience on this occasion was partly conditioned by some false expectation, or if it was affected by a hallucinogenic drug, and if our description of the way the subject arrived at his perceptual belief makes reference to this fact, the mode of arrival will be represented as unreliable. Once more, then, we face the problem of how the epistemologically relevant description is to be selected and how the selection is to be justified.

In the examples we have considered, Ayer would see some descriptions as too specific – as giving weight to details which are best regarded as incidental. On the other hand, he could hardly set a premium on generality as such. For there is no mode of arrival which would not turn out to be unreliable if it were described in sufficiently generic terms: whatever factors sustain truth-reliability in a particular case, we could find a description which, by its generality, allowed those factors to vary. If we were always obliged to choose the most generic description, we would have to conclude that it is impossible to arrive at a belief in a truth-reliable way – and this, as well as undermining the truth-reliability thesis, would be manifestly absurd.

One possible solution, and at first sight quite plausible, would be to say that a mode of arrival is truth-reliable, for the purposes of epistemological appraisal, if and only if it is truth-reliable under *some* description. On this proposal, there is no premium on generality or specificity as such. In each case, a defender of the truth-reliability thesis will look to see whether there is *some* way of representing the belief-inducing process as reliable, and, acording to whether or not there is, he will grant or deny the subject the right to be sure. This solution, of course, does not accord with Ayer's intuitions in every case. In particular, it involves conceding the right to be sure in cases where a perceptual or recollective apparatus which is prone to malfunction happens to work efficiently on the given occasion. But perhaps this is something we can tolerate, even if Ayer would like to exclude it. In any case, it is hard to see by what general principle it could be excluded without generating worse anomalies in other cases.

However, the solution has other consequences which we cannot tolerate. Thus suppose that there is a chemical which, when injected into someone's bloodstream, causes him, in certain circumstances, to acquire a belief. The chemical works like this: if, at the time when it is injected, the subject happens to be imagining some kind of event, it causes him to believe, subsequently, that an event of that kind occurred at that time; otherwise, it has no effect. Now normally, if the chemical induces a belief at all, it induces one which is false. Moreover, even when it induces a true belief, the explanation of its doing so will normally involve citing factors which are extraneous to the way in which the belief has been acquired, however specifically that way is described. For normally the fact that such an event did occur at the time when the chemical was injected will have nothing to do with the acquisition of the belief. But now suppose the following situation: the subject is blindfolded and, without his knowledge, the chemical is injected into his anaesthetized arm; at the same time he happens, purely by chance, to be imagining such an injection occurring. The chemical then takes effect, causing him to believe that such an injection occurred at just the time it did. So the belief is true. Moreover, its truth is ensured by its mode of acquisition, if the mode is described in sufficient detail, so as to take account of the content of the subject's imagination at the time of the injection. So under this description the mode of acquisition is truth-reliable. But, clearly, we should not regard it as reliable for the purposes of epistemological appraisal. For these purposes we should take the content of the imagination to be irrelevant and the mode of acquisition to be the same as it would have been had the imagination been different. We should say that the mode is hopelessly unreliable and achieves truth in this instance by the merest coincidence. And, consequently, a defender of the truth-reliability thesis cannot afford to say that the way someone arrives at a belief is truth-reliable, from the standpoint of the thesis, if and only if it is reliable under *some* description, of whatever specificity.

The problem remains, then, of finding some rationale for deciding which factors in the process of arriving at a belief are epistemologically relevant – for selecting the description of the mode of arrival relative to which its truth-reliability is to be assessed. It is not a problem which

Ayer considers. Nor do I know how he would answer it. Perhaps he would say that there is no general answer: we simply have to examine each type of case on its merits, allowing it, in the context of all our theoretical and practical concerns, to fall into its natural perspective; if this perspective still presents alternative descriptions, yielding different assessments of reliability, we are free to choose either as a basis for epistemological appraisal. In effect, this would be to concede that the problem is insoluble, but blame it on the untidiness of the concept of knowledge rather than on some defect in the truth-reliability thesis. I regard this as a position of last resort, but, from the standpoint of the thesis, I cannot see what other reply is available.

A quite different response, of course, would be to abandon the truth-reliability thesis altogether. For without this thesis there is no problem: we simply allow truth-reliability to be relative to a description. It is only if there is something else (like the right to be sure) which cannot be thus relativized, but which depends on truth-reliability, that we are forced to select some description as the relevant one. So we might see the problem as a symptom of the fact that the thesis is fundamentally mistaken. What we must now do, therefore, is take a fresh look at the question 'What gives someone the right to be sure?' and see whether, from first principles, we are led to Ayer's position (i.e. the truth-reliability thesis) or to something quite different. This brings us to what I earlier described as the central issue.

5 *The reason-furnishing thesis*

It is plausible to claim that if, at a certain time, a subject has the right to be sure of something, he possesses this right solely in virtue of his state of mind at that time. After all, it will be said, for someone to have the right to be sure is for him to have an adequate reason for being sure. And what could furnish him with such a reason except his state of mind at the time in question? Of course, factors extraneous to this state may indirectly contribute to his having such a reason, since they may be, or be in part, causally responsible for his current mental condition or the relevant aspect of it. Typically, it will be as a result of past observations and past processes of reasoning that he has come now to have a sufficient reason for accepting the proposition as true. But surely this is only because such past observations and processes are in some way reflected in his current state of mind. How else could they supply a rational basis for his *current* conviction?

All this might pass without much comment in another context. But what must be obvious is that the view it suggests is in radical conflict with the view we have attributed to Ayer. On this latter view, we are to determine whether a person is justified in being sure of something by focusing on the way he has arrived at his belief: his certainty is justified just in case the mode of arrival is truth-reliable – can be relied on, generally, to yield the truth. In certain special cases, focusing on the mode of arrival will involve nothing more than focusing on the subject's current state of mind. It will, presumably, involve no more in the case of current introspective belief or current *a priori* intuition. But these cases are the exception. Normally, evaluating the reliability of the mode of arrival involves appealing to factors extraneous to the subject's current mental condition; and sometimes it involves only an appeal to such factors. In such cases, a subject may be justified in being sure by the criterion of truth-reliability even if his current state of mind fails to furnish him with an adequate reason for being sure – or, indeed, with an adequate reason for believing.

We have already introduced the name 'truth-reliability thesis' to designate Ayer's view. And I shall now give the name 'reason-furnishing thesis' to the view which is radically opposed to it. According to the truth-reliability thesis, a subject has the right to be sure of something he believes if and only if he has reached his current state of belief in a truth-reliable way. According to the reason-furnishing thesis, a subject has the right to be sure of something if and only if his current state of mind furnishes him with an adequate reason for being sure. The question which now confronts us is which, if either, of these views is correct. We have, of course, already noted a difficulty for the truth-reliability thesis and mentioned a point in favour of its rival. The difficulty for the truth-reliability thesis is the one we elaborated in the last section: the question of whether someone has arrived at his belief in a truth-reliable way may receive different answers according to how the mode of arrival is described, and we have yet to find a rationale for selecting one description rather than another. The point in favour of the reason-furnishing thesis is, as we noted at the outset, its initial plausibility. But these considerations are hardly decisive. In particular, we have yet to subject the conflict between the rival theses to any detailed scrutiny. It is possible that, when we do, factors will emerge which will make us see things in a new light.

There are two preliminary points to be noted. The first is that while, as alternatives, the truth-reliability and reason-furnishing theses are mutually exclusive, they are not jointly exhaustive. In particular, there is a middle position which combines elements of both. To see how this position arises, we must bear in mind the distinction between the acquisition of a belief and its subsequent retention. According to the reason-furnishing thesis, a subject has the right to be sure of something if and only if his current state of mind furnishes him with an adequate reason for being sure. So if someone acquires a belief at a certain time, and then subsequently retains it, the reason-furnishing thesis makes two claims: first, that the subject acquires a right to be sure at the initial time just in case he is furnished with an adequate reason for being sure by his state of mind at that time; and second, that having acquired such a right, he continues to possess it just so long as he continues to be furnished with an adequate reason by his subsequent states of mind. The truth-reliability thesis, of course, rejects both these claims. It holds that the subject acquires a right to be sure at the initial time just in case he acquires his belief truth-reliably and that, having acquired such a right, he continues to possess it just so long as he retains the belief by a type of process which is reliably belief-retentive (and thus reliably truth-retentive if the belief is true). At neither the stage of acquisition nor the stage of retention does it require that the subject be furnished with an adequate reason for being sure. The middle position, occupied by what I shall call the 'compromise thesis', sides with the reason-furnishing thesis in respect of the first claim and with the truth-reliability thesis in respect of the second. It insists on the furnishing of an adequate reason at the point of acquisition, but allows truth-reliability to suffice over the period of retention. More precisely, the compromise thesis asserts that someone has the right to be sure of a proposition if and only if one of two conditions obtains: either (a) his current state of mind furnishes him with an adequate reason for being sure, or (b) his state of mind at some earlier time furnished him with such a reason, he came to believe the proposition at that time on the basis of that reason, and he has retained that belief to the present time by a type of process which is reliably belief-retentive. One may suspect that, by combining elements of both extremes, such a position is almost certain to lack an adequate rationale. If truth-reliability suffices over the period of retention, why must a reason be furnished at the point of acquisition? Or if a reason is needed at the point of acquisition, how can truth-reliability be sufficient there-after? But at this stage it will be useful to keep the compromise thesis in play, if only for the light it sheds on the extremes. In effect, by comparing the compromise in turn with each extreme, we can divide the issue which confronts us into two questions. First, is the compromise preferable to the truth-reliability thesis? Second, is the reason-furnishing thesis preferable to the compromise? The first question concerns the relative merits of the two extremes in respect of acquisition. The second concerns their relative merits in respect of retention. We know that a negative answer to the first question will entail a negative answer to the second, and we may expect an affirmative answer to the first to prompt an affirmative answer to the second. But it is important to see that there are two questions to be considered – two areas in which the different claims of the truth-reliability and reason-furnishing theses must be investigated.

Before we turn to these questions, there is, as I mentioned, a further preliminary point to be made. Nominally, the issue between the truth-reliability and reason-furnishing theses is concerned with the conditions under which someone has the right to be sure. And we have been led to this specific issue because the possession of such a right is taken by Ayer, and I think correctly taken, to be one of the requirements of knowledge. But obviously the issue over the right to be sure is only one aspect of a more general issue over the justification of belief. And we could hardly expect to settle the specific issue without also reaching a conclusion on the more general. In one respect, of course, this is quite trivial. For whatever suffices to justify certainty, thereby suffices to justify belief. But, more importantly, we can also expect that, to a large extent, the requirements for justified certainty will reflect the requirements for justified belief. In particular, we can expect that if someone needs to be furnished with an adequate reason for being sure in order to have the right to be sure, then he needs to be furnished with an adequate reason for believing in order to be justified in his belief. In short, we can expect that whichever of the rival theses proves correct on the narrow issue, some generalized version of that thesis will also prove correct on the broader one. The reason I mention this is that, although we have concentrated on the narrow issue hitherto, the broader issue of the justification of belief will turn out to be our main concern – as indeed it is the main concern of Ayer's own epistemological work.

Let us now turn to the evaluation of the rival theses. As we have seen, there are two areas to be investigated – one concerning the acquisition of belief, where we have to compare the truth-reliability thesis with the compromise, and the other concerning the retention of belief, where we have to compare the compromise with the reason-furnishing thesis. We will consider these areas in turn.

To investigate the first area, we need to focus on cases in which the subject acquires a belief truth-reliably but without being furnished, by his state of mind at the time, with an adequate reason for being sure. A clear-cut case of this type is Ayer's example of the mind-reader (already referred to in section 3), though we need to develop it in a way which makes the mechanism of truth-reliability clear. We shall suppose that our subject – call him Jones – has never had hitherto the slightest indication of his telepathic powers. Along with other randomly selected subjects he agrees to take part in an experiment. His contribution is as follows. Another subject, Smith, is put in a room and asked to think of a number. Jones is put in another room, handed a photograph of Smith, and asked to identify the number. In response, he focuses his mind on Smith, whom he identifies by the photograph, and suddenly finds himself believing that the number is 47. He does not reach this belief on any rational basis: prior to acquiring it, he has no indication of what is going on in Smith's mind and absolutely no reason to choose one number rather than another. But, as it happens, the belief is correct and truth-reliably acquired. For, although no one knows it, Smith's brain is so constructed as to emit waves which encode the content of his thoughts, and Jones's brain is so constructed as to be able to decode such waves and generate true beliefs about Smith's thoughts, whenever Jones focuses his mind on Smith in the relevant way. It might be objected that the truth-reliability is only relative to a description and that the selection of that description has still to be justified. But this objection is beside the point. For whatever the requirements of truth-reliability, if they are to serve the purposes of the truth-reliability thesis in general, then we can devise the present example in a way which meets them. Thus if it is required that Jones should have a similar mind-reading capacity in respect of subjects other than Smith or that his capacity should be able to span greater distances of space, we can adapt the example accordingly.

We have, then, a clear-cut case of someone acquiring a belief truth-reliably, but without deriving from his mental condition at the time an adequate reason for being sure or even any reason for reaching that belief. According to the truth-reliability thesis, Jones acquires the right to be sure. According to the reason-furnishing thesis, in company with the compromise, he does not. Clearly, our intuitions support the second conclusion. After all, suppose that (understandably) Jones himself has doubts. He *thinks* that the number is 47 and, to that extent, *thinks* he is correctly reading Smith's mind, but, not being convinced of his telepathic powers, is less than completely certain. Do we really want to say that his doubts are unjustified? To say this would seem quite absurd. Moreover, in one respect, we could have made the example even more difficult for the truth-reliability thesis to accommodate. As we stated it, Jones was furnished with no reason for choosing one number rather than another. But we could have made it that he had a reason to select the wrong number, though a reason which got overruled by the telepathic process. Thus suppose we alter the story in the following way. Smith's room is not properly sound-proof, and, just before the experiment begins, Jones overhears him telling one of the experimenters that he is going to think of the number 58. As it happens, this is a lie: Smith has already decided he is going to think of 47, which he duly does. But Jones has, at this stage, no reason to suspect Smith of lying, and so, at the very moment when he is telepathically caused to acquire the correct belief on no rational basis, he is furnished (by his memory of what he overheard) with a reason for rejecting the proposition in question. It would surely be preposterous to maintain that, just because he acquires the belief truth-reliably, he acquires the right to be sure.

It also seems clear, on either version of the example, that Jones is not even justified in his *belief*. But here we need to be careful; in particular, we need to bear in mind the distinction between the acquisition of the belief and its retention. Certainly, it seems clear that, since he has no rational basis for selecting the number 47, we cannot see Jones as justified in acquiring his belief (though to say that he is not justified might give the false impression that he could, and should, have done something to avoid it). And if this is so, and if there are no further considerations, we cannot see him as justified in retaining it either – unless he acquires independent confirmatory evidence. But perhaps there are further considerations. After all, Jones could legitimately feel that his situation calls for some explanation: what, he may ask, has induced him to acquire this belief, without any evidence to support it, or even, as in the second version of the example, with positive evidence against it? Maybe the very strangeness of his situation could furnish him with a reason for thinking that telepathic contact has been achieved – that he has reached his ground-less belief because Smith's thought has, in some way, imposed itself on his mind. If so, then, after the initial acquisition, he could have a reason for thinking that his belief was true – though in no sense an adequate reason for being sure – and thus, to that extent, could be justified in retaining it. None of this, of course, provides any comfort for the truth-reliability thesis. It is not just that this thesis accords Jones the right to be sure rather than merely a justified belief. It is also that the justification we have just envisaged, such as it is, is itself sustained by the furnishing of a reason rather than by mere truth-reliability. The crucial point remains that in so far as Jones lacks a rational basis for his belief, we see the belief as unjustified.

Assuming our intuitions are sound, we must conclude that the truth-reliability thesis is mistaken, and that it is mistaken not only on the issue with which it is nominally concerned – the issue of the right to be sure – but also on the broader issue of the justification of belief. For, as our example shows, a subject may acquire a belief truth-reliably without gaining a right to be sure and without even being justified in his belief. We can also conclude, I think, that in the respects in which the truth-reliability thesis is shown to be mistaken, the reason-furnishing thesis is correct. To acquire a justified belief, the subject needs to be furnished, by his state of mind at the time, with an adequate reason for believing; and to acquire the right to be sure, he needs to be furnished with an adequate reason for being sure. Admittedly, this conclusion goes beyond what is strictly shown by the example. For it could still be said that Jones would have been justified in his belief if he had been furnished with *some* reason for belief, however inadequate. And, likewise, it could be said that he would have gained the right to be sure if he had been furnished with a reason which was adequate for *belief*, but not for certainty. But while such views are formally available, they can be quickly set aside. For there would be no point in requiring the furnishing of a reason unless it was to provide an adequate basis for the degree of conviction which the subject would be justified in possessing. The reason why Jones fails to gain the right to be sure or even a justification for his belief is, indeed, that he has no reason at all for accepting the proposition in question, but only because, in having no reason, he lacks an adequate rational basis for either certainty or belief.

Let us assume, then, that the reason-furnishing thesis is correct on the questions we have so far considered. It still does not follow that it is correct altogether. What we have so far established (if our intuitions are sound) is that, at the time when he acquires a belief, a subject must be furnished with an adequate reason for being sure if he is to have the right to be sure, and with an adequate reason for believing if he is to be justified in his belief. But we have not yet established that, once he has acquired such a right or justification in that way, the furnishing of such a reason has to continue if the right or justification is to continue. It might still be said that, once the right or justification has been rationally earned, all that its continuance requires is that the belief should be retained in a reliably belief-retentive way – retained, that is, through the operation of some internal system which can be relied on, when operative, to preserve an existing belief until some new evidence comes to light. Such a position is advocated by what we have called the compromise thesis, which agrees with the reason-furnishing thesis on the question of acquisition, but, in effect, endorses the truth-reliability account on the question of retention. What we must now consider, and this brings us to our second area of investigation, is whether we should adopt this compromise or accept the reason-furnishing thesis in full.

Two points are not in dispute. The first, and this is obvious, is that a person may be justified in retaining a belief without retaining the reason which justified its acquisition. For the fact that he has not preserved *that* reason does not mean that he is furnished with *no* reason, or no reason adequate to justify his current state of belief. Thus a mathematician who has come to accept a certain theorem by proving it may still be justified in accepting it at a later time when he can no longer remember the proof; for he may now know some other proof, or remember that he once proved it, or in some other way have evidence that it has been proved. The second point is that a person may be justified in retaining a belief even though he can derive from his current mental condition nothing which, if he did not already possess the belief, would justify its acquisition. For he may be furnished with a reason which justifies his acceptance of the proposition in question, but only by reference to the fact that he already believes it. This point is less obvious than the first, but we can make it clear by the following example.

Suppose someone learns at school that Charles I was executed in 1649 and retains this information to a later time when he can no longer remember the circumstances in which he acquired it. Let us also assume that, over the period of retention, while he has come across various references to Charles's execution and the circumstances which led up to it, he has acquired no further confirmation of the date – at least to the exact year. It is quite likely that he can find nothing in his current mental condition which would afford an adequate reason for believing that the execution occurred in 1649, if he did not already believe it. But, at the same time, he might still have an adequate reason to endorse the belief, given that he already possesses it. He might clearly remember that he was taught history at school and that Charles I featured prominently in the syllabus. He might clearly remember that his teacher laid great stress on the learning of dates, and he might clearly remember learning various other dates under his teacher's instruction. He might have independent evidence that he is usually very accurate in his recollection of dates and that he is not in the habit of acquiring historical beliefs unless he has derived his information from some accredited source. And while, apart from his belief, he has no evidence of the *exact* date of Charles's execution, this belief might form part of a large and coherent system of historical beliefs, for many of which he does have independent evidence – among them, perhaps, some which fix the date of the execution to some broader period (e.g. the middle portion of the seventeenth century) within which the year 1649 falls. All this – and we could go on adding to it – might furnish him with an adequate reason for believing that his belief is correct. If so, he is justified in retaining it, even though, if he did not already possess it, he would not be justified in acquiring it.

I have said that these points are not in dispute, and by this I mean that they are points on which the defender of the reason-furnishing thesis and the defender of the compromise thesis can agree. For they concern cases in which the alleged justification for the subject's belief stems from the furnishing of an adequate reason at the time in question, even though the reason is different from that which justified the original acquisition of the belief and even if, as in the second case, it would not justify the acquisition of such a belief if it were not already held. The reason I have drawn attention to them is that they help to put the issue between the rival theses in perspective. This is especially true of the second point. It is easy to overlook the distinction between having an adequate reason for believing (or being sure of) something, but one which depends on the fact that the belief is already held, and having an adequate reason which is not thus dependent – a reason which would justify the acquisition of the belief if it were not already held. And when this distinction is overlooked, cases in which the subject only has a *dependent* reason for his belief (or certainty) may appear to be cases in which he has no reason at all. This, in turn, can make the compromise thesis appear more plausible than it is. For cases of this sort are very common – indeed, I suspect the majority of our beliefs are ones which, if we did not already possess them, we would have no adequate reason to acquire. And since it is counterintuitive to count all such beliefs as unjustified, we may be tempted to appeal to the compromise thesis to account for their justification.

Once we have noted the distinction, however, and seen where the real issue between the rival theses lies, our intuitions clearly support the reason-furnishing thesis. To see this, we have to focus on a case in which, though the subject acquired his belief on an adequate rational basis and has since retained it in a reliably belief-retentive way, his current mental condition does not furnish him with an adequate reason to accept the proposition in question – not even a reason which makes reference to his holding of the belief. We can construct such a case by altering our recent example in certain crucial respects. Let us again suppose that someone learns at school that Charles I was executed in 1649 and, in a relevantly reliable way, retains this information to a time when he can no longer remember the circumstances in which he acquired it. But, in our new version, we will suppose that he does not remember having had lessons on Charles I (as far as he can recollect, his history instruction stopped at the Tudors), that he has retained virtually no other information on Charles I or the circumstances which led up to his death (so the belief in question does not form part of a coherent system), and that he has no independent evidence that he is usually accurate in his recollection of dates. If this is not sufficient, we can suppose that, a few days ago – and he can still recall the incident – he had a dispute with someone over the date of the execution, and though he stuck to his original belief, the other person, who seemed rather more knowledgeable on this period of history, was convinced it was mistaken. Or again, we can suppose that only yesterday he was proved wrong about the date of Magna Carta, and though he is, in general, accurate over dates, this is the only occasion, in recent years, when his accuracy has been put to the test. By such stipulations we can reach a situation in which the subject lacks an adequate reason for endorsing his belief. And when we reach it, our intuitions are that the subject is no longer justified in his belief – let alone has the right to be sure – even though he was justified in his original acquisition and has, in respect of both acquisition and retention, arrived at his current state of belief in a truth-reliable way.

We have seen, then, that, on both the question of acquisition and the question of retention, our intuitions are in favour of the reason-furnishing thesis and, thereby, against the truth-reliability thesis which I have attributed to Ayer. Moreover, this conclusion not only covers the specific issue with which these rival positions are nominally concerned (i.e. the conditions under which someone has the right to be *sure*), but also extends to the broader, and I think more important, issue of the justification of *belief*. There remains, however, one way in which a defender of the truth-reliability thesis might try to explain these intuitions away, and it is this which we must now, and as the final topic in this section, consider.

The defender of truth-reliability might claim that the contrary intuitions result from a confusion of two things which are really distinct, namely: (1) someone's being justified in believing (or being sure of) something, and (2) someone's being in a position to justify his belief (or certainty), i.e. to establish that he is justified in holding it. Obviously, a person who believes something, but is not furnished by his current state of mind with an adequate reason for believing it, is not in a position to justify his belief – much less to establish his entitlement to certainty. But this does not show that he is not justified in holding it; for he might be justified in holding it, yet unable to discern the justification. At the same time, the distinction is one which it is easy to overlook. For in the business of ordinary life the issue of justification is normally raised as a challenge to the subject himself: where it is unclear whether a belief is justified, the onus is put on the subject to show that it is. This may lead us to suppose that justification must always be looked at from the viewpoint of the believer and thus to exclude any form of justification which is not currently accessible to him. And this, the defender of the truth-reliability thesis will claim, is the crucial mistake: it is what explains our erroneous intuition that a person is not objectively justified in believing something unless his current state of mind furnishes him with an adequate reason for belief. Once we have seen the distinction, it will be said, we can see that, whatever his current mental condition, the subject is *objectively* justified in his belief just in case he has reached it in a truth-reliable way.

I do not find this argument convincing. It is true that a subject's being justified in believing something is not the same as his being in a position to justify his belief. But even when we take account of this distinction, our intuitions against the truth-reliability thesis remain. It still seems wrong to say that someone could be justified in believing something – let alone possess the right to be sure – if he has no reason to believe it. And it still seems clear that he could not possess such a reason unless, in some way, it is furnished by his current mental condition. This does not destroy the distinction between being justified in believing and being in a position to justify one's belief, though, of course, in comparison with the truth-reliability account, it lessens the contrast. To be justified in believing is to be furnished with an adequate reason for believing; to be in a position to justify one's belief is to be able to cite the reason and make clear its adequacy. Since the reason is furnished by his current

115

mental condition, the subject will normally be equipped to give some account of it. But perhaps not *always*, and perhaps only rarely a *complete* account. The fact that it is in virtue of his current mental condition that the subject is justified in his belief does not guarantee that he can discern the justification. This is partly because, at least on some theories of mind, the subject's current mental condition may contain aspects which are not accessible to introspection. It is also, and less controversially, because even if the subject can discern all the relevant aspects of his mental condition, he may fail to see how they fit together to form a rational basis for his belief.

6 *The furnishing of reasons*

The reason-furnishing thesis claims that a person is, or would be, justified in believing (or being sure of) something if and only if his current state of mind furnishes him with an adequate reason for believing (or being sure of) it. At least, this is what the thesis claims as we have so far formulated it. An alternative formulation, and one which is arguably better, would be to drop the indefinite article before 'adequate reason' – to speak of the subject's being furnished with *adequate reason* for belief, rather than of his being furnished with *an* adequate reason. Another alternative, along the same lines, would be to speak of the subject's mental condition making it *rational for him* to hold the belief. What makes these alternatives arguably better is that there are certain cases where we clearly want to count a belief as justified under the conditions of the reason-furnishing thesis (or under the conditions which the thesis is intended to express), but where it is, or might be thought to be, slightly misleading to speak of the subject as having *an* adequate reason for his belief. In itself, this point is of no real importance, but, as we shall see, there is something important which lies behind it.

The reason-furnishing thesis involves two central notions: first, the notion of someone's having an adequate reason for belief or certainty (and for the time being I am following the original formulation); second, the notion of such a reason's being furnished by the subject's current state of mind. It is time to examine these notions in greater detail. Such an examination may seem to be leading us away from our discussion of Ayer. But this is not so. It is, in fact, a way of leading us into the topic, that of scepticism, which forms Ayer's predominant concern. And, as we shall see, as he becomes more involved in the issue of scepticism, so his conception of justification changes from his original position to that of the reason-furnishing account.

When we say that someone has a reason for believing something we sometimes mean that he has a *practical* reason – a reason in the sense in which someone who has a motive for doing something has a reason. It is this sort of reason for belief which is involved in cases of wishful thinking and self-deception – where the subject believes something because he finds it agreeable or because he cannot bear to acknowledge what, deep down, he knows to be the case. But normally, when we speak of reasons for belief, it is a different sort of reason which we have in mind. What we have in mind is not a practical, but a *theoretical*, or, as we might say, *truth-relevant*, reason – a reason in the sense in which someone who has *grounds* for believing something has a reason. This is what we normally have in mind and it is this sort of reason with which the reason-furnishing thesis is exclusively concerned.

If a truth-relevant reason is the sort of reason possessed by someone who has grounds for belief, it might seem that we should simply equate the possession of such a reason with the possession of grounds. This would lead us to reformulate the reason-furnishing thesis as a grounds-furnishing thesis: a person would be justified in believing something if and only if his current state of mind furnished him with adequate grounds for believing it. But while this reformulation is on the right lines, and has the merit of making the truth-relevant character of the reason explicit, it is in one respect unsatisfactory. For it sometimes happens that a person has (in the truth-relevant sense) adequate reason for believing something simply because the truth of the proposition is directly evident to him; and in such cases it seems wrong to speak of the subject as furnished with *grounds*. Admittedly, it may also seem wrong – at least to put a strain on ordinary usage – to speak of him as having *an* adequate reason for belief. But if this is so (and I am not completely sure that it is), it just means that we should have started from one of the alternative formulations I mentioned at the beginning. For what is clear is that we want to count the subject as justified in his belief, under the reason-furnishing thesis, even though he does not have grounds for belief in the ordinary sense.

The clearest example is the case of those truths of logic and mathematics which are so simple as to be self-evident to anyone of sufficient intelligence and conceptual sophistication. Thus we want to say, I assume, that any normal adult has adequate reason (if not *an* adequate reason) to believe – indeed to be certain – that 1 is greater than 0 and that everything is identical with itself. These are propositions which it is rational for him to believe because his very rationality reveals their truth. But it would surely be wrong (on a strict interpretation) to say that the subject has *grounds* for believing them – or at least wrong to say that his possession of grounds is what makes it rational for him to believe them. For this would imply that he could base his acceptance of these propositions on other facts which are more immediately apparent to him and that it is the availability of this basis which makes it rational for him to accept them. But, in the present case, there is nothing more immediately apparent to the subject than the truth of the propositions in question. Their truth is self-evident to him, as it is self-evident to anyone who understands them.

It might be objected that it is the very self-evidence of these propositions which affords the subject his grounds for believing them. But what does this mean? If it means merely that it is their self-evidence to the subject which makes it rational for him to believe them, we can agree. Our point would then be that the term 'grounds' is being used in a very loose sense. On the other hand, if it means, what it seems to mean, that it is the subject's *recognition* of this self-evidence which makes it rational for him to believe them, then this is surely mistaken. Indeed, not only mistaken, but incoherent. For how could the recognition that a proposition was self-evident to one afford one grounds for accepting it unless the self-evidence on its own made acceptance rational? The only way round this would be to reconstrue the recognition as a recognition that the propositions *seem* self-evident. We could then take the subject's grounds for accepting them as supplied by the combination of this recognition and his knowledge that his capacity for rational intuition was normally very reliable. But it would be absurd to suppose that the subject needs grounds of this sort. If he did, he could never achieve rational belief at all, since he could never find grounds which were sufficiently secure. How, for example, could it be rational for him to believe that he has a *reliable* capacity for rational insight if it is not rational for him to believe, without further grounds, that 1 is greater than 0? The provision of grounds has to start somewhere. If it cannot legitimately start with (perhaps amongst other things) such simple truths of logic and mathematics, it cannot start at all. Unless these truths are directly evident to him and therefore rational for him to believe without further grounds, there is nothing which it is rational for him to believe.

Another objection – and one which could be extracted from Ayer's anti-rationalist position in *LTL* – might be that it is the subject's linguistic knowledge which supplies his grounds for believing such propositions. After all, if someone were to claim, in all seriousness, that 1 is *not* greater than 0, we should presume that it was a misunderstanding of language which had led him astray. We should try to explain to him what the terms '1', '0', and 'greater than' mean and hope thereby to demonstrate the falsity of his claim. Does not this show that it is our linguistic knowledge – our knowledge of the meanings of words and expressions – which constitutes our grounds for believing that 1 is greater than 0 and thereby makes it rational for us to believe it? The answer is that it does not and that the supposition that it does is based on a confusion. Obviously, it is through our linguistic knowledge that we know what proposition the sentence '1 > 0' expresses, and so partly through our linguistic knowledge that we know that this sentence expresses a truth.

But once we have identified the proposition, we do not need any linguistic knowledge to perceive its truth; for its truth is then self-evident. It is on linguistic grounds that it is rational for us to believe that '1 > 0' expresses a true proposition; but it is not on linguistic grounds, or on any grounds at all, that it is rational for us to believe that 1 > 0. Of course, it may be that the proposition is only self-evident to subjects who have linguistic knowledge. For it may be that it is only by acquiring such knowledge that one can achieve the conceptual sophistication needed to grasp the proposition. But this, whether or not it is correct, is a point about the genesis of concepts, not about the rationality of beliefs. It no more challenges the self-evidence of the proposition to those who understand it than the claim that concepts are only acquired through experience challenges the view that some knowledge is *a priori*.

The self-evident truths of logic and mathematics provide one example (and the clearest) of propositions which someone may have, in the truth-relevant sense, adequate reason to believe without possessing grounds for belief. (Incidentally, I am not claiming that *all* the truths of logic and mathematics are self-evident to us, though, presumably, all of them, or at least all that are knowable *a priori*, would be self-evident to a being of *supreme* rationality.) Perhaps a further example is provided by propositions about the subject's current state of mind, or at least about those aspects of it of which he is, or by introspection could become, directly aware. Thus when someone is in pain, or is feeling depressed, or is thinking about something, the propositions which record these aspects of his current mental condition are ones which he has, or through introspection could come to have, adequate reason to believe – indeed, to be sure of. (I am assuming, of course, that the propositions make no reference, explicit or implicit, to anything contingent but extraneous to that current mental condition.) But perhaps it is inappropriate to speak of his having grounds for such beliefs. Certainly, we cannot take his possession of adequate reason to consist in his knowledge of other facts which support them; in this sense at least, his knowledge of the psychological facts is direct and not mediated by his knowledge of something else. Perhaps we should say, then, that the truth of these psychological propositions is directly evident to him, through his capacity for self-consciousness, just as the simplest truths of logic and mathematics are directly evident to him, through his capacity for rational insight. And to say this would be to treat the case as a further example of rational but ungrounded belief.

I think this position is defensible, but not obligatory. An alternative, which I think is also defensible, would be to say that the subject does have grounds for believing these propositions, but that his possession of such grounds consists, not in some further knowledge, but in the psychological states of affairs themselves – that it is his being in pain, or

119

feeling depressed, or having a certain thought, which constitutes his grounds for believing that he is. All in all, I think we are free to choose between these alternatives. If we wish to restrict the possession of grounds to cases in which the subject has some further knowledge from which the relevant proposition can be legitimately inferred, or in which there is some further state of affairs to which the subject has more immediate access and which constitutes evidence for the truth of the proposition, we will characterize introspective beliefs as ungrounded. If we are willing to lift this restriction, we may count the psychological states of affairs themselves as the subject's grounds for belief. Obviously, if we do count this as a case of possessing grounds, it will be a quite special and distinctive case.

However we decide this case, the fact remains that we cannot reformulate the reason-furnishing thesis as a grounds-furnishing thesis. A person who has adequate (truth-relevant) reason for believing something does have reason *in the sense in which* someone who has grounds for belief has reason (this distinguishes truth-relevant reason from practical reason). But, as the case of logic and mathematics shows, he may have adequate reason without having grounds. What we can say, I think, is that someone has adequate reason for believing something if and only if *either* he has adequate grounds for believing it *or* the truth of the proposition is directly evident to him. It is crucial here, of course, to give the notion of a directly evident truth the right interpretation. In particular, it does not mean merely (what in the context of the truth-reliability thesis it might be taken to mean) an ungrounded true belief induced in a truth-reliable way. We have to interpret the notion in such a way that, where a truth is directly evident to someone, he has thereby adequate reason for believing it – indeed for being certain of it – in the sense in which someone who has adequate grounds for belief has adequate reason. It is presumably only self-evident *a priori* truths and (if we choose to characterize the case in that way) current first-person psychological truths which can be directly evident in that sense.

If these are the only propositions whose truth can be directly evident, then, in the case of all other propositions, a person can only have adequate reason for belief through, in some form, the possession of adequate grounds. We must now consider in what circumstances, if any, such grounds are available and, if they are available, what form they take.

In considering these questions, we must turn our attention to the second of the two central notions involved in the reason-furnishing thesis – the notion of a reason's being furnished by the subject's current state of mind. Ostensibly, the role of this notion is to provide an additional requirement for the justification of belief: to be justified in believing something, the thesis claims, the subject must not only *possess* adequate reason for belief, but must possess such reason solely in virtue of his current mental condition. Strictly speaking, however, this extra requirement is not needed at this point. We could have said simply: 'A person would be justified in believing something if and only if he has adequate reason to believe it.' For the possession of adequate reason suffices, on its own, for justification. The real purpose of the requirement is to make explicit what is involved, from the standpoint of the thesis, in the possession of reason: having adequate reason suffices for justification, but a person can only *have* reason to the extent that it is furnished by his current state of mind. This claim may seem obviously correct – and indeed, I think it is. But, as we shall now see, it does impose a more severe restriction on the possession of reason than is ordinarily appreciated. This restriction does not affect the rationality of belief in the case of self-evident truths and introspective propositions: in these cases, it is clear how the subject's current state of mind furnishes him with adequate reason. But it does seem to challenge the rationality of belief in almost every other area.

Let us begin by focusing on a typical example of someone reaching a belief on grounds and where there is no way in which the truth of the proposition believed could be thought of as directly evident. Thus suppose a detective, investigating a murder, discovers Smith's fingerprints on the gun and concludes, on this basis, that Smith has handled it. We would ordinarily say that, given his evidence, the detective has adequate grounds for reaching this conclusion. But how exactly are we to represent the grounds as furnished by his current state of mind? How can we represent the rationality of his belief as sustained solely by his current mental condition? Well, as our first shot, we might say this: the detective knows that Smith's prints are on the gun and from this, together with his knowledge of how such prints are caused, he can legitimately infer that Smith has handled it. But the knowledge that Smith's prints are on the gun is not something which the detective possesses solely in virtue of his current mental condition. For, since knowledge entails truth, the possession of this knowledge depends, in part, on the fact that Smith's prints *are* on the gun, and this fact is something extraneous to the detective's mental condition. It would be logically possible for his mental condition to be exactly as it is, in all intrinsic respects, without this fact obtaining, and hence logically possible for his mental condition to be exactly as it is without him possessing the knowledge in question. Clearly, then, to represent his grounds for belief as depending solely on his current state of mind, we have to describe the situation in a different way. Instead of saying that he *knows* that Smith's prints are on the gun, we should presumably say that he believes (or, perhaps, is sure) that they are and has adequate reason for this belief (or conviction). But now we face the new question as to how, purely in terms of his current state of mind, the rationality of this further belief is to be explained. How does his current mental condition furnish him with adequate reason for holding it?

Once again, our immediate response might be to appeal to some further knowledge which the detective possesses and which constitutes adequate grounds for the belief. The detective, we can suppose, has taken Smith's fingerprints, has compared them with the prints on the gun and has seen that they match. All this he now knows, through his faculty of memory, to have taken place, and this knowledge, we may say, gives him sufficient grounds for concluding that the prints on the gun are Smith's. But, of course, in saying this, we are no longer confining ourselves to a description of the detective's current mental condition. For the possession of this knowledge, if it is to be *knowledge*, depends, in part, on facts which are extraneous to this condition. It could have been with him, mentally, exactly as it is, even if he had never taken Smith's fingerprints, or not compared them with the prints on the gun, or, having compared them, not seen that they matched. For his current mental condition leaves open the possibility that his memory is deceiving him or that, though his memory is veridical as a record of his earlier experiences, these experiences misrepresented the physical situation. Once again, then, we shall have to replace the knowledge-claim by something weaker, which does not go beyond a description of the detective's current mental condition. But what is the replacement to be? If we settle merely for the claim that he holds certain beliefs (beliefs that he has conducted certain tests and obtained certain results), but make no provision for their rationality, we seem to undermine the rationality of the conclusion he derives from them. On the other hand, if we add the claim that these beliefs are ones which it is rational for him to hold, we have still to explain how such rationality is sustained by his current mental condition. And how can we do this other than by appealing to further beliefs – an appeal which, on its own, seems inadequate for the purpose?

It might be thought that, given certain additional assumptions about the case, our final appeal could be not to the detective's beliefs, but to his current experiences. Thus let us assume, for the sake of argument, that at the very time when he reaches his final conclusion, and when we want to say that he does so on adequate grounds, the detective is comparing the prints on the gun with his own record of Smith's prints and sees that they match. Let us further assume that he simultaneously recalls, in some perceptual way, the occasion on which, by taking Smith's prints, he obtained the record now in front of him. Could we not say that these current experiences, sensory and recollective, constitute, on their own, adequate grounds for his belief that Smith's prints are on the gun and, thereby, adequate grounds for concluding that Smith has handled it? The answer is that we could not. We could not, even if we grant, what could well be challenged, that the detective is entitled, without any further evidence, to take these experiences to be veridical. For, even if we grant this, the experiences can constitute adequate grounds for the belief in question only when interpreted in the framework of other beliefs whose rationality is already secure. Without this interpretative framework, the information which the detective can extract from the experiences as such is, even granted their veracity, minimal. They tell him, at most, how, on two occasions – one current, the other earlier – a portion of the physical world is sensibly arrayed. From this he can infer nothing about guns or fingerprints, nor even a causal connection between a certain portion of the colour-pattern he currently sees (i.e. the record of Smith's prints) and the event (i.e. the taking of Smith's prints) whose sensible features he recalls. To have adequate grounds for believing that Smith's prints are on the gun, he must know, or have adequate reason to believe, that what he is currently seeing are the prints he then took and a gun, that certain marks on the gun can only be plausibly explained as fingerprints, and that it is extremely rare (if it ever happens at all) for the fingers of different people to produce qualitatively identical prints. The rationality of such beliefs is not sustained by the experiences themselves and we have yet to show how it can be sustained at all by the detective's current mental condition.

The appeal to current experience does not work. And even if it did, it would hardly provide the solution we want. For it depends on the assumption that the detective has the appropriate kinds of sensory and recollective experience at the time when the rationality of his belief is supposedly sustained, and such an assumption seems unduly restrictive. We would like to be able to show how he has adequate reason to believe that Smith has handled the gun even when he is not currently scrutinizing the two sets of fingerprints nor engaged in mentally re-living his earlier activities. In this sense, the failure of the appeal to current experience is hardly a setback, though this is not to say that we are any nearer to a solution.

Nor, at the moment, shall I try to offer a solution. The point of considering the case of the detective was to bring out the problem – to show just how restrictive the furnishing requirement turns out to be. As things stand at the moment, there seems to be no way in which the detective can have adequate reason for believing that Smith has handled the gun, if such reason has to be furnished by his current state of mind. And this, of course, is not an isolated example. If there is a problem for this case, there is the same problem for almost all cases of allegedly rational belief. Indeed, on the face of it, it seems that the only cases which escape the problem are those in which the proposition in question is either one which the subject can know *a priori*, whether as something self-evident or by deduction from what is self-evident, or one which he can know by introspection, as something exclusively concerned with his current state of mind. In all other cases, where the proposition is not knowable *a priori* and where its truth depends on some state of affairs extraneous to the subject's current state of mind, there seems to be no way in which this state can furnish him with adequate reason for believing it. The upshot of this is that the reason-furnishing thesis seems to force us into an almost total scepticism – a scepticism which claims that almost all our ordinary beliefs are unjustified and, indeed, that, outside the narrow sphere of *a priori* knowledge and introspection, justified belief is unattainable.

In the face of this problem, we may be tempted to fall back on the truth-reliability account. For on this account there is no problem in seeing how someone can be justified in holding empirical beliefs about matters extraneous to his current state of mind. The detective, for example, would be justified in his belief that Smith has handled the gun, since, through normal processes of perception, interpretation, retention, and reasoning, he has reached it in a truth-reliable way. And he could even be said to have, in one sense, adequate *grounds* for this belief, in that it is adequately supported by other beliefs (about the course of his investigation) which he would be justified in holding. Quite generally, it seems that, by adopting the truth-reliability account, we can avoid the scepticism which the reason-furnishing thesis appears to generate. And since, by the standards of common sense, such scepticism is implausible, in that respect the adoption of the account becomes an attractive option.

Certainly we may feel tempted to revert to the truth-reliability account. But, for a number of reasons, the temptation must be resisted. In the first place, we have not yet *established* that the reason-furnishing thesis forces us into the sceptical position; it is just that, on present considerations, it *seems to*. It may be that, when we come to examine the sceptical challenge in more detail, we will find some way of escape without abandoning the thesis. Secondly, even if the thesis does entail scepticism, this does not, in itself, show that the thesis is mistaken. It would only show this on the further assumption that scepticism is itself mistaken. And this assumption, though it is in line with common sense, is not one which, as philosophers, we are entitled to make at this stage. Thirdly, and most importantly, we have already developed over the last two sections a powerful case against the truth-reliability thesis. However tempting the thesis may seem in the perspective of the sceptical challenge, this contrary case has not been answered. In view of these points, all we can do at present is to retain the reason-furnishing thesis, while registering a certain perplexity over its apparent implications.

In fact, even the temptation to revert to the truth-reliability account will soon disappear. As things currently stand, it seems that the sceptical challenge is a consequence of the reason-furnishing thesis and could be avoided if we adopted a different account of justification. But we shall soon see that the threat of scepticism is not thus restricted. It arises in some form however we construe the notion of justification, and the defender of the truth-reliability thesis is no better equipped to meet it than his rival. It is to the nature of this threat that we must now turn, and, in doing so, we rejoin Ayer's discussion in *PK*.

7 The nature of scepticism

'What the philosophical sceptic calls in question is not the way in which we apply our standards of proof, but these standards themselves' (*PK*, 36). Thus Ayer introduces the topic of scepticism at the start of the second chapter of *PK*. The contrast which he has in mind, between challenging some application of our standards of proof and challenging the standards themselves, can be readily illustrated both in the field of *a priori* reasoning and the field of empirical investigation. Thus suppose I want to solve a simple algebraic equation. There are certain standard procedures which I can employ and which, we ordinarily assume, can be relied on to yield the right answer. Someone who accepts the validity of these procedures may still doubt whether, in the particular case, I have correctly applied them. He may agree, for example, that if the same number is subtracted from each side, the equation remains true, but he may still doubt whether, in applying this principle, I did my arithmetic correctly. Doubts of this kind are not the province of the philosophical sceptic. The philosophical sceptic directs his challenge at the procedures themselves. He denies that these procedures can be relied on to yield the truth, or at least denies that we have sufficient warrant for supposing that they can. In this sense he is calling in question our standards of proof, not the accuracy with which an individual has applied them in a particular case. To take another example, this time from the empirical realm, suppose I want to know what is inside a certain parcel I have just received. Again there are certain standard procedures for finding out. They begin (and typically end) by my unwrapping the parcel and having a look – sometimes a feel, smell or taste as well. Someone who accepts the reliability of the procedures may still deny that, on this occasion, I have followed them correctly. He may claim that I did not look carefully enough, or that, while I looked carefully enough, I was careless in my interpretation. Again, these are not the challenges of the philosophical sceptic. What the latter denies or doubts is not the success of my attempt to apply the procedures, but the validity of the procedures themselves. He may concede that my application has been impeccable, but claim that such procedures are not a reliable way of discovering the truth, or, at least, that there is no good reason to think that they are.

Having stated that what the philosophical sceptic calls in question are our standards of proof, not the way in which we apply them, Ayer goes on to note a further restriction. For not all questioning of the standards is philosophical:

> There was a time when people believed that examining the entrails of birds was a way of discovering whether a certain course of action would be propitious, whether, for example, the occasion was favourable for joining battle. Then any sceptic who doubted the value of such a method of divination would have been questioning an accepted canon of evidence. And it is now agreed that he would in fact have been right. But the justification for his doubt would have been not philosophical, but scientific. It might have been the case that these so-called omens were systematically connected with the events which they were supposed to presage: but experience shows otherwise. (*PK*, 36)

'The peculiarity of the philosopher's doubts is that they are not in this way connected with experience' (*PK*, 36). They are founded not on empirical evidence, but on *a priori* reasoning. They are also, and this is intimately connected with their *a priori* character, more far-reaching than the empirical scepticism illustrated above. The empirical (or scientific) sceptic challenges some reputed source of knowledge by appealing to the empirical evidence obtained from some other and more fundamental source. Thus he may argue that divination is not even a remotely reliable method of predicting the future because an impartial empirical investigation shows that it is unsuccessful in practice. In conducting this empirical investigation, he is relying on other sources of empirical knowledge – perception, memory, and perhaps testimony – sources whose credentials he is taking for granted. But it is characteristic of the philosophical sceptic, at least in respect of the empirical realm, to take nothing for granted. He directs his challenge against those reputed sources of knowledge which we regard as fundamental. This, indeed, is why the basis of his challenge has to be *a priori*. For he has already called in question the very standards of proof on which any empirical scepticism would be based.

Ayer goes on to concede that empirical investigation does reveal that even the most fundamental sources of empirical knowledge are fallible. They can sometimes lead us into error (as judged by the preponderance of our empirical evidence), even when we are applying the standard procedures correctly. But once again the challenge of the philosophical sceptic is more far-reaching: not only is it directed against the most fundamental sources of empirical knowledge, but it seeks to discredit those sources *entirely*. These two thoughts are interwoven in the following passage, which summarizes the sceptic's position in the main areas of Ayer's epistemological concern.

> . . . the philosophical sceptic is not concerned, as a scientist would be, with distinguishing the conditions in which these sources are likely to fail from those in which they can normally be trusted. Whereas the enlightened thinker who casts doubt upon the reliability of omens is suggesting that they do not yield good enough results, that this method of prognostication does not reach a standard which other methods could, and perhaps do, satisfy, the philosophical sceptic makes no such distinction: his contention is that any inference from past to future is illegitimate. Similarly, he will maintain not merely that there are circumstances in which a man's senses are liable to deceive him, as when he is suffering from some physiological disorder, but rather that it is to be doubted whether the exercise of sense-perception can in any circumstances whatever afford proof of the existence of physical objects. He will argue not merely that memory is not always to be trusted, but that there is no warrant for supposing that it ever is: the doubt which he raises is whether we can ever be justified in inferring from present experiences to past events. In questioning one's right to believe in the experiences of others he will not be content with producing empirical evidence to show how easily one may be mistaken; so far from encouraging us to be more circumspect, his argument is designed to show that however circumspect we are it makes no difference: it puts the thoughts and feelings of others behind a barrier which it is impossible that one should ever penetrate. (*PK*, 36–7)

The arguments of the philosophical sceptic will obviously vary in detail according to the source of knowledge which he is calling in question. Our main concern, like Ayer's, will be with the realm of empirical knowledge. And in this realm, with the exception of scepticism about induction, Ayer sees the various sceptical arguments as exemplifying a common pattern. The pattern involves four steps. The sceptic begins by claiming that, to obtain the kind of knowledge in question, we are entirely dependent on our knowledge of certain other premises – premises whose subject-matter is quite different from that of the conclusions we draw from them. In his next two steps, he argues that the inferences from our premises to our conclusions cannot be justified either deductively or inductively: the conclusions do not logically follow from the premises; nor, without begging the question, can we find evidence of a systematic correlation between the states of affairs in the two subject-matters. As his final step, he concludes that, 'since these inferences cannot be justified either deductively or inductively, they cannot be justified at all' (*PK*, 78) and that, consequently, we should abandon our claims to knowledge, or even justified belief, in the relevant area.

To illustrate this pattern of argument, let us focus on the particular case of our knowledge, or supposed knowledge, of other minds. I ordinarily assume that I can, to some extent, discern the thoughts and feelings of other people, not, admittedly, through any special telepathic powers of the sort attributed to the mind-reader, but simply by observing how they behave and what they say. If one of my children falls over and cuts his knee, starts crying and says that his knee hurts, I have no serious doubt that he is really in pain, even if, as I sometimes suspect, his reactions exaggerate its severity. If I see someone at a bus stop put out his arm as a bus approaches, I conclude, other things being equal, that he wants the driver to stop, and I become quite confident that I have correctly interpreted his arm-movement if I subsequently see him get on the bus and buy a ticket. If someone affirms (or, at least, makes an utterance which satisfies all the overt conditions for affirming) that Charles I was executed in 1648 and is prepared to wager £100 that this is so, I am convinced that his affirmation expresses his own belief, whether or not it is one which I endorse. These are just some among a potentially infinite number of cases in which I am confident of being able to discern the mental states of other people. But is my confidence justified? In each case, it seems that I reach my conclusion about the mental condition of the other person by (in some sense) inference from something I perceive in the physical realm – from his bodily condition, his physical circumstances, his behaviour, his utterances. Admittedly, the inference need not be an explicit step of reasoning, in which I mentally formulate the premises and consciously draw the conclusion. More often than not, the move from the physical premises to the mental conclusion is automatic: I simply put a certain psychological interpretation on the physical facts without stopping to ask what these facts indicate. Nevertheless, if I am asked to justify the conclusion, it is to the physical evidence that I am obliged to appeal. And if the conclusion cannot be legitimately inferred from such evidence, perhaps in the light of other things I know, then it seems that my confidence in its correctness is misplaced.

The sceptic will now argue that such steps of inference are not deductively valid. When my child falls over and behaves in the way described, I may be correct to conclude that he is in pain. But the conclusion is not one which the physical facts I register logically entail. There is no logical inconsistency in conceding that his knee is damaged and that he evinces what we would normally take to be pain-behaviour, while denying that he is genuinely in pain. Moreover, the sceptic will say, the inference remains deductively invalid even if we allow the premises to draw on additional sources of evidence, e.g. what is occurring in the child's brain, how he has reacted in similar situations in the past, what sort of sensation *I* feel when I hurt my knee, what sort of sensation is the normal precursor of pain-behaviour in *me*. Even a total description of the physical world (past, present, and future), together with a complete record of my mental biography, would not allow me to deduce that my child is in pain or, indeed, to deduce anything at all about his mental condition.

Likewise, the sceptic will argue that the steps of inference are not inductively valid. His point here is not that inductive reasoning is itself invalid (this would be a different kind of scepticism), but that, even if valid, such reasoning cannot help us in the present case. Thus, in the example of the child, if my inference were to be justified inductively, I should need to know that in all or almost all the cases so far examined, children in these circumstances and evincing this sort of behaviour have been in pain. But to obtain such knowledge, I would, in each case examined, have to rely on the very methods of inference whose validity is in question. Admittedly, there is one person for whom I can establish the past correlation without recourse to such inference. For at least I know, without such inference, that *in my own case* this sort of behaviour in these sorts of circumstances has always been an expression of pain. But the most I can inductively infer from this, the sceptic will insist, is that the correlation is likely to hold for *me* in the future. I am not entitled to make any inductive inference to the case of others, for whom the past correlation has not been established. For how can I reach a conclusion about other people if all my evidence is confined to my own case? How can I assume that I and others are similar in this respect if I have no independent access to their mental life?

Granted that the steps of inference are neither deductively nor inductively valid, the sceptic now concludes that they have no justification, and that, consequently, in the case of other minds, our claims to knowledge or justified belief must be abandoned. In place of these claims, we are to acknowledge that we have no way of discovering what states and episodes occur in the minds of others and that we do not even have adequate grounds for believing that they have minds at all.

The case of other minds is just one among several examples which Ayer uses to illustrate the common pattern of sceptical argument. Some of the other examples he offers are:

(1) scepticism about the physical world, where the relevant inference is from premises about sense-experience to conclusions about physical objects;
(2) scepticism about the past, where the inference is from premises about current states of affairs (e.g. current memories and records) to conclusions about the past;
(3) scepticism about imperceptible scientific entities, such as atoms and

electrons, where the inference is from premises about the overt qualities and behaviour of observable physical objects (ignoring the more
radical scepticism in (1)) to their internal, but unobservable,
structure.

In each of these cases, as in the case of other minds, the sceptic argues
that the steps of inference are illegitimate. They cannot be justified
deductively, since the premises do not logically entail the conclusions.
And they cannot be justified inductively; for since we have no *independent* access to the domain of facts which the conclusions concern (independent, that is, of the methods of inference in question), we can never
establish the kind of correlations needed for an inductive argument. And
in each case the sceptic concludes that our ordinary claims to knowledge
or justified belief have to be renounced. In addition, of course, there is
scepticism about induction itself. Here again what is at issue is the
justification of a certain kind of inference – in this case, an inference
from the premise that a certain correlation has held in the sample of
instances so far examined to the conclusion that it will hold for some
instance, or set of instances, yet to be examined. But obviously, in this
case, the sceptic does not claim that the inference cannot be justified
either deductively or inductively, since it just is an application of inductive reasoning. Rather, he claims that inductive reasoning itself lacks any
justification. For the time being, I shall put the problem of induction on
one side and focus exclusively on those cases of scepticism which
conform to the common pattern we have outlined.

The first thing we need to look into, at this juncture, is the nature of
the sceptic's conclusion. On the face of it, the sceptic is not merely
calling in question, but actually denying the claims to knowledge or
justified belief which we ordinarily make. I would ordinarily claim to
be justified in believing, perhaps even to have the right to be sure, that
my child is in pain when I observe him in the circumstances described.
The sceptic seems to be saying not merely that such a claim *may be*
mistaken or that I have no warrant for making it, but that it actually *is*
mistaken and that the justification I claim is something I do not possess.
For he seems to be saying that my belief would be justified only if a
certain inference were justified, and that this inference (from physical
premises to a psychological conclusion) has no justification. Likewise in
the other areas, the sceptic seems to be denying that our ordinary beliefs
or convictions are justified. Thus he seems to be saying that we are not
justified in our beliefs about the physical world or the past or the
submicroscopic entities of physics, because the propositions in question
cannot be legitimately inferred from our evidential premises.

This is more or less how Ayer *ends up* characterizing the sceptic's
position. The only qualification is that he envisages the sceptic as, in

practice, losing his nerve at the last moment and shrinking from 'carrying his argument to what appears to be its logical conclusion' (*PK*, 78):

> It is scarcely to be imagined that anyone should seriously maintain that we had no right whatsoever to be sure, or even moderately confident, of anything concerning physical objects, or the minds of others, or the past. (*PK*, 78)

None the less, it is this strong claim – the one 'it is scarcely to be imagined that anyone should seriously maintain' – which Ayer here takes to be the conclusion of the sceptic's argument. In his earlier remarks, however, the sceptic's position is sometimes characterized in significantly weaker terms. Thus, as we have seen, he speaks of the philosophical sceptic as *calling in question* our standards of proof and *casting doubt* on our reputed sources of knowledge. All that the sceptic about physical knowledge is reported as claiming is that 'it is to be *doubted* whether the exercise of sense-perception can in any circumstances whatever afford proof of the existence of physical objects' (*PK*, 37; my italics). Likewise, all the sceptic about memory is reported as claiming is that 'there is no *warrant* for supposing' that memory is ever to be trusted, and in claiming this he is said to be raising a '*doubt*' as to 'whether we can ever be justified in inferring from present experiences to past events' (*PK*, 37; my italics). Even the sceptic about other minds, though he 'puts the thoughts and feelings of others behind a barrier which it is impossible that one should ever penetrate', is only said to be '*questioning* one's right to believe in the experiences of others' (*PK*, 37; my italics).

Now it might seem that the difference between these two ways of expressing the sceptic's position – the stronger way in which the sceptic *denies* our claims to knowledge or justified belief and the weaker way in which he merely casts *doubt* on them – is of no philosophical import-ance. After all, however it is formulated, the sceptic's position poses a challenge to our ordinary views. We ordinarily assume that we do possess the knowledge or justification which is being doubted or denied, and, presumably, the main business will be to try to vindicate that assumption in the face of the sceptic's arguments, however strongly or weakly we formulate his own conclusion. However, I think that the difference in formulation is of some significance in the context of Ayer's discussion. Ayer leads us into the topic of scepticism via a discussion of the nature of knowledge – in particular, via a discussion of the right to be sure, which is one of the three requirements for knowledge, as he defines it. As we have seen (or, at least, as I have interpreted him), he thinks that what gives the believing subject the right to be sure is that he has arrived at his belief (i.e. at his current state of believing) in a truth-reliable way – a way which can be relied on, in general, to yield the truth. This is why Ayer is able to envisage the cases of the lottery-predictor and the mind-reader as cases of genuine knowledge: the subject, if he is consistently successful, may be supposed to have a reliable capacity to get the right answers, even though he has no evidence to guide him. As Ayer puts it, 'we should grant him the right to be sure, simply on the basis of his success' (*PK*, 33). Now assuming that Ayer really does accept the truth-reliability thesis and still has that thesis in mind as he turns to the issue of scepticism, it is not difficult to see why he should, at this stage, prefer to state the sceptic's position in its weaker form. For if the truth-reliability thesis is correct, the most that the sceptic's arguments could establish is that we have no warrant for supposing that our beliefs, in the relevant area, are justified. They do not establish that our beliefs are *not* justified; for they do not establish that we have not arrived at them in a truth-reliable way.

The point can be illustrated by focusing again on the problem of other minds. The sceptic claims that the steps of inference from our physical evidence to our psychological conclusions cannot be justified either deductively or inductively. But obviously this claim does not entail, nor would the sceptic think that it entails, that the whole process of acquiring beliefs about other minds, which terminates in such inferences (or in interpretations which implicitly embody such inferences), is not, under an appropriate description, truth-reliable. For example, it might be that we are psychophysically designed (partly by nature and partly by nurture) in such a way that, by and large, a stimulus which is painful to one subject is also painful to others and behaviour which is a symptom of pain in one subject is also a symptom of pain in others. Given this framework of psychophysical agreement, it is not hard to see how, using myself as a model, I have a generally reliable way of detecting pain in others: I simply have to put the same psychological interpretation on the physical circumstances and behaviour of the other subject as fits my own case. This does not mean that my inferences from the physical evidence to the psychological conclusions are deductively or inductively valid. It just means that, given the whole psychophysical set-up, my inferences, if they conform to the appropriate pattern, are assured of success. And this is all that is required, on the truth-reliability account, to render the beliefs which I reach by such inferences justified. In a similar way, we can easily see how, despite the invalidity of the relevant modes of inference, our beliefs about the physical world and the past could turn out to be justified on the truth-reliability account, given the right kind of causal mechanisms governing their acquisition and retention.

Does this mean that we can protect ourselves against scepticism by adopting the truth-reliability account? At the end of the last section it seemed that it might. But we can now see that this is not so. The sceptical challenge remains, however we construe the notion of justification. What varies is the form in which the challenge is expressed. The basis of the sceptic's challenge is his claim that, in each of the areas of reputed knowledge, the acquisition of belief is, explicitly or implicitly, inferential and that in each case the inference as such is unsound – the premises do not provide adequate grounds for accepting, with even moderate confidence, the conclusion. On any intuitive understanding of the notion of justification, this claim would have the consequence that we are not justified in holding the beliefs in question; for how can we be justified if we hold these beliefs on grounds which are insufficient to support them? But even if we construe justification in accordance with the truth-reliability account – a construal which, as we have seen, is counter-intuitive – there is still a sceptical consequence. For though our beliefs may then be justified, we are not in a position to tell that they are. In so far as we lack adequate grounds for holding the beliefs, we also lack adequate grounds for believing that they have been truth-reliably acquired.

Once again, the case of other minds will serve to illustrate the point. Let us suppose, for the sake of argument, that we and the sceptic accept the truth-reliability account. The sceptic cannot then claim, without begging the question, that our beliefs about other minds are not justified. But he can and will claim that we have no reason to suppose that they are. For how could we have reason to suppose that our beliefs have been acquired in a truth-reliable way if any inference from physical evidence to psychological conclusion is itself unsound? Only by acquiring evidence that things are so psychophysically organized as to ensure that, despite the invalidity of our inferences, we manage to reach the truth. But, *ex hypothesi*, the only evidence we can acquire concerning the psychophysical organization, in so far as it relates to other subjects, is physical. We have no access to the mental condition of others except through their physical circumstances, bodily condition, and behaviour. If such physical evidence is, as the sceptic claims, inadequate, then we have nothing by which the truth-reliability of the way in which we acquire our beliefs could be independently established. It may be that, from a God's-eye view, the mode of acquisition is reliable. But we cannot survey things from such a viewpoint. Of course, we might say that if we are justified in our other-minds beliefs and can, from them and our physical knowledge, legitimately infer that the appropriate psychophysical organization obtains, then we do, in one sense, have adequate grounds for accepting that the beliefs are truth-reliably acquired. But this would only be a verbal manoeuvre, in which the requirements for the possession of grounds are made to fit what is available on the truth-reliability thesis. If the sceptic's premises are correct, we do not have adequate grounds for the beliefs; and, except by relying on the beliefs, we cannot show that they are truth-reliably acquired. This is all the sceptic needs to make his point.

Given that Ayer has endorsed the truth-reliability thesis in his discussion of the nature of knowledge, we can understand why he begins by formulating the sceptic's conclusion in its weaker form, which claims not that we are not justified in believing what we do, but that we have no good reason to suppose that we are – a conclusion which casts doubt on our possession of justification, but does not positively deny it. I think we can also understand why, as the issue of scepticism becomes his dominant theme (the theme, indeed, from which his book derives its title), the stronger formulation eventually emerges. Part of the reason, presumably, is that the very issue of scepticism helps to expose the peculiarity of the truth-reliability account – the peculiarity of saying that we may be justified in believing something, indeed have the right to be sure of it, even when our current mental condition furnishes no adequate reason for belief. But, more importantly, within the issue of scepticism, the kind of justification which we might possess in virtue of truth-reliability is simply irrelevant. It is not something to which we could appeal in meeting the sceptical challenge; for it is not something which helps us to defend our beliefs once the sceptic has called them in question. It is hardly surprising that, in considering the issue of scepticism, Ayer should come to adopt a concept of justification which is relevant to that issue – that he should come to think of the sceptical position as a *denial* that we are justified in our beliefs and as putting knowledge of the things in question beyond our reach.

8 *The four possible solutions*

As I have already mentioned, Ayer sees the sceptical position as only a hypothetical position, rather than as one which someone might seriously adopt. The problem, then, is how, given the sceptic's arguments, the sceptical conclusion can be avoided.

> No doubt we do know what he says we cannot know; we are at least called upon to explain how it is possible that we should. (*PK*, 78)

The rest of the book is, in effect, Ayer's attempt to provide the solution.

Ayer begins by setting out what he regards as the four main ways in which, traditionally, a solution has been sought. In each case we are concerned with sceptical arguments which conform to the four-step pattern already outlined, and each supposed solution is distinguished by the particular step which it denies. This way of correlating the range of possible solutions with the structure of the sceptical arguments, and seeing each in the perspective of the other, is both elegant and illuminating. It typifies the artistry and lucidity of Ayer's philosophical technique.

The first solution, which Ayer calls *naive realism*, counters the sceptical argument by denying its very first step, the step in which the sceptic claims that the supposed knowledge is (if only implicitly) inferential – that we are entirely dependent for it on our knowledge of certain other premises whose subject-matter is quite different from that of the conclusions which we draw. Thus, as Ayer characterizes him, the naive realist

> will not allow that our knowledge of the various things which the sceptic wishes to put beyond our reach is necessarily indirect. His position is that the physical objects which we commonly perceive are, in a sense to be explained, directly 'given' to us, that it is not inconceivable that such things as atoms and electrons should also be directly perceived, that at least in certain favourable instances one can inspect the minds of others, that memory makes us directly acquainted with the past. The general attitude displayed is that of intuitionism. It is in the same spirit that philosophers maintain that they intuit moral values, or try to justify induction by claiming the power of apprehending necessary connections between events. But of course it is possible to take up the naive realist's position on any one of these questions, without being committed to it on the others. (*PK*, 79)

In effect, then, the naive realist's solution is to deny that there is even a *prima facie* problem. The inferences which the sceptic claims are unwarranted may indeed be unwarranted. But according to the realist, that is neither here nor there. For we do not (even implicitly) depend on such inferences for our primary knowledge of the facts in question. In appropriate circumstances, the facts are directly accessible to us – knowable without inference from anything else.

Obviously, the notion of direct and non-inferential knowledge which the naive realist employs is not the notion supplied by the truth-reliability account. It would not suffice for direct knowledge, in the relevant sense, that the subject should arrive at his belief, without inference, in a truth-reliable way. For this would not provide any defence against scepticism. This becomes clear if we consider again the case of the mind-reader as we earlier envisaged it. We supposed that, perhaps through some neural sensitivity to the wave-signals emitted by the other subject's brain, the mind-reader has a reliable capacity to reach the truth about this subject's mental states, without recourse to any kind of evidence. By the truth-reliability criterion, this counts as direct knowledge. But it is not the kind of direct knowledge which the naive realist needs, since it does not equip the subject who possesses it to meet the sceptic's challenge. It does

135

not give the subject any reason for holding his beliefs or for thinking that he has arrived at them in a truth-reliable way. Clearly, what the naive realist needs is a form of knowledge in which the facts are directly evident to the subject in the way in which first-person psychological facts are, or may be said to be, directly evident – a way which certifies the truth of the convictions formed and puts them beyond the reach of the sceptic's doubt.

It is hard to see how anyone could think that such knowledge was available in the case of other minds. It would involve, I take it, claiming that we have, in appropriate circumstances, the same kind of introspective access to the minds of others as we have to our own minds – that I can be, in some way, conscious of someone else's mental states from the inside, as I am conscious of my own. And it is very hard to see how such a claim could be sustained without also claiming that what we take to be different minds are really different portions of a single mind, distributed over several bodies. But it is easier to understand how someone could think such knowledge was available in the case of the physical world – at least in respect of its sensible aspects. Prior to detailed investigation, it is not unnatural to assume that, in standard conditions, sense-perception directly displays to a subject certain sensible aspects of his physical environment – that, through vision, the subject is directly aware (in the perspective of his viewpoint) of the physical arrangement of colours, and that, through touch, he is directly aware of physical texture and shape. And, given this assumption, it might then be claimed that this direct perceptual awareness constituted a source of physical knowledge immune from the sceptic's doubt. By taking this position, the naive realist would, in effect, be treating this perceptual knowledge as a special kind of introspective knowledge. He would be assuming that since the subject is directly aware of these physical items, their presence in his environment is part of the very content of his experience, so that the subject only has to know the intrinsic nature of his experience to know that such items exist. Whether this realist view is tenable in the case of the physical world is something we shall examine in detail later.

The second solution, which Ayer calls *reductionism*, is one which we have already discussed in some detail in our examination of *LTL* – though there the role of the reductionist's programme was not so much to defeat scepticism as to secure the factual significance of ordinary discourse in the restrictive framework of the verification principle. In the context of our present discussion, the reductionist is seen as rejecting the second step in the sceptic's argument. He accepts that our knowledge in the relevant area is (at least implicitly) inferential, but claims that the inferences are (or will be if we are sufficiently careful) deductively valid. He does this by maintaining that the conclusions thus inferred turn out on analysis to be logically equivalent to statements about the subject-matter of the premises. Thus he may claim that statements about the physical world are equivalent to statements about sense-experience, or that statements about the minds of others are equivalent to statements about their behaviour and behavioural dispositions, or that statements about the past are equivalent to statements about current memories and records. By such claims, he tries to absorb the subject-matter of the conclusions, which the sceptic says we cannot know, into the subject-matter of the premises, which the sceptic concedes that we do know, and thus defend our knowledge in the relevant area from the sceptic's attack. In this sense, as Ayer points out, he has something in common with the naive realist, since 'both of them try to close the gap which the sceptic relies on keeping open' (*PK*, 79). But 'whereas the naive realist does so by bringing the evidence up to the conclusion, the reductionist's policy is to bring the conclusion down to the level of the evidence' (*PK*, 79).

As in the case of naive realism, reductionism in one area does not commit one to reductionism in another. And in certain cases reductions in different areas would be incompatible unless the scope of one of them were specially restricted. Thus a complete reduction of statements about the mind to statements about the physical world would be incompatible with a complete reduction of statements about the physical world to statements about sense-experience. The only way of combining the two reductions, without making the analysis viciously circular, would be by limiting the scope of one of them. For example, it might be claimed that psychological statements *other than those about sense-experience* are reducible to physical statements and that physical statements are reducible to statements about sense-experience. Alternatively, adopting a first-person perspective, I might claim that psychological statements (including experiential statements) about *other* subjects are reducible to physical statements and that physical statements are reducible to experiential statements about *me*. The second is, in effect, Ayer's position in *LTL*.

The third solution is what Ayer calls the *scientific approach*. This is how he describes it:

This is the position of those who admit the first two steps in the sceptic's argument but deny the third. Unlike their predecessors, they accept the existence of the gap between evidence and conclusion, but they hold that it can be bridged by a legitimate process of inductive reasoning. Thus they will maintain that physical objects, though not directly observable in the way the naive realists suppose, can be known to us indirectly as the causes of our sensations, just as the existence of scientific entities can be inferred from their effects, without our having to identify the two. On this view, the deliverances of memory, and other records, make the existence of the past an overwhelmingly probable hypothesis. Knowing that we ourselves have inner thoughts and feelings, we can attribute them to others by analogy. (*PK*, 80).

From this brief specification, it is not entirely clear what kind or kinds of inductive reasoning Ayer has in mind. In the cases of physical objects and scientific entities, he is obviously thinking of some kind of causal inference: we are directly aware of our sensations and postulate physical objects, of which we are not directly aware, as their causes; we perceive certain physical events, characterized by their sensible qualities, and interpret them as the effects of certain underlying physical processes involving imperceptible particles. But if this is all that is to be said about the inferences, it is quite unclear why anyone should take them to be legitimate. Why is there even a *prima facie* case for supposing that our sensations are caused by external objects of which we have no direct awareness or for supposing that observable physical events are the effects of underlying processes that are unobservable? Ayer's remarks about the case of the past and the case of other minds are even less revealing. The scientific approach, we are told, sees the deliverances of memory and other records as making the existence of the past an overwhelmingly probable hypothesis. But how so? By some kind of causal inference? And if so, what equips it to meet the sceptical challenge? Again, we are told that, following the scientific approach, we attribute mental states to others by analogy with ourselves. But how is this supposed to be an answer to the sceptic? If I cannot directly discern the mental condition of others, why should I suppose that the analogy holds?

In the case of physical objects and scientific entities, I assume that the kind of causal inference which Ayer has in mind is what is known as *explanatory induction* or *inference to the best explanation*, and that, in particular, he is thinking of the use of such inference as a means of justifying (or trying to justify) an expansion of our ontology beyond the domain of what can be directly observed. In this ontologically expansive form, the explanatory inference works, in broad outline, in the following way:

(1) There is a domain of objects and events which are (or for the purposes of the argument are assumed to be) directly observable. We may call this the *observable domain*.

(2) There is something about the observable domain which calls for explanation. Typically, what calls for explanation will be a certain degree of detected orderliness and predictability too great and too consistent to be attributed to chance.

(3) No satisfactory explanation can be found if we confine our ontology to the observable domain itself. Thus if what calls for explanation is the orderliness of events in this domain, the orderliness is not so simple and self-contained that we can fully and adequately account

for it by postulating laws exclusively concerned with these sorts of events.

(4) A satisfactory explanation can be found if we expand our ontology to include, in addition to the observable domain, a domain of objects and events which are not directly observable and for whose existence we have no independent evidence – independent, that is, of their explanatory role. Thus it might be that, within the framework of this larger reality, we can postulate general laws governing events in the unobservable domain and causally linking such events with events in the observable domain, such that these laws fully and adequately account for the detected orderliness which needs explaining.

(5) A satisfactory explanation constitutes the best explanation if there is no other explanation which is better or as good. Typically, one explanation is deemed to be superior to another if it postulates simpler laws or, while postulating laws of equal simplicity, involves a smaller expansion of the ontology.

(6) The best explanation is then deemed to be the correct one – though, since the merits of an explanation may be altered by subsequent evidence, any verdict is only provisional.

I am fairly sure that, in the cases of physical objects and scientific entities, it is an explanatory inference, along these lines, that Ayer has in mind. In the first case, the observable domain would be the domain of human sense-experience, and the physical world would be postulated to explain, via physical and psychophysical laws, the orderliness it exhibits. In the second case, the observable domain would cover the sensible aspects of the physical world, and the underlying physical reality of scientific entities would be postulated to explain, through physical laws (including those causally linking underlying properties with sensible properties), the orderliness at the sensible level. I also suspect that it is this sort of inference which he has in mind in the case of the past, if only because I cannot see what else, in this case, the scientific approach could be.

What of the case of other minds? Here too one might suppose that what is envisaged is an inference to the best explanation – unobservable mental states being postulated to explain observable behaviour. And certainly this is what Ayer envisages in his later book *The Central Questions of Philosophy* (*CQ*), where, describing the same four possible solutions to scepticism, he writes of the scientific approach:

The existence of physical objects or of the experiences of other persons or of past events is represented in each instance as a probable hypothesis which one is justified in accepting because of the way in which it accounts for one's experiences. (*CQ*, 66)

However, this is not what Ayer envisages in *PK* when he says, in the passage already quoted, that 'knowing that we ourselves have inner thoughts and feelings, we can attribute them to others by analogy'. What he is here envisaging is an inductive inference of the ordinary (non-explanatory) kind, in which a correlation which has been observed to hold in a certain sample of instances (i.e. a correlation between physical states of affairs and mental episodes in one's own case) is taken to hold quite generally (i.e. to hold in the case of other people as well). Since all the evidence for the correlation has to be drawn from one's own case, it might seem that such an inference is clearly illegitimate. But Ayer would deny that the issue is that clear-cut. As we have already seen in our earlier discussion of Ayer's verificationism,[6] he has by now come to think that, at the level of *statements*, demonstrative references to persons disappear. When I ascribe a mental state to someone, whether to myself or to another, all that the statement I make records is that someone who satisfies a certain description is in that mental state; whether it is I or someone else who satisfies this description is left open. So, while my evidence is exclusively drawn from my own case and the conclusion I base on it concerns someone else, this is not something which, when canonically formulated, the premises and the conclusion express, and it is not relevant to the logic of the inference.

> The inference is not from my experience as such to his experience as
> such, but from the fact that certain properties have been found to
> be conjoined in various contexts to the conclusion that in a further
> context the conjunction will still hold. This is a normal type of
> inductive argument; and I cannot see that it is in any degree
> invalidated by the fact that, however far one is able to extend the
> positive analogy, it always remains within the compass of one's own
> experience. (*PE*, 214)

This passage comes from his essay 'One's Knowledge of Other Minds',[7] but he makes the same point in the final chapter of *PK*. Of course, even if the inference can be represented as of the normal inductive type, it does not follow that it is justified – even by the standards of inductive reasoning. For the evidence, though supporting the conclusion, may still be too weak to justify belief. This is something which has to be separately evaluated, and Ayer tries to do this in his later discussion.

The fourth solution is what Ayer calls the *method of descriptive analysis*:

> Here one does not contest the premises of the sceptic's argument,
> but only its conclusion. No attempt is made either to close or to
> bridge the gap: we are simply to take it in our stride. It is admitted
> that the inferences which are put in question are not deductive and
> also that they are not inductive, in the generally accepted sense. But

this, it is held, does not condemn them. They are what they are, and none the worse for that. Moreover, they can be analysed. We can, for example, show in what conditions we feel confident in attributing certain experiences to others: we can evaluate different types of record: we can distinguish the cases in which our memories or perceptions are taken to be reliable from those in which they are not. In short, we can give an account of the procedures that we actually follow. But no justification of these procedures is necessary or possible. (*PK*, 80–1)

On the face of it, this seems a very strange position. The sceptic claims that the inferences cannot be justified; the descriptive analyst agrees, but insists that the inferences are legitimate. But why should he suppose that they are legitimate if he cannot justify them? The only answer Ayer gives, on behalf of the analyst, is one which, in effect, grounds the legitimacy on the impossibility of a justification:

One may be called upon to justify a particular conclusion, and then one can appeal to the appropriate evidence. But no more in these cases than in the case of the more general problem of induction, can there be a proof that what we take to be good evidence really is so. *And if there cannot be a proof, it is not sensible to demand one.* The sceptic's problems are insoluble because they are fictitious. (*PK*, 81; my italics)

But the sceptic is hardly likely to be impressed by this. After all, he is not demanding a proof on his own behalf; he is simply asking those who accept the legitimacy of the inferences to justify their position. And why not? How can it be rational to endorse the inferences if no justification is forthcoming?

However, the method of descriptive analysis should not be just dismissed. After all, we are bound in the end to fall back on processes of reasoning for which we can offer no independent justification. The only question is at what point we can legitimately do this. Many philosophers, including Ayer himself, think that this is legitimate in the case of induction – that induction is inherently rational, although it cannot be justified in terms of anything else. And while this is controversial (an issue which I shall consider in Part III), all would agree that we can legitimately assume the validity of deduction, since without the framework of deductive logic we could not reason at all. It does not follow, of course, that we should take a similar view of the sorts of inference which the sceptic is here calling in question; and, given the specificity of their subject-matter, our initial intuition is that we should not. But there is at least the possibility that we should. It is an issue which can only be finally settled by examining each case on its merits.

These then – naive realism, reductionism, the scientific approach, and the method of descriptive analysis – are the four main ways in which, as Ayer sees it, philosophers have sought an answer to the sceptic's challenge. Whether any of them is successful for any of the cases of scepticism considered remains to be seen.

Before we look into this question, however, there is a point which needs to be stressed. Obviously, the different forms of scepticism can be combined; and, when they are, they yield a more general scepticism, which challenges our beliefs in all the areas separately considered. Thus scepticism about other minds, scepticism about the physical world and scepticism about the past combine to form a general scepticism which challenges all our beliefs about empirical matters of fact, except for a person's knowledge, at any time, of his own current mental condition. This general scepticism, of course, is just what we encountered earlier, as an apparent consequence of the reason-furnishing thesis, before we had even considered Ayer's account. Now what needs to be stressed is that not only do the different forms of scepticism combine to form a more general scepticism, but the sceptical problems in one area may be aggravated by the problems in another. For, while each specific form of scepticism denies the legitimacy of a certain kind of inference, but does not deny our entitlement to believe the premises from which the conclusion is inferred, the beliefs which we are permitted to retain as premises by one form of scepticism may be part of what is called in question by another. Thus what the sceptic about other minds allows us to retain, namely our physical evidence, is part of what is called in question by the sceptic about the physical world, and part of what the physical sceptic allows us to retain, namely our knowledge of earlier sense-experiences, is part of what is called in question by the sceptic about the past. So the problem of other minds is aggravated by the problem of the physical world, which is, in turn, aggravated by the problem of the past. Moreover, for a given pair of problems, the aggravation may be mutual. Thus just as, by denying our access to the physical evidence, scepticism about the physical world exacerbates scepticism about other minds, so also, by denying our access to the sense-experiences of others, other-minds scepticism exacerbates scepticism about the physical world. And just as, by denying our access to earlier experiences, scepticism about the past exacerbates scepticism about the physical world, so also, by denying our access to current physical records (and other relevant physical evidence), physical scepticism exacerbates scepticism about the past.

The upshot of this is that the general problem of scepticism turns out to be even more difficult than (at least from Ayer's account) we might have supposed. We might have thought that since scepticism has been divided into different forms, each of which concerns a specific area of putative knowledge, all we have to do, in order to find an answer to the general problem, is to find an answer to each specific form of scepticism, considered in its own terms, and then combine the results. For surely the combining of the answers to the specific forms would provide an answer to the general scepticism which these forms, in combination, generate. But we can now see that this is not so. An adequate answer to scepticism A, taking for granted all that A does not call in question, together with an adequate answer to scepticism B, taking for granted all that B does not call in question, need not provide an adequate answer to $A + B$. For we may find that in answering A we have relied on assumptions undermined by B and that in answering B we have relied on assumptions undermined by A. And even if our answers to A and B do combine to form an adequate answer to $A + B$, we may still find that our answers to A, B, and C do not combine to form an adequate answer to $A + B + C$. It follows that if we are seeking a solution to the general problem, then, in dealing with each specific form of scepticism, we should make no assumptions which are vulnerable to scepticism at some other point – unless, of course, we have already defeated this further scepticism (without begging similar questions) at an earlier stage. It is this which makes the general problem so difficult. For it seems that everything is vulnerable to scepticism except (perhaps) for certain forms of *a priori* knowledge and each person's knowledge of his own current mental condition.

Ayer seems to be unaware of this aspect of the problem. He is content to divide the issue of scepticism into its separate topics, without considering how scepticism in one area may add to the sceptical problems in another. Thus, in his treatment of scepticism about the physical world, he sees the problem exclusively in terms of whether a person can legitimately reach physical conclusions on the basis of his sensory evidence. The fact that a sceptic about the past (i.e. in this context, a sceptic about memory) would insist on restricting the sensory evidence to the person's *current* sense-experiences is not allowed to affect the issue. Likewise, in dealing with scepticism about the past, he focuses exclusively on the status of the inference from knowledge of current states of affairs to conclusions about earlier ones. The question of what restrictions a physical sceptic would place on the premises is not, at this point, considered. In one sense, this is a perfectly legitimate procedure. In each case, Ayer is highlighting a specific sceptical problem and seeing what can be done to meet it if the rest of our knowledge is left intact. But it also means that, in following this procedure, he fails, in each area, to come to grips with the full force of the sceptic's challenge. And, as a result, he fails to show how, in the final analysis, anyone can be justified in holding any empirical belief about matters extraneous to his current mental condition – at least justified in any sense (unlike what is captured

by the truth-reliability thesis) which protects the subject from the sceptic's attack. This is not to deny the importance of what he achieves in
his discussion of the separate sceptical topics; nor is it to claim that his
achievements in these areas make *no* progress towards a solution of the
general problem.

9 Perception

As I have said, Ayer divides the issue of scepticism into separate topics
concerned with specific disputed areas of knowledge or justified belief.
Apart from induction itself, the main areas he considers are our knowledge of the physical world, our knowledge of the past, and our knowledge of other minds. It would be interesting and instructive to follow
his discussion in each of these cases. But because I want to examine his
arguments in some detail, I am forced to be selective. And since our
knowledge of the physical world is the predominant concern of his
epistemological writings, I shall focus my attention on this area.

It is uncontroversial that knowledge of the physical world, if we truly
possess it, is in some way derived from sense-perception. It is hardly
surprising, then, that, in this area, the issue of scepticism is intimately
connected with questions about the nature of perception and its putative
role as a source of knowledge. Ayer indeed, throughout his writings,
often speaks of the sceptical problem about the physical world as the
'problem of perception'. And it is with this label that he introduces us
to the problem in the third chapter of *PK*:

> The problem of perception, as the sceptic poses it, is that of justifying
> our belief in the existence of the physical objects which it is
> commonly taken for granted that we perceive. In this, as in other
> cases, it is maintained that there is a gap, of a logically perplexing
> kind, between the evidence with which we start and the conclusions
> that we reach. If the conclusions are suspect, it is because of the
> way in which they seem to go beyond the evidence on which they
> depend. The starting-point of the argument is, as we have seen,
> that our access to the objects whose existence is in question must be
> indirect. (*PK*, 84).

However, as Ayer immediately points out, it is by no means clear that,
in the case of perception, this starting-point is acceptable. Why should
we suppose that our access to physical objects is always indirect and that
we can only know of their existence by inference from something else?
Surely there are many kinds of physical object, e.g. tables, trees, and
houses, which we can directly perceive by sight and touch, and whose
existence is directly revealed by such perception. There may indeed be
certain types of physical object, e.g. atoms and subatomic particles,

which we cannot directly perceive and whose existence we can only infer from their perceptible effects. But such cases only serve to emphasize, by contrast, the apparent directness of our perception of physical objects of the common-sense sort. In what sense could I now be said to be only indirectly perceiving this sheet of paper when I see it quite clearly in front of me and feel its surface with my hands?

That physical objects can be directly perceived and their existence thereby directly revealed is, of course, the position of the naive realist. And, as Ayer represents him, the sceptic is ready with a reply. He argues that in every case where we might take ourselves to be directly perceiving a physical item, the immediate object of perceptual awareness is something else (variously called an *idea*, or an *impression*, or a *sense-datum*) which is private and mental – something which, unlike a physical object, has no existence outside the content of the awareness itself. Accordingly, he claims that our perception of a physical object is always indirect, since it is always mediated by the awareness of a non-physical item which represents it. And this, he claims, is what creates the epistemological problem – the problem of justifying our belief in the existence of physical objects and our beliefs about their properties. For if the immediate objects of perceptual awareness are mental, how can we tell whether there are, as it were beyond them, physical items which they represent? And even if there are such items, how can we tell what properties they possess? It seems that, ultimately, we have nothing but our knowledge of the mental objects to go on and that any belief about the physical world will have to be justified by inference from this.

Whether, to make his epistemological point, the sceptic needs to adopt this sense-datum account of perception is something we shall consider presently. For the moment, I want to focus on the account itself. On what basis does the sceptic claim that the immediate objects of perceptual awareness are always private and mental? As Ayer notes, the basis which is most commonly employed is the so-called argument from illusion. And it is this argument which he now proceeds to formulate and assess.

The starting-point of this argument is that physical objects sometimes sensibly appear to us in ways which misrepresent, or at least differ from, their true character. For example, when partially immersed in water, a straight stick may look crooked, and, when viewed at an oblique angle, a round coin may look elliptical. It is then claimed that whenever a physical object is perceived, the immediate object of perceptual awareness is something which really possesses the sensible qualities which the physical item appears to possess. Thus when a straight stick looks crooked, the immediate object of awareness is not the stick, which is straight, but something which is actually crooked, and when a round coin looks elliptical, the immediate object of awareness is not the coin, which is round, but something which is actually elliptical. But apart from the physical object perceived, there is no physical item which could form an immediate object of awareness in this way. So where the sensible appearance of a physical object differs from its true character, the immediate object of awareness must be something non-physical: it must be a sensible object internal to the episode of awareness itself, something momentary and mind-dependent, something whose *esse* is *percipi* – in short, to use the modern jargon, a *sense-datum*. Now from this, of course, it does not immediately follow that in *every* case of perception the immediate object of awareness is a sense-datum. For one could still say that in cases where the perceptual experience is wholly veridical – where the physical object sensibly appears the way it really is – the immediate object of awareness is the physical item itself. To exclude this possibility, the argument appeals to the similarity between cases, if there are any, in which the appearance is veridical and cases in which it is not.

> From different angles the coin may appear a variety of different shapes: let it be assumed that one of them is the shape that it really is. There will be nothing to mark off this appearance from the others except a difference of aspect which may be extremely slight. There will in any case be no such difference between the way in which the coin is perceived in this instance and the way in which it is perceived in all the others as to render it at all plausible to say that they are generically distinct; that the object which is directly perceived in this instance is of a different kind altogether from that which is directly perceived in all the others . . . In this way we are brought to the conclusion that, even granting that physical objects may sometimes be perceived as they really are, what is directly perceived is always something else. (*PK*, 88–9)

In other words, we are brought to the conclusion that the immediate object of perceptual awareness is always a sense-datum – a mental or mind-dependent entity internal to the awareness itself. This conclusion is known as the *sense-datum theory*.

As Ayer remarks, this argument is plainly not conclusive. Its main weakness comes near the beginning, where it claims that whenever a physical object is perceived, the immediate object of perceptual awareness is something which really possesses the sensible qualities which the physical object appears to possess. For why should we accept this claim?

> It makes perfectly good sense to talk of perceiving things which look in some way different from what they are, and there is at least no obvious reason why we should here feel bound to add that these things are not perceived directly. (*PK*, 89)

Why not, then, say, in the cases we mentioned, that the immediate object of awareness (i.e. what we directly perceive) is a straight stick which looks crooked or a round coin which looks elliptical? What reason is there for reifying the look as a mental object, which is detached from the physical item perceived and prevents any direct vision of it? Certainly it is not enough just to appeal to the fact that looks, and appearances in general, may be deceptive.

However, as Ayer sees, a further reason for accepting the sense-datum theory is provided by the possibility of complete hallucination.

> The case which we have so far been considering is that in which a physical object looks to have some quality that it does not really have: there has been no question of its not being really there to be perceived. But it may also happen that one 'perceives' a physical object which is not there at all. Let us take as an example Macbeth's visionary dagger . . . There is an obvious sense in which Macbeth did not see a dagger; he did not see a dagger for the sufficient reason that there was no dagger there for him to see. There is another sense, however, in which it may quite properly be said that he did see a dagger . . . But still not a real dagger; not a physical object; not even the look of a physical object, if looks are open to all to see. If we are to say that he saw anything, it must have been something that was accessible to him alone, something that existed only so long as this particular experience lasted; in short, a sense-datum. But then, it is argued, there would not have been anything in the character of the experience, considered simply in itself, to differentiate it from one that was not delusive. It is because an experience of this sort is like the experience of seeing a real physical object that hallucinations are possible. But in so far as the experiences are alike, their analysis should follow the same pattern. So if we are bound in one case to say that what is seen is a sense-datum, it is reasonable to hold that this is so in all. (PK, 90)

It might be objected that, contrary to what this argument claims, hallucinations of the sort envisaged are not, in their intrinsic psychological character, just like veridical perceptions – that the experience of 'seeing' a visionary dagger, at a time when the balance of one's mind is disturbed, is not exactly like the experience of genuinely seeing a real dagger, when such a dagger is before one's eyes. The fact that the hallucination may, and typically does, delude the subject into thinking that he is genuinely perceiving a physical object does not show that it is, as an experience, indistinguishable from a genuine perception. For such delusion could be explained by the fact that, with the balance of his mind disturbed, the subject's powers of judgment are impaired.

However, despite Ayer's formulation of it, the argument from hallucination does not need to claim that hallucinations of Macbeth's kind are, as experiences, exactly like genuine perceptions. All it needs to claim is that, for any genuine perception, i.e. for any perceptual experience in which some real physical object is perceived, there *could be* (i.e. it is logically possible for there to be) a hallucination which is, as an experience, exactly like it. And this, surely, can be easily established. Indeed, we can even envisage how, in practice, such hallucinatory replicas could be produced. Thus it is not difficult to foresee a time when it is technically possible, by electrically stimulating a person's optic nerves, to produce the same coordinated pattern of neural firings as would be produced, by photic stimulation of his eyes, if he were observing a certain type of physical object under certain conditions of illumination. Now, obviously, the visual centres in the brain are going to respond in the same way to the same type of input from the optic nerves, however that input was itself caused. So, given any genuine visual perception, produced in the normal way by photic stimulation of the eyes, we can envisage a situation in which, with the subject blindfolded, a visual experience of exactly the same intrinsic kind is produced by electrically stimulating the optic nerves, though no physical item of the sort which such an experience would normally represent is present in the subject's environment. In other words, given any genuine visual perception, we can, in this way, envisage a situation in which the subject would have a visual hallucination which was, as an experience, exactly like it. And clearly, by appropriately varying the details, the same result can be obtained for every other sense-realm. This is enough to establish that if sense-data are the immediate objects of awareness in the case of hallucination, they are also the immediate objects of awareness in the case of genuine perception. For since sense-data are, by definition, internal objects of awareness, their existence, whenever they do exist, depends on nothing more than the intrinsic character of the experiences in which they occur. Consequently, since each genuine perception could be experientially replicated by a hallucination, it is impossible to recognize sense-data as the immediate objects of hallucination without also recognizing them as the immediate object of perceptual awareness in every case.

The only way of avoiding this conclusion would be by drawing a distinction between the *subjective* character of an experience and its *intrinsic* character. Thus it might be claimed that although, for any genuine visual perception of a physical object, it would be possible, by artificially stimulating the optic nerves, to produce a hallucination of the same subjective character, i.e. an experience which could not, even in principle, be introspectively distinguished from the genuine perception, none the less the genuine perception and the hallucination are not experiences of the same intrinsic type, the former being the direct awareness of a physical item and the latter being the direct awareness of a sense-datum. The fact that the two experiences are subjectively indistinguishable would be explained by the fact that, although they are entities of different ontological types, the two immediate objects of awareness, i.e. the physical item and the sense-datum, have the same sensible qualities – or rather, that the sensible qualities of the sense-datum match the way the physical item sensibly appears to the subject, given his viewpoint and conditions of observation. However, such a position would be very hard to sustain, not only because the distinction between the subjective and the intrinsic character of an experience is dubious, but also because to exploit the distinction in the way proposed would involve giving a very peculiar and implausible account of the causation of experience. For if we say that, even as experiences, genuine perception and hallucination differ in their intrinsic character, we are forced to say that the very same type of brain-process, which causes an experience of one intrinsic sort when it is produced in the normal way (by photic stimulation of the eyes), causes an experience of a different intrinsic sort when it is produced in the artificial way (by electrical stimulation of the optic nerves) – as if the brain has some way of telling, without any neural record, how its current state was brought about and that it uses this information to decide on the appropriate experiential effect. Such a position may be logically tenable, but it is scarcely one which anyone would want to adopt.[8]

Ayer, however, sees a quite different way in which the argument from hallucination can be resisted:

> . . . the fact is that in giving an account of such hallucinations we are not bound to say that anything is seen. It would be perfectly legitimate to describe Macbeth's experience by saying that he thought he was seeing a dagger, whereas in fact he was not seeing anything. It is just as natural a way of putting it as the other. And even if we insist on saying that he was seeing something, though not of course a physical object, we are not bound to infer from this that there *was* something which he saw; any more than we are bound to infer that ghosts exist from the fact that people see them. In general, we do use words like 'see' in such a way that from the fact that something is seen it follows that it exists. For this reason, if one does not believe in ghosts, one will be more inclined, in reporting a ghost story, to say that the victim thought he saw a ghost than that he did see one. But the other usage is not incorrect. One can describe someone as having seen a ghost without being committed to asserting that there was a ghost which he saw. And the same applies to Macbeth's visionary dagger or to any other example of this sort. It is only if we artificially combine the decision to say that the victim of a hallucination is seeing something with the ruling that what is seen must exist, that we secure the introduction of sense-data. But once again there seems to be no good reason why we should do this. (*PK*, 90–1)

Here, I do not find Ayer's reasoning compelling. To begin with, although it may be perfectly correct to say, in a case like Macbeth's, that the subject *thought he saw* a physical object of a certain sort, this seems to be not so much a description of the visual experience itself, as a description of the judgment which the experience induced him to make. Admittedly, granted the assumption that the subject is not wholly demented, we can infer something about the character of the experience from the description of the judgment. But this does not mean that the expression 'thought he saw . . . ' is, directly, a description of the visual experience as such. Moreover, and this is decisive, we can easily envisage a case in which someone has a visual hallucination but does not think that he sees any physical object at all. Suppose, for example, the subject *knows* that his visual experiences are being artificially induced by the electrical stimulation of his optic nerves and, consequently, *knows* that they are hallucinations. In such a case, we cannot record his experiences in the way Ayer envisages – e.g. 'he thinks he sees a dagger', 'he thinks he sees a bus' – since all such descriptions would simply be false. The subject knows that he is not seeing anything physical at all.

At this point Ayer might appeal to his other locution, where we say that someone sees something, without implying that there is something which he sees. For even in the case of the subject who knows he is having hallucinations, we can still say that he 'sees' a dagger or 'sees' a bus in this special sense and thereby characterize his visual experiences without the introduction of sense-data. But it would be wrong to take such locutions as the basic way of describing the experiences. For their grammatical form misrepresents the logical structure of the propositions they express. Grammatically, 'sees' is a transitive verb, taking both a grammatical subject and a grammatical object. Going by grammar alone, we expect it to signify a genuine relation – one which obtains if and only if there are two entities which are thus related, an entity x and an entity y such that x sees y. But in the case of Ayer's locutions, even if they are sanctioned by ordinary usage, this expectation fails. 'Sees' continues to function grammatically as a transitive verb, with subject-term and object-term, but it no longer signifies a relation. If it did, then from 'S sees a dagger', in Ayer's sense, we could deduce 'there is a dagger which S sees' – in logical notation, '$\exists x(x$ is a dagger and S sees $x)$'. And this is just what, *ex hypothesi*, we cannot deduce. The conclusion to be drawn from this is that, to render them logically perspicuous, Ayer's locutions stand in need of analysis. And the analysis, indeed, is not hard to find. Presumably, what is meant by saying that the subject sees a dagger in Ayer's sense is that it is with him visually as if he sees a dagger in the ordinary sense – that his visual experience is exactly as if there were a real dagger which he really sees. But, thus analysed, Ayer's locutions offer no escape from the argument from hallucination, since they do not even purport to give any account of the nature of visual experience. To say that someone's visual experience is exactly as if he sees a dagger is merely to say that his experience is, intrinsically, just like the experience of one who really sees a dagger. It does not tell us in what the intrinsic character of such an experience consists. Consequently, it is not offering a positive alternative to the claim of the sense-datum theorist that, in hallucination, the immediate objects of awareness are sense-data. Of course, it does not follow from this that the sense-datum theory is true. But the onus is very much on its opponents to show how it can be avoided, by providing some alternative account of the nature of hallucination. And this, in my view, Ayer has failed to do.

Finding the argument from hallucination inadequate, Ayer goes on to consider whether a stronger case for sense-data could be made out by bringing in what he calls 'the causal aspect of the argument from illusion' (*PK*, 91). Under this aspect, the argument lays stress on the fact, attested by physical science, that 'the way in which things appear to us is causally conditioned by a number of factors which are extraneous to the thing itself' (*PK*, 92).

> If, for example, this carpet now looks blue to me it is because light of a certain wave-length is being transmitted from it to my eyes, from which impulses pass along the appropriate nerve fibres to my brain. In a different light, or if my eyes or brain were injured, it might appear to me a different colour, or no identifiable colour at all. (*PK*, 92)

From this it is inferred that 'we do not perceive things as they really are, that, for example, the physical object which I refer to as 'this carpet' is not really blue' (*PK*, 92). The underlying assumption behind this inference is that if a thing's appearing to have a certain property is caused, in part, by factors extraneous to the thing's intrinsic condition – factors such as the character of the illumination and the state of the observer's sense-organs and brain – then the appearance is illusory and does not accurately depict what the thing is like in itself.

Even if this inference were valid, it is not immediately clear how it serves to strengthen the argument from illusion as originally formulated. It is uncontroversial that objects sometimes sensibly appear in ways which belie their true character. This fact, according to Ayer, is not sufficient to establish the existence of sense-data, since we can continue to speak of the physical objects as what we directly perceive even when their appearance is deceptive. But all the causal argument shows, if it shows anything at all, is that appearances are more generally deceptive than we ordinarily suppose. And why should this be considered decisive if the original cases of the crooked-looking stick and the oval-looking coin are not? Ayer is somewhat vague here, but I take his thought to be something like this. If we concede that, where it is conditioned by extraneous factors, sensible appearance is deceptive, we shall be forced to conclude that all appearances are thoroughly deceptive, since all are, and in every respect, thus conditioned. But, given this conclusion, it becomes hard to see how physical items could still qualify as direct objects of perception. How, for example, could it be said that I directly see this sheet of paper if it has not the slightest resemblance, in either colour or shape, to how things visually appear to me? How, indeed, could I be said to see it at all in any ordinary sense? It seems that once we have conceded that all sensible appearance is deceptive, all physical objects assume the same status as the insensible particles of physics and only sense-data are left to serve as the immediate objects of perceptual awareness.

Whether or not this reasoning is sound, Ayer correctly notes that the principle underlying the causal argument is not. From the fact that a thing's appearing to have a certain property is caused, in part, by factors extraneous to the thing itself, we cannot legitimately infer that it does not really have it. Indeed, such an inference would lead to absurdity. For since any appearance is bound to be causally dependent, in part, on the state of the observer and conditions of observation, we could establish that an object lacked a certain property solely on the basis of its appearing to possess it. Thus we could establish that two objects were qualitatively different simply because they looked qualitatively identical or that they were qualitatively identical simply because they looked qualitatively different. And we could establish that two objects were contiguous simply because they appeared to be separated or that they were separated simply because they appeared to be contiguous. All this is manifestly absurd.

It is so absurd that I am doubtful whether anyone has maintained the causal principle in quite the form which Ayer envisages. What certainly has been maintained, and with considerable plausibility, is a causal principle of a different kind, namely that if our only grounds for supposing that an object has a certain property is that, when it is observed in appropriate conditions, it appears to have it, and if we have established, perhaps by scientific investigation, that the object's possession of this property, if it does possess it, is causally irrelevant to its having this appearance, then we have no valid reason to believe that the object does possess the property. This principle, together with certain scientific findings, could be invoked in support of a Lockean view of secondary qualities; or more precisely, it could be invoked to show that we have no good reason to suppose that physical objects possess colour, flavour, odour, or any other of the secondary sensible qualities, except in the form of powers to induce certain kinds of experience in us. Whether such a conclusion would help the sense-datum theorist is another question and one which I shall not at the moment pursue.

Ayer does not think that the argument from illusion, in any of the forms so far developed, establishes the truth of the sense-datum theory or even provides a reasonable basis for accepting it. None the less, he goes on to claim that, by focusing on the case of illusion, or more accurately, on the possibility of illusion, we can find a legitimate method of introducing sense-data as a way of formulating, in the form which best serves the interests of philosophical inquiry, the facts which are epistemologically given in sense-experience. Here is how, in *PK*, he takes his first step towards this position:

> We have already remarked . . . that the ordinary way of describing what one perceives appears to make a stronger claim than the perception itself can cover. This follows indeed from the fact that illusions are possible. If I can be undergoing an illusion when, on the basis of my present experience, I judge, for example, that my cigarette case is lying on the table in front of me, I may, in saying that I see the cigarette case, be claiming more than the experience strictly warrants: it is logically consistent with my having just this experience that there should not really be a cigarette case there, or indeed any physical object at all. It may be suggested, therefore, that if I wish to give a strict account of my present visual experience, I must make a more cautious statement. I must say not that I see the cigarette case, if this is to carry the implication that there is a cigarette case there, but only that it seems to me that I am seeing it. We are not here concerned with the question whether such statements are incorrigible . . . Their point is not that they give us complete security from error; it is that, if they are true, they serve as descriptions of the contents of our sense-experiences, irrespective of any larger claims that these experiences may normally induce us to make. (*PK*, 95–6)

So far, not a whiff of sense-data. But Ayer continues:

> The next step, continuing with our example, is to convert the sentence 'it now seems to me that I see a cigarette case' into 'I am now seeing a seeming-cigarette case'. And this seeming-cigarette case, which lives only in my present experience, is an example of a sense-datum. Applying this procedure to all cases of perception, whether veridical or delusive, one obtains the result that whenever anyone perceives, or thinks that he perceives, a physical object, he must at least be, in the appropriate sense, perceiving a seeming-object. These seeming-objects are sense-data; and the conclusion may be more simply expressed by saying that it is always sense-data that are directly perceived. (*PK*, 96–7)

As Ayer immediately acknowledges, there is no genuine conflict between this conclusion, given the way it has been reached, and the claim of the naive realist that we directly perceive physical objects. It is true that there is a conflict of terminology – a conflict over the use of the expression 'directly perceive'. But there is no conflict about the *nature* of perceptual experience, since sense-data have been introduced by terminological fiat, not by considering what perceptual experience is really like. Nor does Ayer claim that the sense-datum terminology is needed if we are to deal with cases of illusion. For, as we have seen, he accepts that, by speaking of how it appears or seems to the subject, we can describe such cases, and even cases of complete hallucination, without introducing sense-data at all. His motive in adopting the sense-datum terminology is, rather, that it is philosophically illuminating. For, as he sees it, it brings to light, in a way that the naive realist's terminology tends to conceal, the true nature of our epistemological situation. By introducing sense-data as the only immediate objects of perceptual awareness, it clearly reveals the way in which our knowledge of the physical world is at best indirect; and it thus draws attention to the fact that, to the extent that the inferences from sense-data to physical objects are problematic, our physical beliefs can be called in question. It might be thought that the realist's terminology has the advantage of shielding us from this sceptical challenge. But it shields us not by meeting the challenge, but by obscuring its force. As Ayer remarks:

> . . . philosophical problems are not settled simply by our taking care that they should not arise. If the introduction of sense-data is permissible, then there exists a problem about the way in which they are related to physical objects. If this question can be raised, it is philosophically entitled to an answer. (*PK*, 98)

That he is only advocating the adoption of a sense-datum *language*, not a sense-datum *theory*, is something which Ayer makes more explicit in his earlier book, *The Foundations of Empirical Knowledge* (*FEK*). Having sketched a slightly different, but similarly stipulative, procedure for introducing sense-data (the differences between it and the *PK*-procedure are of no philosophical importance), he writes:

> This procedure is in itself legitimate; and for certain purposes it is useful. I shall indeed adopt it myself. But one must not suppose that it embodies any factual discovery. The philosopher who says that he is seeing a sense-datum in a case where most people would say that they were seeing a material thing is not contradicting the received opinion on any question of fact. He is not putting forward a new hypothesis which could be empirically verified or confuted. What he is doing is simply to recommend a new verbal usage. He is proposing to us that instead of speaking, for example, of seeing a straight stick which looks crooked, or of seeing an oasis when there

is no oasis there, we should speak of seeing a sense-datum which really has the quality of being crooked, and which belongs to a straight stick, or of seeing a sense-datum which really has the qualities that are characteristic of the appearance of an oasis, but does not belong to any material thing. If we accept this recommendation it will not be because our ordinary language is defective, in the sense that it does not furnish us with the means of describing all the facts, or in the sense that it obliges us to misdescribe some of them; but simply because it is not so good an instrument as the sense-datum language for our special purposes. For since in philosophizing about perception our main object is to analyse the relationship of our sense-experiences to the propositions we put forward concerning material things, it is useful for us to have a terminology that enables us to refer to the contents of our experiences independently of the material things that they are taken to present. And this the sense-datum language provides. (*FEK*, 25–6)

There is one crucial point which needs to be made here. In introducing a sense-datum language, Ayer is not merely introducing a new *notation* for formulating the propositions which are normally formulated in terms of the perception or apparent perception of physical objects. Thus although in *PK* sense-data are introduced by converting sentences of the form 'it now seems to me that I perceive a φ', where 'φ' is a noun or noun-phrase signifying a certain kind of physical object, into sentences of the form 'I am now perceiving a seeming-φ', we are not to construe the latter sentences as mere notational variants of the former. We are not to interpret the step of conversion as the stipulation that the new sentences are to have the same meaning as the original sentences, which are already understood. For, thus interpreted, the introduction of the sense-datum language would be of no interest at all. It would not be a genuine alternative to the language of naive realism, since it would just be the naive realist language in disguise. It would not be a genuine method of introducing sense-data, since any apparent reference to such entities would disappear once the new notation was decoded.

In stressing that what he is introducing and defending is a new language, rather than a new theory, what Ayer intends to convey, I think, is that the nature of perceptual experience can be conceptualized in alternative ways – one way being expressed by the terminology of naive realism, the other by the terminology of sense-data. The two sentences 'it now seems to me that I see a cigarette case' and 'I am now seeing a seeming-cigarette case' do not express the same proposition; for the latter, unlike the former, involves a genuine ontology of seeming-objects, i.e. sense-data. But, as Ayer sees it, each is a correct way of recording, in the perspective of its own conceptual scheme, the content

155

of one's experience. Nor is there, Ayer thinks, any question of one of these conceptual schemes being objectively right and the other objectively wrong: abstracted from these perspectives, the nature of perceptual experience is, as it were, indeterminate. On such a view, philosophers who have construed the question 'Do we directly perceive physical objects or sense-data?' as a question of fact, are just confused. In so far as there is a question at all, it is one which calls for a conceptual decision, and, though the decision need not be entirely arbitrary, the only reason for preferring one option to the other is that it serves one's philosophical purposes better.

Why Ayer should take this position is not entirely clear. In *FEK* his reason seems to be that the question of what we directly perceive cannot be settled empirically. This is suggested by something in the passage I quoted, where, having claimed that the philosopher who employs the sense-datum terminology 'is not contradicting the received opinion on any question of fact', he continues, apparently by way of explanation: 'He is not putting forward a new hypothesis which could be empirically verified or confuted' (*FEK*, 25). And the point is made explicit in the following paragraph, where he argues that the sentence 'I never see material things but only sense-data' (it is clear from the context that 'see' here means 'directly see') does not express a genuine proposition – one with objective truth-value – since, unlike the sentence 'I never see gold sovereigns but only Bank of England notes', it is not subject to empirical tests. But I do not see how this argument meets Ayer's own requirements. It is true that, at the time of writing (*FEK* was published in 1940), Ayer's thought was dominated by the verificationism of *LTL*. But even in *LTL*, in which his empiricism assumed its most uncompromising form, he never maintained that the only genuine propositions are empirical. On the contrary, he accepted the *a priori* truths of logic and mathematics and defended their *a priori* (non-empirical) status against those, like Mill, who would interpret them as empirical hypotheses. Admittedly, he held that such truths are devoid of factual content; but by this he meant no more than that the propositions in question are analytic – that is, they owe their truth solely to the meanings of the symbols which they, or the sentences which express them, contain. He did not suppose that such sentences as '2 + 2 = 4' and 'everything is identical with itself' fail to have objective truth-values or that our acceptance or rejection of them is a matter for decision. Rather, he held that we could establish their truth by appealing to the definitions of their constituent terms. Now, of course, the sentence 'I never (directly) see material things but only sense-data' does not express a proposition of logic or mathematics. If it expresses a proposition at all, it expresses a philosophical proposition. But, as we have already noted (in Part I, section 1), Ayer himself classifies the truths of philosophy as analytic and hence *a priori* (see, for example, the preface of *LTL*). So the fact that the sentence does not express an empirical proposition is not decisive. Even from Ayer's standpoint, there is no reason to insist that, to be factual in the ordinary sense (i.e. to be objectively resolvable), the issue over sense-data has to be empirical.

It does not follow, of course, that Ayer is wrong in seeing the issue as terminological in his sense – as calling for a choice between alternative descriptions, or conceptualizations, which are equally true to the (as it were indeterminate) pre-conceptualized facts. Nor should we assume that his only reason for holding this view was that the issue could not be settled empirically. No doubt a further reason, and I suspect the main one, was that, having looked into the issue with some care and finding himself unable to establish any definite theory of perception by *a priori* reasoning, he came to the conclusion that there was nothing to be established. My own view is that, despite the care, Ayer came to this conclusion too hastily and that there are some crucial considerations of which he failed to take account. In particular, as I have already indicated, I think that the argument from hallucination is more powerful than he supposed. Whether it suffices to establish the sense-datum theory is something I shall examine in the next section.

The introduction of sense-data as the immediate objects of perceptual awareness was supposed to validate the first step in the sceptic's argument – the step of claiming that our knowledge of the physical world is at best indirect. But as Ayer remarks, and as must be clear from our whole discussion, sense-data 'are not strictly needed for the formulation of the sceptic's problem' (*PK*, 112).

> Even if one refuses to take the final step of transforming 'seeming to perceive an object' into ' "perceiving" a seeming-object', and inferring from this that there is a seeming-object which is directly perceived, there will still be the gap between evidence and conclusion which the sceptic requires. It is the gap between things as they seem and things as they are; and the problem consists in our having to justify our claims to know how physical objects are on the basis of knowing only how they seem . . . A problem of this sort must arise once it is admitted that our ordinary judgements of perception claim more than is strictly contained in the experiences on which they are based. (*PK*, 112–13)

It might seem to follow from this that, unless the sceptic chooses to formulate his first step in terms of the sense-datum theory, the position we have labelled 'naive realism' is not in conflict with the sceptical argument. But we must be careful here. For naive realism, as we originally characterized it, involves *two* claims: first, that physical objects can be directly perceived; second, that, through perception, we can acquire direct knowledge of physical facts. The first claim, which asserts the directness of our *perceptual* access to the physical world, is in conflict with the sense-datum theory (taken as a *theory*), but is perfectly compatible with a suitably formulated sceptical argument. The second claim, which asserts the directness of our *epistemological* access to the physical world, is an explicit rejection of the sceptic's first step, however this step is formulated. For it denies that our primary knowledge of the physical world – knowledge supplied by perception – depends, even implicitly, on the validity of some kind of inference, as the sceptic asserts. Of course, the naive realist sees these two claims as intimately connected: he thinks that it is by directly perceiving physical objects that we acquire direct knowledge of physical facts. But we can now see that this connection does not hold – at least in any sense of 'knowledge' which would protect us from the sceptical challenge. For even if I am directly perceiving a physical object on a certain occasion, how do I know that my perception is veridical? And how do I know that I am perceiving a physical object at all, granted that a hallucination could have exactly the same subjective character? Our perceptual access to the physical world may be direct, in the sense that, when a physical object is perceived, there is no intervening object of perceptual awareness; but this does not remove the epistemological problem, once it is recognized that our physical judgments, based on our perceptual experiences, go beyond the evidence which these experiences supply. This is the point which Ayer is making in the passage above.

It might also seem to follow that, even if it is of interest in its own right, the issue over the nature of perception is ultimately irrelevant to our epistemological concern. The sceptical problem can be formulated with or without a sense-datum theory; and so it might be thought that the introduction of sense-data would only serve to *underline* the problem (underline the gap between evidence and conclusion), in the way Ayer suggests. However, this would be to overlook a crucial point. For even though scepticism about the physical world does not depend on the sense-datum theory, the theory could make a difference to whether such scepticism can be satisfactorily met. After all, one of the four possible answers to scepticism, as previously outlined by Ayer, is that of the reductionist, who, in the present case, claims that statements about the physical world turn out, on analysis, to be logically equivalent to statements about sense-experience. Whether or not it is acceptable, such an analysis would not even be an option if, as the naive realist claims, the basic way of describing the content of sense-experience were in terms of the perception or apparent perception of physical objects. Clearly, for the possibility of this analysis to arise, the primitive experiential language must be one which dispenses with physical concepts and physical ontology. And if the sense-datum theory were true, such a language would, it seems, be available. In this way, ironically, though not required for the formulation of the sceptical problem, the sense-datum theory might be invoked as a step towards its solution.

10 *The nature of perceptual experience*

The naive realist claims that, in appropriate conditions, we directly perceive physical objects. But what exactly is meant here by 'directly perceive'? There are, I think, two possible interpretations, one of them considerably more naive than the other. According to one interpretation, a subject S directly perceives an object O if and only if S perceives O and his perceptual awareness of O is not mediated by his awareness of something else. According to the other, a subject S directly perceives an object O if and only if S perceives O and his perceptual awareness of O is not mediated by anything at all. It is the second of these interpretations which is the more naive. But before we can appreciate why this is so, we need to be clear about what is meant by *mediation*.

When I say that S's perceptual awareness of O is mediated by something x, what I mean is given by the conjunction of three conditions: first, x is some psychological event or state in S at the time in question; second, it is logically possible for S to undergo an event or have a state of x's intrinsic type without being perceptually aware of O or of any object of O's intrinsic type; third, S's perceptual awareness of O consists in x together with some further state of affairs. Typically, this further state of affairs consists, at least in part, in the obtaining of some relation – though not that of awareness – between x and O, or, if x itself is an awareness of something, between the object of this awareness and O.

To understand this definition of mediation, it will help to begin by considering an example which is uncontroversial – or, at least, neutral with respect to the controversy over sense-data. Smith, we will suppose, is watching a football match on television and one which is being shown 'live'. We want to say that, at each moment of his viewing, he is, in some sense, visually aware of a certain pattern of colours on the screen. In saying that he is visually aware of this pattern, we do not, of course, mean that he is thinking about it or paying attention to it. He is unlikely to be doing this unless the picture is conspicuously defective. The better the picture, the more likely he is, as it were, to look through it, rather than at it, and to focus his mind on the football-events it depicts. None the less, if the sequence of colour-patterns is to reveal these events to him, as it surely does, these patterns have to be, in some rudimentary way, visually registered and thus, in some sense, recorded in the content of his visual awareness. Thus, at a particular moment, what he notices and takes an interest in is (say) the event of two opposing players competing for the ball. But part of what enables him to notice this is that, with the two players wearing shirts of different colours, he visually

159

registers the contrast of colours in two portions of the screen. Granted that Smith is, in some sense, visually aware of the colour-patterns on the screen, we also want to say that such episodes of awareness mediate, in the sense defined, his perceptual awareness of the match. At each moment, his visual contact with the match consists in his visual awareness of the current pattern, together with some further state of affairs; the main component of this further state of affairs is the qualitative and causal relationship between the pattern and some time-slice of the match – that relationship, in short, which renders the pattern a televisual representation of the match at the relevant time from a certain viewpoint. This then is a clear-cut and philosophically uncontroversial case of mediation. The subject sees the football match and at each moment his visual awareness of the match is mediated by his visual awareness, in some rudimentary sense, of the colour-pattern on the screen.

Now that we understand the notion of mediation, let us return to the two interpretations of 'directly perceive'. As I said, according to one interpretation, a subject directly perceives something just in case he perceives it and his perceptual awareness of it is not mediated by his awareness of something else, while, according to the other, a subject directly perceives something just in case he perceives it and his perceptual awareness of it is not mediated by anything. To distinguish these interpretations, let us henceforth use the expression 'directly$_1$ perceives' when we wish to speak of direct perception in the first sense and 'directly$_2$ perceives' when we wish to speak of it in the second sense. Corresponding to these different forms of direct perception, we have two forms of direct realism: one which claims that, in appropriate conditions, physical objects are directly$_1$ perceived, and one which claims that, in appropriate conditions, they are directly$_2$ perceived. Let us label these as, respectively, 'direct realism$_1$' and 'direct realism$_2$'. It may be wondered why I am now speaking of '*direct* realism' rather than '*naive* realism'. One reason is that, as we have seen, naive realism (as we have characterized it) makes two claims, one concerning the directness of perception, the other concerning the directness of knowledge, and 'direct realism' is being used to signify the perceptual claim alone. A further reason is that while direct realism is divided into two versions, corresponding to the different senses of 'directly perceives', it is, I think, only direct realism$_2$ which would qualify as '*naive* realism' (or its perceptual component) in the customary sense.

Obviously, direct realism$_2$ is stronger than (i.e. entails but is not entailed by) direct realism$_1$. It is sufficient for truth of direct realism$_1$ that, in appropriate conditions, our perceptual awareness of physical objects is not mediated by our awareness of something else. But it is necessary for the truth of direct realism$_2$ that, in appropriate conditions, our perceptual awareness of physical objects is not mediated by anything at all. Indeed, direct realism$_2$ is so strong that I cannot see how anyone could wish to assert it once he has realized what it involves. The problems of asserting it have already been exposed by the argument from hallucination formulated in the previous section. When we consider the possibility of artificially inducing perceptual experiences by electrical stimulation of the subject's nervous system, it seems impossible to deny that, for each genuine perception, i.e. for each perception of a physical object, there could be a hallucinatory experience of exactly the same intrinsic psychological character. If this is so, then whenever someone perceives a physical object, his experiential state is, in itself, logically neutral between genuine perception and hallucination, and his perceptual awareness of the physical object is mediated by this experiential state in the sense defined. His perceptual awareness of the object consists in this state together with something else – presumably, as the main factor, the way in which the state causally results from, and, by its intrinsic features, represents, the object. This conclusion is, of course, incompatible with the claim that the object is directly$_2$ perceived, since direct perception of this sort requires the perceptual awareness to be wholly unmediated: it requires that perceptual contact with the object is part of the very intrinsic character of the experiential state – that the state is, as such, the awareness of the object.

The possibility of hallucination, or more precisely, the fact that, for any genuine perception, there could be a hallucination of the same experiential character, refutes direct realism$_2$ – and thereby refutes naive realism as, I think, it is ordinarily understood. But it does not refute direct realism$_1$. It does not refute the claim that, in appropriate conditions, we directly$_1$ perceive physical objects, i.e. we perceive them and our perceptual awareness of them is not mediated by our awareness of something else. For we have not established that the experiential state which mediates the perceptual awareness of a physical object is itself to be specified as the awareness of something. In short, the possibility of hallucination refutes direct realism in its naive form, but it does not, without some further argument, establish the sense-datum theory.

But what alternatives to the sense-datum theory are there? If the mediating state is not the awareness of a sense-datum, what could it be? Before we try to answer this, we need to get somewhat clearer about what the sense-datum theory is claiming.

The first thing which needs to be stressed is that in any normal perceptual experience there is a large element of interpretation – interpretation which in some way overlays and enriches something else which we may call, for want of a better name, the presentational content. The name 'presentational content' is, perhaps, somewhat tendentious, since it seems to presuppose something like the sense-datum account. But for the moment I just want to use this expression, in conjunction with the term 'interpretation', to mark an intuitive distinction between two elements in perceptual experience, however that distinction is to be ultimately analysed.

The distinction I have in mind can perhaps be best brought out by considering again the case of the man who is watching a football match on television. We have already noted that his perception of the match is mediated by his visual awareness of the colour-patterns on the screen: at each moment, his visual contact with the match is secured by his visual registering of the current pattern and by the way in which, through its causal origins and intrinsic features, this pattern qualifies as a televisual picture of some momentary stage in the match. However, we do not want to say that, at each moment, this visual registering of a colour-pattern on the screen exhausts the content of the man's perceptual experience. Clearly it does not. For he not only registers the pattern, but interprets it in a way which is strikingly different from its actual character. The pattern, in itself, is two-dimensional. But he interprets it as a three-dimensional pattern viewed in a certain perspective; and not just as a three-dimensional pattern of colours, but as an arrangement of material objects with coloured surfaces; and not just as an arrangement of material objects, but as people kicking a ball around on a grass pitch; and not just this, but as two teams playing football, with all that that involves. Moreover, these interpretations of the pattern on the screen are not just accompanying judgments, extraneous to the perceptual experience itself. It is not that he sees the two-dimensional pattern and infers from it, together with his knowledge of the principles of televisual photography, the sorts of objects and events it represents. In some way, the interpretation is fused with the awareness of the pattern – fused so perfectly that, to the viewing subject himself, it seems that what is visually presented is not the pattern itself, but the pattern-as-thus-interpreted. It is only by switching the focus of his attention from the football match to the televisual process that he can come to distinguish the presentational from the interpretative elements in his perceptual experience – come to appreciate the extent to which the content of his experience consists in his own conceptualization of what is sensibly given.

Now when the sense-datum theorist introduces sense-data as the immediate objects of perceptual awareness, these objects are only intended to furnish the presentational content of perceptual experience, not its element of interpretation. For it would be not merely extravagant but incoherent to suppose that, in addition to the purely sensible item which is strictly presented, there is some non-physical, mind-dependent object of awareness which embodies the physical characteristics we attribute to the sensible item by our interpretation. This is why I think it is infelicitous for Ayer to speak of his 'seeing a seeming-cigarette case' and to claim that 'this seeming-cigarette case, which lives only in my present experience, is an example of a sense-datum' (*PK*, 96). For such a claim suggests that the sense-datum, the immediate and internal object of awareness, has to incorporate not only the visual appearance of the cigarette case to Ayer, i.e. the pattern of colours which is visually presented, but also the content of his perceptual interpretation, i.e. his seeing this pattern as a physical object of a certain sort, namely a cigarette case. And I do not see how the object of awareness can incorporate this interpretative content without forfeiting its awareness-dependent character. Obviously, it is not possible for something to have the physical properties of a cigarette case without being a genuine physical object. But how, if not by possessing these physical properties, could the sense-datum embody the content of the interpretation? Of course, it might be said that, as Ayer introduces it, the sentence-schema '*S* sees a seeming-φ' has the same meaning as 'It seems to *S* that he sees a φ', and that, consequently, we can understand the way in which a sense-datum embodies the content of a perceptual interpretation in terms of the way in which this content is part of how things seem to the subject. But to say this is to admit that the sense-datum terminology is just a *façon de parler*, whose meaning is given by sentences in which no objects of awareness, other than physical items, are mentioned: it is to concede that, in the final analysis, all references to sense-data disappear. This would certainly not be a way of supporting a sense-datum *theory*, nor even a philosophically interesting way of introducing a sense-datum language. Moreover, as I indicated in the previous section, I am sure it is not what Ayer intends.

The upshot of this is that if the sense-datum theory is to have any chance of success, we must take the sensory items it postulates to be what remain, as the immediate and internal objects of awareness, when all elements of perceptual interpretation are subtracted. Exactly what does remain may be a matter of some dispute even among those who accept the theory. There may be disagreement as to where the line between presentation and interpretation is to be drawn. For example, sense-datum theorists may differ among themselves as to whether in the visual realm the presented colour-pattern is purely two-dimensional, or whether it includes, in addition, some structuring in phenomenal depth. But such disagreements need not concern us. All that matters, at present, is that there is a line to be drawn and that the sense-datum theorist is not attempting to absorb the whole content of a perceptual experience into the sense-datum which forms the object of awareness.

Having, in this respect, clarified the nature of the sense-datum theory, let us now return to the question we posed earlier: what alternatives to the sense-datum theory are there? How might we construe the experiential state which mediates the perception of a physical object if not as, in part, the unmediated awareness of a sense-datum?

The main alternative is the cognitive theory proposed by D. M. Armstrong, a theory which he originally developed in *Perception and the Physical World*[9] and which he subsequently endorsed, with certain refinements, in *A Materialist Theory of the Mind*[10]. With certain important qualifications, which I shall mention presently, this cognitive theory asserts that for a subject to have a perceptual experience is just for him to acquire some belief or beliefs about the current state of his physical environment, where at least some of the beliefs thus acquired are acquired non-inferentially (i.e. without any inference, either conscious or unconscious), and where any belief which is acquired inferentially is acquired at least partly on the basis of those which are acquired non-inferentially. Thus take the example of Ayer looking at a cigarette case on the table in front of him. There is a certain experiential state which mediates his visual perception of this object – a state which Ayer initially describes, in accordance with common sense, as its seeming to him that he sees a cigarette case. According to the sense-datum theorist, this experiential state divides into two components: a *presentational* component, consisting of the awareness of a visual sense-datum – a sense-datum which embodies the visual appearance of the cigarette case to Ayer at that time – and an interpretative component, whereby the colour-patch or colour-pattern which forms the visual sense-datum is, as part of the experience itself, interpreted as the coloured surface of a material object of a certain kind, namely a cigarette case. The cognitivist also divides the experiential state into two components and ones which, in a sense, correspond to the two components recognized by the sense-datum theorist. First, there is a certain complex of beliefs, acquired non-inferentially, about the spatial arrangement of colours in the current environment, where each of these beliefs is the belief that a certain colour is physically realized at a certain (often not precisely identified) distance and in a certain direction from the subject. Second, and partly based on this complex of non-inferential beliefs, there is a belief that there currently exists, at a certain distance and in a certain direction and orientation, a material object of a certain shape, colour, and functional character, namely a cigarette case. This second component can still be thought of as interpretative, since it is, in effect, an interpretation of the content of the beliefs which form the first component – an interpretation of the spatial arrangement of colours which is, in the first component, believed to be physically realized. And in this sense, the distinction between the presentational and interpretative elements of the perceptual experience is maintained, even though the term 'presentational', if strictly interpreted, is no longer appropriate. This term is no longer appropriate, since the element which we might ordinarily think of as presentational turns out to be not the awareness of some object, but a complex of beliefs that things are thus and thus, and it is the propositional content of these beliefs that then gets overlaid by a further level of conceptualization.

It is clear how this cognitive theory manages to preserve direct realism₁, though not, of course, direct realism₂. When a subject perceives a physical object, his perceptual awareness of it is mediated by a psychological state which is itself neutral between genuine perception and hallucination. But, according to the cognitivist, this state is not the awareness of something else, but rather certain beliefs about the current state of the environment, and whether it yields a genuine perception or a hallucination depends on the extent to which these beliefs are true and the manner in which their acquisition has been caused. In this way, the cognitivist maintains that, in appropriate conditions, we directly₁ perceive physical objects; and, indeed, in his earlier book, Armstrong describes his theory as a version of direct realism, though he later abandoned this title to avoid confusion with the naive version, in which the perceptual awareness of physical objects is wholly unmediated.

I have represented the cognitivist as asserting that for a subject to have a perceptual experience is just for him to acquire certain beliefs about the current state of his physical environment. But, as I indicated, this assertion is made with certain important qualifications, to which we must now turn.

It does not take long to see that, *as so far formulated*, the cognitivist theory is indefensible. For obviously it is possible for someone to have a perceptual experience without thereby acquiring any belief about the current state of the physical world – or at least any which could conceivably count as part of the experience itself. One only has to go back to the case, mentioned in the previous section, of someone who knows that his experience is hallucinatory. Or, to take an even simpler case, when I look at a ruler half-immersed in water, I do not acquire the belief that it is crooked: I know that straight sticks look crooked in such circumstances and discount the appearance accordingly. Clearly, in this sense, seeing is not necessarily believing and the cognitivist should not claim that it is.

One way in which the cognitivist could modify his position would be by saying that where a perceptual experience does not consist in the acquisition of beliefs, it consists in the acquisition of an *inclination* to hold certain beliefs. Thus even when I know that I am undergoing some kind of illusion or hallucination, I may still be expected to feel some inclination to believe that things are, physically, as my experiences seem to indicate – an inclination which I resist because of what I independently know. But, as Armstrong himself concedes, this modification does not go far enough. For there are cases where the illusory character of the experience is so familiar that the subject does not even feel any inclination to hold the relevant belief. Armstrong gives the example of someone looking in a mirror. So long as the person is thoroughly familiar with mirrors, he will not feel any inclination at all to believe that the face he sees is in the place, beyond the mirror, where it visually appears to be. It will be part of his perceptual experience to interpret this face as his own, reflected by the mirror, rather than as that of his double, located at some distance in front of him.

Armstrong's answer is to introduce the concept of *potential* belief.

> Nevertheless, we may reply, in such cases of perception without belief and even without inclination to believe, it is possible to formulate a true counter-factual statement of the form 'But for the fact that the perceiver had other, independent, beliefs about the world, he would have acquired certain beliefs – the beliefs corresponding to the content of his perception.' We do not believe that our mirror-double stands before us *only* because we have a great deal of other knowledge about the world which contradicts the belief that there is anything like the object we seem to see behind the surface of the glass . . . In cases of 'perception without belief', we can now argue, an event still occurs in our mind, an event which can be described as one that would be the acquiring of belief but for the existence of other, contrary, beliefs that we already hold. The event might perhaps be called the acquiring of a *potential belief* . . . In this way, perception without belief or inclination to believe might be fitted into our analysis.[11]

But this answer is surely inadequate. It is true that where a perceptual experience does not induce the beliefs or belief-inclinations that corre-spond to its content, it does, at least normally, induce potential beliefs in Armstrong's sense. But it seems obvious that the perceptual experience does not just consist in the acquisition of such potential beliefs. It is difficult enough to accept that, in normal cases, it just consists in the acquisition of actual beliefs. But to claim that when I look in a mirror, my visual experience just consists in the fact that, if I did not know about the reflective character of mirrors, I would acquire the relevant complex of beliefs about the arrangement of colours in front of me and would, on this basis, believe that my double stands before me, seems crazy. Surely, this counterfactual fact obtains precisely because I have, independently of it, a visual experience of a certain sort – an experience which, because of its intrinsic character, would lead me to acquire these beliefs if, in ignorance of the properties of mirrors, I took it to be wholly veridical. Ayer, in effect, is making this criticism (though his use of the term 'inclination' is inappropriate) when, in his *Philosophy in the Twen-tieth Century* (*PTC*), he writes of Armstrong:

> . . . he treats the case of seeing an object in a looking-glass as one

in which the potential acquisition of the belief that the object is behind the glass is inhibited by one's previous knowledge of the effects of reflection. But why should we have any inclination at all to believe that the object is behind the glass unless that is where it appears to be? (*PTC*, 183)

In one sense, admittedly, Armstrong himself allows that the counterfactual fact obtains only because I have, independently of it, a visual experience of a certain sort. For, at least in his later book, he identifies a perceptual experience with a brain event, an event which qualifies as the acquisition of certain actual or potential beliefs in virtue of the causal role of events of that intrinsic type in the whole sensory–neural–muscular system. A perceptual experience is thus construed as an acquisition of certain actual or potential beliefs, but this acquisition is a concrete event with a certain intrinsic physical character – a character which is not specified by specifying the content of the beliefs (actual or potential) which the subject thus acquires. In this way, Armstrong too would deny that, when I look in a mirror, my visual experience just consists in the fact that, if I did not know about mirrors, I would acquire the relevant beliefs. Rather, he would say that this experience is a certain neural event whose functional properties, in the context of the sensory–neural–muscular system, make that counterfactual true.

However, I cannot see how this avoids the problem. For even if we allow a perceptual experience to have an intrinsic physical character (and I think this itself is a mistake[12]), we cannot take this physical character to be part of its psychological character or to be something which could be discerned by introspection. The psychological character of a perceptual experience does, on Armstrong's theory, consist in no more than the fact that the subject acquires certain actual or potential beliefs, and, if the theory is true, this fact is all that the subject can introspectively discern. But it is this which seems intuitively absurd, especially in the case where the acquired beliefs are only potential. It seems quite clear that what introspection reveals is not only the fact that I hold certain beliefs, or would hold them but for other things I know, but also the intrinsic character of a certain experience on which the actual or potential holding of these beliefs is based. Armstrong's theory seems, in the last analysis, to be a denial that we have *experiences* at all. And this, again, is how Ayer sees it in his recent review:

The important question is why Armstrong says that perception is nothing but the acquisition of a belief. What is the force of the 'nothing but'? The astonishing answer is that it serves to deny that the belief is acquired through sensory experience. (*PTC*, 182)

Perhaps this point can be made more clearly by switching our attention from cases of perception without belief to cases of belief without perception. Let us imagine the case of someone who, in addition to his eyes, has been given (presumably artificially) a pair of photo-sensitive receptors at the back of his head. The receptors are wired up to the cognitive centres in his brain in such a way as to convey to him the same kind of information about the current state of his posterior environment as he receives, through the use of his eyes, about the current state of his anterior environment. Thus the photic stimulation of these receptors causes him to acquire, non-inferentially, a complex of (normally true) beliefs as to the physical arrangement of colours behind him and, based on this complex, certain 'interpretative' beliefs concerning the location, character and behaviour of certain sorts of material object. In short, these receptors, when operative, furnish the subject with what would qualify, on Armstrong's account, as visual experiences. However, we can easily imagine that, by the standard of his *eye*-induced experiences, they would not seem to the *subject* to be visual experiences. We can imagine him saying something like this: 'By using these special receptors I can tell how things are behind me, just as by using my eyes I can tell how things are in front of me. And I have the same kind and the same amount of information in both cases. But there is an important difference. When I use my eyes, I actually *see* what lies in front of me: there is a visual display and it is this display – this presentation of the colour-arrangement – which is the source of my knowledge. But I do not *see* what lies behind me: I just know, without any display, what is there. The difference is like the difference between perceptual recall and ungrounded factual memory – between, for example, knowing that someone was wearing a red hat because I can visually recall the occasion and just remembering, without the basis of any perceptual recall, that this was the case. When I use my special receptors, I do not have sense-experiences at all. I just gain factual information.' Surely we can imagine the subject drawing this distinction, and drawing it correctly on the basis of a genuine difference which his introspection discerns. But it is a distinction which Armstrong's theory cannot accommodate, since, on this theory, there is, at the psychological level, nothing more to a visual experience than the acquisition of the appropriate sort of belief.

To some extent, I think, Armstrong is aware that his position is counterintuitive and that the sense-datum theory is *initially* more plausible. His reason for adopting the cognitive theory (apart from his wish to have a theory which is consonant with his materialist world-view) is that, as he sees it, it avoids certain conceptual and epistemological problems to which the sense-datum theory is vulnerable. On the epistemological side, he sees the sense-datum theory as generating scepticism, by confining our non-inferential knowledge to facts about sense-data and thus leaving us with no legitimate method of reaching conclusions about the physical world. But here he is just confused. The problem of scepticism remains however the nature of perceptual experience is construed. For the sceptic will always raise the question of how we can establish that our perceptual experiences are ever, or ever come near to be being, veridical perceptions of an external reality, whether the perceptual contact with this reality is wholly unmediated (the position of direct realism₂) or mediated by the awareness of internal objects (the position of the sense-datum theory) or mediated by the acquisition of beliefs (the position of the cognitive theory). Indeed, in one sense, the cognitive theory exacerbates the problem, since by eliminating sense-data, or any genuinely presentative element in perceptual experience, it eliminates our only independent source of evidence for the truth of the physical beliefs we acquire. The evidence may be inadequate, but, apart from the beliefs themselves, there is no other available. How Armstrong could think that the beliefs become easier to defend when they are not grounded on anything, I cannot imagine.

More important are what Armstrong sees as conceptual problems for the sense-datum theory, and it is these which we must now consider. He raises two problems, both very familiar, and we shall look at them in turn.

The first problem concerns the relation of exact similarity as it applies to sense-data. Armstrong invites us to consider a case in which three samples of cloth, A, B, and C, differ very slightly in colour in such a way that, when we focus our attention, in turn, on each pair, we cannot see the difference between A and B or the difference between B and C, but can (because it is the sum of these differences) just see the difference between A and C. He argues that, according to the sense-datum theory (or as he calls it 'the sensory item view'), the two visual sense-data A_1 and B_1, which occur in our perceptions of A and B, must be identical in colour. 'For the sensory items are what are supposed to make a perception the perception it is, and here, by hypothesis, the *perceptions* are identical.'[13] In the same way, he argues that B_1 must be identical in colour to C_1, the visual sense-datum which occurs in our perception of C. But, of course, since we visually detect the difference between A and C, A_1 and C_1 are not identical in colour. So the sense-datum theorist is apparently forced to deny that, in its application to sense-data, the relation of exact resemblance in colour is transitive, and this denial, Armstrong plausibly contends, is plainly contrary to logic.

In *FEK*, Ayer anticipates this objection to the sense-datum theory, but claims that the denial of transitivity is not, after all, paradoxical:

To say that a sense-datum a, which belongs to a material thing A, has the relation R to a sense-datum b, which belongs to a material thing B, is not to say that A really has R to B, but only that it appears to have R to B. Accordingly, the model that we must take for the relation of exact resemblance between sense-data is not the relation of exact resemblance between material things, but the relation between material things of appearing to be exactly resemblant; and this relation, though it too is symmetrical, is not transitive. For it is admitted that a material thing A can appear exactly to resemble a second thing B, and that B can appear exactly to resemble a third thing C, in respect of some sensible property, without its being the case that A and C appear in this respect exactly to resemble one another. We must therefore conclude that the relation of exact resemblance is not a transitive relation when it is applied to sense-data. (*FEK*, 133).

But this reasoning is fallacious. To say that a sense-datum x, which belongs to (i.e. is presented by) a material thing X, exactly resembles in some respect a sense-datum y, which belongs to (i.e. is presented by) a material thing Y, is not, as Ayer supposes, merely to say that X appears exactly to resemble Y in that respect. Rather, it is to say that the appearance of X in that respect exactly resembles the appearance of Y in that respect. Thus, in Armstrong's example, when we say that A_1 and B_1 have exactly the same colour, what we mean, in terms of the appearance of the samples, is not merely that A and B appear to have exactly the same colour, but that the colour-appearance of A is exactly the same as the colour-appearance of B. But once this is recognized, the paradox remains. For the relation of exact resemblance should be transitive in the domain of appearances, as much as in any other domain. It makes no more sense to suppose that the colour-appearances of A and C are different but exactly the same as the colour-appearance of B, than to suppose that the colours of A and B are different but exactly the same as the colour of B. If the sense-datum theory is committed to denying the transitivity of this relation, as applied to sense-data or appearances, then, as Armstrong claims, the theory is false.

Before we consider in what other ways a sense-datum theorist might try to meet the objection, we should pause to ask why Armstrong thinks his own theory is not vulnerable in a similar way. His answer is rather curious:

When we look at A and B we acquire an inclination to believe (falsely) that they are exactly the same colour. When we look at B and C we also acquire an inclination to believe (falsely) that they are exactly the same colour. But when we compare A and C we acquire an inclination to believe (truly) that they are slightly different in colour. In other words we are inclined to believe p and q which together entail r, and yet we are also inclined to believe not-r. This sort of thing is quite frequent in our mental life, and not at all puzzling.[14]

What Armstrong says here is true, but it does not give a fair representation of the original problem from the standpoint of the cognitive theory. And it is unfair in much the same way as Ayer's representation was unfair. Just as Ayer tried to avoid the problem by focusing exclusively on the appearance of a relation and ignoring the relation between the appearances, so Armstrong now tries to avoid it by focusing exclusively on the belief about a relation and ignoring the relation between the beliefs. Thus Armstrong claims that if, by direct comparison, we cannot visually detect any difference in colour between two physical items, then, on the sense-datum theory, the sensory items they present must be identical in colour. But if this is so, how can Armstrong avoid saying that, on his own theory, the two belief-acquisitions which the physical items cause are, with respect to colour-concepts, identical in propositional content – that, for the same colour-property P, each belief is the belief that P is physically instantiated? And if he has to say this, he faces the same problem. For he would have to conclude that, while the colour-concepts employed in the beliefs caused by A and C are different, each is the same as the colour-concept employed in the belief caused by B. And this conclusion denies the transitivity of identity.

The problem then is not confined to the sense-datum theory, and though the sense-datum theorist cannot afford to ignore it, the cognitivist cannot use it as an argument against him until he has put his own house in order. Moreover, I think that the sense-datum theorist has a simple solution. The problem only arises if it is assumed that two sense-data cannot differ in their intrinsic character unless the difference is one which the subject can detect on direct comparison. But why should this assumption be made? It does not seem to me to be surprising that if two sense-data are sufficiently similar in some sensible respect, the difference between them is only detectable *indirectly*, by finding some third sense-datum which can be directly distinguished from the one but not from the other. The usual objection to this is that sense-data are purely phenomenal objects (the reification of appearances) and that their phenomenal status excludes the possibility of their intrinsic character transcending what is apparent to the subject who has them. But this objection trades on an ambiguity in the notion of what is apparent. If a total visual sense-datum includes two colour-patches x and y which differ in colour, then obviously, as this difference is an intrinsic feature of the sense-datum, it is part of what is *phenomenally* apparent to the subject – it is an aspect of the sensible appearance of which the sense-datum is the mental reification. But this does not mean that the difference is *cognitively* apparent to the subject – that it is one which he can judgment-

171

ally detect by introspectively focusing on the nature of his experience. Nor can I see why an undetectable difference should be thought problematic. Why should we not leave room for the case in which the colours of x and y are so similar that the subject cannot tell them apart except by comparing each with some third colour which is detectably different from just one of them?

Ironically, it is the cognitive theory which faces the genuine problem here. For while it is not difficult to see how a subject may be unable, by direct comparison, to detect the qualitative difference between two simultaneous sense-data, it *is* difficult to see how he could be unable, by direct comparison, to detect the conceptual difference between two simultaneous beliefs. If the colour-concept he employs in the belief caused by A is different from that which he employs in the belief caused by B – and, to preserve the transitivity of identity, the cognitivist must surely concede that it is – how, on suitable (and, of course, directly comparative) reflection, could he fail to detect the difference? How could a difference in cognition be inaccessible to his cognitive awareness? I do not think that the cognitivist has any adequate answer to this. It might be objected that since the sense-datum theorist will also have to accept the occurrence of the relevant beliefs (though he will take them to be grounded on sense-data), he too faces a similar problem. But this is not so. For in the content of the beliefs which the sense-datum theorist attributes to the subject, the *exact* shades of colour will only be identified by reference to the presented sense-data which instantiate them, and thus there will be no undetectable difference between the beliefs over and above the undetectable difference between the sense-data.

The second problem which Armstrong raises is concerned with the question of whether sense-data have a fully determinate character. He refers us to the classic case of the speckled hen. 'I may be able to see that it has quite a number of speckles, but unable to see exactly how many . . . The hen has a definite number of speckles, but the perception is a perception of an indeterminate number.'[15] Armstrong argues that, in such cases as this, the sense-datum theorist would have to take the sensory items to be, in the relevant respects, indeterminate in nature. 'The non-physical item that exists when we perceive the physical speckled hen will have to have an indeterminate number of speckles.'[16] And this, he again plausibly contends, is contrary to logic.

Once again, this is a problem which Ayer considers in *FEK*, and his response is the same: he accepts the indeterminacy, but regards it as unparadoxical. Thus concerning the case of someone who, having been struck on the head, has the experience of 'seeing stars', but is not aware of exactly how many, he writes:

We may . . . be tempted to assert that if he saw stars at all he must have seen a definite number; but that perhaps he was too dizzy to count them. But this would be a mistake. We should be assuming unjustifiably that what could be said about material things could also be said about sense-data. It is true that if the stars in question were physical objects, there would be a definite number of them, whether the observer was aware of it or not. But if we use the expression "seeing stars" to refer only to the sensing of certain sense-data, then, if the sense-data do not appear to be enumerable, they really are not enumerable. (*FEK*, 124)

Ayer thinks he can say this because, having introduced sense-data by terminological fiat, he feels free to fix their properties in the way he finds most convenient. And he finds it convenient to stipulate that sense-data are as they appear and appear as they are and thus to draw no 'distinction between that which is really given to an observer and that which he is aware of' (*FEK*, 125).

What Ayer seems to have overlooked, however, is that even stipulations must be subject to the rules of logic, and it is a rule of logic that any group of objects, of whatever sort, contains a definite number of members. To claim that a particular visual sense-datum contains finitely many components of a certain kind (e.g. speckle-shapes or star-shapes), but that the number of components is neither 0 nor 1 nor 2 nor 3 nor . . . , is just self-contradictory, and we cannot remove the contradiction by stipulating that sense-data are, unlike physical objects, to be entities which can be numerically indeterminate in this way. Admittedly, we do sometimes speak as if something is numerically indeterminate. We say, for example, that the average family contains between two and three children, without meaning that it contains two whole children and some portion of a third. But all this shows is that we do not intend the expression 'the average family' to refer to a genuine entity. In saying 'The average family contains between two and three children' we merely mean 'The average of the numbers of children contained by different families is a number between two and three.' Likewise, if the sense-datum terminology were just a *façon de parler*, so that all references to sense-data disappeared when sense-datum statements were re-expressed in plain terms, it would be possible to retain the indeterminacy thesis. But this would be to abandon the sense-datum theory, or the introduction of a sense-datum language in any interesting form.

As Armstrong himself notes, the sense-datum theorist has another line of defence, namely 'to say that the sensory items do have perfectly determinate characteristics, but that we are only *aware* of something less'.[17] Armstrong finds this unsatisfactory since it 'has the paradoxical consequence that objects specially postulated to do phenomenological justice to perception are now credited with characteristics that lie quite outside perceptual awareness'.[18] But here Armstrong is guilty of confusion. He is failing to distinguish between awareness-*of* and awareness-*that* – between the sensory awareness of a phenomenal object with certain characteristics and the cognitive awareness that the object has those characteristics. This distinction is the same as that which we drew in the case of the first problem, between what is phenomenally apparent and what is cognitively apparent. It is true that, by defending the sense-datum theory in the suggested way, we credit sense-data with characteristics which lie outside the scope of the subject's *cognitive* awareness, in that the subject does not know, and perhaps even with introspective attention cannot tell, what determinate characteristics obtain. But we do not credit sense-data with characteristics which lie outside the scope of the subject's sensory awareness. Precisely because sense-data are internal objects of sense-awareness, two episodes of sense-awareness are experiences of different intrinsic types if the determinate properties of the two sense-data are different. And this is so whether or not the difference is one which the subject can, by introspection, detect. There is no problem for the sense-datum theory here.

We must conclude, then, that not only is Armstrong's own theory wrong, but, in failing to take account of the distinction between sensory and cognitive awareness, his criticisms of the sense-datum theory are misconceived. It does not, of course, follow from this that the sense-datum theory is correct. For although the cognitive theory is its main rival, there are other theories to be considered, and it is possible that one of these will turn out to be preferable to either. This is not a question which I have time to look into in any detail. But I shall end by briefly reviewing the other options. As far as I can see, there are only four which deserve consideration; and in my view all but the last, which is no more than a modification of the sense-datum theory, should be rejected.

Firstly, someone who is basically sympathetic to the cognitive theory might claim that there is some kind of propositional attitude ψ such that:

(1) ψ-ing is an experiential state in a way that believing is not;
(2) ψ-ing that p inclines one to believe that p, or would do so in the absence of any contrary beliefs;
(3) like believing, ψ-ing does not entail truth, i.e. 'S ψs that p' does not entail 'It is true that p'.

He might then claim that the correct theory of perceptual experience is what results from the cognitive theory by substituting ψ-ing for believing. The idea would be that, because ψ-ing is an experiential state, the theory would not be vulnerable to the objections which undermined the cognitive theory.

All I can say about this proposal is that I cannot think of what this ψ-state would be. It is true that we can introduce some locution such as

'It experientially seems to the subject that . . .' which appears to express what is required. But the problems emerge when we try to unpack what this means. I cannot see what the experiential seeming could be other than either the subject's having some experience which inclines him to believe that . . ., or his having some experience which constitutes *prima facie* evidence that. . . . And, either way, we are left with no account of the nature of the experience as such.

Secondly, it might be suggested that while sense-experience is to be characterized not as some kind of propositional attitude, but as the awareness of something, the objects of this awareness are only 'intentional'. That is to say, sense-awareness is to be thought of as a special kind of experiential conceiving. Just as I can, in the ordinary way, form a conception of a unicorn, without there having to be a real unicorn which is thus conceived, so, when I have a visual experience, what occurs in my mind is a visual conception of a physical colour-arrangement, without there having to be an actual arrangement of that sort which is thus conceived. The mistake of the sense-datum theorist is to construe sense-awareness as a genuine relation, between a subject and a really existent object. For it is this, together with the possibility of hallucination, which forces him to postulate his non-physical sensory items.

The main drawback of this proposal is that it leaves no room for a distinction, with respect to intrinsic character, between sense-experience and mental imaging. For if sense-awareness is only a special kind of experiential conceiving, there can be no intrinsic difference, when they are directed onto the same sensible quality-pattern, between visual sense-awareness and 'seeing in one's mind's eye' or between auditory sense-awareness and 'hearing with one's mind's ear'. The undermining of this distinction is problematic in more than one way. To begin with, the distinction itself is, I think, a genuine one. There does seem, introspectively, to be a difference in intrinsic character between my awareness of a colour-patch when I am looking at something and my awareness of a colour-patch when I am merely visualizing it. And, in my view, attempts to explain away this apparent difference are unsatisfactory.[19] Moreover, unless we preserve this distinction – by taking sense-awareness to be something different from mere experiential conceiving – it will not, as far as I can see, be possible to give an adequate account of imaging itself. For surely what gives imaging its distinctive character, in relation to ordinary, non-imagist modes of conceiving, is that there is something else, not itself a form of conceiving, of which it is, as it were, the conceptual replica. In short, and putting both points together, if we construe sense-awareness as a form of conceiving, we cannot do justice either to the distinctive character of sense-experience or to the distinctive character of mental imaging.

Thirdly, some philosophers[20] have suggested that we should think of the sensible qualities as characterizing sense-experience in an 'adverbial' way, so that instead of saying 'S visually senses a red triangular patch' and 'S visually senses a chequered pattern of white and black squares', we should say 'S visually senses red-triangularly' and 'S visually senses chequer-patterned-white-and-black-squarely'.

Unless this adverbial account is just a prelude to something more radical (such as a cognitive or an intentional account), the difference between it and the sense-datum theory is not, from a metaphysical standpoint, of much importance. Both theories accept that sensible qualities are genuinely *realized* in sense-experience, as opposed to just featuring in the content of some propositional attitude or conception. Where they differ is over the ontological character of this realization, the sense-datum theorist taking the qualities to characterize an internal object of awareness, the adverbialist taking them to characterize the mode of awareness. With respect to all the major philosophical issues concerned with perception and the physical world, there is not much at stake here. None the less, to the extent that it does differ from the sense-datum theory, I think that the adverbial theory is clearly wrong. There are, indeed, a number of technical difficulties in even constructing an adverbial terminology for describing the content of sense-experience in the required way.[21] But even if these difficulties can be overcome, the adverbial theory is simply not in keeping with the phenomenology of experience as introspection reveals it. Indeed, if sense-experience were as the adverbialist construes it, there would be no way of explaining why, prior to philosophical reflection, we find it so natural to be naive realists. For how could we suppose ourselves to have a wholly unmediated awareness of physical objects unless there is something presented – some internal object of awareness – which we mistakenly interpret as an item in the external world?[22]

Finally, some philosophers who are basically sympathetic to the sense-datum theory find it more natural to take the immediate and internal objects of sense-awareness to be not (as we have defined sense-data to be) private and momentary particulars, but intersubjective and repeatable universals. Thus when someone visually senses a certain colour-array, instead of construing this array as a sensory particular, confined to that momentary episode of awareness, these philosophers construe it as a sensory universal, which can be empirically realized in different minds and at different times. This is a strategy which Ayer himself comes to favour in his later writings,[23] where, adopting the terminology of C. I. Lewis and Nelson Goodman, he calls these universals 'qualia'.[24]

The only point which needs to be made about this proposal is that it does not constitute a rival to the sense-datum theory in any deep sense – not even in the sense in which the sense-datum and adverbial theories are rivals. Both the sense-datum theory and the qualia theory accept that sensible qualities are experientially realized and both accept that they are realized as elements of phenomenal objects. They differ only in the identity-conditions they impose on these objects – the one tying the identity of an object to the occasion of its presentation, the other allowing the same object to be presented on any number of occasions. If there are subtle reasons for preferring the qualia theory (and I am inclined to think that there are), they need not concern us in our present investigation.

11 *Sense-experience and the physical world*

One way of trying to avoid scepticism about the physical world is by adopting the reductionist strategy of the linguistic phenomenalist. In its strongest form, linguistic phenomenalism claims that statements about physical objects can be translated into equivalent statements about sense-data, where the latter statements make no explicit reference to physical entities and are entirely devoid of any distinctively physical vocabulary. It also claims that the concepts employed in sensory statements are more basic than the physical concepts employed in the statements they translate, so that we are to see the rules of translation into the phenomenal language as constituting an exhaustive analysis of physical concepts in sensory terms. If we want fully to understand the content of a physical statement, it is to its sensory translation that we must turn. Consequently, we might call phenomenalism in this strong form 'analytical phenomenalism', and this is how I shall refer to it in what follows.

The way in which analytical phenomenalism might be thought to offer an escape from scepticism is clear. If physical statements can be translated into sensory statements, then, by consulting the translation manual, we can expect to be able to deduce physical conclusions from a record of our sensory evidence. Of course, even to yield the simplest physical conclusion, the sensory evidence will presumably have to be fairly extensive. To establish that there is a desk in this room, I cannot simply appeal to my current visual experience, or even the series of experiences which I have had since entering the room a few minutes ago. For these experiences could be illusory. But if a particular experience, or series of experiences, is illusory, it is so, according to the phenomenalist, only because it deviates from, and thus misrepresents, some larger sensory theme. It is by surveying the whole course of sense-experience, with a view to discovering what is regular and predictable, that we can hope to establish, via the phenomenalistic analysis, what physical facts obtain. Where exactly this leaves the sceptic is something which we shall examine in due course.

As we saw in Part I, analytical phenomenalism is not the only form of phenomenalism, though it is the only one to which Ayer accords the title. In a sense, of course, this is just a question of terminology. But in default of any other term to play this role, it is convenient to use the term 'phenomenalism' in a broad sense, to cover any position which takes physical facts to be nothing over and above sensory facts. And some of these positions would not allow for a full analytical reduction of the sort which Ayer requires. For example, someone might claim that, for each physical statement S, there is an infinite range R of possible sensory situations such that:

(1) each R-situation would, if it obtained, logically suffice for the truth of S;
(2) the truth of S logically requires that some R-situation obtain;
(3) there is no sensory statement, however complex, which expresses the infinite disjunction of all R-situations.

Such a position counts as a form of phenomenalism in the broad sense, since it takes physical facts to be nothing over and above sensory facts. But it does not meet the conditions of analytical phenomenalism, which claims that physical facts can be exactly expressed in sensory terms. In effect, it allows the physical language a certain kind of conceptual autonomy, in that what physical sentences express cannot be expressed in any other way, but, as a form of phenomenalism, it insists that whatever physical facts obtain, obtain solely in virtue of sensory facts.[25]

We have already seen how, under the influence of his verification principle, Ayer accepted analytical phenomenalism in *LTL*, and we have examined in some detail his unsuccessful attempt to elaborate this position by his 'analysis of the notion of a material thing' (*LTL*, 66). But it did not take Ayer long to abandon phenomenalism in this analytical form. He soon came to see that, even from the standpoint of his strong verification principle, a strict translation of physical statements into sensory statements was unnecessary. And, more crucially, he also came to think that such translation was in principle impossible. Part of what influenced him, with respect to this latter conclusion, was the apparently unlimited number of ways in which a physical state of affairs can manifest itself through sense-experience. Even if the truth of a physical statement could be logically established on the basis of purely sensory evidence, there seem to be infinitely many different kinds of possible sensory evidence that would serve equally well (if any of them serve well) for the same physical statement, and Ayer despaired of being able to find, within the confines of the phenomenal language, a finite way of covering the range.

> . . . if we try to describe what at any given moment would afford
> us direct evidence for the truth of a statement about a material thing

by putting forward a disjunction of statements about sense-data . . .
this disjunction will have to be infinite. (*FEK*, 241)

This would force the would-be phenomenalist into the position we envisaged above, which claims that, for each physical statement, there is an
infinite range of possible sensory situations which are individually
sufficient and disjunctively necessary for its truth, but concedes that
there is no sensory statement which exactly expresses the generic situation
defined by their disjunction.

This objection to analytical phenomenalism is one which we have
already encountered in our earlier discussion, and, as far as I can see, it
is correct. But Ayer also claims, in the same book, to have found a
further, though analogous, objection. For he argues that not only would
we need, for each physical statement, an infinite disjunction of sensory
statements to cover the range of situations which suffice for its truth,
but also each of these sensory situations would itself be one which could
not be finitely specified in the phenomenal language. He takes this to be
a consequence of the fact that physical statements cannot be *conclusively*
verified: by undergoing a series of sense-experiences, someone can
accumulate evidence in favour of some physical statement, but 'he can
never reach a stage at which it ceases to be conceivable that further sense-
experience will reverse the verdict of the previous evidence' (*FEK*, 239).
And from this he correctly infers that 'no finite set of singular statements
about sense-data can ever formally entail a statement about a material
thing' (*FEK*, 239). (His use of the word 'formally' here is somewhat
deviant. What he means is 'genuinely, i.e. logically, entail' as opposed
to 'materially imply'.)

In a later article entitled 'Phenomenalism',[26] Ayer expressed doubts
about the premise of this argument. He came to think that perhaps, after
all, a finite series of sense-experiences could conclusively establish the
truth of a physical statement, despite the possibility of further contrary
evidence. But even if the premise is correct, it does not establish as much
as Ayer supposes. It does indeed establish, as Ayer claims, that no
physical statement is entailed by any finite set of *singular* statements
about sense-data – a singular statement being one which records, or
purports to record, the occurrence of a single sense-datum to a particular
subject at a particular time. But since the phenomenal language will have
resources for generalization – both simple generalization by means of a
universal quantification (e.g. 'all sense-data are . . .') and, maybe, more
complex forms employing set-theory and mathematics – many sensory
statements will entail more than is entailed by any conjunctive list of
singular statements. And, for all Ayer has shown, some of them may
entail statements about material things. This is not just a quibble. After
all, Ayer's point seems to be that, however extensive it is, a finite

series of sense-experiences favourable to the truth of a certain physical statement might turn out to be deviant and evidentially misleading in the context of the total sensory story. If so, then to provide sensory statements with the required entailments, the phenomenalist must take care to construct them in such a way that the possibility of deviance is excluded. And it is precisely by employing forms of generalization which transcend any mere listing of sensory singularities that he can hope to achieve this.

At all events, in *FEK* Ayer rejects analytical phenomenalism on the grounds that the factual content of a physical statement cannot be finitely expressed in sensory terms. It may be that, for each physical statement, there is a range of possible sensory situations which are individually sufficient and disjunctively necessary for its truth. But Ayer thinks that nothing short of an infinite disjunction of sensory statements would be sufficiently weak to cover the full range, and that nothing short of an infinite conjunction of sensory statements would be sufficiently strong to specify a given situation. Either of these points would preclude a translation of physical statements into sensory statements, in the way which analytical phenomenalism requires.

In his later article, Ayer advances a further objection to analytical phenomenalism. The objection is repeated in *PK*, and I shall follow the text of the book, where it is expressed more simply. He begins by noting that, because physical objects, unlike sense-data, can exist unperceived, the analytical phenomenalist is obliged 'to hold that the statements about sense-data, into which, according to his programme, statements about physical objects are to be translated, are themselves predominantly hypothetical' (*PK*, 119).

> They will for the most part have to state not that any sense-data are actually occurring, but only that in a given set of circumstances certain sense-data would occur. In other words, the majority of the statements will not describe how things actually do seem to anyone, but only how they would seem if the appropriate conditions were fulfilled. (*PK*, 119–20)

Some critics of analytical phenomenalism object to this procedure on the grounds that it allows unperceived physical objects and events only a hypothetical existence. Ayer rightly dismisses this objection as mere confusion:

> It is quite true that sentences which express hypothetical statements about sense-data are not being used to assert that any sense-data are occurring, but it does not follow that they are not being used to assert that any physical events are occurring, or that any physical objects exist. On the contrary, this is just what they do serve to

assert, if phenomenalism is correct. (*PK*, 121; by 'phenomenalism', of course, Ayer means *analytical* phenomenalism.)

However, he does see the procedure as problematic in another way. The problem concerns the vocabulary used in formulating the antecedent clauses in these hypothetical statements – the clauses which specify the circumstances in which the relevant types of sense-data would occur.

It is not enough for the phenomenalist to make such vague assertions as that what he means by saying that there is a table in the next room is that if he were there he would perceive it. For his being there is a matter of a physical body's being in a certain spatial relationship to other physical objects, and, on the assumption that to talk about physical objects is always to talk about sense-data, this situation must itself be described in purely sensory terms. But it is not at all easy to see how this could be done. (*PK*, 123)

Indeed it is not. Perhaps we could try by reformulating the conditional in some such way as this: 'If *n* seconds ago [or the equivalent in experiential time] I had embarked on a sensory course of *n* seconds [or its experiential equivalent] and of such and such a type [intuitively, a sensory course corresponding to my walking to and into the next room], I should now be having such and such sense-data [intuitively, those appropriate to perceiving a table].' But one objection to this is that there is no guarantee that the pursuit of this sensory course will take the subject to the room in question. It may be that, if the physical environment is sufficiently homogeneous, there is more than one physical destination that he could reach by a series of experiences of the specified type; and, in any case, if he were having a protracted hallucination (which would still be possible even from a phenomenalist standpoint), he could have this series of experiences without physically moving at all. A further objection is that, even if the pursuit of this sensory course did ensure his arrival at the relevant room, this is hardly something which is implicit in the content of the physical statement. In merely saying that there is a table in the next room, the subject is surely not, even implicitly, saying anything about the scenic character of a hypothetical journey to it. Indeed, if we had chosen a different example (e.g. 'there is a church ten miles due north'), the subject might have virtually no idea of what such a journey would be like. Of course, this is not the only way of trying to reformulate the conditional. We could try specifying the subject's hypothetical location in the next room not in terms of a sensory journey, but in terms of the experiences (apart from that relating to the table) which he would have if he were there. But exactly the same objections would apply. The specification would not guarantee the physical location; and even if it did, the fact that the room has that distinctive sensible appearance is not something which can be deduced from the original statement.

Nor do the difficulties stop there. Even if we could specify, in purely sensory terms, what it is for the subject to be in the appropriate place at the appropriate time, his location at that place and time, together with the truth of the physical statement, would not guarantee the occurrence of the relevant sense-data. Someone might be in the room without perceiving the table it contains. Ayer makes the point with respect to a different example drawn from a famous passage in Berkeley's principles. Berkeley, in what amounted to a modification of his doctrine of *esse est percipi*, claimed that to say that the earth moves (although its motion is not actually perceived) is to say that 'if we were placed in such and such circumstances, and such or such a position and distance, both from the earth and sun, we should perceive the former to move'.[27]

> But, setting aside the difficulty . . . of describing the circumstances in purely sensory terms, it might very well happen that when we were placed in them we did not perceive the earth to move at all, not because it was not moving, but because we were inattentive, or looking in the wrong direction, or our view was in some way obscured, or because we were suffering from some physiological or psychological disorder. It might indeed be thought that such obstacles could be provided for. Thus we might attempt to rule out the possibility of the observer's suffering from a physiological disorder by adding a further hypothetical to the effect that if a physiologist were to examine him, or rather, were to seem to be examining him, it would seem to the physiologist that his patient's vision was unimpaired. But then we should require a further hypothetical to guard against the possibility that the physiologist himself was undergoing an illusion: and so *ad infinitum*. (*PK*, 127–8)

Ayer concludes that, for all these reasons, as well as those already elaborated in *FEK*, the programme of the analytical phenomenalist 'cannot be carried through' and that 'statements about physical objects are not formally translatable into statements about sense-data' (*PK*, 129). In this, I am sure he is correct.

The failure of analytical phenomenalism does not, of course, entail the failure of phenomenalism as such, in the broad sense in which I am using the term. We could still hold that physical facts are wholly sustained by, and nothing over and above, sensory facts, while recognizing that no physical statement can be exactly re-expressed in sensory terms. And indeed Ayer's initial response is, in effect, to retain this phenomenalist position, though in his terminology it does not qualify for that title. Thus in *FEK*, having argued against the translation-thesis on the grounds that physical facts cannot be finitely expressed in the phenomenal language, he writes:

> . . . one must not then conclude that to speak about a material thing is to speak about something altogether different from sense-data, or that it is to speak about sense-data but about something else besides. For that would be a mistake analogous to that of supposing that . . . because sentences referring to "someone" cannot be translated into a finite disjunction of sentences referring to particular persons, therefore "someone" is the name of a peculiar being . . . who is distinct from any person that one can actually meet. If we cannot produce the required translations of sentences referring to material things into sentences referring to sense-data, the reason is not that it is untrue that "to say anything about a material thing is always to say something about sense-data", but only that one's references to material things are vague in their application to phenomena and that the series of sense-data that they may be understood to specify are composed of infinite sets of terms. (*FEK*, 241–2)

A similar thought occurs in the much later *PK*:

> It is because this process [that of sensory verification] is fluid that phenomenalism comes to grief. It is not that physical objects lurk behind a veil which we can never penetrate. It is rather that every apparent situation which we take as verifying or falsifying the statements which we make about them leaves other possibilities open. The phenomenalists are right in the sense that the information which we convey by speaking about the physical objects that we perceive is information about the way that things would seem, but they are wrong in supposing that it is possible to say of the description of any particular set of appearances that this and only this is what some statement about a physical object comes to. Speaking of physical objects is a way of interpreting our sense-experiences; but one cannot delimit in advance the range of experiences to which such interpretations may have to be adjusted. (*PK*, 131–2; again 'phenomenalism' here means *analytical* phenomenalism.)

If Ayer is right, then what is wrong with analytical phenomenalism is not its phenomenalism, but its strict analytical character. It fails not because physical statements describe a reality external to human minds, but because they describe the realm of human sense-experience in ways which the phenomenal language, with its explicit confinement to an ontology of sense-data, cannot exactly express. In speaking of physical objects, we do not ultimately commit ourselves to the existence of entities external to human experience, but the apparent commitment to such entities enables us to say things about sense-experience which cannot be said in any other way. It enables us to reach a level of theory with respect to sense-experience which we cannot reach in the phenomenal language itself.

But what is this level of theory? If the sensory realm is ontologically exhaustive and analytical phenomenalism is false, what descriptive purpose does the physical language serve? Well, the first point to notice is that there is something orderly and predictable about human sense-experience. This must be so, since if sense-experience were purely random, we would never be led to make physical judgments on its basis. In some way, our physical theories are a response to the systematic character of our experience – to the fact that, in a multiplicity of different ways, experience is regular and thematic. But there is a second and more important point. Although, human sense-experience is in some way orderly, and has to be if it is to form a basis for physical judgments, the orderliness cannot be specified, except very roughly and partially, in purely sensory terms. To achieve an adequate specification, or anything approaching it, we have to relate the experiential realm, if only hypothetically, to some external reality. We have to begin by thinking of ourselves, at least hypothetically, as observers in a three-dimensional space, which contains objects with sensible qualities, and we have to think of our sense-experiences as (predominantly) veridical presentations, or representations, of these objects, in respect of their sensible qualities, subject to the perspective of our current viewpoint and conditions of observation. And, to bring out the orderliness in full, we have eventually to think of these objects as possessing other and non-sensible qualities, such as properties of internal constitution, in virtue of which they causally interact with each other in various ways and through which, via the stimulation of our sense-organs, they are perceptible to us in their sensible guise. In short, we have to envisage the experiential realm as part of a much larger reality – a reality containing not only human minds and their experiences, but also an external world, with laws controlling the events in it and the effects of these events on human experience. And we can then specify the sensory order, to whatever level of detail is required, by specifying the relevant aspects of this larger reality and saying that our sense-experiences are as they would be if such a reality obtained. Saying this does not, of course, imply that such a reality does obtain. Experience could be orderly in this way, specified in terms of such a reality, even if the experiential realm is all that there is.

Given this, we can see how, from the phenomenalist standpoint, the physical language gives us access to a new level of theory with respect to sense-experience. For, from this standpoint, physical statements, with their apparent function of describing an external world, become devices for describing the various aspects of the sensory order – an order which cannot be adequately specified within the phenomenal language itself. The only remaining question would be how we come to take advantage of this new level of theory if the facts which it describes cannot be specified in sensory terms. For it seems that it would only be after we had learnt to interpret our experiences in physical terms that the need for such interpretation would become apparent. However, the fact that the sensory order cannot be fully or exactly specified in sensory terms does not mean that it is totally concealed at the sensory level – that the course of experience, described within the limits of the phenomenal language, would appear completely random. Obviously, even at the sensory level certain crude tendencies and partial regularities are discernible, and it is these which prompt our initial steps in physical interpretation, in which we think of ourselves as percipients of an external arrangement of sensible qualities in a three-dimensional space. Once we have made this interpretation, which itself transcends the aspects of order which prompted it, then further aspects of order become discernible, prompting us to higher levels of physical theory, and so on. At each stage, the success of our physical theories shows the need for, and points us in the direction of, further theoretical developments.

It is to the task of specifying the earliest stages in this process that Ayer turns in the final sections of *FEK*, where he tries 'to explain what are the relations between sense-data that make it possible for us successfully to employ the physical terminology that we do' and to show 'what are the general principles on which, from our resources of sense-data, we "construct" the world of material things' (*FEK*, 243). The construction he outlines, with characteristic elegance, is not a 'logical' construction of the kind which, as an *analytical* phenomenalist, he sought in *LTL*: it does not involve translating statements about material things into statements about sense-data, since the possibility of this has already been rejected. Rather, it is, as Ayer himself notes, reminiscent of the imaginative process by which Hume thought that we come to attribute a continued and distinct existence to the sensible objects we immediately perceive, in response to their relations of 'constancy' and 'coherence'. The main difference, apart from the details of the construction, is that while Hume took himself to be causally explaining the genesis of a false and indeed incoherent belief, Ayer, as a phenomenalist, claims to be showing, in outline, what the continued and distinct existence of these objects amounts to: he is claiming to show how the postulation of these ostensibly external continuants merely serves to characterize, in a form which we cannot adequately reproduce in the phenomenal language, certain aspects of the sensory order. In this way, Ayer sees himself not as explaining away, but as justifying our physical beliefs, by showing that their ultimate subject matter is experience itself.

All this is very ingenious, but there is still the fundamental question of whether the phenomenalist standpoint itself is correct. One obvious objection to it, which we have already encountered in our discussion of *LTL*, is that phenomenalism of any sort seems to be in conflict with what our physical statements actually mean. When I say that there is a desk in this room, my statement will indeed be based, in some way, on my current and previous sense-experiences. And I may, in some sense, be conveying information about the character of my experiences and about the character of the experiences potentially available to myself and others in suitable conditions of observation. But my statement does not seem to be, as such, a statement about experience – at least not exclusively about experience. Rather, it seems to be a statement about some external and mind-independent reality, and if such a reality does not exist, it seems that the statement is simply false. In short, it seems that physical statements have a realist conception of the physical world built into their meaning.

This is not the only problem for the phenomenalist. For if the physical world is just the product of the sensory order, what explains the order? Why should our experience be organized exactly as if there were a certain kind of external reality, if no such reality exists? This question could perhaps be evaded if the organization could be specified in purely sensory terms. Maybe in such a case the phenomenalist could take the laws of experience to be autonomous and deny that the sensory order needs to be explained in terms of anything else. But if the sensory order can only be adequately specified in terms of the sort of reality whose existence is being denied, the situation is much more perplexing. The sort of experiential laws which would be needed to sustain such an order would be of an exceedingly peculiar kind. Of course, if he is prepared to accept the existence of God, the phenomenalist does have a fairly straightforward solution. He can, like Berkeley, claim that human experience is directly controlled by divine volition and that its orderliness is explained by the consistency of God's volitional policies and the purpose they are designed to serve. I myself find such an account congenial. But it has not, in general, found favour with modern phenomenalists. And it would certainly not be palatable to Ayer.

This problem about the sensory order is relevant to our discussion in another way. The phenomenalist might be tempted to plead that, even if there are difficulties in his position, it at least has the merit of avoiding the sceptical problem which other theories, by acknowledging the 'veil of perception', create. However, the realist might well reply that the very need to explain the sensory order provides a justification for our ordinary physical beliefs, as he construes them. As we saw in section 8, one way of trying to answer the sceptic's challenge is by adopting what Ayer calls the 'scientific approach', an approach which, in the case of the physical world, is founded on an inference to the best explanation.

186

Thus taking the experiential realm to be what we called the 'observable domain', the realist could argue that the orderliness of experience is something which calls for explanation, that no satisfactory explanation can be found within the experiential realm itself, and that the best explanation is achieved by expanding our ontology to include an external reality of just the kind which our ordinary physical beliefs, realistically construed, specify. Such an argument is intuitively plausible, and its plausibility is enhanced by the fact that it is only by reference to the realist's explanation that the sensory order can even be specified. The only way we have of adequately describing the respects in which sense-experience is orderly and systematic is by saying that our experience is as it would be if the realist's explanation were correct. Of course, this does not prove that the realist's explanation *is* correct. We could still fall back on Berkeley's position, which provides a different explanation for the sensory order and one which (taking into account God's purposes) explains why it is only in terms of the realist's (allegedly mistaken) explanation that the order can be specified. But unless there are independent arguments for the phenomenalist position (which, of course, Berkeley thought there were), it would be perverse to regard this as the best explanation. Given the possibility of a mind-independent physical world, the realist's explanation does seem to be the most plausible one. And in that respect, the realist does have, from his own standpoint, a *prima facie* defence against the sceptic, though whether it is fully adequate is something which we shall examine presently.

Curiously, even in his phenomenalist period, Ayer sometimes speaks of our physical beliefs as a theory to explain sense-experience. Thus in 'Phenomenalism', having argued against the possibility of exact translation, he concludes:

If this line of argument is correct, then the solution of the 'problem of perception' may be to treat our beliefs about physical objects as constituting a theory, the function of which is to explain the course of our sensory experiences. (*PE*, 165)

But he sees this solution not as a form of realism, postulating a mind-independent physical world, but as a way of preserving the essential core of phenomenalism. Thus he continues:

The statements which are expressed in terms of the theory may not then be capable of being reproduced exactly as statements about sense-data; that is, it may not be possible wholly to rewrite them as statements about sense-data. Nevertheless, they will function only as a means of grouping sense-data. (*PE*, 165)

Obviously, in saying that the theory *explains* the course of our sensory experience, Ayer is using the term 'explains' in an unusually weak sense.

It is not that the theory offers any causal explanation of sense-experience or tells us why it is organized as it is. The explanation, in Ayer's sense, is just the description of the organization – a description which transcends the resources of the phenomenal language, but does not imply the existence of a reality beyond sense-experience itself.

There are similar remarks in *PK*, where Ayer speaks of our physical beliefs as forming a 'theory which accounts for our experiences' (*PK*, 133), a theory which is 'richer than anything that could be yielded by an attempt to reformulate it at the sensory level', but without having 'any other supply of wealth than the phenomena over which it ranges' (*PK*, 132). But he also adds something which, by its apparent equivocation, makes the nature of his position harder to discern:

> Accordingly, it does not greatly matter whether we say that the objects which figure in it [the theory] are theoretical constructions or whether, in line with common sense, we prefer to say that they are independently real. The ground for saying that they are *not* constructions is that the references to them cannot be eliminated in favour of references to sense-data. The ground for saying they *are* constructions is that it is only through their relationship to our sense-experiences that a meaning is given to what we say about them. (*PK*, 132)

At first sight, this passage suggests some weakening of Ayer's commitment to phenomenalism. For how else could he countenance saying that physical objects are independently real? However, I think that on closer scrutiny, both of the passage and of its context, we can see that the phenomenalist position is being retained. Ayer has already said, in the passage we quoted earlier, that 'the phenomenalists are right in the sense that the information which we convey by speaking about the physical objects that we perceive is information about the way that things would seem' and that consequently physical objects do not 'lurk behind a veil which we can never penetrate' (*PK*, 131). The only error he found in phenomenalism was its commitment to *translation*, and, in my terminology, this is a commitment of only one version of phenomenalism, not a commitment of phenomenalism as such. Consequently, in allowing us to speak of physical objects as independently real, his only point, I think, is to underline the conceptual autonomy of the physical language. He sees that physical objects pose as entities with an ontological life of their own, since 'the references to them cannot be eliminated in favour of references to sense-data' (*PK*, 132). But I think he is still endorsing the phenomenalist's claim that the existence of such entities is wholly sustained by facts about sense-data.

At the same time, I think we should see, in the apparent equivocation, a certain tension which is developing in Ayer's thought. He has, of course, always been aware of the intuitive objection that phenomenalism does not do justice to the actual meanings of our physical statements. But, with the failure of analytical phenomenalism, he is beginning to appreciate the difficulty of finding an adequate answer to it. Our physical language *seems* to represent physical objects as independently real. If we cannot reformulate our physical statements in sensory terms, why should we regard this appearance as illusory? In *FEK*, Ayer could fall back on the verification principle in its content-restricting form: physical statements, if they are to be meaningful at all, have to be construed in conformity with the phenomenalist standpoint, since otherwise they would not have a purely observational content. But by the time of *PK* his commitment to this principle has become weaker: even if the principle has not been entirely abandoned, there is a growing reluctance to rely on it in cases where its consequences are counterintuitive. This does not mean that Ayer is any less firm in his conviction that if physical statements are to be meaningful, they must be open to empirical verification (though not necessarily conclusive verification). But just as he is beginning to appreciate the intuitive difficulties with phenomenalism, so he is also beginning to see that, given the explanatory role of our physical beliefs, there may be a way of securing the verifiability of physical statements within the framework of realism.

At all events, *PK* marks the end of Ayer's phenomenalistic phase. For, from now on, his thought develops in the direction of realism; and this development reaches its fruition in his book *The Origins of Pragmatism* (*OP*), and its sequels *The Central Questions of Philosophy* (*CQ*) and *Russell and Moore*, where a realist position is explicitly defended. Admittedly, the presentation of this new position retains much of the phenomenalistic flavour of his earlier work. Once again we find Ayer outlining the general principles on which, from our resources of sense-experience, we 'construct' the physical world. And once again we find, in the stage-by-stage construction, the physical theory being developed through different levels of sophistication to cover, with increasing scope and precision, the various aspects of the sensory order. The crucial difference is that, as Ayer now sees it, the world which emerges by this constructive process becomes ontologically independent of its sensory origins. The theory is developed to a point where the physical objects it postulates are thought of not just as representations of the sensory order, but as independently real, and, indeed, as causally responsible for the 'percepts' from which they have been constructed.[28] Indeed, as Ayer sees it, the physical theory, though epistemologically derivative, becomes ontologically dominant.

. . . once the theory . . . has been developed . . . we are entitled to

let it take command, in the sense that it determines what there is.
(CQ, 105–6)

We are entitled to do this, he thinks, even at the cost of downgrading
the sensory starting-point, by re-interpreting percepts as states (though
not necessarily *physical* states) of corporeal observers and thus logically
dependent for their occurrence on the existence of the physical world.

In the end, then, Ayer comes, as he puts it, 'to forsake phenomenalism
for a sophisticated form of realism' (CQ, 108). He accepts the realist's
conception of the physical world (the conception of the physical world
as objective and mind-independent), because it is the conception which
the physical theory itself imposes.

> Under the dominion of the theory which is erected on the basis of
> our primitive experiential propositions, the existence of visuo-
> tactual continuants becomes a matter of objective fact. (CQ, 108)

And, in addition, he thinks that we are justified in accepting the physical
theory (thus realistically construed), because, as his account of the
construction reveals, it best explains the course of our experience. It may
be wondered why Ayer describes the form of realism he now accepts as
'sophisticated'. For the world of objective visuo-tactual continuants is
just the physical world of common sense. But the sophistication lies not
in the common-sense view itself, but in Ayer's method of vindicating it.
It lies in the fact that the common-sense view is represented as something
which we can reach, by steps of imaginative construction, from the
starting-point of sensory experience, and as something which we can
justify, in retrospect, by an appeal to its explanatory role.

Given this, it is not surprising that he sees the course he has followed,
in answer to the sceptic, as 'a variant of . . . the scientific approach'
(CQ, 108) – the approach in which, as he earlier put it, 'the existence
of physical objects . . . is represented . . . as a probable hypothesis which
one is justified in accepting because of the way in which it accounts for
one's experiences' (CQ, 66). But he adds a qualification:

> It would, indeed, be somewhat misleading to say that we are
> representing the existence of physical objects as a probable
> hypothesis, since this description would ordinarily be taken to apply
> to propositions that lie within the framework of our general theory,
> rather than to the principles of the theory itself. (CQ, 108)

His point is that while we can represent such statements as 'There is a
desk in this room' or 'Some trees are deciduous' as probable hypotheses,
supported by our sensory evidence, the fundamental ontological postulates of the theory, such as the postulation of a three-dimensional space
and space-occupying continuants, form the very framework in which

the evidential significance of our experiences is assessed. And this point, of course, reflects the fact that, until we have constructed the ontological framework, we cannot even specify the organization of sense-experience in any but the roughest and most desultory fashion. This does not mean that on Ayer's view, as on Kant's, the 'general theory' has an *a priori* status. Like the more specific physical beliefs which presuppose it, it has to prove its validity through the test of experience.

> The theory is vindicated not indeed by any special set of observations but by the general features of our experience on which it is founded, and since these features are contingent, it could conceivably be falsified, in the sense that our experiences might in general be such that it failed to account for them. (*CQ*, 108)

And it is in this sense that Ayer sees the justification of our belief in the existence of physical space and physical objects as resting on an inference to the best explanation, even though the need for such an explanation only becomes fully apparent in the perspective of the belief itself.

Whether Ayer's new-found realism is correct is not something which I shall further pursue (though I have tried to defend my own version of phenomenalism elsewhere[29]). But I want to put on record my admiration for the way in which he expounds it. His characterization of the steps by which the realist physical theory evolves from its sensory origins (in *OP*, II, 3, C, and *CQ*, V) is philosophical writing of the highest calibre, in which analytical rigour and constructive artistry are perfectly blended. If I have been unable to explore this work in sufficient detail, I would encourage the reader to pause and sample it for himself.

12 *Scepticism reconsidered*

Our recent discussion might suggest that, depending on one's conception of the physical world, either the 'scientific approach' or phenomenalism would provide an effective defence against the sceptic's attack. As Ayer represents him, the sceptic is denying the legitimacy of the inference from sensory premises to physical conclusions. But given the sensory order, it seems we can justify that inference in either of the suggested ways. If we conceive of the physical world realistically, we can regard our physical beliefs as affording the best explanation of the sensory order, and if we conceive of it phenomenalistically, we can take physical facts to be what the sensory order logically sustains. Either way, it seems we have a secure route from the premises to the conclusions, whether by bridging the gap by a form of explanatory reasoning or by closing it altogether.[30]

However, the issue is not quite so simple. For, as we noted earlier (in section 8), by focusing exclusively on the status of the inference, Ayer understates the force of the sceptical challenge. The sceptic is concerned not only with the legitimacy of the inference, but also with whether we are justified in believing the premises. And, as we shall see, it is far from clear that we are; or, at least, it is far from clear that we are justified in believing a sufficient number and range of premises to support any physical conclusion.

One problem here is that most of our information about the course of human sense-experience is itself evidentially grounded on our information about the physical world. This is obviously so in the case of one subject having information about the experiences of another. For such information is only available to the extent that the character of the other subject's experiences is revealed by his verbal and non-verbal behaviour and his physical circumstances. But it is also true in the case of a subject's knowledge of his own past experiences. I believe that my past experiences have collectively exhibited a certain orderliness – an orderliness which, depending on whether one adopts a realist or a phenomenalist position, is either best explained by or most fully and exactly described by the physical theory I accept. But I only believe this to be so because I already accept the existence of a physical world and accept a certain account of the way in which my experiences and physical circumstances are systematically linked. It is true that I can, or think I can, directly remember (whether perceptually or factually) a number of my past experiences. But even here I rely heavily on my recollection of physical circumstances in fixing their temporal order, the temporal distances between them, and their remoteness from the present. Divorced from my physical knowledge, or what I take to be such, the evidential value of these memories would be very slight. In short, while I believe that my past experiences have been organized in a way which accords with the physical theory, I do so only because I believe this theory to be true.

The point I am making here is not just the point we have already stressed, that it is only in the perspective of the physical theory that the sensory order becomes apparent. This earlier point does not as such create an epistemological problem. If someone had, through memory, a complete record of his previous sensory biography, formulated in purely sensory terms, and also had mastery of the physical conceptual scheme, he could discern the sensory order without relying on the truth of his physical beliefs. For he could recognize that his experience was organized as if some physical theory were true, without basing that recognition on an acceptance of the theory. And in this way he could appeal to the sensory order (discerned in the perspective of the theory) to justify an acceptance of the theory in one of the two ways we have envisaged. The new point I am making is that because, in practice, the subject does not have anything approaching a comprehensive recollective record of his past experiences, he has to rely on the truth of his physical beliefs to gain access to the relevant sensory evidence. And for this reason the anti-sceptical argument, as we have so far envisaged it, becomes viciously circular.

Nor is this the only problem. Even if the subject did possess an adequate recollective record of his own past experiences, the sceptic would challenge the credentials of the record. For what reason does the subject have for taking his apparent memories to be veridical? If there is a logical gap between the occurrence of a sense-experience and the judgment that a certain physical state of affairs obtains, there is a corresponding logical gap between an apparent memory of an earlier experience and the judgment that such an experience occurred. So what entitles the subject to pass from his introspective awareness of the apparent memory to some conclusion about his experiential past? It is no good objecting that this is a different sceptical problem – that we are only concerned, at present, with the status of the inference from sensory premises to physical conclusions. What we are concerned with is the status of our beliefs about the physical world. We cannot justify those beliefs simply by telling the sceptic to confine his attack to a particular kind of inference. Nor is it any good saying that our memory-faculties have shown themselves to be reliable by their success on previous occasions. For how can we tell that they have been successful without relying on them? Every conceivable way in which one might try to check up on the accuracy of a given memory involves the use of memory itself – and usually, in addition, a reliance on information about the physical world.

Perhaps this second problem could be solved by adopting the same kind of anti-sceptical strategies that we have envisaged for the physical world. If it is possible to justify an inference from the sensory order to the physical world by either the reductive or the explanatory methods, perhaps someone with an adequate recollective record could employ one of these methods to justify an inference from the recollective order – i.e. from the respects in which his apparent memories are systematic – to his experiential past. Of these two methods, only the explanatory one has any plausibility: to collapse the subject's experiential past into his current memories seems tantamount to denying that he had any previous experiences at all. But an explanatory inference looks more promising. If the subject's apparent memories are, in combination, conspicuously orderly, this seems to call for explanation; and if the orderliness is of the requisite type, the hypothesis that they are veridical memories of a genuine past might be taken to offer the most plausible account.

There remains, of course, the problem that, in practice, the subject does not possess anything approaching a comprehensive recollective record of his former experiences, and that what he does possess is too small and fragmented to allow the explanatory inference to work.

However, once we have seen the possibility of employing an explanatory inference in this way, another possibility suggests itself. For why should we restrict the premises of the inference to propositions recording the subject's recollections of his earlier experiences? Why not allow the premises to range over all facts concerning the subject's current state of mind, so long as by 'state of mind' we mean *intrinsic* state of mind and do not include anything (like *knowledge* of the physical world or the past) which depends on things external to his momentary mental condition? After all, what we are looking for is a way in which someone's current state of mind can furnish him with adequate reason for holding certain physical beliefs. If the provision of such reason turns on the legitimacy of some inference to the best explanation, we are entitled to include any aspect of the current state of mind in what has to be explained, if this makes the inference more effective.

In particular, a promising approach would be to take as the main component of what needs to be explained the subject's own current physical beliefs. For these beliefs (we may assume) exhibit a striking coherence and orderliness. They are very far from being just a random selection of possible physical beliefs or even a random selection of physical beliefs which are mutually consistent. They are, in effect, just the sort of beliefs which one would expect the subject to hold if the propositions believed were, by and large, true – the sort one would expect him to hold if there were a physical world of the type believed, acting on his senses in the way believed, and if the subject were disposed to develop a system of belief appropriate to the sense-experiences thus produced. This would be an astonishing fact if there were no explanation for it. And the most natural explanation (and the one suggested by the very specification of what needs to be explained) is that the beliefs are, by and large, true; that they have been acquired on the basis of, and accurately reflect, a past sensory history which itself accurately represents (or, as a phenomenalist would prefer to say, contributes to the existence of) the subject's physical world. If this is the best explanation, then, in this sense, the subject is furnished by his current physical beliefs with an adequate reason for holding them. And since he has introspective access to the beliefs, it seems that, by citing the reason, he could justify his beliefs in the face of the sceptic's attack. In so doing, of course, he would be appealing to the beliefs in order to justify them. But there is no circularity here, since what he is appealing to is his possession of these beliefs, not their truth.

I think that this is the best defence which can be offered against the sceptic. But I am not convinced that it is successful. One residual problem is that although the subject has introspective access to his physical beliefs, he would scarcely be able to focus his attention on all of them simultaneously, much less to discern, in that moment of comprehensive attention, the need to explain them in the envisaged way. The business of constructing the explanatory a gument – of drawing up a comprehensive (or sufficiently comprehensive) list of his physical beliefs, of seeing that they are coherent and orderly in the relevant way, and of showing that they are best explained by a theory which entails their truth – all this business will take a considerable time. Consequently, by the time it is completed, the subject will be relying on his memory to know that he has done the job properly, and to the extent that he is relying on his memory, the sceptic will have a further opportunity to call the whole procedure in question. How seriously we should regard this problem I am not sure. Certainly it does not give the sceptic complete victory. For even if the subject cannot *show* that he is justified in holding his physical beliefs without becoming vulnerable to a further sceptical challenge, this does not mean that he is *not* justified in holding them by the standards of the reason-furnishing thesis. So long as he does hold the beliefs and they are best explained by the supposition of their truth, then the subject is furnished by his current mental condition with an adequate reason for holding them, whether or not he can establish that this is so.

But perhaps the most serious problem is that the envisaged explanation is not the only one. To begin with, there is Descartes's hypothesis of the malignant demon. All the coherence and orderliness of our physical beliefs – the fact that they are just the sort of beliefs we could expect to have if there were a physical world of the kind believed – could be explained by the supposition that a powerful being is trying to deceive us and to cover up all traces of the deception. How can we show that this explanation is inferior to the one which our beliefs themselves entail? Here I confess myself at a loss. One might say that anyone sufficiently malignant to deceive us on such a scale would have made the content of the deceit less pleasant. Indeed, since our physical beliefs are an essential part of what gives human life its value, we might expect the demon to induce scepticism about the physical world rather than belief in it. But the sceptic can reply that the demon's purpose in inducing this belief is to prepare for some future day of disillusionment. Alternatively, he may simply change his hypothesis – replacing the malignant demon by a benevolent god, but one who is not sufficiently powerful to create a physical world to match the beliefs which he benevolently induces.[31] Compared with the common-sense view, such hypotheses strike us as absurd. But it is very difficult to find rational grounds for dismissing them. *Ex hypothesi*, they are eccentric. But this as such does not show that they are less worthy of acceptance than what we ordinarily believe.

Ayer himself, not surprisingly, thinks that such hypotheses *can* be dismissed. With his verificationist outlook, he regards the Cartesian version of the sceptical argument as incoherent.

195

The hypothesis of there being such an arch-deceiver is indeed empty, since his operations could never be detected. (*PK*, 44)

And, of course, this criticism would apply whether the hypothesized deceiver was motivated by malignancy or benevolence. But even Ayer would have to make room for the modern variant of this argument, in which the arch-deceiver becomes a team of unscrupulous scientists and the deluded victim is someone whose experiences, from birth, they artificially control. The scientists control the subject's experiential biography in such a way as to induce him to acquire a predominantly false set of beliefs about the physical world and his situation in it. Ayer would have to acknowledge the significance of such a story, since what it describes could be empirically detected by anyone other than the victim – and presumably even by the victim himself, in retrospect, if he were released from the experiment. The sceptic's challenge will then be to each of us: 'What reason do you have, on reflection, for believing that you are not in the position of such a subject?'

Perhaps both this and (if it is coherent) the Cartesian challenge can be met by showing that these alternative explanations are not as satisfactory as the common-sense one. Certainly in one sense they are not. For, whether or not we can defend our physical beliefs, we have them; and we are not led to discard them by an awareness of the sceptical problem. In default of a proof that such beliefs are incoherent, the common-sense explanation is the only one we can find credible. But this, of course, does nothing to undermine the logic of the sceptic's case. It just means that, even if the sceptic's argument is the logically irresistible force, our physical beliefs constitute the psychologically immovable object. Whether, in the last analysis, the sceptic's argument is logically irresistible, I do not know.

Part III

Man and Nature

---

1 *The problem of induction*

Imagine that I am holding a coin. I believe, indeed am quite sure, that if I release it, the coin will fall. Why? After all, there are infinitely many directions it could take. Why should I believe that it will fall? Why, for that matter, should I believe that it will move at all?

The proposition that, if released, the coin will fall is not one which I know, or could know, *a priori*. It is conceivable that the coin will stay put or move in some other direction. If I have reason to believe what I do, the reason is empirical – a reason drawn from past experience. I believe that the coin will fall because I have discovered, from past observations, that this is how coins, and indeed, with a few explicable exceptions, all material objects, are disposed to behave. Experience has taught me that it is in the nature of unsupported bodies of this type to fall.

But how exactly has experience taught me this? Certainly, I have found in the past that whenever I have released a coin, or similar object, in conditions of this sort, it has fallen. But what entitles me to infer from this that coins will continue to behave in this fashion in future? Obviously, the inference is not deductively valid. There is no contradiction in conceding that unsupported coins have always fallen hitherto but denying that they will do so hereafter. If, on the basis of my past observations, I conclude that they will fall, I seem to be relying on the principle that nature is uniform, i.e. that regularities which have held for all the cases we have so far examined will hold for other cases too. But why should this principle be accepted? We have already, in effect, conceded that it cannot be established *a priori*, since there is no inconsistency in supposing that the way unsupported bodies behave in the future will be different from the way they have behaved in the past. So presumably, if it is to be acceptable at all, the principle must derive its support from experience: we are to accept the principle because, in the cases we have examined, it has held hitherto. But to accept it on this basis is to argue in a circle, since we are using the principle to justify our acceptance of it.

This, of course, is the problem of induction. Induction, in its simplest form, is that method of inference whereby, from the premise that every examined F is G, it is inferred that a particular unexamined F is G, or, more strongly, that every F is G. The problem is that such inferences seem to lack any rational justification. Or, more precisely, the problem is this, combined with the fact that we seem to need such inferences to justify most of our empirical beliefs. For, without the backing of induction, it seems that no one is justified in believing any empirical proposition beyond the data supplied by his current perceptions, memory and introspection. Of course, in so far as they purport to give information about the physical world or the past, perception and memory themselves are (as we have seen) subject to a sceptical challenge. But it is scepticism about induction which now concerns us, though our discussion of this will lead into a range of further issues about nature and the human mind. Naturally, the focus of our discussion throughout will be on the views and arguments of Ayer.

2 Hume's argument

It was Hume who provided the first systematic formulation of the problem of induction, and in his book *Probability and Evidence* (*PAE*) Ayer himself sets out to examine the issue in the light of Hume's account. Much of the discussion is repeated in *The Central Questions of Philosophy* (*CQ*) and I shall move freely between both texts.

Ayer begins by providing a summary of Hume's sceptical argument as a proof in the following nine stages:

(1) 'An inference from one matter of fact to another is never demonstrative.' (*PAE*, 4)
(2) 'There is no such thing as a synthetic necessary connection between events.' (*PAE*, 4)
(3) 'So the only ground that we can have for believing, in a case where A is observed by us and B not yet observed, that B does exist in such and such a spatio-temporal relation to A is our past experience of the constant conjunction of As and Bs.' (*PAE*, 4)
(4) The inference from a past constant conjuction to its future continuance is not logically valid.
(5) To make the inference logically valid we need, as an extra premise, the principle that nature is uniform.
(6) The truth of this principle cannot be established *a priori*.

(7) Nor, without circularity, could we argue for the principle on empirical grounds, since any empirical argument will presuppose it.

(8) We cannot bypass the principle and argue that the inferences in their original form, 'though admittedly not demonstrative, can nevertheless be shown to be probable' (*PAE*, 5). For such a probability could only be established by an appeal to past experience and the principle.

(9) Consequently, the inferences are not rationally justified at all.

Ayer describes this argument as 'one of the most brilliant examples of philosophical reasoning that there has ever been' (*PAE*, 6). His procedure is then to use it as the framework for his subsequent discussion. In particular, he thinks that 'by going through it in detail, we shall be able to see . . . how different theories of induction arise from the attempt to challenge different stages in Hume's argument' (*PAE*, 6).

The first step in the argument, as Ayer has formulated it, is the claim that an inference from one matter of fact (i.e. empirical proposition) to another is never demonstrative (i.e. never deductively valid). As Ayer notes, Hume's own formulation has a narrower focus, being concerned with a special type of factual inference – that from cause to effect or from effect to cause. Hume's claim is that, because cause and effect are always distinct events, it is never possible to deduce the existence or character of the one from the existence or character of the other. But, of course, behind this claim is the more general Humean principle which denies the existence of such deductive links between any events which are genuinely distinct. And it is this principle which Ayer is trying to express.

Taken literally, of course, Ayer's formulation is clearly defective. The fact that I am holding a penny is different from the fact that I am holding a coin, but the inference from the first to the second is clearly demonstrative, and would have been regarded as such by Hume. In this respect, he would have done better to have retained Hume's own formulation of the principle, in terms of distinct events, since the event of my holding a penny is presumably the same as the event of my holding a coin. As it turns out, none of this matters, since Ayer is only using his initial formulation as a kind of shorthand and soon makes it clear that it is the principle of distinct events which is at issue.

Even Hume's own formulation, as Ayer sees, needs refinement. For the question of what can or cannot be deduced from the occurrence of a certain event depends crucially on how the event is described. Even if two events are wholly distinct (e.g. they occur at different times or in different places), it is still possible to describe them in terms which allow the occurrence of one to be deduced from the occurrence of the other; for example, we can deduce the occurrence of B from the occurrence of A if A is identified by the description 'the cause of B'. Ayer's response is to limit the relevant descriptions to those which are *intrinsic*, where an 'intrinsic' description of something *x* is one which exclusively concerns the character of *x* in itself and carries no implications about how *x* is actually or potentially related to anything else. He then reformulates Hume's principle as the proposition that if two events are distinct, in the sense of having no common part, then 'an intrinsic description of either of them entails nothing at all about the existence or character of the other' (*PAE*, 6). Thus reformulated, the principle becomes a tautology. He then takes Hume's substantive claim to be that such intrinsic descriptions can be provided and that 'they are sufficient to describe everything that happens' (*PAE*, 6).

Ayer thinks that this claim is, strictly speaking, false. For he thinks that it is not possible to describe an object or event in terms which are sufficiently observational and non-theoretical to carry no implications about anything else. This holds, he thinks, even at the level of the phenomenal language, since 'the possibility of starting with sense-qualia depends on our being able to locate them in a spatio-temporal system', with the result that 'the identification of an individual will presuppose that there are others to which it stands in some spatio-temporal relation' (*PAE*, 9). None the less, he has no doubt that Hume's position is right in spirit. If we are to extend our knowledge beyond what we currently observe or remember, we need to invoke a method of inference of a non-deductive kind. And while it may be impossible to provide descriptions which are fully intrinsic, we can at least provide ones which are, as it were, sufficiently intrinsic for Hume's purposes. In particular, given two distinct events, we can describe each of them in a way which entails nothing at all about the existence or character of the other.

A point on which Ayer lays particular stress, in this connection, concerns the use of predicates which have implications of a causal or dispositional kind. If I describe something as a *magnet*, I imply that it has the causal property of attracting iron. If I describe something as a *match*, I imply that it is disposed to ignite when suitably struck. It might be thought that such implicity causal or dispositional descriptions could help us to rebut Hume's sceptical argument at its first stage. If it is a conceptual truth that magnets attract iron, then, merely from the knowledge that a magnet is in proximity to a heap of iron filings, I can deduce that the filings will move towards it. If it is a conceptual truth that matches ignite when suitably struck in appropriate conditions, then, merely from the knowledge that I have struck a match in such a way and in such conditions, I can deduce that it will produce a flame. It seems that, merely by attending to the natural description of the event which I already know to have occurred, I can gain knowledge of some further event by deduction alone. Moreover, by introducing new predicates or altering the meanings of our existing predicates in the appropriate way, it seems that we can confer a similar deductive security on all the inferences which Hume saw as problematic. If it is not a conceptual truth that the coin, when released, will fall, we can make it so by making gravitational behaviour a defining characteristic of material objects. If being poisonous is not a defining characteristic of arsenic, we can introduce the term 'parsenic' of which it is. Such procedures may seem artificial. But why not exploit them if they put our empirical beliefs on a firmer foundation?

But, as Ayer clearly sees, the suggestion that we could rebut Hume's argument in this way is entirely misconceived. For any security we may gain for the inferences, we forfeit in the assertion of the premises. If it is a conceptual truth that magnets attract iron, the empirical question becomes: 'How do you know that this is a magnet?' If we make gravitational behaviour a defining characteristic of material objects, the empirical question becomes: 'How do you know that this object is material?' The point is not that these questions are clearly unanswerable, but that any answers will involve the very forms of non-deductive reasoning which Hume is challenging us to justify and which we had hoped, by the appropriate formulation of our premises, to bypass. We cannot know that what we observe is a magnet, or in the relevant sense material, without making an inference from its sensible qualities to its causal powers or dispositions. And, whether or not we can justify it, this inference is clearly not demonstrative. In short, whatever descriptions we use, the empirical questions, and the sceptical challenge they invite, will remain. The advantage of employing intrinsic descriptions, or ones which are as nearly intrinsic as possible, is that it makes the epistemological situation clear.

Having made the first step in Hume's argument secure, Ayer now turns to the second, the contention that there is no such thing as a synthetic necessary connection between events. He begins by reformulating this as the claim that, apart from those of comparison, the only relations between events are spatio-temporal, that 'everything that happens in the world can be represented in terms of variations of scenery in a four-dimensional spatio-temporal continuum' (*PAE*, 10–11). He then proceeds to defend the claim by elaborating an example of Hume's, that of a cannon in billiards:

> We think of the cue striking the billiard ball, and so imparting motion to it, of the ball hitting a second ball, and rebounding on to a third. All these forceful expressions, 'striking', 'hitting', 'imparting motion', 'rebounding', are expressions of causal agency, and their use in this context is perfectly correct. But everything that actually happens can be wholly described in purely undramatic spatio-temporal terms. First there is a period of time in which there is a

concordant movement, that is, a relative change of place, of the player's body and the cue, then an instant at which the cue and the cue ball are in contact, or in other words, share a common spatial boundary, then a period in which this ball is in motion relatively to the other balls, the sides of the table, and so forth, then an instant at which the first ball is in contact with the second, then a period in which both balls are in motion, then an instant at which the first is in contact with the third. However long this story is continued, there is nothing in the situation that calls for anything more than the identification of various objects and the specification of their changing spatio-temporal relations. In particular there is nothing of which such terms as 'power', 'force', 'energy', 'agency' could be names. As Hume would put it, there are no impressions from which any such ideas could be derived. (*PAE*, 11)

Ayer's claim that the use of the causal expressions is perfectly correct, combined with his claim that what actually happens can be wholly described in spatio-temporal terms, seems to imply that the causal description says no more than the spatio-temporal. But he is quick to correct this impression. The causal description does add something, for it 'brings in an element of greater generality' (*PAE*, 12).

We are in some way implying that this situation is typical; that this is what normally happens or would happen in these circumstances. (*PAE*, 12)

But the analysis of causal statements is not Ayer's present concern. The point he wants to stress is that, whatever our causal statements imply, the events themselves are only connected by spatio-temporal relations.

What is not yet clear is why Ayer should think that this is so. The argument seems to be that only the spatio-temporal relations are observable: there are impressions of motion and contact, but none of causal connection – no impression of agency or necessitation. But why should this be thought decisive? After all, physicists postulate unobservable entities and unobservable properties, and take themselves to be responding to the empirical evidence. If causal agency can be empirically detected in some way, however indirect, the fact that it is unobservable (if this is so) is not problematic. And even if it is not detectable, the most that seems to follow is that we *cannot tell* whether events are linked by relations of agency, not that they are not.

The reason why Ayer is sure that there are no such relations is that he regards the very notion of them as incoherent. Or put another way, he thinks that we can form no conception of what it is that such terms as 'agency' and 'necessitation' are supposed to signify. A hint of this is given at the end of the passage we quoted, where he says that 'as Hume would put it, there are no impressions from which any such ideas [of power, force, energy, agency] could be derived' (*PAE*, 11). The reference is to Hume's empiricist principle that every genuine idea must be either a copy of a previous impression or divisible into ideas which are copies of previous impressions – a principle which Hume himself uses to eliminate any genuine idea of agency or necessitation. Not that Ayer accepts Hume's principle as it stands. He recognizes that, as Hume has formulated it, the principle is only an empirical generalization and, indeed, one which is falsified by the very counter-example which Hume supplies. Nor does he even accept, without qualification, the amended version of Hume's principle (as we formulated it in Part I, section 5), that, for every primitive concept, there is a *type* of impression in terms of which it could be ostensively grasped. For even this he regards as too restrictive. What he accepts, as most recently expressed in his book *Hume* (*H*), is that every genuine concept must be capable of featuring non-redundantly (and non-redundantly with respect to every aspect of its supposed content) in some empirically confirmable theory.[1] He acknowledges that this principle takes us 'rather far from Hume' (*H*, 32); in effect it is Hume's atomistic principle substantially re-shaped to fit Ayer's verificationist outlook. But at least it preserves the basic empiricism of Hume's approach. Like Hume, Ayer is insisting that all genuine concepts must be ones which we can ultimately grasp by reference to experience. And, like Hume, he thinks that the supposed notions of agency and necessitation fail the empiricist test. Not only can they not be ostensively defined (there being no corresponding impression) or analysed into concepts which can be ostensively defined; but, unlike the theoretical concepts of physics, we cannot even grasp them indirectly, by their contribution to the confirmation-conditions of empirically confirmable theories. They are, as he sees it, notions wholly devoid of empirical content.

As it turns out, Ayer does not think that the rejection of causal agency is crucial to Hume's sceptical argument. Even if, *per impossibile*, we could make sense of such a notion, it would not, he claims, help us to avoid the sceptical problem. This claim turns on the fact that if agency is to help, two conditions must be satisfied. First, and obviously, agency must be something which we can detect in a situation without reliance on induction – otherwise, our claim to detect it will simply beg the question. Second, it must be something whose presence in one situation, linking a cause E_1 with an effect E_2, logically ensures either (a) that whenever there is an event of the same type as E_1 in relevantly similar conditions (specified without the use of causal terms), there is, or is very likely to be, an effect of the same type as E_2, or (b) that whenever there is an event of the same type as E_2 in relevantly similar conditions, there is, or is very likely to be, a cause of the same type as E_1. Otherwise, the detection of agency in a situation where both events are observed would not help to justify an inference from one type of event to the other in situations where only one was observed. Ayer's point then, in effect, is that these two conditions cannot be jointly satisfied. If agency is an intrinsic feature of a situation, it may be possible to detect it non-inductively (e.g. by direct observation), but then its presence will carry no implications about the course of events on other occasions. Conversely, if it is to carry such implications, its presence will involve the truth of some causal generalization, whose confirmation depends on induction. Of course, by suitably fixing the meanings of its terms, we could turn this generalization into a conceptual truth. But, as Ayer has already shown, this only transfers the need for induction to another point.

This argument is certainly very plausible. But our final assessment of it may depend on our assessment of a related argument concerned with a different sort of natural necessity. At all events, it is this related argument which brings us to the real issue and which must become our main concern.

So far the only sort of natural necessity we have considered is one which relates particulars – the relation of one event's causally producing or necessitating another. However, there is commonly supposed to be a further kind of natural necessity, which relates not particulars but universals – the kind of necessity which is involved in general laws of nature, such as the law of gravity. Philosophers who recognize both kinds of necessity usually take the first kind to be reducible to the second. They usually hold that the only sense in which one event causally necessitates another is that these two events fall under a general law of nature, whereby it is nomologically necessary that any event of the first type is followed, in the appropriate spatio-temporal relation, by some event of the second type. But the acceptance of both kinds of necessity does not as such commit one to accepting this reduction. It would still be possible to hold that causal relations between particulars are not reducible to nomological relations between types. And it would also be possible to hold that causality itself forms part of the subject-matter of certain laws, in the sense that the obtaining of causal relations is part of what the laws explicitly control. These are matters which we shall examine later, when we consider the nature of causation in more detail.

Given his radically empiricist outlook, it is hardly surprising that Ayer, in company with Hume, rejects the notion of objective nomological necessity, just as he rejects the notion of relations of causal agency or necessitation between events. But the point I want to focus on is that, as in the case of agency, he does not regard the rejection of nomological necessity as crucial to Hume's sceptical argument, since the acceptance of such necessity 'does not help us at all in dealing with the problem which Hume raises' (*PAE*, 17). If it were to help us, it would be, presumably, by providing a basis for the step of induction, in which we predict that some unexamined case will conform to the regularity we have so far observed. And, so far from helping us in this respect, Ayer thinks that an appeal to necessity only makes things worse. As he explains more fully in *CQ*:

> If on the basis of the fact that all the A's hitherto observed have been B's, we are seeking for an assurance that the next A we come upon will be a B, the knowledge, if we could have it, that all A's are B's would be quite sufficient; to strengthen the premiss by saying that they not only are but must be B's adds nothing to the validity of the inference. The only way in which this move could be helpful would be if it were somehow easier to discover that all A's must be B's than that they merely were so; and perhaps this is what its advocates believe. But how can they possibly be right? . . . It is no good claiming that empirical hypotheses of this or any other sort are known to be true by intuition. . . . But then, if it is a matter of evidence, it must be easier to discover, or at least find some good reason for believing, that such and such an association of properties always does obtain, than that it must obtain; for it requires less for the evidence to establish. (*CQ*, 149–50)

Once again, Ayer's argument looks very plausible. If we are going to use nomological necessity to validate the inductive step, we have to establish that the relevant necessity obtains. And surely we could only do this by a further step of induction. Moreover, this further step of induction seems even more problematic than the step we were seeking to validate. For we are now trying to get the evidence to yield a stronger conclusion: not merely that all *A*s are *B*s, but that they *must* be.

None the less, I think that Ayer's reasoning is fallacious. To see why, we must begin by reminding ourselves of something which we have already had cause to stress in our earlier discussion of scepticism, namely that there is a form of empirical inference which is supposedly rational, but not inductive in the sense we are presently considering. In the sense we are considering, we make an inductive inference when, from our knowledge that all the examined *A*s are *B*s, we infer that all *A*s are *B*s or that some particular unexamined *A* is a *B*. In such cases, the inductive inference is just an extrapolation from the evidence; it is just an extension to the unexamined cases of what we have found to obtain in the examined cases. But not all supposedly rational empirical inferences are of this kind. Consider, for example, the way in which chemists have supposedly established that water is H_2O. No doubt there is a step of extrapolative induction, from the chemical composition of the water-samples examined to the composition of water in general. But this is not the only step of inference. For the composition of the samples is not directly observed: it is detected by inference from how the samples respond to certain tests. The rationale for such an inference is the explanatory power of the conclusion it yields. The conclusion is accepted because it explains the experimental findings – at least it does so in the framework of a more comprehensive chemical theory which is itself accepted largely on explanatory grounds. Thus the conclusion is reached not by extrapolation, but by an inference to the best explanation. And this is how, quite generally, scientists reach conclusions about things not directly observable.

Ayer is well aware that there can be empirical inferences of this explanatory kind, and in his later writings, as we have seen, he sometimes employs such inferences in answering other types of sceptical argument. Thus in CQ he tries to justify our ordinary physical beliefs by the way in which their truth accounts for the organization of sense-experience, and to justify our ascription of mental states to others by the way in which such states account for observed behaviour. But he never considers the possibility of employing an explanatory inference to answer scepticism about (extrapolative) induction. If he had, he might not have been so swift to dismiss the notion of nomological necessity as irrelevant.

The crucial point emerges when we reflect on Ayer's claim that 'if it is a matter of evidence, it must be easier to discover, or at least find some good reason for believing, that such and such an association of properties always does obtain, than that it must obtain; for it requires less for the evidence to establish' (CQ, 150). Now, of course, on the assumption that it is only by means of an extrapolative inference that the evidence can be used, this claim, or at least the point it is trying to make, is clearly correct. An extrapolation to the stonger conclusion (which associates A and B across all nomologically possible worlds) already includes an extrapolation to the weaker (which merely associates A and B in the actual world), and hence cannot serve to mediate it. If the smaller extrapolation is doubtful, then eo ipso the larger is doubtful, and presumably more so. But suppose we drop the assumption that the only route from the evidence to the two conclusions is by extrapolative induction. Suppose, instead, we think of reaching these conclusions by an inference to the best explanation. It is by no means obvious then that an inference to the stronger conclusion might not be the means of justifying an acceptance of the weaker. For it might be precisely because the stronger conclusion is stronger that it has the explanatory power required to make it worthy of acceptance, and thus precisely because we are justified in accepting the stronger conclusion on explanatory grounds that we are justified in accepting the weaker conclusion it entails. It is this possibility which Ayer has overlooked. Whether we shall be able to make anything of it is a question I shall consider later, after I have completed my survey of Ayer's exposition of Hume's argument.

The third step in Hume's argument, which is seen as a consequence of the first two, is (as Ayer now reformulates it) the claim that 'the only ground we can have for believing either that all As are conjoined with Bs or that a particular A is conjoined with a particular B, in a case where A has been observed but B not, is our past experience of the constant conjunction of As and Bs' (*PAE*, 19). Ayer rightly notes that this claim is false as it stands, since often our grounds for accepting some generalization are less direct. Sometimes we have reason to accept a generalization not because we have observed it to hold hitherto, but because it is a consequence of a more general theory which has been experientially confirmed at other points. Sometimes, again, we have reason to accept a generalization about something unobservable to explain something observable. But while Hume's claim is false as it stands, Ayer believes that it is right in spirit: the only grounds for accepting an empirical generalization are that it 'squares with' the observed facts – in a sense which requires not only compatibility, but also relevance, so that the generalization has observational consequences which are experientially confirmed. In *CQ* he expresses the point more cautiously: it is at least necessary for the acceptability of a generalization that it should square with the observed facts, though, of two generalizations or theories which alike square with these facts, 'one may be thought superior . . . on the ground that it is simpler, or more far-reaching, or that it explains the facts more systematically' (*CQ*, 157). But the mere fact that an acceptable generalization has to square with the observed facts is, as Ayer sees, 'all that we need to be able to pursue Hume's argument' (*CQ*, 157).

Reformulated in these terms, Hume's fourth step becomes: from the fact that a certain generalization squares with all hitherto observed facts we cannot logically deduce that it squares with all observable facts nor even that it squares with the observable facts in respect of some particular and as-yet-unexamined case. This claim is clearly correct, as Ayer sees. It is a rephrasal of 'the tautology that an extrapolation from a certain body of evidence is not a deduction from it' (*PAE*, 20).

It is over the fifth step that Ayer finds himself in more serious disagreement with Hume. Hume claims that to make the inductive inference logically valid we need as an extra premise the principle that nature is uniform, 'that instances of which we have had no experience must resemble those of which we have had experience, and that the course of nature continues always uniformly the same'.[2] Ayer objects that such a principle cannot do the work that is here required of it:

> Let us take as an example the false proposition that all swans are white, and let n be the date at which the first black swan was

observed. Then the syllogism will run: Nature is uniform. All swans observed before *n* are white. Therefore, all swans are white. Since the conclusion is false, one of the premisses must be false, if the syllogism is valid. But *ex hypothesi* the minor premiss is true. Consequently, it is false that nature is uniform. Since we do not draw this inference, it follows that the syllogism is not thought to be valid. The uniformity of nature is not so rigidly conceived as to be at the mercy of an exception to what has so far seemed to be a true generalization. (*CQ*, 162)

Of course, we could construe the principle in such a way as to make the syllogism valid. For example, we could take it as equivalent to the proposition: 'For any *F*, any *G*, and any *t*, if all *F*s observed before *t* are *G*, then all *F*s are *G*.' But such a manoeuvre would be pointless. For any construal which renders the syllogism valid automatically renders the principle false. There is no getting away from the fact that all swans observed before *n* are white but some swans observed after *n* are not.

It does not follow from this that any acceptable principle of uniformity will be wholly irrelevant to the justification of induction. It is true that if the principle is to be acceptable, it cannot be so strong as to entail the truth of the induced conclusion when combined with the other premises of the inference. For, as we have just seen, inductive inferences are not always successful. But it could still be the case that an acceptable principle of uniformity shows inductive inference to be rational; that it shows how the premises genuinely support the conclusion, how the conclusion is at least probable given the truth of the premises.

But can we find a principle of this kind? As we have already said, it cannot be so strong as to entail that inductive inferences are always successful. But nor can it be so weak that no alteration in the course of nature would falsify it. Thus, as Ayer points out, we cannot construe the principle as the proposition that every event comes under some true generalization, since 'if no restriction is set upon the form and complexity of the generalizations, or upon the choice of the terms which enter into them, we can always adjust them to any finite series of events' (*CQ*, 161).

It is like our ability to draw a curve through any finite series of points. We may come to grief when we try to extend the curve to points which have not yet been supplied to us, but once they have been supplied, we can always make it fit them retrospectively. If we have complete freedom in the coinage of predicates, we can cause any two events to share a common quality just by introducing a predicate which is so defined that its extension covers them both. (*CQ*, 161)

And if we try to avoid this problem by restricting ourselves to generalizations which attribute, in some intuitive sense, a 'genuine' resemblance
to the instances they cover, we can still make every event come under
some true generalization simply by choosing a generalization of
sufficiently narrow scope. If necessary, as Ayer notes, we can choose
one which, by the specificity of its antecedent predicate-expression (the
'*A*' in 'All *A*s are. . . '), covers only the event in question.

Even if we could formulate a uniformity-principle of just the right
strength – sufficiently strong to make inductive inference rational, but
sufficiently weak to accommodate the fact that such inferences sometimes
fail – there would still be the question of how the principle could be
justified. Since it has to attribute some non-trivial form of uniformity to
nature, whereby it would be falsified by a radical alteration in the course
of events, it cannot be an *a priori* truth. But in so far as its acceptance
rests on empirical evidence, it seems to presuppose the rationality of
induction. For how, except by reliance on induction, can we have
grounds for expecting the uniformity we have so far observed to continue
in the future? And if we need induction to justify the principle, we
cannot, without circularity, use the principle to justify induction. This
is the core of Hume's argument in steps (6) and (7), and it is not touched
by Ayer's criticisms. Nor, of course, does Ayer think that it is. Ayer's
only objection is that Hume has misunderstood the role which we would
want the principle to play and (presumably because of this) has failed to
appreciate the difficulties in formulating a principle of the required sort.

When we add in step (8), Hume's argument becomes the classical
sceptical argument that *any* attempt to justify induction is circular. We
may try to 'by-pass the general principle of the uniformity of nature and
argue that inferences from one matter of fact to another, though admittedly not demonstrative, can nevertheless be shown to be probable'
(*PAE*, 5). But 'this judgment of probability must have some foundation'
and 'this foundation can lie only in our past experience' (*PAE*, 5). And
consequently, 'we have to assume the very principle that we are trying
to by-pass' (*PAE*, 5). Thus my only grounds for believing that, if
released, the coin I am holding will fall is my knowledge that (at least
as far as my evidence extends) bodies have always, or nearly always,
behaved gravitationally hitherto.[3] But if I am asked to say why such
knowledge gives me grounds for the belief, I can only appeal to the
rationality of induction itself or to something, like the principle of
uniformity, whose acceptability, in turn, depends on induction. I cannot
even make use of the fact (if it is a fact) that inductive inferences have
usually been successful in the past. For without relying on induction, I
can infer nothing from this about the likelihood of their success in the
future.

Ayer accepts this circularity argument. What conclusion he draws from it with respect to the status of induction we shall see presently. But first we need to look a little more deeply into the argument itself. For there are those who think that it can be resisted. In particular, there are those who think that it can be resisted by recourse to some *a priori* theory of probability. It is to the views of these philosophers that Ayer now turns.

3 *A priori probability*

Can we find a non-circular justification of induction by appealing to some *a priori* theory of probability? Ayer considers various ways in which such a justification has been attempted. In each case he concludes, and I think correctly, that the attempt fails: it fails either because it establishes nothing which is even relevant to the issue of induction or because, although purporting to be an *a priori* argument, it tacitly relies on some empirical assumption whose acceptability depends on induction itself. And Ayer believes that all such attempts are bound to fail in one of these two ways. It would be interesting and instructive to look in turn at each of the attempts which Ayer considers, along with his refutation. But since we have much else to discuss (including what I regard as a much more plausible way of trying to avoid the circularity argument), I shall restrict myself to just two cases. These will serve to illustrate Ayer's general approach and, in particular, the alternative ways in which, as he sees it, any attempt to derive induction from an *a priori* theory of probability is vitiated.

The first of these attempts,[4] which Ayer attributes to J. M. Keynes, involves an appeal to the 'axiom of multiplication'. This states that, for any propositions P, Q, and R, the probability of (P and Q) relative to evidence R equals the probability of P relative to R multiplied by the probability of Q relative to (P and R) – or put succinctly:

$$\text{Prob } (PQ/R) = \text{Prob } (P/R) \times \text{Prob } (Q/PR)$$

The axiom as such is uncontroversial, and, on certain mathematical treatments of probability, truistic. The whole issue turns on an argument which purports to establish, on the basis of the axiom, the rationality of induction. I shall formulate this argument by means of an example.

Suppose we are interested in the inductive support for the generalization, G, that all ravens are black. Let E be our existing evidence, which we will assume to be compatible with G, and let Rupert be some particular raven, such that E includes the fact that Rupert is a raven, but leaves open the question of whether Rupert is black. If we now take S as the singular proposition that Rupert is a black raven and assume that there are only finitely many ravens, we know that both Prob (G/E) and Prob (S/E) are greater than 0 and less than 1. It is at this point that we can, it seems, exploit the multiplication axiom. By two applications of the axiom, we have:

$$\text{Prob } (GS/E) = \text{Prob } (G/E) \times \text{Prob } (S/GE)$$
$$\text{Prob } (SG/E) = \text{Prob } (S/E) \times \text{Prob } (G/SE)$$

Since 'Prob (GS/E)' and 'Prob (SG/E)' are synonymous ('GS' and 'SG' being just notational variants for the conjunction of G and S), we get:

$$\text{Prob } (G/E) \times \text{Prob } (S/GE) = \text{Prob } (S/E) \times (G/SE)$$

And this can be re-expressed as:

$$\frac{\text{Prob } (G/E)}{\text{Prob } (G/SE)} = \frac{\text{Prob } (S/E)}{\text{Prob } (S/GE)}$$

But since E includes the fact that Rupert is a raven, G and E jointly entail S. So Prob $(S/GE) = 1$. But, *ex hypothesi*, Prob (S/E) is less than 1. Hence to preserve the equation, Prob (G/E) must be less than Prob (G/SE) – i.e. the addition of S to the existing evidence increases the probability of G. When generalized, this means that, in a finite domain, the probability of a generalization's being true increases with each new instance in which it is found to hold. And this seems to be just what we need to establish the rationality of induction.

However, as Ayer clearly sees, this is just an illusion. There is nothing wrong with the formal proof that Prob $(G/E) <$ Prob (G/SE), given the assumptions which were made. And this indeed does show, quite generally, that, in a finite domain, the probability of a generalization increases with each new favourable instance. But it has nothing to do with induction. It merely reflects the trivial fact that, with each new favourable instance, there are fewer cases left in which the generalization could fail. The point is most easily seen if we focus on the example of drawing balls from a bag. Let us assume, for simplicity, that we already know that there are ten balls in all and that each is either black or white. When we have drawn one ball and found it to be black, we have more reason to believe that all the balls are black, simply because there are now only nine possible counter-instances remaining. When we have drawn two balls and found them both to be black, we have still more reason, since there are only eight left. And so on. This has nothing to do with induction, since it does not involve using the examined cases as a basis for predicting the properties of the unexamined cases. It tells us that the probability that *all* the balls are black increases, as the number of black balls drawn increases, but not that the probability that the *next* ball will be black increases, as this number increases. Thus it does not tell us that, having drawn nine black balls, we are entitled to be more confident about the colour of the tenth ball than when we first began the experiment. For this reason, the multiplication axiom has no bearing on the problem of

211

induction. It offers absolutely no grounds for extrapolating past regularities into the future.

The second attempt to justify induction by reference to *a priori* probabilities appeals to the so-called law of large numbers, according to which,
as Ayer puts it, 'in the case of any sufficiently large sample which is
drawn [at random] from a larger population, there is a high probability
that the ratio in which a given character is distributed in the sample
approximately matches its distribution in the parent population' (*PAE*,
41) – the probability approaching unity as the size of the sample
increases. Once again, the principle to which appeal is made is undoubtedly correct if properly interpreted.

> To say that if the sample is sufficiently large, there is a high
> probability that it approximately matches the parent population,
> with respect to the distribution of any given character, is just a way
> of saying that if we take all the possible selections from the parent
> population which yield a sample of its size, we shall find that those
> which roughly match the parent population in the respect in question
> very greatly outnumber those which do not. In short, deviant samples
> are untypical, and become more untypical the larger the sample.
> (*PAE*, 41).

And, one might add, they become more untypical the more they are
deviant. Thus if there are a hundred balls in a bag, fifty white and fifty
black, and we consider the class of all fifty-ball samples, the largest
subset of this class will comprise samples with twenty-five of each colour,
the next largest will be the two subsets which respectively comprise
samples of twenty-six whites and twenty-four blacks and samples of
twenty-four whites and twenty-six blacks, and so on till we reach the
two smallest subsets, one containing a single sample of fifty whites and
the other containing a single sample of fifty blacks.

All this is trivially true. And yet it seems, at first sight, to provide a
rational basis for induction. For suppose I know that there are exactly
a hundred balls in a bag, each either white or black, and I now draw at
random fifty, which turn out to be white. I have no further information
about the fifty remaining balls: my evidence leaves open the possibility
that they are all white, the possibility that they are all black, and all the
possibilities in between. But by the law of large numbers, it seems that
I can be reasonably confident that, even in this unexamined group, there
are comparatively few blacks. For my sample is sufficiently large to make
it highly probable that its colour-distribution (100% whites) approximately matches the distribution in the total population. In effect, I can,
it seems, be reasonably confident that there are not many blacks, since,
if there were, an all-white fifty-ball sample would be extremely untypical

in the class of possible fifty-ball samples and would therefore have had only a very slight chance of being drawn.

How should we respond to this argument? Well, even if it were successful for the case of the balls, it would be difficult to generalize it to cover the cases of induction which primarily concern us. The main difficulty here is that, in the case of the balls, we have assumed that I drew my sample *at random*. And, at least implicitly, we have taken this to mean that each of the possible fifty-ball samples had the same chance of being drawn as any other. In effect, we have assumed that if a particular sample-distribution is (given the actual distribution in the population) untypical, it is, to the extent of its untypicality, less likely to show up in the sample drawn. And it is on this basis that my sample gives me grounds for believing that even the unexamined balls are predominantly white. But, whether this assumption is legitimate in the case of the balls, no comparable assumption of fair-sampling can be made in the standard cases of induction.

> So far from its being the case that we are as likely to make any one selection as any other, there is a vast number of selections, indeed in most instances the large majority, that it is impossible for us to make. Our samples are drawn from a tiny section of the universe during a very short period of time. And even this minute part of the whole four-dimensional continuum is not one that we can examine very thoroughly. (*PAE*, 42)

For these reasons, Ayer thinks that, if we are to use our samples as a basis for estimating the distribution of properties in the whole universe, 'we need to make two quite strong empirical assumptions' (*PAE*, 42).

> They are first that the composition of our selections, the state of affairs which we observe and record, reflects the composition of all the selections which are available to us, that is to say, all the states of affairs which we could observe if we took enough trouble; and secondly that the distribution of properties in the spatio-temporal region which is accessible to us reflects their distribution in the continuum as a whole. (*PAE*, 42)

He is willing to concede the first assumption. For he is content to rely on scientific method to shuffle, as it were, the bag of observable states of affairs and thus 'prevent our selections from being biased by the circumstances in which they are made' (*PAE*, 42). But the second he finds troublesome, since 'it postulates the uniformity of nature, not trivially but in quite a strong fashion' (*PAE*, 42). He admits that we could avoid some of the trouble by restricting our predictive concern to what primarily interests us, for practical purposes, namely the character of the universe 'in our fairly close neighbourhood and in the fairly immediate future' (*PAE*, 42). But even here he sees that we need a non-trivial assumption of uniformity to have any assurance that the distribution of properties among the unexamined cases is similar to that among the examined. We cannot obtain any such assurance from the law of large numbers, simply because our existing sample has not been randomly selected in the relevant sense. Most of the unexamined cases were not candidates for selection in the way required by the model of the balls in the bag. Indeed, the future cases were not candidates for selection in any sense at all.

To illustrate the point, consider the two hypotheses: H_1, that all ravens up to the year 2000 are black; and H_2, that all ravens up to the present time are black and all ravens from the present time up to the year 2000 are white. All the ravens we have so far examined have been black. But how, from principles of sampling, can we use this fact to show that H_1 is more probable than H_2? It is true that if all the future ravens are white, our current sample is less typical than if they are all black. But this does not help if, as is clearly the case, the future ravens had no chance of being selected. The analogy would be this: after we have drawn all the balls from the bag, it is refilled with a new set of balls and we are asked to estimate the distribution in this new population from that in the old. Obviously, the law of large numbers is of no assistance here, since the new balls have not been subjected to any sampling test. In the same way, we can infer absolutely nothing about the colour of ravens in the future from their colour hitherto, unless we can independently assume that ravens are likely to have the same colour in different periods of history, which is just to assume a raven-specific version of the uniformity of nature.

But does the law of large numbers at least provide a non-circular justification for induction in the case of the balls and other cases (like opinion polls) of the same type? The answer is that it does not. For even in these cases we need the empirical assumption that the possible samples have equal chances of selection, and this assumption can only be justified by reasoning of an inductive sort (or, if there is some further justification of induction, by the sort of reasoning to which induction itself is ultimately reducible). Thus I may shuffle the bag before each extraction, draw out the balls without looking inside, and take whatever other measures I can to facilitate an unbiased selection. But none of this affords me grounds for believing that the selection is unbiased unless I already know, or have grounds for believing, certain propositions about how the world works – e.g. that shuffling does not make white balls group together at the top of the bag; that the balls do not imperceptibly adjust their positions, as my hand enters the bag, in a way which makes the extraction of a white ball more likely; and so on. These are not propositions which I know *a priori*. My grounds for believing them rest on my past experience (or perhaps *our* past experience) of how objects of this sort have behaved in these circumstances. Thus it is only in so far as I can extrapolate from past regularities to my current situation that I can legitimately take my sample to be a fair one. And so the rationality of induction has to be assumed before the *a priori* principles of sampling are applied.

4 *Ayer's own position*

Ayer believes that any attempt to justify induction by appealing to an *a priori* theory of probability is bound to fail in one of the two ways which the arguments we have just examined exemplify: either, as in the case of the multiplication axiom, the argument will establish nothing which is even relevant to the issue of induction, nothing relevant to using the examined cases as a basis for prediction; or, as in the case of the law of large numbers, the argument will tacitly rely on some empirical assumption about the uniformity of nature which can only be justified by induction itself. And, taking into account the whole of Hume's argument, he concludes that we cannot provide a non-circular justification of induction at all. Nothing can show that induction is rational which does not itself involve the reliance, at some point, on inductive reasoning. This conclusion, indeed, is not unique to Ayer. In fact, it is almost universally accepted by those philosophers who have examined the issue. The only point where there is much disagreement is over the further conclusions which should be drawn from it.

The most obvious conclusion to draw would be that induction is irrational: since we can find no non-circular justification for it, we have no good reason to accept the conclusions which it yields. The fact that it has served us well hitherto cannot help us to avoid this consequence, since, without induction, we cannot take this as a reason for expecting it to be successful in future. The honest thing is to admit that the sceptic is right, even if we find it impossible to break the inductive habit. This, as Ayer notes, is Hume's official position, though it is not one which Hume consistently applies when dealing with other philosophical problems.

Among modern philosophers, the most notable exponent and defender of this sceptical position is Karl Popper.[5] Popper's repudiation of induction is combined with a further and more interesting claim, namely that induction is not an essential or even an actual ingredient of scientific method. Science, according to him, does not aim at the verification of generalizations, but at their falsification. The theories which the scientist advances are not advanced as certain or worthy of acceptance; they are advanced as hypotheses which are compatible with the data so far collected and which are to be retained, as hypotheses, until some counter-instance is forthcoming. Once the hypothesis has been advanced, the business of the scientist is to try to falsify it, to try to find a counter-instance by subjecting the hypothesis to experimental tests. A hypothesis which persistently survives the tests, and which thus shows itself to be, at least in those respects, resistant to falsification, acquires a sort of respectability – it becomes, as Popper puts it, 'corroborated' or 'attested'. But this does not increase the probability that it will survive future tests or give us any grounds for believing that it will. All we have done is to extend the number and range of empirical data with which it is compatible, without finding any datum which refutes it. According to Popper, science can and does proceed satisfactorily on this basis, without any appeal to the validity of inductive inference.

However, Ayer has detected a serious weakness in Popper's position. For even if Popper is right in thinking that scientific tests are attempts at falsification, rather than verification, this does not remove the need for induction. Ayer first makes this point in *PK*, though it is repeated in *PAE* and *CQ*:

> For what would be the point of testing a hypothesis except to confirm it? Why should a hypothesis which has failed the test be discarded unless this shows it to be unreliable; that is, except on the assumption that having failed once it is likely to fail again? It is true that there would be a contradiction in holding both that a hypothesis had been falsified and that it was universally valid: but there would be no contradiction in holding that a hypothesis which had been falsified was the more likely to hold good in future cases. Falsification might be regarded as a sort of infantile disease which even the healthiest hypotheses could be depended on to catch. Once they had had it there would be a smaller chance of their catching it again. But this is not in fact the view that we take. So far from approaching nature in the spirit of those gamblers at roulette who see in a long run of one colour a reason for betting on the other, we assume in general that the longer a run has been the more it is likely to continue. (*PK*, 74)

The fact that scientific method does depend on induction does not, of course, mean that induction is rational or that Popper was wrong to reject it. But Ayer, at any rate, takes a quite different view. While recognizing that induction is needed, and that we can provide no non-circular justification for it, he does not see this as yielding the conclusion that scientific method is irrational.

> It could be irrational only if there were a standard of rationality which it failed to meet; whereas in fact it goes to set the standard: arguments are judged to be rational or irrational by reference to it . . . When it is undersood that there logically could be no court of

superior jurisdiction, it hardly seems troubling that inductive reasoning should be left, as it were, to act as judge in its own cause. (*PK*, 75)

The same thought recurs in *PAE*:

Where I differ from Hume is in not seeing this [the lack of a non-circular justification of our inductive procedures] as a reason for scepticism. The conclusion that all non-contradictory judgements about the future are equally credible is simply false, if we assess it by our own standards. And Hume has not supplied us, and indeed on his own correct principles could not have supplied us, with any logical reason for adopting a standard of rationality which would make it true. (*PAE*, 88)

Thus the conclusion which Ayer draws from Hume's argument is not that induction is irrational, but that its rationality is *primitive*. Induction is rational, not because it can be shown to be so by appeal to more fundamental principles, but because it sets the ultimate standards of rationality in the area in which it is employed. In this respect induction is no worse off than deduction. Deduction cannot be validated by any argument which dispenses with deductive reasoning, and induction cannot be validated by any argument which dispenses with inductive reasoning. If this does not make deduction irrational, it does not make induction irrational either. It just means that both deduction and induction are primitive, *sui generis* forms of rational inference, which we are obliged to acknowledge without further justification: they are, as we may put it, *inherently* rational. This, at least, is how Ayer sees it.

One problem with this position is that not all inductive inferences are ones which we intuitively regard as rational. Take, for example, Hempel's paradox of the ravens. The sentence 'all ravens are black' (construed as meaning 'for all x, if x is a raven, x is black') is logically equivalent to the sentence 'all non-black things are non-ravens' (construed as meaning 'for all x, if x is not black, x is not a raven'). So whatever counts as inductive evidence for the truth of one of these sentences must count as equal inductive evidence for the truth of the other. Now suppose that, although we have never so much as caught sight of a raven, we have checked through all the non-black things we have so far encountered, of which there have been a vast number, and established that none of them are ravens. This, by inductive standards, seems to provide considerable support for the hypothesis that all non-black things are non-ravens; and any support for this hypothesis is equal support for the hypothesis that all ravens are black, if the two hypotheses are equivalent. But, could we seriously maintain that we had good reason, or even any reason at all, to accept the second hypothesis on the basis of such data – data which never involved the examination of a single raven? Surely not. But why not, if induction is inherently rational?

The reason, according to Ayer, is that, for the purposes of inductive confirmation, we are tacitly treating generalizations as conjunctions. The generalization 'all ravens are black' becomes, in effect, the conjunction 'R_1 is black and R_2 is black and . . . and R_n is black', where '$R_1, R_2 . . . R_n$' is an exhaustive list of all the ravens. The credit of the generalization is not increased by finding cases of non-black non-ravens, since such cases fall outside the scope of the conjunction. Ayer concedes that this account has to be modified in the case of what he calls an 'open' generalization, where the number of instances is potentially infinite. If 'all ravens are black' is construed as open in this sense, 'what is confirmed by the discovery of n black ravens, and none not-black, is the truth of any consistent finite set of propositions which includes the sequence of propositions stating that these particular ravens are black' (*PAE*, 81). And he sees this as indirectly confirming the generalization by confirming, in the case of each such set, 'the security of the inference from being a raven to being black' (*PAE*, 81).

Even so, Ayer sees a residual difficulty. For 'why should not the discovery of a number of white handkerchiefs serve equally well as confirming the inference from not being black to not being a raven?' (*PAE*, 81). And surely it does not. His answer is:

> The existence of the white handkerchiefs would indeed confirm a summative generalisation which predicated of a list of non-black objects, in which they were included, that they were not ravens, but it does not confirm any rule of inference which proceeds from the property of not being black, because we do not operate with any such rule . . . If this is right, the solution to Hempel's paradox is that if the propositions that all ravens are black and that all non-black things are non-ravens are treated as summative generalisations they are not equivalent, and that if they are treated as open generalisations, they sustain only a single rule of inference which proceeds in the direction from being a raven to being black and not the other way around. Why this should be so is a complicated question. All that I can say here is that it depends upon our beliefs about the way the world is organised. (*PAE*, 81–2)

I find it difficult to follow Ayer's reasoning here. In the first place, even if 'all non-black things are non-ravens' is treated as a summative generalization in Ayer's sense, I do not see how the discovery of a number of white handkerchiefs would contribute to its inductive confirmation. It would, of course, leave fewer cases to be examined and thus, in a trivial sense, increase the probability that the generalization is true. But as we have already noted in discussing the multiplication axiom

– and this was Ayer's own point – such confirmation has nothing to do with induction, since it provides no basis for prediction: the credibility of the generalization with respect to the unexamined cases has not been strengthened. Curiously, it seems that, in the present case, Ayer is only thinking of confirmation in this trivial sense. For in relation to the treatment of generalizations as conjunctions, he writes:

> The process of confirmation then consists in working through the conjuncts. When one of them is verified, the credit of the generalisation is strengthened, not in the sense that the remainder of the race which it has to run becomes any easier, but just in the sense that there is one fewer obstacle at which it can come to grief. (*PAE*, 80)

But confirmation in this sense has no bearing on the problem. What is at issue is the status of extrapolative induction, and, in particular, why such induction seems legitimate when we extrapolate from the observed blackness of the examined ravens to the blackness of the unexamined ravens, but illegitimate when we extrapolate from the observed non-ravenhood of the examined non-black things to the non-ravenhood of the unexamined non-black things.

I am also puzzled by Ayer's point about the direction of the rule of inference. He seems to be saying that if they are treated as open generalizations, the propositions that all ravens are black and that all non-black things are non-ravens are indeed equivalent, but sustain a single rule of inference which runs exclusively from the property of being a raven to the property of being black, and that because the rule only runs in that one direction, its confirmation has to come from testing ravens for colour rather than testing non-black things for ravenhood. But this seems strange. Given the framework of classical logic, which Ayer himself is taking for granted, there is simply no difference between a rule of inference from being a raven to being black and one from being non-black to being a non-raven. Either rule will allow us to classify an object as black on the basis of its being a raven and to classify an object as a non-raven on the basis of its being non-black. Presumably, all Ayer means is that we are to think of the rule as running in a certain direction for the purposes of confirmation; in other words, that the rule, however we are to formulate it, acquires its credibility from tests involving the sampling of ravens rather than the sampling of non-black things. No doubt this is true, but it is just the re-statement of the problem, not its solution.

If Hempel's paradox is troublesome, the inductivist also faces another and more fundamental problem, namely that *any* inference from the examined to the unexamined cases can be represented as inductively sound given a suitable choice of predicates. The classic illustration is the case of the 'grue' emeralds devised by Nelson Goodman.[6] The predicate 'grue' is defined as true of all things examined before t just in case they are green and to all other things just in case they are blue, where t is some arbitrarily selected time in the near future. Now let us assume that all the emeralds so far examined are found to be green. Then our current evidence inductively supports the hypothesis that all emeralds are green. The trouble is that it also seems to support the hypothesis that all emeralds are grue; for if all the emeralds so far examined are green, they are also, according to the definition, grue. But these two hypotheses make incompatible predictions about the colour of emeralds examined after t – one claiming that they are green, the other that they are blue. We are in doubt as to which of these incompatible predictions we should accept, but the problem is that both seem to be equally sanctioned by inductive reasoning. Nor does the problem stop there. For Goodman shows that, by choosing an appropriate predicate, we can represent our evidence as inductively supporting any prediction we like about emeralds or anything else. It is quite clear that if induction licenses all such inferences, induction is not inherently rational. Indeed, it is just about as irrational a method of inference as one could devise, since it is guaranteed, over the range of its possible applications, to yield infinitely many false predictions for every true one.

Ayer has no real answer to this problem other than to acknowledge that we have to place restrictions on the types of predicate we are to regard as 'projectible' and, more generally, on the sorts of hypothesis we should regard as inductively confirmed, given certain sorts of data.

> It is only by legislation of this kind which takes account of extra-logical considerations, such as simplicity, that we can make it rational to accept any given hypothesis rather than any one of the others that can be devised to accord with our existing information. The point is that our way of looking at the world, as evinced by our conceptual system, our methods of interpreting our observations and our selection of general hypotheses, goes together with our standard of rationality. If someone has an altogether different way of looking at the world, and correspondingly different standard of rationality, we can not prove the superiority of our standpoint except by begging the question. We can only gamble on being more successful and then wait to collect our winnings, or possibly not collect them. (*PAE*, 87–8)

A more intuitive response would be to deny that the non-standard extrapolations of the sort which Goodman envisages are applications of the inductive method in any but a nominal sense. The essence of induction, it might be said, is to use our existing data as a basis for generalization in accordance with the principle that nature is *uniform* – the principle, as Hume put it, 'that instances of which we have had no experience must resemble those of which we have had experience'.[7] To claim (and here I am slightly altering Goodman's own example) that before t all emeralds are green and after t all emeralds are blue is hardly to attribute a uniformity to nature in respect of the colour of emeralds. And while this claim is compatible with our data, it is not one which has any inductive support, if induction involves the attribution of uniformity. It is true, of course, that by choosing an appropriate predicate to describe our data and formulate the claim, we can make it seem that the claim is an extrapolation from the data in an inductive way. Taking 'grue' to apply to green things before t and blue things after t, we can say: 'The emeralds we have so far observed have been grue; so we hypothesize that all emeralds are always grue.' But the choice of this predicate only serves to conceal the counter-inductive status of the inference by building the colour-difference into the predicate itself. To say that all emeralds are always grue is just a contrived way of saying that the earlier ones are green and the later ones are blue. Any appearance of a colour-resemblance between pre-t and post-t grue things, closer than the resemblance between green and blue, is just a linguistic artifact.

It might be objected that even though grueness is a linguistic artifact for *us*, it is not so *essentially*. What makes it a linguistic artifact for us is the particular system of colour-classifications which we find it natural to adopt. As we imaginatively reflect on possible instances of colour in the past, present, and future, we find ourselves matching the pre-t instances of green with the post-t instances of green (not with the post-t instances of blue) and matching the pre-t instances of blue with the post-t instances of blue (not with the post-t instances of green). But surely there could be beings who found it natural to adopt a different classificatory system – beings who, while visualizing such instances in the same way as we do, matched the earlier green with the later blue and the earlier blue with the later green. For such beings, Goodman's (that is, our slightly revised version of Goodman's) predicates 'grue' and 'bleen' (where 'bleen' applies to blue things before t and green things after t) would be the natural terms of colour-classification. They would interpret the preservation of greenness in emeralds from $t - 1$ to $t + 1$ as involving a genuine change in colour, from grue to bleen, and the preservation of blueness in sapphires as involving a parallel change in colour from bleen to grue. Such a classificatory system is alien to us, but this does not mean that it has less claim to validity in absolute terms. And why should we suppose that it does? As Ayer remarked in the passage just quoted, 'if someone has an altogether different way of looking at the world, and correspondingly different standard of rationality, we can not prove the superiority of our standpoint except by begging the question' (*PAE*, 88).

We need to approach this issue with some care. No doubt it is possible

to envisage beings who find it natural to classify in accordance with grue
and bleen rather than blue and green. No doubt too, if we set up the
example carefully enough, there would be no way in which we could
prove to *them* the superiority of our system. But this does not oblige
us, or even provide us with any reason, to question the absolute correctness of our system and the absolute incorrectness of theirs. Indeed, we
cannot coherently do so. For as the hypothetical case is described – of
course from *our* standpoint – these other beings are making, for reasons
we may or may not be able to understand, a classificatory blunder. When
they focus on the dated colour-samples in their imagination, they have
the same phenomenal evidence as we have; yet they fail to see that it is
by staying green or blue, not by staying grue or bleen, that objects
remain, at the critical time, qualitatively unchanged. We have no choice
but to describe this as an objective mistake, sustained by some kind
of conceptual illusion and presumably stemming ultimately from some
structural defect in their cognitive hardware. Of course, this is a judgment
which we make from within our own conceptual scheme. But this can
hardly be taken to diminish its authority. How else, if not from within
our own conceptual scheme, can we make any judgment as to what is
objectively the case? The fact that from within this scheme we can
envisage the possibility of other beings who have a different one does
not mean that we should or could move to some neutral standpoint. As
Ayer himself says in another context:

> It is vain to attempt to dissociate the world as it is in itself from the
> world as we conceive it. Alternative conceptual systems may be
> possible, but we can only criticize one from the standpoint of
> another. We cannot detach ourselves from all of them and compare
> them with a world which we envisage from no conceptual standpoint
> at all. (*CQ*, 12)

The upshot of this is that our dependence on a certain conceptual scheme
is something which, once noted, can be thereafter ignored. For it cannot
lead to any weakening of the absoluteness of the judgments which we
make, even when those judgments concern the validity of other schemes.
Of course, in acknowledging this point, we must be careful not to
construe our own scheme as more extensive or more rigid than it actually
is. One of the less fortunate tendencies of mid-twentieth century British
philosophy, with its stress on 'ordinary language', has been to treat
certain non-mandatory aspects of our common judgmental practice as if
they were requirements of our conceptual system. And another has been
to forget that even aspects of this system may be shown to be defective by
reference to more fundamental conceptual principles. On these matters, it
must be stressed, Ayer himself is not to be criticized. Indeed, he has

probably done more than anyone to expose these tendencies and fight against them.

All things considered, then, I am inclined to think that the claim that induction is inherently rational is not vulnerable to Goodman's paradox, since we should not regard the projection of grueness onto future emeralds as an inductive step in the relevant sense. This is not to say that the projection of grueness is less rational than the projection of greenness; only that the projection of grueness is not a way of interpreting nature as genuinely uniform and therefore not something which is sanctioned by our inductive standards. And consequently someone who maintains that these standards are inherently rational is not thereby committed to endorsing all the incompatible predictions which appear, in the paradox, to be equally confirmed. Moreover, it seems that a similar approach would enable the inductivist to deal with Hempel's paradox. The generalization 'all ravens are black' and 'all non-black things are non-ravens' are indeed equivalent. But a sample of non-black non-ravens will either fail to exhibit any genuine uniformity at all (there being such a wide range of ways in which things can fail to be black and fail to be ravens) or, if it does exhibit a genuine uniformity (e.g. if it consists of white handkerchiefs or yellow primroses), will fail to exhibit one whose extrapolation would sustain the generalization that all non-black things are non-ravens. And for this reason, the inductivist could claim that the inference from such a sample to the generalization (or even to the ascription of non-ravenhood to some unexamined non-black thing) is not a genuine step of induction.

However, there is a further difficulty for the claim that induction is inherently rational and, in my view, the appreciation of this difficulty is the first step towards a solution of the whole sceptical problem. Suppose we have what we know to be an unbiased coin – one which is evenly weighted and has no other property which makes it more likely to come down on one side rather than the other when tossed. In addition we have what we know to be an unbiased coin-tossing machine – one which is scrupulously designed to vary in a random way the force with which it tosses a coin from one occasion to the next. And let us assume, for the purpose of the example, that, given an unbiased coin, the force of the toss is, and is known to be, the only factor which influences the outcome (heads or tails) on any occasion. Suppose we then get the machine to toss our coin a hundred times and, to our surprise, the coin comes up heads each time. Can we use this run of heads as a basis for predicting the outcome of the next toss? It is easy to see how someone might think that we can. Thus, on the one hand, we can envisage someone who, focusing on his knowledge that the coin and machine are unbiased and believing that this requires in the long run an approximately equal distribution of heads and tails, thinks that, to help even things out, tails is the more likely outcome. On the other hand, we can envisage someone who, focusing on the long run of heads and believing in the uniformity of nature, expects the run to continue to the next trial. But, on reflection, we can see that both these responses are irrational. If there is any reason for expecting in the long run an approximately equal distribution of heads and tails, it is not that the coin and machine have an egalitarian bias, but that they have no bias at all. And this automatically excludes any rational prediction about any particular toss, however uneven the distribution in the preceding series. Likewise, given the knowledge that the coin and machine are unbiased, we cannot interpret the consistency of the previous outcomes as anything more than coincidence. And if it is purely coincidental, we have no reason to expect it to continue to the next trial. Thus, however you look at it, the only rational response with respect to the next toss is to acknowledge our complete ignorance – to admit that the outcome is wholly unpredictable and that the previous run of heads is evidentially irrelevant. That is, this is the rational response given our initial information.

The problem is that one of the two responses which we have rejected as irrational seems to be the response which counts as rational by inductive standards. Someone who predicts heads for the next toss on the basis of the previous run of heads seems to be doing just what induction tells him he should do – projecting a past regularity onto the future. So if, as we have agreed, such a prediction is irrational, how can we accord a rationality to the method of reasoning which it exemplifies? How can induction be inherently rational if the prediction which it here generates is not?

One reply might be that while induction is inherently rational, we need to take account of *all* our observational knowledge about the behaviour of the relevant sorts of object before we can use it to derive a rational prediction. In the present instance, we already know, from other observations, that the distribution of heads and tails for unbiased coins has been hitherto approximately equal. So perhaps the reason we cannot legitimately predict a continuation of the run for this particular coin is just that the evidence drawn from this coin gets swamped by the evidence drawn from coins in general: induction is rational, but a prediction of heads is not something which, all things considered, induction supports. But this reply misses the central point, namely that, irrespective of our other evidence about coins, the assumptions we have made about this coin ensure that any prediction is unwarranted. If it were merely a question of the insufficiency of our inductive evidence when set against our evidence about coins in general, we could remedy this by supposing a larger number of previous trials over which the run of heads had been maintained. We could suppose that the coin had been tossed a thousand or even a million times and come up heads on each occasion. At some point we would be bound to get sufficient evidence of the uniform behaviour of this coin to outweigh the evidence drawn from coins in general. But the fact is that, in assuming that the coin and machine are unbiased, and that we know this, we make any run of heads, however protracted, predictively irrelevant. If the only factor which influences the outcome on any occasion is randomly selected, the run of heads, however protracted, is purely coincidental and must be discounted as a basis for prediction.

This immediately suggests another reply: induction is inherently rational, but obviously we cannot apply it to a case where we start with an assumption which denies the validity of its application. In assuming that the coin and machine are known to be unbiased, we are assuming that, for this case, induction is not appropriate – that any regularity which is found in a given sample of trials is of no evidential value in estimating the distribution of heads and tails over the trials that remain. This, of course, is true. But the question is: how is it to be explained by someone who holds induction to be inherently rational – to be a primitive form of rational inference? In claiming that the coin and machine are unbiased we are not thereby claiming or implying that induction cannot be successfully employed, nor, in particular, that it cannot be successfully employed in extrapolating from the regularity observed in the initial series of tosses. Indeed, in claiming that there is no bias, we explicitly leave room for any degree of uniformity among the outcomes: if there is no bias, there is nothing to prevent or resist a uniform sequence of heads for an indefinite period of time. So if induction is inherently rational, why should the assumption of no bias preclude its application? Why should the coincidental character of the run block the extrapolative step?

The true character of the situation becomes clear when we consider how we would respond to the coin-tossing example if the assumption of no bias were dropped. Thus in this new version, we do not know, in advance of our investigation, that the coin and machine are unbiased. We may believe that they are, but the belief is one which we are permitted to revise in the light of our empirical findings. As before, the coin is tossed a hundred times and comes up heads on each occasion. And, as before, the question is: can we rationally predict the outcome of the next toss? Well, the dropping of the assumption does seem to facilitate a step of extrapolation: it does seem to legitimize the inference from the past regularity to its future continuance. But what is interesting is the way in which it does this. Our reasoning would not be: 'Now that we have dropped the assumption, we have removed the only obstacle to what is, other things being equal, an inherently rational mode of inference.' Rather, we would try to justify the extrapolation by an argument which explicitly involved the postulation of a bias. We would argue that the previous run provided convincing evidence of a strong, and perhaps overriding, bias in favour of heads. And having inferred the bias from the run, we would then appeal to the bias to justify the prediction of heads for the next toss. Thus we would regard the step of extrapolation as rational not because it exemplifies a mode of inference which is, other things being equal, *inherently* rational, but because we can justify it on the basis of two other steps of inference of a quite different kind – an inference from the previous regularity to the presence of a bias and an inference from the bias to the outcome of the next toss. And the reason why the assumption of no bias would block the step of extrapolation is simply that the legitimacy of this step depends on an inference to a conclusion which this assumption explicitly denies.

We can now see that the example of the coin is interesting in more than one way. It was originally offered as a case which posed problems for the view that induction is inherently rational. This point still stands. Given the assumption that there is no bias, and hence that the run of heads is merely a coincidence, the extrapolation is not legitimate; and, as far as I can see, someone who accepts the inherent rationality of induction cannot explain why this is so. But there is now a further point, and one which promises to be of crucial importance. For once we drop the assumption of no bias, we try to justify the extrapolative step by dividing it into two other steps of inference of a non-extrapolative kind. The first of these steps, that from the previous run to the presence of a bias, is, presumably, an inference to the best explanation; the thought, presumably, is that a run of that length cannot be credibly attributed to chance and that the most plausible explanation is that the design of the coin or the machine (or both) is such as (for any arbitrary toss) overwhelmingly to favour, perhaps even to necessitate, a heads-outcome. The second step, from the bias to the outcome (or probable outcome) of the next toss is purely deductive: if we accept the bias in favour of heads, then, unless we have some special contrary evidence concerning the circumstances of the next toss, we are logically committed to accepting heads as the likely outcome. The importance of this is the possibility that we have, in this method of reasoning, a solution to the whole sceptical problem. For might it not be that, in all cases where we regard extrapolation as rational, we can justify our position in a similar way, by falling back on explanatory and deductive modes of inference which are not vulnerable to the sceptic's attack? Clearly, as things presently stand, this is no more than a possibility. We have yet to test this method of reasoning on other cases. And even in the case of the coin, it might be thought that the explanatory inference depends on certain background assumptions whose acceptability in turn depends on extrapolative induction in other areas. But at least there is something here which is worth investigating.

If this points our discussion in a new direction, it also links up with something mentioned earlier. Ayer, it will be recalled, argued that even if there could be such a thing as nomological necessity, it would not help in dealing with the problem of induction. An appeal to natural law, he argued, could only be used to justify a step of extrapolation 'if it were somehow easier to discover that all A's must be B's than that they merely were so' (CQ, 150). And this he took to be clearly impossible: there must be an easier (if you like, shorter) route from the evidence to the ordinary generalization than from the evidence to the law, simply because the generalization is the weaker conclusion. What Ayer overlooked, as we saw, was the possibility of using an explanatory inference. For if such an inference were available, it would not be surprising if it took us to the stronger conclusion first. It might be precisely because the statement of law is stronger that it has the explanatory power required to make it worthy of acceptance, and thus it might be only because we are first justified in accepting this stronger statement on explanatory grounds that we are justified in accepting the weaker generalization it entails. In effect, it is this possibility which we have begun to develop in the case of the coin. For by explaining the past regularity in terms of a bias, we are, in effect, explaining it in terms of natural law: we are supposing that the laws of nature, together with the intrinsic properties of the coin and the machine, are such as to make heads the probable or inevitable outcome in any arbitrarily selected toss. What we must now consider is whether we can extend this reasoning to other and less contrived cases, and, most crucially, whether it affords a general solution to the sceptical problem.

5 The nomological-explanatory solution

The general solution which our discussion suggests, and which I have called elsewhere the *nomological-explanatory solution* (NES),[8] can be summarized by the following three claims:

(1) The only primitive rational form of empirical (non-deductive) inference is inference to the best explanation.

(2) When rational, an extrapolative inference can be recast as the product of two further steps of inference, neither of which is, as such, extrapolative. The first is an inference to the best explanation – an explanation of the regularity whose extrapolation is at issue. The second is a deductive inference – an inference which takes as its premises the explanatory theory, sometimes together with certain additional statements and theories whose acceptability is already established, and which yields the conclusion that the regularity will, or will probably, continue.

(3) A crucial part of the inferred explanation, and sometimes the whole of it, is the postulation of certain laws of nature, or, sometimes,

the postulation of certain quasi-nomological constraints which are derived, in ways not fully specified by the explanation, from laws of nature and stable features of the situation. In either case these laws, and the constraints which depend on them, are not mere generalizations of fact, but forms of objective natural necessity.

How this solution works out in detail will vary considerably from case to case. But to present the issue in its clearest light, I shall focus on the simplest type of case, in which a single law is postulated as the complete explanation of some past regularity and in which the continuance of this regularity is deduced from the statement of law alone. To make things even clearer, I shall focus on this type of case by way of a particular, and suitably accessible, example.

Let us assume that hitherto, as far as experience reveals, bodies have always behaved gravitationally – and here I use the expression 'gravitational behaviour' to cover all the various kinds of behaviour, such as unsupported stones falling to the ground and planets following elliptical orbits, which are normally interpreted as manifestations of gravitational force. Can we use NES to justify our belief that this regularity will continue? The argument that we can would run like this: 'The past consistency of gravitational behaviour calls for some explanation. For given the infinite variety of ways in which bodies might have behaved non-gravitationally and, more importantly, the innumerable occasions on which some form of non-gravitational behaviour might have occurred and been detected, the consistency would be an astonishing coincidence if it were merely accidental – so astonishing as to make the accident-hypothesis quite literally incredible. But if the past consistency is not accidental, how is it to be explained? The most plausible explanation is that gravitational behaviour is the product of natural necessity: bodies have always behaved gravitationally because it is a law of nature that bodies behave in that way. But if we are justified in postulating this law to explain the past consistency, we are justified, to the same degree, in expecting gravitational behaviour in future. For the claim that bodies have to behave gravitationally entails the weaker claim that they always do.'

This argument is, of course, reminiscent of the reasoning employed in the case of the coin. In the latter case, it was claimed that the run of heads was too long to be credibly attributed to chance and that, consequently, we should see it as resulting from a built-in bias in favour of one outcome. In our new example, it is argued that the past consistency of gravitational behaviour is too extensive to be credibly regarded as accidental and that, consequently, we should see it as resulting from a law of gravity. The main difference is that the new example is simpler: we are explaining the regularity directly in terms of a law, whereas in the earlier example, we were explaining it in terms of something (the bias) which depended on laws and conditions in ways not yet specified. A further difference, of course, is that in the gravitational case the demand for some explanation seems that much stronger, since the past regularity is vastly more extensive. But this is only an incidental difference. For we could have set the previous run of heads at a thousand, or a million, or any large number we like.

The question we have to consider is whether the argument is sound and offers an adequate defence against the sceptical challenge. But before we turn to this, there is a point which needs to be stressed. As indicated in claim (3) above, laws of nature, as they feature in the context of NES, are to be construed as forms of objective natural necessity. This is crucial. If the postulated laws were mere factual generalizations, or such generalizations set in the perspective of some attitude we have towards them,[9] they would not be explanatory in the relevant sense. In particular, there would be no question of their postulation being justified by an inference of a non-extrapolative kind. Thus suppose we construed the law of gravity as merely the fact that bodies always behave gravitationally. There is, I suppose, a sense in which the postulation of this 'law' might be taken to explain the past consistency of gravitational behaviour – the sense in which we explain a fact when we subsume it under something more general. But it cannot be this sort of explanation which is involved in NES. For if it were, the inference to it would be an ordinary step of extrapolative induction and hence vulnerable to the sceptic's attack. In subsuming the past regularity under a universal regularity we would not be diminishing its coincidental character, but merely extending the scope of the coincidence to cover a larger domain. And it is just this kind of extension which the sceptic calls in question. The reason we can hope to do better with laws of a genuinely necessitational kind is that, arguably, their postulation can be justified by reasoning of a quite different sort. Thus, arguably, we are justified in postulating a law of gravity, as a form of objective natural necessity, because it removes what would otherwise be an astonishing coincidence: it enables us to avoid the seemingly incredible hypothesis that the past consistency of gravitational behaviour, over such a vast range of bodies, occasions and circumstances, is merely accidental.

Having settled this point, let us now try to evaluate the argument itself. Obviously, the issue is going to turn on the legitimacy of the explanatory inference, and I shall begin by formulating what I take to be the most obvious objection.

The past consistency of gravitational behaviour, does, on the face of it, call for some explanation. Let us agree, for the sake of argument, that this explanation has to be nomological: bodies have always behaved gravitationally, within the scope of our observations, because, by natural necessity, they had to. But why should we suppose that this natural necessity holds constant over *all* bodies, *all* places and *all* times? Why should we postulate a *universal* law of gravity rather than one which, while covering our data, is restricted in its scope to some particular set of bodies or some particular portion of the space-time continuum? To take the most obvious example, consider the following three nomological hypotheses, with t as the present moment:

(A) It is a law that bodies always behave gravitationally.
(B) It is a law that at all times before t bodies behave gravitationally.
(C) It is a law that at all times before t bodies behave gravitationally; and there is no stronger gravitational law (i.e. relevant to times later than t).

To justify our belief that bodies will continue to behave gravitationally in future, we have to justify an acceptance of (A) in preference to (C). But how can this be done by an explanatory inference? For both (A) and (C), by including (B), account for the gravitational regularity so far. It seems that to justify an acceptance of (A) we have to fall back on extrapolative induction, arguing that because gravitational behaviour has been necessary hitherto, it is likely to be necessary in future. But if so, we have not yet solved the sceptical problem. Nor, indeed, do we seem to have made any progress at all. For if we have to resort to induction at this point, we might just as well apply it directly to the past regularity without bringing in nomological explanation at all.

Is this objection decisive? Well it is certainly true that (B), and hence both (A) and (C), offer explanations, in the relevant sense, of the past regularity. But this alone is not enough to sustain the objection. What the objector must show is that, as explanations, (C) is not inferior to (A); or put another way, that (B) is not inferior to (A) as a terminus of explanation. And it is on this point, I think, that the defender of NES has a reasonable case. For it seems to me that a law whose scope is restricted to some particular period is more mysterious, inherently more puzzling, than one which is temporally universal. Thus if someone were to propose (C), our response would be to ask why the fundamental law should be time-discriminatory in that way. Why should t have this unique significance in the structure of the universe that bodies are gravitationally constrained in the period up to t but not thereafter? Barring the postulation of a malicious demon, these questions are unanswerable: any answer we could receive would only serve to show that the fundamental laws were not as suggested – that there was a deeper explanation in terms of time-impartial laws and a difference, relevant to the operation of these laws, in the conditions which obtain in the two periods. Because these questions seem pertinent and yet are *ex hypothesi* unanswerable, we are left feeling that, as hypothesized, nature is inherently puzzling and precludes an explanation of our empirical data which is both correct and, from the standpoint of our rational concerns, fully satisfactory. And it is for this reason that, presented with the data (the past gravitational consistency) and the alternatives (A) and (C), we are justified in preferring (A). We are justified in preferring (A) because it is the *better* explanation. And it is the better explanation because, unlike (C), it dispels one mystery without creating another: it dispels the mystery of past regularity without creating the mystery of capricious necessity. For the same reason, we are justified in preferring (A) to other hypotheses of a similar kind to (C), such as those which restrict the scope of the gravitational law to some particular set of bodies or some particular region of space.

The objector might reply that I am guilty of double standards. I am claiming that in the case of behaviour we should avoid unexplained regularity, while in the case of necessity we should avoid unexplained caprice. But why should our expectations for behaviour and necessity be so strikingly different? If there is no problem in expecting irregular behaviour when there are no laws to forbid it, why should there be a problem in building a measure of irregularity into the laws themselves? Or if it is reasonable to expect the laws to be uniform over bodies, space and time (given no evidence against it), why should it not be reasonable to expect uniformities of behaviour without the backing of laws? It seems that I am relying on opposite standards of rationality in the two cases.

Well, in a sense I am. But that is just because the cases are quite different. What makes them different is that, unlike the concept of behaviour, the concept of necessity has some notion of generality built into it. Thus try to imagine a world in which there are no conspicuous uniformities, but in which, for each object x and time y, there is a separate law prescribing how x is to behave at y. In such a world everything that happens has to happen, by natural necessity, but there is no uniform system of necessity, or anything remotely resembling one, which imposes the same constraints on situations of the same kind. Each law is concerned with the behaviour of a unique object at a unique time. Now it seems to me that such a world is not possible, not because we cannot conceive of such randomness in behaviour, but because we cannot conceive of such singularity in the scope of the laws. And this is not just a trivial point about the meaning of the word 'law' – a point which we could avoid by choosing another term. Rather, we cannot make sense of the claim that it is naturally necessary for a particular object to behave in a certain way at a particular time except as a claim which is implicitly more general, concerning how it is naturally necessary for objects of a certain type to behave in situations of a certain kind. This is not to say that we cannot conceive of laws which are to some degree restricted by singular reference. We can, I think, conceive of the law postulated by

231

(C), whose scope is restricted to a certain period. But this is only because the restriction leaves room for enough generality of scope for the notion of law to gain purchase. In itself, a singular restriction is something which runs counter to the direction of nomological explanation. This is why we serve the purposes of explanation better, if there is a need for explanation at all, by postulating laws without such restrictions, so long as we can do so compatibly with our data. And in particular, this is why, given the past consistency of gravitational behaviour, we rightly regard (A) as a more satisfactory explanation than (C) or any other explanation of a similarly restricted kind, whether the restriction is to a period, to a region, or to a sample of bodies. None of these considerations, which apply to our concept of natural necessity, carry over to our concept of behaviour. There is no implicit notion of generality in our concept of an object's behaving in a certain way at a certain time. Indeed, our rational expectation is that, without the backing of laws, the total pattern of behaviour will be more or less random, not because there is anything to ensure this, but because there is nothing to ensure or encourage regularity, and because, if it is left to chance, the probability of any significant amount of regularity is very small. In short, there is something *a priori* perplexing about an arbitrary restriction in the laws and something *a priori* surprising about a coincidental regularity in behaviour.

However, if the sceptic's first objection fails, he can offer an alternative one along similar lines. For even if the past regularity should be explained in terms of some law which is universal in scope – with no *singular* restriction to some particular period, region or set of bodies – the sceptic can still impose what will amount, for predictive purposes, to the same kind of restriction, but by the use of general predicates. All he needs is some general description 'φ', not involving any explicit or implicit singular reference, such that 'φ' applies to the circumstances of the past regularity, but, as far as we know, does not apply to other circumstances or to those particular circumstances with which we are predictively concerned. He can then claim that the past regularity is adequately explained by the hypothesis:

(D) It is a law that in φ-circumstances bodies behave gravitationally.

This postulates a universal law, covering all bodies, places and times. But it does not entail anything about the behaviour of bodies in non-φ circumstances, i.e. in precisely those circumstances with which, given the evidence of the past regularity, we are predictively concerned. The sceptic will argue that because (D) adequately explains the past regularity, then, to the extent that (A) goes beyond (D), we have no grounds for accepting (A) – in other words, that we have no grounds, other than inductive, for preferring (A) to the alternative hypothesis:

(E) It is a law that in φ-circumstances bodies behave gravitationally; and there is no stronger gravitational law (ensuring gravitational behaviour in any other circumstances).

Obviously, the same objection could be applied to any case in which NES was invoked to justify an inductive inference.

It is not easy to evaluate this objection. One difficulty is that we need some general but reasonably detailed account of what makes one explanation better than another. Clearly there is at least one factor on the side of the sceptic: if two hypotheses both explain the data and one hypothesis is stronger than the other (i.e. entails but is not entailed by it), then, other things being equal, the weaker hypothesis is to be preferred (thus if other things were equal, (D) would be preferable both to (A) and to (E)). What is far from clear is how we are to determine whether other things are equal. It is easy enough to say something very general and non-committal, e.g. that other things are not equal if the weaker hypothesis, while explaining the data, postulates some state of affairs which itself calls for further explanation of a kind which the stronger hypothesis supplies, or if the conjunction of the weaker hypothesis and the negation of the stronger postulates a state of affairs which is inherently more puzzling than the state of affairs which the stronger hypothesis postulates. But what we need, to evaluate the objection, is a set of more specific principles, justified independently of induction, which will enable us to decide, case by case, whether a state of affairs does call for explanation or is inherently puzzling. And the formulation of such principles would be a large and difficult task, if it is possible at all. A further difficulty, at least for a defender of NES, is that there is an infinite range of non-equivalent descriptions which could play the role of 'φ'. To rebut the objection entirely, it would be necesary to divide this range into a finite number of categories, show that the differences within each category were, relative to the present issue, irrelevant, and then rebut the objection for each category. This too promises to be a difficult and perhaps impossible task, even if, for each separate description, the objection could be shown to fail.

All I can do here is to examine some of the more obvious cases on their own merits. One such case would be to model (D) and (E) on the cases of (B) and (C) considered earlier. Thus suppose S is the total state of the universe at t (i.e. at the present moment) and 'Fx' is defined as 'the universe is in state S at time x'. Then we have as examples of (D) and (E):

(D1) It is a law that at any time before an F-time bodies behave gravitationally.

(E1) It is a law that at any time before an F-time bodies behave gravitationally; and there is no stronger gravitational law.

For all we know, an F-time will not occur in the future. So explaining the regularity by (D1) provides no basis for extrapolation. The question is: are there non-inductive grounds for claiming that (A) serves better than (D1) as a terminus of explanation? And this question becomes: is the state of affairs postulated by (E1) inherently more puzzling than that postulated by (A)? I think that it is, for two reasons. Firstly, what (E1) postulates involves, in effect, action at a temporal distance. For if (E1) were true then (and here, for simplicity, I assume that t is the only F-time) each past instance of gravitational behaviour would directly causally depend, in part, on the intrinsic state of the universe at t, there being no continuous causal chain mediating this causal dependence and spanning the temporal interval between t and the time of the behaviour. Secondly, since t is subsequent to the past instances of gravitational behaviour, the direction of the causal influence involved would be from later to earlier: the occurrence of gravitational behaviour in the past would be partly the causal result of the state of the universe now. In both these respects, and especially the second, what (E1) postulates is inherently more puzzling than what (A) postulates; and, consequently, (A) is a better explanation than (E1) and better, as a terminus of explanation, than (D1).

One way for the sceptic to eliminate both these defects would be as follows. Take each occasion i of observed gravitational behaviour and form a very detailed description 'F^i' of the intrinsic conditions obtaining immediately prior to this behaviour – a description sufficiently detailed to distinguish it, as far as we know, from the conditions which will obtain on any future occasion or on those future occasions with which we are predictively concerned. We then let 'ϕ' be the disjunction of these descriptions, so that 'in ϕ-circumstances' means 'either in F^1-circumstances or in F^2-circumstances or . . . or in F^n-circumstances', where the disjunctive list exactly covers all the specific conditions in which gravitational behaviour has occurred and been detected so far. Let us call (D) and (E) thus interpreted (D2) and (E2). Then (E2) avoids the two mentioned defects of (E1). It does not postulate any backward causation or any direct causation at a temporal distance. If (E2) were true, each past instance of gravitational behaviour would causally depend solely on the intrinsic conditions obtaining on that occasion.

Are there any other grounds for claiming that (A) is a better explanation than (E2) and better, as a terminus of explanation, than (D2)? I think there are. The first point to notice is that, in effect, (D2) explains the past regularity of gravitational behaviour by providing a separate explanation of each past instance. Because 'ϕ' does not signify a natural generic property, but rather a disjunctive list of the complex properties separately drawn from the different instances, it would be less misleading to reformulate (D2) as a long list of separate hypotheses: 'it is a law that in F^1-circumstances bodies behave gravitationally; it is a law that in F^2-circumstances bodies behave gravitationally; . . . .' The whole list would provide an explanation of the past consistency only in the sense that each hypothesis provided an *ad hoc* explanation of one behavioural instance. How then should we respond to someone who offers (D2) as a terminus of explanation, i.e. who asserts (E2)? Well, we are likely to find the state of affairs he postulates inherently puzzling, since the way in which the D2-law (or laws) discriminates between φ and non-φ circumstances is not based on any natural mode of classification: it seems peculiar that just the listed circumstances should be gravitationally efficacious when they are no more similar to each other than they are to other circumstances. Still, it may be hard to establish that the grounds for this puzzlement are non-inductive, and for this reason I would put the stress on a different point. Even though in a sense (D2) explains the past consistency of gravitational behaviour (by separately explaining each instance), it leaves us with another consistency which calls for explanation and which it would be very hard to explain if we accepted (E2). For although there are infinitely many types of circumstances (all those that are non-φ) to which the (D2)-law does not apply, whenever we have checked for gravitational behaviour the circumstances have always been of a type (φ) to which the law does apply. This would be an astonishing coincidence if it were purely accidental, and, on the face of it, it would be purely accidental on the supposition of (E2). Of course, it was not accidental that the sceptic chose to postulate a law which exactly covered the examined cases. But that is beside the point. What would, it seems, be accidental and exceedingly improbable is that the range of examined cases should exactly match the law which actually and independently obtained. No such surprising coincidence arises on the supposition of (A), and for this reason, if no other, (A) seems to be the more plausible hypothesis.

These are, of course, only two examples of the way in which the sceptic might pose the objection and the fact that we can apparently rebut them does not mean that he cannot turn to others. I do not have space here to look into this issue any further. But I suspect that, whatever the sceptic chooses for 'φ', there will be some way of vindicating our preference for (A).

However, the sceptic still has one further and more fundamental line of objection. For he might claim that the very notion of objective natural necessity is incoherent. This would be the position of many empiricist philosophers, including, as we have seen, Hume and Ayer.

Ayer himself does not go so far as to reject the concept of a law of nature altogether or to deny that there is a valid distinction between generalizations of law and mere generalizations of fact. But he thinks that the distinction between them lies not in a difference in what they assert, but in a difference in the attitudes they express. The difference is that when someone says 'It is a law that all *F*s are *G*s', he is, in addition to asserting the factual generalization, expressing a willingness to extend it to hypothetical cases – a willingness to say not merely that all actual *F*s are *G*s, but also, for any further *F*s which he might imagine, that they too are *G*s. This willingness is reflected in the fact that the subject's belief in the generalization is equipped to withstand certain kinds of additional information which would otherwise destroy or weaken it. As he explains in his essay 'What is a Law of Nature':[10]

> . . . I believe that all the cigarettes in my case are made of Virginian tobacco, but this belief would be destroyed if I were informed that I had absent-mindedly just filled my case from a box in which I keep only Turkish cigarettes. On the other hand, if I took it to be a law of nature that all the cigarettes in this case were made of Virginian tobacco, say on the ground that the case had some curious physical property which had the effect of changing any other tobacco that was put into it into Virginian, then my belief would not be weakened in this way. (*CP*, 231)

The belief would not be weakened, because, in treating the generalization as a law, the subject is already prepared to extend it to the hypothetical situation in question: he is willing to say, even with respect to the imaginary world in which it has been filled from a box of Turkish cigarettes, that the contents of the case are exclusively Virginian.

This attitudinal analysis of our concept of natural law is of some interest, and we shall be looking at it again in the context of Ayer's account of causation. What matters more at this stage, however, is the negative thesis from which it stems, i.e. the denial that we can form any coherent notion of objective natural necessity. For it is this which poses the threat to NES. As I have already stressed, it is essential to the rationale of this solution that the laws it postulates should be forms of objective necessity; otherwise, they would not have the explanatory power required to justify their postulation by means of a non-extrapol-ative inference. If the notion of such necessity is incoherent, so is the solution.

But why should this notion be thought incoherent? The traditional empiricist argument, stemming from Hume and endorsed by Ayer, is based on two claims: first, that the associations of properties which are alleged to be objectively necessary cannot be established *a priori*; second, that there is no way of explicating the notion of objective natural necessity by reference to actual or possible experience. This second claim, of course, depends, for its relevance, on some empiricist criterion of significance. The underlying assumption is that unless we can in some way explicate the notion experientially, we cannot make sense of it at all.

Of these two claims, the first is uncontroversial and its only purpose is to indicate where the real issue lies. Since the objective necessity in question is *natural* rather than *logical*, it goes without saying that necessities of this kind, if they obtain at all, could only be discovered empirically, through observation and experiment. The only thing which might obscure this point is that some of our predicates are so defined that they only apply to objects which are disposed to behave or causally affect other objects in a certain way. For this might make it seem that certain generalizations (we have already discussed Ayer's example of 'magnets attract iron') both specify natural associations of properties and are conceptual truths. This, as we have seen, is just an illusion. The natural association of properties remains non-conceptual, and, to specify it, the generalization has to be reformulated in terms of predicates which do not have this dispositional sense.

The real issue, then, turns on the second claim and the underlying empiricist assumption on which its relevance depends. Both the claim and (correspondingly) the assumption can take different forms, according to the nature of the empiricism. An empirical atomist will rely on the principle that all genuine concepts must either be, or be analysable in terms of, concepts whose content can be defined ostensively; and he will argue that, since there could be no impression of objective natural necessity, or anything else (like power, agency, force) in terms of which it might be analysable, the notion of such necessity turns out to be spurious. A verificationist, in contrast, will rely on the principle that any genuine concept must be capable of featuring non-redundantly in some empirically verifiable theory (its content being fixed by what it contributes to the verification-conditions of the theories in which it occurs); and he will say that since statements of natural necessity cannot be, even weakly, empirically verified, the notion of such necessity does not meet his requirements. Ayer himself does not, as far as I know, explicitly formulate either of these arguments. Indeed, whenever he discusses the issue, he seems to think that the onus is on the defender of natural necessity to justify his position rather than on the empiricist to refute it. But the verificationist argument is clearly in accord with Ayer's general outlook and the principle it relies on is, as we noted earlier, one which he explicitly endorses even as late as his book on Hume.[11]

But how could the verificationist argument be relevant to the present dispute? Even if we accepted the underlying principle, that any genuine concept must be capable of featuring non-redundantly in some empirically verifiable theory, this would not count against the supposed concept of objective natural necessity, unless we had some independent argument against NES. For the whole burden of NES was to argue that nomological theories, which employ this very concept, can be verified by means of an explanatory inference. Of course, the verification is not conclusive. But conclusive verification is not what is required. If it were, then almost all supposed empirical concepts would turn out to be spurious. The only way in which the verificationist argument could become relevant would be if the phrase 'empirically verifiable theory' were interpreted, in accordance with Ayer's original position in *LTL*, as meaning 'purely observational theory' – in the sense explained in Part I, section 3. For certainly there is no way in which the relevant statements of necessity could fall within the scope of an observational language. But this would hardly be an embarrassment to the defender of NES, since, as we have already shown, the verification principle in that strong, content-restricting form is indefensible.[12]

This still leaves the argument of the empirical atomist. But here again the defender of NES can afford to be complacent unless the atomist can make good his principle, and our earlier discussion (Part I, section 5) suggests that he cannot. All I would now add, by way of reinforcement, is that the atomist principle has implausible consequences in other areas. Perhaps the most crucial point, in this connection, is that, if the principle excludes a concept of *natural* necessity, it equally excludes a concept of *logical* necessity. For there is clearly no way in which such a concept could be analysed, or even in some weaker sense explained, in terms of concepts which are ostensively definable. And this point holds even if, as we earlier envisaged, we allow the notion of ostensive definition a liberal interpretation. The atomist might plead that the concept of logical necessity, and other concepts of a similarly formal and meta-theoretical character, are a special case. We need not require them to yield to empirical analysis, since they form part of the very framework of human rationality. But if so, why should not this framework also include a concept of *natural* necessity, or, at the very least, a generic concept of necessity which can be developed into its distinct species by further modification? If reason generates its own non-empirical concepts, it would not be surprising if some of them served, in the Kantian sense, as interpretative categories for the empirical realm. And among these categories, it would be plausible to include a concept of natural necessity (or perhaps just a generic concept of necessity), unless this concept (or, if generic, its application to the empirical realm) can be discredited in some other way.

All in all, I am fairly confident that the notion of objective natural necessity is coherent and, as such, will serve the purposes of NES. We can make sense of the claim that bodies have to behave gravitationally and we can advance this claim as an explanation of the past regularity. I am also fairly sure (though I have not investigated the issue fully) that the past regularity calls for explanation, that this claim provides the most plausible explanation, and that its plausibility does not depend on any prior acceptance of extrapolative induction.[13] And so, for this case at least, I see NES as providing an answer to the sceptical problem. Moreover, I cannot see why, if the solution works in this case, it should not work quite generally, though its application to other cases will often be much more complicated.

A point on which I am much less sure is whether we can plausibly, or even coherently, regard these objective necessities as autonomous. We are justified in postulating an objective law of gravity to explain the past regularity. But are we justified in regarding this law as the terminus of explanation – as just a brute fact of necessity which explains, but does not itself have, or stand in need of, any further explanation? Perhaps we are. Certainly, the law does not call for explanation in the way that the regularity does: the law, if unexplained, would not involve an astonishing coincidence. Nor, provided it is universal in scope, does it have the distinctively perplexing character of a restricted law. None the less, we may still feel that the very idea of an autonomous law is perplexing. How can it be, we may ask, that bodies have to behave gravitationally, if there is nothing to compel them? And, of course, in the sense of this question, the law itself does not compel them: the law is just the abstract fact that they have to behave in that way. What we were seeking, in posing the question, was, as it were, a concrete mechanism for the necessity, an agent of compulsion.

Maybe the question is spurious; or maybe it disappears into the more general question of why there is a natural world at all and has no special force as a distinctive question. On these points, I have at present no firm intuitions. If the question is well posed, then the proposed solution to the problem of induction might well turn into an argument for the existence of God. If it did, Ayer would no doubt see this as a further objection to the solution rather than as the vindication of theism.

6 *Ayer's account of causation*

As we have seen, Ayer, in the footsteps of Hume, denies that causation, as it obtains or could obtain in the world, involves any relation of objective necessary connection – and this, indeed, is just part of his more general thesis that any notion of objective natural necessity, whether as a causal relation between events or as a nomological relation between universals, is incoherent. Thus if we consider a typical case of a causal sequence of events, such as a cannon in billiards, Ayer thinks that while we use expressions of causal agency, like 'striking', 'hitting', 'imparting motion', and 'rebounding', to describe the sequence, 'everything that actually happens can be wholly described in purely undramatic spatio-temporal terms' (*PAE*, 11) – in terms of the movements of the cue and the balls.

> . . . there is nothing in the situation that calls for anything more than the identification of various objects and the specification of their changing spatio-temporal relations. In particular there is nothing of which such terms as 'power', 'force', 'energy', 'agency' could be names. (*PAE*, 11)

And quite generally, 'everything that happens in the world can be represented in terms of variations of scenery in a four-dimensional spatio-temporal continuum' (*PAE*, 10–11).

Whether or not there are or could be objective necessary connections, it is plausible to claim that our ordinary causal judgments assert or imply that there are. It is plausible to claim that our actual concept of causation includes a notion of objective necessity, even if, for that reason, it is incoherent. Ayer works on the assumption that this is not so – that, to the extent that they are assertive, our causal judgments are frequently true and should be construed in a way which makes that possible. He concedes that the reason for this assumption is partly charitable:

> . . . I should prefer to avoid saddling the public with such confusion of thought that its concept of causality had no application. (*H*, 59)

But there is also, I think, a further reason. For his own account of the meaning of causal statements would, if true, explain why we are led to suppose (mistakenly) that such statements do assert the existence of objective necessities. This is an important point, about which I shall say more in due course. In contrast, the question of whether our actual concept of causation does or does not include a notion of objective necessity is of no real concern, given Ayer's metaphysical position.[14] For on the assumption that such a notion is incoherent, then if our actual concept of causation includes it, our actual concept needs to be revised. Ayer's account of what our causal statements assert can then be recast as an account of what they *should* assert, i.e. of what they come to assert when their conceptual defects are corrected.

Ayer's account of the meaning of causal statements is based on two main ideas. The first is that even singular causal statements are implicitly general. The second is that causal judgments are not purely assertive. I shall explain these points in turn.

Although Ayer holds that 'everything that happens in the world can be represented in terms of variations of scenery in a four-dimensional spatio-temporal continuum', he does not think that in giving a causal description of some sequence of events we are merely describing the variations in scenery contained in that sequence. Thus he does not think that a causal description of the sequence in billiards merely records the succession of movements of the cue and the balls, though this is all the sequence in itself involves.

> . . . I am not maintaining that, when we say that the impact of the first ball causes the second ball to move, we are saying no more than that there is first a period in which the first ball is in motion and the second at rest . . . , then an instant at which they share a common spatial boundary, and then a period in which the balls are both in motion. . . . Exactly what more we are saying is not easy to specify, except that the answer has to do with the fact that the use of causal expressions brings in an element of greater generality. We are in some way implying that this situation is typical; that this is what normally happens or would happen in these circumstances. But the point is that the other situations with which this one is linked are of the same character. The only relations involved in them are spatio-temporal. (*PAE*, 11–12)

Later in the same book, he tries to specify the element of generality more precisely:

> The factual content of a singular causal statement consists in an assertion of the existence, in such and such a spatio-temporal relation, of the states of affairs which it conjoins, together with whatever generalisation is the basis for the conditional that one of these states of affairs would not in the circumstances have occurred without the other; this may be a universal generalisation, but it may also be a statement of tendency. (*PAE*, 132)

The exact interpretation of this is unclear, particularly over the question of how precise the relevant generalization has to be. But I take Ayer to be saying something along the following, broadly Humean, lines: if someone makes a causal statement of the form 'state of affairs A (e.g. the movement of ball X) caused state of affairs B (e.g. the movement of ball Y), and if 'caused' here means (though without involving any notion of an objective necessary connection) 'was, in the circumstances, causally necessary and sufficient for', then his statement is, in its factual (assertive) content, equivalent to the conjunction of two other statements. The first of these statements asserts that A and B exist in a certain spatio-temporal relation (e.g. that A is just precedent to and spatially contiguous with B). The second is a generalization which asserts that whenever there is a state of affairs like A in relevantly similar circumstances, there will always, or at least normally, be, in the same spatio-temporal relation, a state of affairs like B, and that whenever there is a state of affairs like B in relevantly similar circumstances, there will always, or at least normally, be, in the same spatio-temporal relation, a state of affairs like A. In cases where the causal statement only implies that A was causally necessary for B (without implying that it was sufficient) or that A was causally sufficient for B (without implying that it was necessary), the relevant generalization would be appropriately shortened, losing one of its two constituent clauses. It is slightly odd that Ayer should include a specification of the spatio-temporal relation in the first of the conjoined statements, since this seems to go beyond what the causal statement actually asserts. If I say that the movement of ball X caused the movement of ball Y, my statement may imply that the first movement was earlier than the second, but it surely does not imply anything about their spatial relationship nor anything more specific about their temporal. For this reason, it would be preferable to leave the spatio-temporal relation unspecified, though, of course, it will still be referred to in the generalization – in the claim that whenever there is a state of affairs of the one type there is always or normally, in the same *spatio-temporal relation*, a state of affairs of the other type. I am not, of course, denying that in more complex causal statements a specification of the spatio-relation is often, explicitly or implicitly, included – e.g. 'By *striking Y, X* caused it to move'. Perhaps it was these cases which Ayer had in mind.

One aspect of the passage which this exposition ignores is the way in which the generalization is seen as forming a basis for the counterfactual conditional – 'the conditional that one of these states of affairs would not in the circumstances have occurred without the other'. The reason I have so far suppressed this aspect is not that it is unimportant, or that it is only intended as an informal way of indicating the character of the generalization, but that we can only understand its significance by taking account of the second of the two main pillars of Ayer's account. And it is to this that we must now turn.

Ayer does not think that causal judgments are purely assertive, that their content is purely factual. Rather, he holds that a crucial part of their meaning is to express certain mental attitudes and dispositions, so that, in addition to asserting that certain facts obtain, they also exhibit a certain mind-imposed perspective in which these facts are viewed – a perspective which, following C. S. Peirce, he speaks of as 'our arrangement of the facts' in contrast with the facts themselves.[15] This point ties in with the point about generality, and indeed it is only in combination with the other that either point can be fully appreciated. Thus Ayer is claiming that when we make a singular causal statement, about two particular events or states of affairs, we are implicitly asserting something more general, to the effect that events or states of affairs of these sorts are, in the relevant kind of circumstances, invariably or normally conjoined. This implicit generality goes some way towards capturing the causal force of the singular statement: part of what makes the statement a causal one, despite its singularity, is its implication that the particular pair of items involved exemplifies a general regularity, whether universal or tendential. But, as Ayer sees it, this is not the whole story. Part of what gives the statement its causal force is that it expresses a certain attitude towards the generalization which it implicitly asserts. This attitude is that of regarding the generalization as a law of nature; and, as we have seen, Ayer takes the distinctive feature of this attitude to be a willingness to extend the generalization to hypothetical cases, in a way that one is not willing to extend any generalization which one is treating merely as a generalization of fact. This is why Ayer speaks of the generalization implied by the causal statement as forming the basis for the counterfactual conditional. It is not that the generalization itself sustains this conditional, but that a willingness to endorse the conditional is sustained by the nomological attitude to the generalization; and this attitude is something which the causal statement, as part of its very meaning, expresses. To say that A caused B is implicitly to assert that A-type items are relevantly conjoined with B-type items; and it is also to express an attitude towards this conjunction which makes it appropriate to endorse the appropriate counterfactual conditional, namely (in the case of a *necessary* cause) that B would not have occurred without A, or (in the case of a *sufficient* cause) that A would not have occurred without B, or both. And it is, in combination, this implicit assertion of the constant conjunction (the implicit generality) and this expression of the nomological attitude towards it (the non-assertoric force) which give the statement its causal meaning.

To be precise, I should say that, on Ayer's account, these factors provide the *core* of the causal meaning. For Ayer recognizes that, in its present form, the account does not allow for all the causal distinctions which we would want to draw. It does not, for example, allow for an adequate distinction between cases in which two events are directly causally related, as cause and effect, and cases in which they are collateral effects of the same cause. And even in the domain of direct causation, it is not clear that it allows for an adequate distinction between the case of A causing B and the case of B causing A. But Ayer is content, for the moment, to leave these points on one side, as not affecting the central issue. His basic thesis, at this stage, can be represented as follows:

(1) Apart from the implication that the items stand in a certain spatio-temporal relation, the central core of the content (both assertoric and non-assertoric) of the statement that A caused B consists in the claim that A was, in the circumstances, necessary (and/or sufficient) for B.

(2) This claim does not imply that A and B stand in any relation of *objective* necessary connection.

(3) Rather, the claim is to be analysed as the combination of three elements: (a) the assertion that A and B exist; (b) the assertion that A-type and B-type items are, in the appropriate way, constantly

243

conjoined (the way must be appropriate to the character of the claim as either a necessity-claim or a sufficiency-claim or both); (c) the expression of a nomological attitude towards this constant conjunction, i.e. of a willingness to extend it to hypothetical cases.

The only aspect of causal meaning which this account makes no attempt to capture is that which renders the claim of *circumstantial* necessity (and/or sufficiency) weaker than the claim of *causal* necessity (and/or sufficiency). This may look like a serious deficiency. But, as we shall see, Ayer thinks that it can be remedied by further refinements, without disturbing his basic strategy.

Some philosophers have suggested that, given a singular causal statement, the central core of its content can be expressed by the corresponding counterfactual conditional.[16] It looks as if this suggestion is very much in line with Ayer's position, as I have represented it. To claim that A was circumstantially necessary for B is surely to claim that, in the circumstances, B would not have occurred without A, and to claim that A was circumstantially sufficient for B is surely to claim that, in the circumstances, A would not have occurred without B. And these claims of circumstantial necessity and sufficiency cover, either individually or in combination, the core of causal content which Ayer is trying to analyse.

In fact, however, the suggestion is one which Ayer would reject. This becomes clear when we contrast his analysis of causal statements (or of the core of their content) with his analysis of counterfactual conditionals. In one respect, the two analyses are similar. For, in both cases, Ayer holds that the relevant statements are only partly factual: they combine an element of assertion with an element of expression. The difference lies in the nature of these two elements. In the case of the counterfactuals, the assertive element, to which a truth-value can be assigned, is merely the corresponding *material* conditional, and the expressive element, to which no truth-value can be assigned, is the expression of a willingness to assert the consequent on the supposition of the antecedent. The crucial point is that, unlike the causal case, neither of these elements involves any implicit generality. Thus suppose, taking out an unused match, I say: 'If this match had been struck five minutes ago, it would have lit.' The assertive component of my statement (which is true, but in the circumstances not very interesting) is expressed by the material conditional 'This match was struck five minutes ago $\supset$ this match lit', which is equivalent to the disjunction 'Either this match was not struck five minutes ago or it lit'. The expressive component (which is what gives the statement its main interest) is the expression of a willingness to assert that the match lit, on the (false) supposition that it was, at the relevant time, struck. Each of these components is only concerned with the actual or hypothetical behaviour of one particular match on one specific occasion. The material conditional carries no implication that, in similar circumstances, matches which are struck light. Nor does the willingness to make the suppositional assertion imply a general willingness to make similar assertions of similar hypothetical cases. It is true, of course, that my commitment to this suppositional assertion would not be rational unless it was based on beliefs and attitudes of a more general kind. I would have no reason to accept *this* outcome for *this* hypothetical case unless I accepted, as a generalization of law, that this is how objects of that sort behave in these circumstances. But this does not make the commitment as such implicitly general. For I could have the commitment, and appropriately express it by uttering the singular counterfactual, without having any justification for it. As Ayer illustrates:

> I make a bet: 'If I toss this penny it will come up heads' . . . . But
> now suppose that I find no takers, and so do not toss the penny,
> I then say: 'You were quite right not to bet with me, for if I had
> tossed the penny it would have come up heads.' I have no grounds
> for this assertion – the penny is not two-headed or known to be
> biased – but I make it all the same. (*PAE*, 120–1)

I have no business to make such a claim. But I can, without misuse of language, do so. And in doing so, I am not, on Ayer's view, implicitly asserting something about the behaviour of coins in general or even about the behaviour of this coin on other occasions. Nor am I implicitly expressing a willingness to assign a similar outcome to other hypothetical tosses. My claim is only concerned, both assertively and attitudinally, with this particular case.

In certain fundamental respects, Ayer's analysis of counterfactuals is highly controversial. In particular, it is far from clear (and, in my view, not the case) that a counterfactual asserts nothing more than the corresponding material conditional. But where I think he is clearly right is in maintaining that the counterfactual idiom does not as such involve any implicit generality. And this alone would, from Ayer's standpoint, vitiate any attempt to express the central core of content in a singular causal statement by means of the corresponding counterfactual. For, given the singularity of their concern, the claims that B would not have occurred without A and that A would not occurred without B are manifestly too weak to match the corresponding claims of circumstantial necessity and sufficiency. This is not to deny, of course, that these latter claims can be re-expressed counterfactually, if we are willing to combine the subjunctive mood with some further modality. We can re-express the claim that A is circumstantially necessary for B as the claim that, in the circumstances, B *could* not have occurred without A, and re-express the claim that *A* is circumstantially sufficient for *B* as the claim that, in the circumstances, *A could* not have occurred without *B*. But in these new formulations, what is doing most of the work is not the counterfactual idiom, but the notion of impossibility employed within it. And it is just this notion which will, to Ayer's way of thinking, import the implicit generality. In claiming that one of these events could not have occurred without the other we are, he would say, implicitly asserting a generalization correlating events of those types and implicitly expressing the corresponding nomological attitude – our willingness to project the correlation onto hypothetical cases.

His claim that singular causal statements are implicitly general, combined with his insistence that the only form of necessary connection they signify is attitudinal rather than objective, gives Ayer's account a strikingly Humean character – and Ayer would be the first to acknowledge the influence of Hume's theory. Like Ayer, Hume denies that we can form any coherent notion of objective natural necessity, and, like Ayer, he offers an analysis of causal statements which dispenses with that notion. The analysis is provided by two alternative definitions of the cause–effect relation, definitions which reflect alternative ways of modifying the notion of objective necessity so as to remove the incoherence. One way of removing the incoherence is to retain the objectivity, but commute the necessity into the weaker but respectable notion of constant conjunction. Instead of speaking of *A* and *B* as necessarily connected, we speak of *A*-type and *B*-type events as invariably conjoined. This yields, in the *Treatise*, the definition of a (sufficient) cause as 'an object precedent and contiguous to another, and where all the objects resembling the former are placed in like relations of precedency and contiguity to those objects that resemble the latter'[17] (or, as he puts it more succinctly in the *Enquiry*, 'an object, followed by another, and where all the objects similar to the first are followed by objects similar to the second'[18]). The other way of removing the incoherence is to retain the necessity, in a manner of speaking, but change it from something objective to something subjective – from something which relates the events as they are in themselves to something which the mind imposes on them by its inferential propensities. We continue to say 'Given *A*, *B must* follow', but we construe the 'must' merely as signifying the mind's disposition to pass from a belief in the one type of event to a belief in the other. This yields, in the *Treatise*, the definition of a (sufficient) cause as 'an object precedent and contiguous to another, and so united with it that the idea of the one determines the mind to form the idea of the other, and the impression of the one to form a more lively idea of the other'[19] (or, as he puts it more succinctly in the *Enquiry*, 'an object followed by another, and whose appearance always conveys the thought to that other'[20]).

Certain commentators, noting the obvious fact that these two definitions are not equivalent, even extensionally, have concluded that either
Hume is guilty of a gross inconsistency or else does not intend both as
genuine definitions. Thus J. A. Robinson, preferring the second of these
alternatives, arrives at the conclusion that the first is Hume's genuine
definition and the second is only an empirical claim about the cause–effect
relation as thus defined, namely that our observation of constant
conjunction induces an association between the corresponding ideas in
the mind.[21] But this completely misses the point. Hume recognizes that
any definition which leaves causation as something of which we can have
a coherent notion is bound to deviate in some way from the direction
in which our initial, pre-philosophical understanding of causation points
us – precisely because our initial understanding points us in the direction
of objective necessity. Whatever definition we choose, we are bound to
feel that we have missed the original target, precisely because the original
target was illusory. This is what Hume means when he says at the end
of his discussion in the *Enquiry*:

> But though both these definitions be drawn from circumstances
> foreign to the cause, we cannot remedy this inconvenience, or attain
> any more perfect definition, which may point out that circumstance
> in the cause, which gives it a connexion with its effect. We have no
> idea of this connexion, nor even any distinct notion what it is we
> desire to know, when we endeavour at a conception of it.[22]

Given that the original target is illusory, the best we can do is to miss
it by the smallest amount. And it is here that the alternatives present
themselves. If what makes this target illusory is that it combines objectivity and necessity, we have a choice between two ways of adjusting
our aim, according to which of these factors we retain and which we
change – a choice between defining a connection which is objective but
not necessary and defining a connection which is necessary but not
objective. This is why Hume offers his two definitions, which are clearly
different but have, as he sees it, equal claims to be what our initial
understanding yields to the extent that we can make sense of it.

The similarity between Hume's account and Ayer's account is clear.
Hume's two definitions of cause correspond to Ayer's discernment of
two kinds of component in the content of causal statements. Ayer's
assertive component is, more or less, the assertion of a constant conjunction, in conformity with Hume's first definition. Ayer's expressional
component is, more or less, the expression of an inferential disposition,
in conformity with Hume's second definition. The differences between
the accounts are also clear. While Hume offers alternative interpretations
of causal statements, according to whether we are more concerned with
causation as it is objectively or causation in the perspective of our inferen-

tial attitudes, Ayer offers a single interpretation which allows for both factors. And while Hume claims that the relevant inferential attitude or disposition is something whose existence a causal statement, construed in the second way, asserts, Ayer takes it to be something whose existence a causal statement merely expresses. In both respects I think Ayer's account is superior to Hume's. It is superior in the first respect because, by combining both factors in a single interpretation, it is bound to come closer than either of Hume's interpretations to the target set by our initial understanding; for it retains both the objectivity, though only of constant conjunction, and the necessity, though only attitudinal. It is superior in the second respect because, even if there has to be some discrepancy between our philosophical analysis of causal statements and our initial understanding of them, to construe such statements as *assertions* about our attitudes or dispositions, or about the attitudes and dispositions of the person who makes them, makes that discrepancy too great. As Ayer himself gently puts it, in commenting on Hume's account:

> On the other hand, it was a venial mistake on Hume's part to include a reference to the mind's propensity in what was supposed to be a definition of causality. In propounding causal judgements, we express our mental habits, but do not normally assert that we have them. An account of our mental habits does enter into the explanation of our ascriptions of causality: but this is not to say that when we attribute causal properties to some physical object, we are also making an assertion about ourselves. (*H*, 68)

The mistake would be similar to construing an aesthetic or moral judgment as an assertion about the judgment-maker's aesthetic or moral feelings. It may be – and, as we saw in Part I, section 8, this is Ayer's view – that in calling something *beautiful* or *good*, I am not ascribing an objective property of beauty or goodness to it, but merely expressing my aesthetic or moral approval. But I am certainly not asserting that I have this feeling of approval. I am not asserting anything about myself at all. Likewise, in saying that A caused B, I may be expressing my willingness to infer a B-type occurrence from an A-type occurrence (in the case of a sufficient cause) or my willingness to infer an A-type occurrence from a B-type occurrence (in the case of a necessary cause). But I am certainly not asserting that I or anyone else has such an inferential disposition. I am not asserting anything about the human mind at all, unless, perchance, either A or B happens to be a mental event.

The upshot of this is that while both Hume's and Ayer's accounts would leave a discrepancy between our pre-philosophical understanding of causal statements and the interpretation assigned to them by the analysis, Ayer could claim with much more plausibility to be revealing what these statements actually mean. He could claim, with much more plausibility than Hume, that his analysis involves no revision of our concept of causality, even though it does involve correcting the vulgar misconception of what that concept actually is. This, of course, is connected with the point mentioned earlier, that Ayer's analysis, if correct, would explain how the misconception arises: it would explain why we ordinarily suppose (falsely, if the analysis is correct) that our causal statements imply the existence of an objective necessary connection between the cause and the effect. The point is that, because the overt form of a causal statement is purely assertoric, the non-factual status of its expressive component would be concealed. This would make it easy to mistake what is really the expression of a nomological attitude, or inferential disposition, for an assertion of how things objectively are – to misconstrue the expression of a willingness to generalize over hypothetical cases as the assertion of some objective necessity. Of course, the fact that such an explanation is available does not mean that we are called on to use it. Even for someone who regards the notion of objective necessity as incoherent, it is arguably more plausible to think that our actual concept of causality involves it. On such a view, Ayer's analysis would be revisionary rather than descriptive.

As I have already stressed, Ayer's analysis, in its present form, is only intended to capture the central core of the content of singular causal statements – the core expressed by such claims as 'A was, in the circumstances, necessary for B' or 'A was, in the circumstances, sufficient for B' or the conjunction of the two. These claims of circumstantial necessity and sufficiency are, in various respects, weaker than the corresponding causal claims. The question we must now consider is whether Ayer can make good the deficiency within the framework of his general strategy.

One respect in which the circumstantial claims fall short of the causal claims is that there are cases where we want to say that one event was circumstantially necessary and/or sufficient for another, but where we regard the events as collateral effects of the same cause, rather than as directly causally related. To take an example of Ayer's, we accept the generalization that, in standard conditions, a fall in a barometer is normally followed by rain; and we regard this generalization (perhaps more precisely expressed) as a consequence of a law of nature and thus as covering hypothetical as well as actual cases. Given this belief and nomological attitude, we would claim, with respect to a particular instance, that a certain barometer-fall was circumstantially sufficient for a certain shower of rain, i.e. that, in the circumstances, the fall could not have occurred without the subsequent shower. But we would certainly not claim that the fall caused, i.e. was causally sufficient for, the shower. Rather, knowing how barometers work, we would say that both these events were independently caused by a fall in atmospheric pressure.

The problem is that, in its present form, Ayer's account does not explain why the case should be treated in the one way rather than the other.

Ayer recognizes this problem, but thinks that his account can be developed to meet it.

> A falling barometer is thought to presage rain and not to cause it, because we possess a more comprehensive theory which accounts both for the fall in the barometer and for the subsequent rain as dependent facts. (*PAE*, 136)

His point is that, to distinguish direct causation from collaterality of effects, what we need is not some new causal concept, signifying a stronger connection than the relations of circumstantial necessity and sufficiency already analysed, but merely the deployment of these latter concepts in a broader context. The reason why we classify the barometer-fall and the shower of rain as collateral effects is not that the circumstantial sufficiency which relates them is, as such, too weak to meet the requirements of direct causation, but that this connection is seen to be the product of more fundamental connections, of a similar type, which oblige us to picture the lines of causation as running in a different way. The constant conjunction of barometer-changes and subsequent weather-changes is seen as the product of two other constant conjunctions, which separately connect both of these changes with earlier atmospheric changes, and our nomological attitude towards the first conjunction is wholly absorbed by, and conditional on, our nomological attitude towards these other two. Thus what prevents us from treating this case as one of direct causation is not that our beliefs and attitudes fail to assign a sufficiently strong connection to the two events in question, but that, in the framework of the whole web of our beliefs and attitudes, embodying, as Ayer puts it, our 'more comprehensive theory', this connection is seen in a perspective which makes the collaterality conspicuous.

This point is well taken. But there is now a further question which arises. Let us agree that by taking account of our more comprehensive theory, we can see that the lines of causation (i.e. the *fundamental* connections of circumstantial necessity and sufficiency) run not between the barometer fall and the shower of rain but between each and the earlier fall in atmospheric pressure. Even so, this does not reveal the precise causal structure of the situation. For we still have to determine the direction in which the causation runs. We want to say that the fall in pressure caused the subsequent change in the barometer and the subsequent shower of rain, rather than *vice versa*. But how can this preference be explained on Ayer's account? If the fall in pressure was, in the circumstances, sufficient for the fall in the barometer, the fall in the barometer was, in the same circumstances, necessary for the fall in pressure. And, if we like, we can envisage the circumstantial relationship as entirely symmetrical – the earlier event being both sufficient and necessary for the later, and the later thus both necessary and sufficient for the earlier. So here we have a further respect in which the causal concept defined by Ayer's analysis seems too weak for our purposes – a further respect in which the content of singular causal statements exceeds the content of the corrresponding circumstantial claims.

One obvious response to this would be to let the temporal relation itself do the additional work. Our intuition is that the cause must precede, or at least be no later than, the effect. All Ayer has to do, it seems, is to build this intuition into his analysis, so that whatever is not covered by the relations of circumstantial necessity and sufficiency, and their interpretation in the framework of the comprehensive theory, is covered by specifying the temporal relation. Admittedly, the temporal relation would not help to fix the direction of causation in cases where the two events were simultaneous. One way of dealing with this would be to deny that such cases can arise – to insist that the cause must always be earlier than the effect. This would not, I think, be implausible. But even if we allow for cases of simultaneous causation, there is no real problem. For if the temporal relation fixes the direction of causation in the case of non-simultaneous events, and if, apart from directionality, the lines of causation are already fixed by the circumstantial relations in the framework of the comprehensive theory, then the direction in the case of simultaneous cause and effect will presumably fall into place – in the same way as the lines of causation fall into place in the framework of the theory. Thus, typically, one would interpret one event as the cause and the other as the effect because the preceding chain of causation led up to the one rather than the other. Indeed, it would surely only be in cases where the surrounding context indicated the direction that there would be any temptation to construe the simultaneous events as directly causally related.

This would, I think, be Ayer's own response, or at least the outer layer of it. Certainly in *PK*, where he discusses the relationship between causality and time, he regards it as analytic that cause cannot succeed effect.

> The use of the word 'cause' is such that if one event is said to be the cause of another, it is implied that it precedes, or at any rate does not succeed, the event which is said to be the effect. (*PK*, 170–1)

And so apart from the case of simultaneous events, he thinks that the temporal relation is bound to reveal the direction of causation. But he also concedes, and I think rightly, that this does not get to the heart of the problem. For if the relations of necessity and sufficiency run in both directions, what is the point of having a concept of causation which has

251

this temporal asymmetry built into it? Of course, one might say that there is no special point other than that of linguistic economy – of having a single term which will indicate the temporal order of the events as well as the other, and more fundamentally causal, factors. But this hardly does justice to our ordinary intuitions. We take it to be a conceptual truth that cause cannot succeed effect; but we also take this truth to reflect some more fundamental asymmetry in the causal process – an asymmetry which coincides with, but is not reducible to, direction in time. If A is the cause and B is the effect, we take this to imply that B depends on A in a way in which A does not depend on B; and this one-way dependence is not captured by specifying the nomological connection between their types and indicating that A is the earlier event, even if the fact that A is earlier explains why, if there is a dependence, it has to run in that direction. Maybe these intuitions are misguided. Certainly on Ayer's account it seems they would have to be. But at least Ayer is called on to explain them. If he is going to reduce the direction of causation to the temporal order, he needs to uncover some significance in the temporal order which accounts for our feeling that causation is asymmetrical in a deeper way, of which the temporal asymmetry is only a manifestation.

One suggestion might be that, at any time, the past is fixed and the future is open, so that, although the relations of necessity and sufficiency run in both directions, we can exploit these relations to influence the future but not to influence the past. However, as Ayer sees, this suggestion is either false or begs the question. The past and future are both closed in the sense that they cannot be *altered* and they are both open in the sense that they cannot be deduced from the present. The only sense in which the past is closed and the future is open is that present activities can causally influence (though not, of course, alter) the future but not the past. And this, of course, just rests on the very principle whose rationale we are trying to discover – that cause cannot succeed effect.

Another suggestion would be that the directionality we think we discern is just a projection of human interests. Human action is always directed towards the future, never towards the past: we act to bring about a later result, never to bring about an earlier. The suggestion would be that, because our intentions are always forward-looking, we come to think of the external processes themselves as running causally from earlier to later. But again, as Ayer points out, we need to explain why our intentions are always forward-looking, why we always set ourselves future goals, never past ones. It is not as if we have no emotional concern about the past; and, in particular, we have hopes and fears about the past, just as we have them about the future. If we thought our present actions could causally influence the past, we would often act with a backward-looking intention. Of course, if we knew, independently of our intentions, that a certain event had occurred, we could not rationally intend to cause its non-occurrence, nor, for that matter, to cause its occurrence. But the same applies to the future as well. It is only where we are ignorant or unsure of the outcome, without relying on our knowledge of how we will act, that we can rationally intend to influence the outcome by our action. This is so whether the outcome is in the past or in the future.

Even so, it is essentially this last point which, in Ayer's view, provides the key to the solution. For he thinks that it is a difference in the extent of our knowledge of the past and of the future which explains the directionality of causation from the human viewpoint.

It is because the future seems to us uncertain that we think that we must strive to bring things about. The past, on the other hand, is not unknown to nearly the same degree; and especially not the immediate past, where the events of which we might discover our present actions to be the necessary or sufficient conditions are mainly located. The reason, then, why we do not allow ourselves to conceive of our actions as affecting past events is, I suggest, not merely that the earlier events already exist but that they are, for the most part, already *known* to exist. Since the same does not apply to the future, we come to think of human action as essentially forward-moving: and this rule is then extended to all other cases of causality. (*PK*, 175)

This, of course, is not intended to justify our attribution of a causal direction to events, but only to explain it. The relations of necessity and sufficiency run in both temporal directions, but we think of the causal processes as running forwards in time because, at any moment, the past is, to a much greater extent than the future, epistemically settled and thus no longer something on which we could rationally hope to exert an influence. This contingent directionality then gets transformed into a definitional requirement, so that it becomes a conceptual truth that cause cannot succeed effect.

I do not find this explanation convincing. If the only thing which differentiates the past and the future, in respect of causal accessibility, is the extent of our knowlege of them, we could, having taken note of this distinction, readily change our judgmental practice to allow for causation in both directions. In particular, where we were ignorant of what happened on some past occasion, as we often are, we could come to make sense of the notion of our doing something now which would causally determine the outcome. The fact that this would involve revising our actual concept of causation would not be an objection, since the revision would be in line with the very factors which give our forward-looking concept its rationale. Indeed, the revised concept would be more in line with these factors than the current concept: if the rationale for directionality is the distinction between what is known and what is unknown, there is really no justification for a concept of causation which never permits the direction to run from later to earlier irrespective of the epistemological situation. However, it does seem that the problems of allowing for the possibility of backward causation run deeper than this, and that, consequently, the rationale for the forward-looking character of our actual concept is not what Ayer suggests.

Exactly what the rationale is remains a difficult question, and one which I shall not try to answer in any detail here. The approach which I would favour is almost the exact opposite of Ayer's. To begin with, I would endorse our ordinary intuition that there is an essential, pre-temporal asymmetry in the causal relation itself – that the cause is asymmetrically responsible for the effect and the effect asymmetrically dependent on the cause, in a way which does not reduce to their temporal order. In one sense this makes the problem harder. For if the direction of causation does not reduce to temporal order, then we have to find some further explanation for their supposedly necessary coincidence – for the fact, as we believe, that cause cannot succeed effect. My suggestion here, reversing Ayer's approach, would be that temporal order is ultimately a product of causal structure. The reason why backward causation is impossible, or, at the very least, conceptually problematic, is that the temporal order of events is logically constructed from their actual and potential causal relations on the basis of the principle that causation runs from earlier to later. This, of course, requires the concept of causality to be logically prior to the concept of time, and, at first sight, this requirement seems objectionable. For how could we have a concept of causality without having a prior concept of an event, and how could we have a concept of an event except as something which occurs in time? I recognize the force of this objection. All I shall say here is that I think we can avoid it by accepting a certain form of phenomenalism. For this will allow the primitive domain of events from whose causal structure time is constructed to be characterizable without the use of temporal concepts, or at least without the use of those temporal concepts which depend on the construction. The details of this construction I have set out elsewhere,[23] along with a defence of the phenomenalist position which it assumes.

7 The reducibility thesis

A central component of Ayer's account of causation, as of Hume's, is the claim that causal relations between particulars are reducible to the nomological relations between their types. I shall call this the *reducibility thesis*. Put more precisely, this thesis asserts that if x and y are events and x is the cause of y, there is a non-causal property F, a non-causal property G and a non-causal relation R – this relation being either temporal, or spatio-temporal, or in some other way locational and partly temporal – such that the causal relation between x and y holds in virtue of, and is nothing over and above, the combination of (1) the fact that x instantiates F, y instantiates G, and x is R-related to y, and (2) some suitable law (or laws) relating F, G and R. To be suitable, this law must have a form corresponding to the nature of the causal relation it sustains. Thus if x (i.e. x's being F) is the *sufficient* cause of y (i.e. y's being G), the law must ensure that any F-event is R-related to some G-event, while if x is the *necessary* cause of y, it must ensure that any G-event has the converse relation to some F-event. In cases where x is both the necessary and the sufficient cause, the law (or laws) must ensure both.

Some philosophers who accept the reducibility thesis regard laws of nature as forms of objective natural necessity. Others, like Hume and Ayer, regard laws of nature as partly subjective – as, in part, the projection of our own inferential attitudes. According to these latter philosophers, the only objective element in a law is constant conjunction, the mere factual association of certain properties; any necessity in the association is derived from the perspective of the human viewpoint – from our willingness to accept the universality of the association without examining all the instances and to extend the association to purely hypothetical cases. Obviously, the difference between the objectivist and subjectivist interpretations of natural law generates, within the framework of the reducibility thesis, a corresponding difference between an objectivist and a subjectivist interpretation of causality. But in what follows such differences will not concern us. For what I want to examine is the thesis itself, irrespective of how laws themselves are construed. Of course, in discussing the thesis, I shall have to adopt a form of speech which appears to assume the objectivist position. I shall have to speak of events as causally related and of its being a law that such and such. There is no more explicitly neutral mode of speech available which would not also be excessively cumbersome. But it has to be remembered that when I speak in this ostensibly objectivist way, I am not excluding a philosophical position of a subjectivist kind, though, for reasons I have already made clear, I myself would reject this position.

One of the problems for the reducibility thesis, as we have seen, is the difficulty of accounting for the directionality of causation. And here the problem is not just that, if the thesis is correct, there seems to be no reason for excluding backward causation or for having a concept of causality which excludes it. It is also, and more fundamentally, that the thesis is in conflict with our ordinary conception of causation as an inherently directional process, involving an asymmetrical dependence of one event (the effect) or another event (the cause). But there is also a further problem for the thesis and it is this which I want now to discuss. I shall begin by sketching a purely fictitious example in which the problem arises, before turning to the central area where it assumes its most interesting form.

Suppose that there is a certain kind of metal K and it is a law of nature that, when any spherical K-lump reaches a specified temperature, a flash occurs half a second later somewhere (unspecified) in the region of points no further from the centre of the sphere than twice its diameter. Suppose further that there is no stronger law which fixes the position of the flash more precisely – that, at the moment when the critical temperature is reached, all positions within the specified region have equal chances of receiving the flash. Now given this law, it is very plausible to construe the relationship between the occurrence of the critical temperature in any K-sphere and the subsequent occurrence of a flash in the specified region as *causal* – plausible to say that the first event causes the second. And normally this causal interpretation creates no problems for the reducibility thesis. But now suppose that two K-spheres, which are sufficiently close together for their specified regions to overlap, reach the critical temperature simultaneously and that, half a second later, two simultaneous flashes occur within the region of overlap. It is still intuitively plausible to suppose that each sphere-temperature is the cause of one of the flashes and that each flash is the effect of one of the sphere-temperatures. But the causal pairings are not determined by the law and the non-causal properties of the events, since each flash falls within the specified region for each sphere. Thus if we call the two temperature events T_1 and T_2 and the two flashes F_1 and F_2, we want to say that either

  (a) T_1 (and not T_2) caused F_1 (and not F_2) and T_2 (and not T_1) caused F_2 (and not F_1),

or (b) T_1 (and not T_2) caused F_2 (and not F_1) and T_2 (and not T_1) caused F_1 (and not F_2).

But the law and the non-causal description of all that happens are neutral between (a) and (b). They are compatible with each pair of causal pairings. So whichever pair of pairings obtains, it involves a causal relationship which is not reducible to a nomological relationship. In other words, the case, if interpreted in the most natural way, refutes the reducibility thesis.

Now, of course, the fact that *on its most natural interpretation* the case refutes the reducibility thesis does not mean that it refutes it *as such*. For the reductionist is not forced to interpret the case in that way. He can insist that there are no causal pairings beyond what the law and non-causal conditions reveal: we are entitled to say that the two temperature events in combination cause the two flashes in combination, but not that each flash is uniquely the effect of one temperature event and that each temperature event is uniquely the cause of one flash. It is true that this interpretation is contrary to our ordinary intuitions. But the reductionist would see this as a case in which our ordinary intuitions need to be corrected. Of course, before he can correct these intuitions, he needs to establish the correctness of his own interpretation, and it is far from clear how he could do this. Perhaps he would employ a verificationist argument – appealing to the fact that any causal pairings beyond what the law and non-causal conditions reveal are undecidable. Or perhaps he would argue that we cannot make sense of causation unless it is analysed in a way which accords with his thesis. My own belief is that neither of these arguments can be developed in a cogent way and, indeed, that the reductionist cannot find any adequate rationale for his position at all. But rather than pursue this question directly, I want to consider the consequences of the reducibility thesis in a quite different area.

However it is to be interpreted, the example of the spheres is purely fictitious. And, for all I know, there may be no actual case in the physical realm which would illustrate the same problem – no case in which there are *prima facie* causal pairings, but ones which the reducibility thesis cannot accommodate. For it may be that in the physical realm the correct causal pairings can always be decided by reference to some determinate spatio-temporal relation which features in the covering law, so that, given a putative cause, the law will tell us exactly where and when to look for its effect and, given a putative effect, the law will tell us exactly where and when to look for its cause. However, there is one important area where the reducibility thesis may have difficulty in accommodating the actual facts. The area in question is that of psychophysical causation – the causation of mental events by physical events or *vice versa*. The reason why this area may be thought to raise special problems for the thesis is that mental events, as traditionally conceived, do not have any genuine spatial location and thus cannot stand in any spatio-temporal relation to their physical causes and effects. The difficulty is then of envisaging laws which relate mental and physical events with sufficient precision to guarantee unique causal pairings. It is this issue which I want to discuss.

It is clear that laws which merely relate the two event-types in *time* will not suffice. Thus suppose that Smith and Jones simultaneously have experiences E_1 and E_2, of exactly the same psychological character ψ, E_1 being Smith's experience and E_2 Jones's. Suppose further that E_1 and E_2 were respectively caused by two brain events half a second earlier, B_1 in Smith's body and B_2 in Jones's body, these two brain events being of exactly the same physical character ϕ. Suppose finally that the only covering law is to be formulated as:

L_1: It is a law that any ϕ-event is ½ second earlier than some ψ-event.

Obviously this law, which only links the relevant types of event by a temporal relation, cannot account for the causal pairing of E_1 with B_1 and of E_2 with B_2. For since both brain events are of type ϕ and both experiences are of type ψ, and since the two brain events occur simultaneously and the two experiences occur simultaneously, the law does not determine which brain event is causally paired with which experience.

Now this does not immediately prove that the reducibility thesis is untenable. For while, apart from the nomological supposition, the situation we have just described is clearly possible, the reductionist might be able to envisage a stronger law which he could plausibly suppose to obtain and which would secure the right causal pairings. It is true that, as traditionally conceived, mental events do not stand in any spatial relation to physical events. But maybe there is some other relation which would serve as effectively as a spatial relation and which could be used, in conjunction with the temporal relation, to strengthen the law in the required way.

And indeed there is an obvious candidate, namely the relation which holds between any mental event in some subject's mind and any physical event in the *same* subject's body – in other words, the relation signified by the expression 'x belongs to a subject in whose body y occurs'. Let us abbreviate this expression to 'x is subject-linked to y'. Then we could suppose that, in the case of Smith and Jones, there is a covering law which nomologically links the relevant types of event both temporally and under this additional relation, i.e.:

L_2: It is a law that, for any ϕ-event x, there is a ψ-event y such that x is ½ second earlier than y and y is subject-linked to x.

L_2 yields unique causal pairings. Given any brain event of type ϕ, the law tells us exactly where in time and 'mental space' we will find its ψ-effect, namely half a second later in the mind of that subject in whose body the brain event occurs; and given any experience of type ψ, the law tells us exactly where, in time and physical space, we will find its ϕ-cause (assuming that it has a cause under that law), namely half a second earlier in the body of that subject in whose mind the experience occurs. So L_2 tells us that B_1 is the cause of E_1 and that B_2 is the cause of E_2. Moreover, it is surely very plausible to suppose that the psychophysical laws controlling the causation of mental events by physical events are of the L_2-form, in which the relevant types of event are connected under the relation of being subject-linked.

However, the reductionist cannot escape so easily. In envisaging psychophysical laws of the L_2-form, we are taking for granted the notion of embodiment: we are assuming that we can speak, unproblematically, of a conscious subject's possession of a body or of the union of a certain mind and certain body in a single person. The trouble is that, as the mind–body relation is traditionally conceived, the very notion of embodiment is, in part, implicitly causal. An essential part of what makes a certain body *my* body, i.e. the body of *me the conscious subject*, is that I am in a special way causally attached to it: it is *my* experiences, and no one else's, which events in this body (or this brain) directly cause and it is *my* decisions, and no one else's, which directly cause events in this body (this brain). But how is this causal attachment to be construed in the framework of the reducibility thesis? Obviously we cannot construe it in terms of laws, like L_2, in which the notion of such attachment already implicitly features. But if we fall back on laws like L_1, in which the only relation is temporal, then in certain circumstances the causal attachment would be indeterminate. Thus if the mental and neural biographies of Smith and Jones coincided on every occasion, these weaker laws would not determine which body was attached to which mind. It may be objected that the hypothesis of systematic coincidence is too far-fetched to be taken seriously. But granted that it is conceivable, the reductionist ought to be able to deal with it. (In any case, it is perhaps not even far-fetched in the case of two babies who are identical twins and have very short lives.)

A quite different line of defence for the reductionist would be to abandon dualism for the mind–brain identity thesis. As I indicated at the outset, the problem of causal pairings only arises because, as traditionally conceived, mental events do not have genuine spatial location. But if we abandoned this conception and identified mental events with brain events, mental events, as physical events, would have spatial location and would thus stand in spatio-temporal relations to other physical events. This would allow us to envisage psychophysical laws which, by incorporating such relations, guaranteed unique causal pairings. Indeed, we could probably settle for purely physical laws, since if mental events are physcial events, it is likely that only their physical properties are causally relevant.

However, although it is currently fashionable, I do not think that the identity thesis is tenable. The decisive refutation was, in my view, provided by Saul Kripke in *Naming and Necessity*.[24] Kripke's argument is exceedingly simple. Suppose E is a particular sensation, e.g. a pain, and B is the particular brain event, e.g. a certain firing of C-fibres, which is alleged to be identical with E. Kripke claims, surely correctly, that being a sensation (and indeed being a pain) is an essential property of E: there is no possible world in which E exists and is not a sensation. He also claims, surely again correctly, that being a sensation is not an essential property of B. For since B is a physical event, all its essential properties would surely be specifiable in purely physical terms, without any implication as to what is taking place in the subject's consciousness.[25] It follows that B and E are numerically distinct. For there is a property, that of being essentially a sensation, which is true of E but not of B. Admittedly, this argument assumes that the property of being a sensation cannot be analysed in a functionalist way. For, on such an analysis, E would possess this property only contingently, in virtue of the causal role which events of E's (presumably physical) intrinsic type played in the whole physical or psychophysical system. But I think that functionalism can be independently refuted. In particular, I think that it cannot accommodate the fact that a congenitally blind physiologist who knew all about the physiology and functioning of the visual system could still not tell what it was like, experientially, for the sighted person to see.[26]

Although Kripke's argument persuades me, it would not persuade Ayer. For Ayer rejects the very notion of an essential property as Kripke uses it. He thinks that the only sense in which an object can be said to possess a certain property necessarily is that its possession of that property is implicit in its mode of designation. In this sense it is correct to say that nine is necessarily a number, since the property of being a number is implicit in the sense of the designator 'nine'. But it is incoherent to think of this property as essential to the object as such, essential *de re*. As he concludes an article directed against Kripke's essentialism:[27]

> . . . there are only *de dicto* modalities. The idea that things possess individual essences, independently of the way they are designated, is a metaphysical absurdity. Having once been discarded, it should never have been revived.

On this view of the matter, which strikes me as needlessly austere, Kripke's argument collapses. The only sense in which E is essentially a sensation is that we are implying it is a sensation when we designate it as E. The fact that the use of 'B' does not carry this implication would not then prevent 'E' and 'B' being different names for the same thing.

Not that Ayer would appeal to the identity thesis to avoid the problem of causal pairings. In the first place, he thinks that even if the thesis is coherent, its acceptability depends on establishing an exact law-like correlation between mental properties and simultaneously instantiated neural properties and showing that the neural properties on their own suffice, in the framework of physical law, to explain all that is going on at the physical level.[28] And he would not want the validity of the reducibility thesis to depend on the outcome of future scientific research in this way. Secondly, even if all the requisite scientific evidence had been gathered and was compatible with the identity thesis, it would also be compatible with epiphenomenalism: we would have a choice between saying that mental events were identical with physical events and saying that they were causal effects of physical events but without any causal efficacy themselves. But, given his verificationist outlook, Ayer does not regard this choice as raising a question of fact, but rather a question of policy.

> The difficulty here is to see what can be meant by saying that our experiences are not merely caused by physical occurrences which take place in our brains, but are literally identical with them. How could this claim be tested? . . . The most that can be empirically established is that our experiences are causally dependent upon the condition of our brains. To go beyond this and maintain that what appears to us as a correlation of the mental with the physical is really an identity, is simply to take a decision not to regard the mental correlates as entities in their own right. (*CP*, 103)

It follows that, even if this decision can be justified on, as Ayer puts it elsewhere, grounds of 'scientific convenience' (*Philosophy in the Twentieth Century (PTC)*, 178), the identity relations would, from Ayer's standpoint, be subject to the same kind of reducibility as causal relations. The identity of a mental event E with a brain event B would be nothing over and above the fact that: (1) E's mental type and B's physical type are nomologically correlated in the appropriate way, (2) all the physical processes can be explained in terms of physical laws, and (3) we have taken the decision to confine ourselves to a physical ontology wherever possible. But this means that the problem of pairings arises for psychophysical identity as much as for psychophysical causation. If E has a simultaneous duplicate E' in some other mind, a psychophysical law employing only a temporal relation (i.e. the law that for each instance of B's type there is a simultaneous instance of E's type and *vice versa*) does not determine whether B is identical with E or with E', and if B has a simultaneous duplicate B' in another brain, such a law does not determine whether E is identical with B or with B'. Indeed, I think that Ayer is making this very point in *PTC* when, having conceded that the move from causal dependence to identity may be justified on grounds of scientific convenience, he remarks:

> But there is a difficulty . . . which it is easy to overlook. Even if it could be established that an experience of a particular kind was always the outcome of some molecular disturbance, and it could also be discovered that the right molecular motions were occurring at a given time in some nervous system, they might be temporally accompanied by many different instances of that sort of experience.

261

We need to select the instance which the theory picks out. Evidently it is one which 'belongs' to the same body as the nervous system in question. But how is this to be determined? What are the criteria for assigning experiences to one body rather than another? (*PTC*, 178)

Of course, some philosophers would deny that the identity of mental with physical events requires any exact law-like correlation between mental and physical types. Donald Davidson, indeed, has argued that it is precisely because there cannot be strict psychophysical laws that the identity thesis must be true. I shall not say anything about this argument here, except to remark that Ayer himself briefly examines it in *PTC* and rejects it, in my view rightly, as fallacious.[29]

Assuming that he cannot invoke the identity thesis, there is, I think, only one way in which the reductionist can make provision for unique causal pairings in cases, like that of Smith and Jones, of simultaneous duplication. What he must do is postulate psychophysical laws which include singular references to a particular conscious subject or mind and to a particular human body or brain. Thus, in the example considered, he must postulate a separate law for each person:

$L(S)$: It is a law that any ϕ-event in N_1 is ½ second earlier than some ψ-event in M_1.

$L(J)$: It is a law that any ϕ-event in N_2 is ½ second earlier than some ψ-event in M_2.

Here N_1 and N_2 are, respectively, the bodies (or brains) of Smith and Jones, and M_1 and M_2 are their minds (or the two persons as conscious subjects). Between them, these two laws would secure the right causal pairings. B_1 and E_1 would be causally linked under $L(S)$, and B_2 and E_2 would be causally linked under $L(J)$. The alternative pairings would not be sanctioned since they fall under neither law.

An apparent drawback of this solution is that laws with singular restrictions are, or so I have claimed, inherently puzzling. However, I do not think that in the present case the puzzle really applies. For one thing, it is not as if the restrictions in question involve any element of caprice. In postulating such laws, we are not making the nomological constraints inexplicably vary from person to person. Quite the reverse. Where there is a law for one person, there are exactly similar laws for everyone else; the only thing which varies is the reference to the particular body and particular mind in question. Moreover, even though the singular references cannot be eliminated in favour of some general relation, there is a sense in which all the restricted laws of the same type can be subsumed under one general and unrestricted law. Thus $L(S)$,

$L(J)$, and the other laws of this type (varying only in their singular references) are all, in a sense, specific instances of the general law:

L_3: It is a law that there is some 1–1 correlation between human bodies (or brains) and human minds such that any ϕ-event in a body x is $\frac{1}{2}$ second earlier than some ψ-event in that mind which is correlated with x.

It is not that the restricted laws can be deduced from L_3; for L_3 does not specify *how* the bodies and minds are correlated. But L_3 ensures that there is some correlation, and the restricted laws are what L_3 yields for the correlation which actually obtains.

Not only are the restricted laws not puzzling, but they are also, and quite independently of the help they afford the reductionist, very plausible. For it seems that we are going to need to postulate laws of this sort to account for the way in which each mind is causally attached to a particular body and each body causally attached to a particular mind. This attachment presumably involves, in each case, more than its just being true that the particular mind (and no other) directly interacts with the particular body (and no other). It presumably involves, in addition, some form of psychophysical arrangement which *ensures* that this is so – something which disposes the body to interact with just that mind and the mind to interact with just that body. It is difficult to see what could provide this arrangement other than restricted laws of the kind envisaged – at least, it is difficult if we retain our dualistic position in which the mind and the body do not stand in any spatial relation.

It seems then that the reductionist has found an adequate solution to the problem. However, there is a complication. If the reductionist is to invoke these restricted laws to ensure unique causal pairings, it is crucial that the assignment of a mental event to a certain mind be logically independent of its causal assignment to a certain body. Otherwise, by their references to particular minds, the laws will presuppose what they are intended to secure. Whether this requirement will prove troublesome remains to be seen. And of particular interest, of course, is whether it will prove troublesome for Ayer.

8 *The unity of the mind*

One way of ensuring that the assignment of mental events to minds is logically independent of their causal assignment to bodies is by adopting the Cartesian view of the self. According to this view, the mental subject – the entity which thinks, perceives, wills, and feels – is a simple non-physical substance, with an irreducible identity and an irreducible capacity for persistence. To say that two mental events occur in the same mind is just to say that they occur in the history of the same non-

263

physical substance. What assigns the events to the same substance rather than different substances is not a question which arises. Each event just is a certain substance's being in a certain mental state at a certain time. And there is no further way in which a substance's persistence through time is to be analysed

This Cartesian view of the self is one which Ayer has always rejected, and rejected on predominantly verificationist grounds. Here, however, we must distinguish between a weaker and a stronger claim. The weaker claim is that because the existence of the Cartesian self is completely unverifiable, the Cartesian view is the merest of fancies: we have not, and could never have, the slightest reason to accept it. The stronger claim is that because the existence of such a self is completely unverifiable, the Cartesian view is nonsensical: we cannot even grasp what it would be for this view to be true. Not surprisingly, it is the stronger claim which Ayer presses in *LTL*.

> The existence of such an entity is completely unverifiable. And accordingly, we must conclude that the assumption of its existence is no less metaphysical than Locke's discredited assumption of the existence of a material substratum. For it is clearly no more significant to assert that an "unobservable somewhat" underlies the sensations which are the sole empirical manifestations of the self than it is to assert that an "unobservable somewhat" underlies the sensations which are the sole empirical manifestations of a material thing. (*LTL*, 126)

The same objection is endorsed twenty years later in *PK*: the view that 'people are differentiated from one another . . . by being different spiritual substances' Ayer finds unintelligible, because he does not see 'by what criterion it could possibly be decided whether any such spiritual substances existed' (*PK*, 184). Thereafter, Ayer continues to condemn the Cartesian doctrine as unverifiable, but without (at least as far as I have been able to discover) explicitly claiming that it is nonsensical.[30] Whether this claim has been abandoned is not entirely clear. My impression is that it has not, though I think Ayer would no longer make it on purely verificationist grounds, in the narrowly empiricist sense. Certainly we find him, in his later works, appealing to what he sees as further considerations – in particular, that the Cartesian view is gratuitous. Thus as he puts it in *OP*, quoting from William James:

> Not only . . . is the existence of a mental substance not verifiable, but 'the substantialist view' is not required 'for expressing the actual subjective phenomena of consciousness as they appear'. It explains nothing that cannot be equally well or better explained without it. (*OP*, 265)

The Cartesian, of course, will not accept that his position is either unverifiable or gratuitous. And here there are at least three arguments he might use. First, he might claim that the existence of a substantive self is revealed by introspection and that its Cartesian character, as a simple and persistent non-physical substance, can, to the extent that it is not introspectively manifest, be established by *a priori* reasoning. Secondly, he might claim that the very notion of mental events without a subject – of perceptions without a perceiver, of thoughts without a thinker, etc. – is incoherent, and that, once again, *a priori* reasoning establishes that the mental subject must be of a Cartesian kind. Thirdly, he might claim that, unless we accept the Cartesian view, there is no adequate account of what it is for two mental events to occur in the same mind – that only a Cartesian self will serve to collect different mental events into a single mind and to distinguish that mind from others. Let us consider these claims in turn.

Ayer's response to the first claim is to deny that introspection reveals a substantive self at all:

> Our reasoning on this point, as on so many others, is in conformity with Hume's. He, too, rejected the notion of a substantive ego on the ground that no such entity was observable. For, he said, whenever he entered most intimately into what he called himself, he always stumbled on some particular perception or other – of heat or cold, light or shade, love or hatred, pain or pleasure. He never could catch himself at any time without a perception, and never could observe anything but the perception. (*LTL*, 126)[31]

The only respect in which he thinks that he can improve on Hume's argument is by stressing the logical rather than the empirical character of our incapacity for self-detection.

> Though this may not have been entirely clear to him, he had hit upon the logical point that nothing would count as one's discovering oneself apart from any perceptions: (*CQ*, 120)

> . . . if this [a mental substance] is what Hume was seeking when he tried to distinguish himself from his perceptions, it is not merely a contingent fact that he was unable to find it; there is no possible way in which such a substance could be identified. (*CP*, 112–13)

It might be urged in reply that even if we cannot detect ourselves *apart from* our perceptions, we can at least detect ourselves *in* them – that when I introspectively detect a perception, what is revealed is the complex of myself-perceiving-something. Indeed, it is not clear in what sense a perception could be introspectively detected without a detection of the subject. Hume seems to be supposing that introspection works like sense-perception: a mental item is presented as the object of introspective awareness in the same way that a colour-pattern is presented as the object of visual awareness. On this presentational model of introspection, it is hardly surprising that Hume finds no room for self-awareness. But it seems that it is the model, rather than our claims to self-awareness, which is at fault. Thus suppose I am looking at something. My visual awareness, divorced from interpretation, is of some spatial array of colours – an array which, according to the sense-datum theorist, is purely internal to the awareness and dependent on it. In addition to having this visual awareness, I am also, let us assume, introspectively aware of it. But I am surely not aware of the visual awareness as a kind of phenomenal object – as something detached from myself but presented to me. Surely, I am aware of it, so to speak, from the inside – not as something presented, but as something which I have. In short, it seems that I introspectively detect my visual awareness by being aware of being visually aware, i.e. by being aware of myself being visually aware. And if this is so, then, even if Hume was right to claim that he could not catch himself without a perception, he should have added that he could not catch a perception without catching himself.

In effect, however, Ayer has already anticipated this objection and taken measures to avoid it:

> To begin with, we must make it clear that we do not accept the realist analysis of our sensations in terms of subject, act, and object. For neither the existence of the substance which is supposed to perform the so-called act of sensing nor the existence of the act itself, as an entity distinct from the sense-contents on which it is supposed to be directed, is in the least capable of being verified. (*LTL*, 122)

Thus Ayer would meet the objection by denying that my visual awareness, as something distinct from the visual colour-array, exists. All that I can introspect and all that my visual experience involves is the occurrence of a visual sense-content. I do not detect myself in the experience, because I only detect the experience as a phenomenal object, not as an experiential act.

I think Ayer's position here is quite plausible; and if we were only concerned with the case of sense-experience, it would allow him to avoid the objection. However, Ayer's opponent has other areas in which he can develop his point. For even if we can eliminate the mental act in the case of sense-experience, it is much harder to see how we could do this in the case of thoughts, judgments, decisions, and other mental events with a propositional or conceptual content. How could Ayer avoid conceding that the subject's introspective awareness of such events is an awareness of doing something – of thinking, judging, deciding, etc?

Surely he cannot think of these events as phenomenal or quasi-phenomenal objects, introspectively presented in the same way as colour-patterns and sounds.

In fact, it is clear that, at least in *LTL*, Ayer does think of the introspectible aspects of these events in just this way. This is why he explicitly allows the term 'sense-content' 'to refer to the immediate data not merely of "outer" but also of "introspective" sensation' (*LTL*, 53). How he would justify this view is not entirely clear, but I assume that, like Hume, he would rest his case on an austerely empiricist account of human psychology. He would say, I think, that the only genuinely conscious, introspectible elements in these events are mental images of the ordinary sensory type and that it is only through their location in the framework of certain capacities and dispositions that these images acquire their conceptual significance. Thus suppose, in the course of solving some arithmetical problem, I make the judgment that $9 \times 7 = 63$. Ayer is likely to say, I think, that the only conscious element in this judgment – all that introspection directly reveals – is a series of mental images, most probably of the sounds in the English sentence, or of the symbols in the arithmetical formula, used to express the proposition in question. And he would then attribute the conceptual significance of these images, as a vehicle for my so-called propositional act, to such things as my capacity to use language, the dispositions of my mind to pass from one sort of image to another, the goal-directedness of my present behaviour, and the particular way in which these current images contribute, or have the potential to contribute, to the reaching of this goal. But if mental images are the only introspectible phenomena, and if, in line with Ayer's account of sense-experience, there is no act of imaging additional to the image itself, then introspection does not reveal a substantive self.

I cannot myself accept this austere account of human psychology. In particular – and I have already drawn attention to this in Part II, section 10 – it seems to me that, even in the case of ordinary sense-perception, there is a large element of conceptual interpretation within the conscious experience itself. And precisely because such interpretation forms part of the conscious experience, I do not think that it can be satisfactorily explained in terms of images, capacities, and dispositions. However, let us, for the sake of argument, assume that Ayer can justify the austere account and in this way avoid the objection. What we must now consider is how Ayer would deal with the other two claims which the Cartesian might advance.

The second claim was that the very notion of mental events without a subject is incoherent and *a priori* reasoning establishes that the mental subject must be of a Cartesian kind. The first part of this claim seems very plausible. For how could there be perceptions, thoughts, and judgments without a perceiving, thinking, and judging subject? But, of course, Ayer has already neutralized the force of this challenge by his austere view of our mental life. No doubt there could not be acts of perceiving, thinking and judging without someone to perform them. But, on Ayer's view, there are no such acts. The mentalistic ontology is exclusively one of sensory items – Hume's impressions and ideas – and these need not be thought of as states or activities of a subject. It may be objected that as *sensory* items, there must still be something to which they are presented, something for which they form objects of awareness. But Ayer would handle this in terms of the relations between different sensory items and the whole functional organization of the sensory mind. Thus he would insist that, for example, a visual colour-array forms an object of awareness only in as much as it is, or could be, monitored by other sensory items (like memory-images) or by introspective judgments which themselves dissolve into sensory items (such as verbal images), capacities, and dispositions.

It is the third Cartesian claim which promises to pose the greatest problems for Ayer – the claim that only the Cartesian view allows an adequate account of what it is for two mental events to belong to the same mind, i.e. to occur in the mental history of the same person. For the Cartesian, the situation is straightforward: the boundaries of the mind are fixed by the identity of the mental subject and the mental subject is a non-physical substance with an irreducible identity and mode of persistence. But how are the boundaries fixed if the Cartesian view is rejected? What determines whether two mental events belong to the same mind or to different minds – to the same person or to different persons? This was a question which even Hume found himself, in the end, unable to answer.

Admittedly, given Ayer's austerely empiricist view of our mental life, there seems to be no problem in fixing the boundaries of the mind at any particular time. For presumably it will suffice to say that two simultaneous experiences (or sense-contents) belong to the same mind or person if and only if they are parts of the same total experience. Ayer implicitly accepts this analysis in *LTL*, though he comes later to reject it as circular. The circularity arises, he thinks, because 'what is meant here by a total experience is just the experience of one and the same person' (*PK*, 195). On the face of it, this seems a rather strange claim. For if we can use the concept of an experience without begging the question – and Ayer seems to think that, once we have freed it from any notion of an act of awareness, we can – then presumably we beg no further questions when we combine this concept with the neutral relation of *being a part of*. And this combination is all we need to define the notion of a total experience (as an experience which is not a part of any other experience) and thus fix the boundaries of each mind at any time.

But I assume Ayer's point is that the very concept of an experience, if it is allowed to apply to complexes which cover more than one sense-realm or which include both sensations and mental images, already presupposes some method of co-conscious grouping, and that the anti-Cartesian is called on to show how such grouping is possible without the substantival ego. At the time of *PK*, he felt unable to meet this challenge, other than by postulating a *sui generis* relation. But subsequently he found the answer in the phenomenal relation of sensible compresence: what makes the various elements of a complex experience elements of a single experience is that they are sensibly compresent, and, as Ayer sees it, this relation no more requires the existence of a subject of awareness than does any other phenomenal quality or relation.

The difficulties arise when we try to specify what it is for two experiences at *different* times to belong to the same mind. For here, it seems, the relation of sensible compresence, or the relation of being parts of the same total experience, will not help us. One possibility would be to say that non-simultaneous experiences belong to the same mind (are 'co-mental') if and only if they are attached to the same body. In effect, this would be to make bodily persistence a necessary and sufficient condition of personal persistence. What gives this position some initial plausibility is that, in practice, we normally identify and re-identify persons, or at least other persons, by their bodies.

Ayer himself adopted a version of this position in *LTL*. For he claimed that 'for any two sense-experiences to belong to the sense-history of the same self it is necessary and sufficient that they should contain organic sense-contents which are elements of the same body' (*LTL*, 125). By 'sense-experiences' he here means *total* sense-experiences and by 'organic sense-contents' he means bodily sensations. What he is then claiming, in effect, is that for two total sense-experiences to be co-mental it is necessary and sufficient that they should contain bodily sensations which are phenomenologically located in the same body. The reason he speaks of these sensations as 'elements of' the body is that, in the framework of his phenomenalism, material objects are logical constructions out of sense-contents, and, in the case of human bodies, bodily sensations (organic sense-contents) are among the elements which feature in the construction. For the purposes of our present discussion, however, this phenomenalist aspect of his position is best ignored.

Even if Ayer is right in thinking that it is their attachment to the same body which assigns two total experiences to the sense-history of the same person, the form of attachment he here envisages is clearly unsatisfactory. In the first place, it is obviously not a necessary truth that every total experience in someone's sense-history includes some bodily sensation. For example, someone might be anaesthetized over a certain period with respect to his body, but continue to have visual and auditory experience. (Nor, indeed, would it be necessary for the content of such visual and auditory experience to contain any representation of his body at all.) This means that for two total experiences to be co-mental it is not a necessary condition that they should contain bodily sensations located in the same body. Moreover, this condition is not sufficient either; for it is possible for the sensations of different persons to be located in the same body. For example, there might be two Siamese twins, whose minds are quite distinct, but who, with the appropriate sensory nerves running to their separate brains, both feel sensations in the region where their bodies coincide. The sensations which each twin feels in this region are distinctively his; but they are located in the other twin's body as much as in this own, and are thus located in the same body as the other twin's sensations.

In view of these objections, it might seem better to construe the attachment of experiences to bodies in causal rather than phenomenological terms. For even if some of a person's total experiences contain no bodily sensations, they are still presumably causally generated by processes in his nervous system. And even if two people feel sensations in the same body, we can still presumably identify each person by some distinct corporeal continuant, whose neural processes generate his and only his experiences. In his much later essay 'The Concept of a Person', Ayer himself comes to think that it is *causal* attachment which is crucial:

> I am . . . inclined to think that personal identity depends upon the identity of the body, and that a person's ownership of states of consciousness consists in their standing in a special causal relation to the body by which he is identified. (*CP*, 116)

He goes on to specify this special relation as one of immediate causal dependence, so that two experiences are co-mental just in case (1) they causally depend on states of the same body, and (2) their causal dependence on these states is not mediated by their causal dependence on anything else. It should be noted that, in this new analysis, unlike the one in *LTL*, attachment to the same body is doing *all* the work: it determines the extent of a person's mental life *at a time* as well as the extent of his mental history *through time*. The reason for this is that by now (after his discussion in *PK*) Ayer has come to regard the notion of a total experience as question-begging, but he has not yet found the solution in the relation of sensible compresence.

Ayer does not tell us exactly what counts as a person's *body* for the purposes of this analysis. Obviously, we are to think of a person's body as persisting even if his arms and legs are amputated. But suppose we remove someone's brain and attach it to some suitable apparatus, in a way which ensures that it continues to perform its psychological functions. Are we to think of this separated brain as the person's (now much depleted) body and regard the experiences it generates as co-mental with those it generated before its removal? Presumably we are. But then how would Ayer's analysis apply to a case in which *A*'s brain is removed and destroyed and *B*'s brain is transplanted into what remains of *A*'s body? Intuitively, this is a case of *A*'s body receiving a new brain, just as it might receive a new heart or kidney. But, equally, if the operation is successful, it is more plausible to think that it is *B*, rather than *A*, who has survived – in analogy with the case in which the functions of an isolated brain are sustained by some special apparatus. So perhaps what Ayer means by *body*, in the context of his causal analysis, is *that corporeal continuant* (whatever part of the whole human body this happens to be) *which is directly responsible for the production of experience*. This would allow him to say, in the case of a brain transplant, that the identity of the resulting person was determined by the identity of the surviving brain – which seems intuitively right.

However, the exact interpretation of Ayer's position need not concern us. For I think that, irrespective of its details, his analysis can be shown to be defective on quite general grounds. Perhaps its most obvious defect stems from the point we have already mentioned, that bodily attachment is being made to do all the work – determining the extent of a person's mind *at a time*, as well as its extent *over time*. The reason why this will not work is that it is a necessary truth that simultaneous experiences are co-mental if and only if they are parts of the same total experience; and (as Ayer himself came later to see), once we have discounted the Cartesian view, it must be in this relation that the co-mentality of simultaneous experiences consists. Now, of course, it may be that, if it is not to be question-begging, the notion of a total experience stands in need of further analysis – for example, in terms of the relation of sensible compresence. But what is quite clear is that for two experiences to be parts of the same experience is for them to be united by some purely mental relation, which cannot be reduced to their standing in a certain causal relation to the same body. This leaves open the possibility that it is when and only when they have an immediate causal dependence on states of the same body that experiences stand in this mental relation. But if this is so, it is so only contingently. We can conceive of cases in which two simultaneous experiences are directly caused by processes in the same body, but fail to be mentally united as parts of a single experience. Likewise, we can conceive of cases in which two experiences are so united, but fail to have the requisite causal dependence on the same body. And all this holds irrespective of what, for the purposes of Ayer's analysis, we take the body to be.

Ayer could try to remedy things by restructuring his analysis on the lines of *LTL*, so that bodily attachment is only invoked to determine the temporal spread of the mind, not its boundaries at each moment.

271

Thus he could say that what makes simultaneous experiences co-mental is that they are parts of the same total experience (e.g. in virtue of their sensible compresence), and that what makes two total experiences co-mental is that they occur at different times and have (or at least the majority of their components have) an immediate causal dependence on states of the same body. But once we have recognized the need for a mentalistic criterion in the case of simultaneous experiences, it is very difficult to retain a causal criterion in the area that remains. In fact there are two difficulties. The first is the general difficulty of seeing how the concept of co-mentality could retain its rationale if its applications in the two areas were governed by two such disparate criteria. How could there be, in any interesting sense, a generic form of mind-unity if its species *at a time* and *over time* were so different? The second difficulty is that, because the causal criterion *could be* extended to cover both areas (as in the original analysis), its proven inadequacy in the one argues against its adequacy in the other. For how could causal dependence on the same body suffice for the co-mentality of total experiences at different times, when it does not suffice in the case of experiences which are simultaneous? If more is needed to unify the mind at any given time, surely more is needed to unify it over time as well. Otherwise, we seem to be allowing causal dependence on the same body to suffice in the case of non-simultaneous experiences simply because, being non-simultaneous, the experiences cannot reveal that they are not co-mental through their failure to be parts of a single experience.

Nor, for Ayer at least, do the problems of the causal analysis stop here. For even if we could make the analysis intuitively plausible, it would not, it seems, be available in the framework of Ayer's general position. The reason for this is that, if our earlier arguments are correct, Ayer, as a champion of the reducibility thesis, would need to fall back on some other analysis of co-mentality in order to have, in cases of simultaneous duplication, an adequate account of causal attachment. Thus returning to the example of Smith and Jones, it seems that the only way in which the reductionist can account for the causal pairings of E_1 with B_1 and of E_2 with B_2 is by postulating separate laws for the two persons involved, one law relating ϕ-events in Smith's body (or brain) with ψ-events in Smith's mind, and the other law relating ϕ-events in Jones's body (or brain) with ψ-events in Jones's mind. And if Ayer has to postulate laws of this kind to ensure that experiences are causally attached to bodies, then he has to accept that experiences are assigned to minds independently of their bodily attachment. Admittedly, if he was determined to retain his causal analysis, he could say that, where there is simultaneous duplication, the experiences are not causally attached to bodies and are consequently not constituents of minds. But

272

this would be a very implausible conclusion, and surely one which he would be unwilling to accept.

If, even in the case of non-simultaneous experiences, Ayer cannot define co-mentality in terms of attachment to the same body, what possibilities remain? The obvious alternative would be to fall back on certain purely mental relations, on ways in which co-mental experiences are psychologically related to one another independently of their connection with the physical world. It is already clear that the non-Cartesian has to do this in the case of simultaneous experiences. So the natural strategy would be to look for some way of extending the mental unity which we discern within each total experience to cover co-mental experiences at different times.

Up to a point, Ayer himself follows this strategy in his more recent work (that is, in OP and subsequently), where he takes over, with some changes and with considerable elaboration, William James's theory of the self. Ayer argues that, just as simultaneous experiences can be grouped into complex experiences by the relation of sensible compresence, so also total experiences can be grouped into streams of experience by the relation of sensible continuity. The concept of sensible continuity is explained in terms of James's theory of the specious present. Essentially, the idea is that a total experience will normally be temporally extended, spanning a series of momentary sense-contents arranged in a phenomenal time-field. In consequence, each total experience will normally overlap the total experiences which immediately precede and follow it within the same mind. And it is this which gives rise to sensible continuity. As James puts it, quoted by Ayer:

> If the present thought is of A B C D E F G, the next one will be of B C D E F G H, and the one after that of C D E F G H I – the lingerings of the past dropping successively away, and the incomings of the future making up the loss. These lingerings of old objects, these incomings of new, . . . give that continuity to consciousness without which it could not be called a stream.[32]

Thus a series of total experiences is sensibly continuous if and only if its successive members overlap, and a stream of experience is any complete series of total experiences which is sensibly continuous in this way.[33]

Since being constituents of the same stream is a logically sufficient condition of co-mentality, Ayer has made some progress here. But, as he sees, the analysis is not yet complete. For a single mind may, and typically will, contain more than one stream.

> There are gaps in consciousness of which we have to take account. When I wake from what I take to have been a dreamless sleep . . . I have no doubt that I am the same person as went to sleep so many

hours before; but what is it that unites my present experiences with those that I had then? (*CQ*, 115)

Assuming we want the uniting relation to be mental, a plausible suggestion would be that they are linked by memory. Such a link could be either direct, where certain experiences in the current stream are recollections of experiences in the earlier one, or indirect, where the two streams are connected by a series (not necessarily in temporal order) of streams, the successive members of which are directly linked.

In *OP*, Ayer tries to make something of this suggestion, as part of his elegant reconstruction of James's theory. But his final verdict is that memory will not suffice:

> It is, indeed, through memory that I discover my self-identity over this period of time, but it cannot be memory that produces it. The reason why it cannot is that if we make the assumption that the experiences which I think that I recall cannot fail to have been my own, we are reasoning in a circle; and if we do not make this assumption, the link is not established; the experiences in question might never have occurred, or they might belong to a different biography. (*CQ*, 115–116)

This objection is partly confused. What is at issue is whether the co-mentality of streams can be defined in terms of the *relation* '*x* is a memory of *y*', and, however it is construed, there is no way in which this relation could hold unless both the items it relates exist. Ayer's real point, I assume, is that either this memory relation has itself to be defined partly in terms of co-mentality, in which case we cannot without circularity define co-mentality in terms of it, or else it will turn out to be something which can hold between items in different minds, in which case it will be useless for the purpose in hand. Here I think he is right. If a memory trace in someone else's brain were appropriately transplanted to mine, I might come to have a 'recollection' of one of his past experiences. This would surely not make the past experience mine. If it is objected that the recollection is only apparent, not real, the objector has to explain the distinction. And surely the only way of doing this would be by stipulating that any *genuine* recollection has to occur in the same mind as the experience it recollects. But this would presuppose some independent account of what it is for two experiences to occur in the same mind.

In any case, given his acceptance of the reducibility thesis, there seems to be a further reason why Ayer could not appeal to the memory relation without circularity. Let us assume, for the sake of argument, that this relation entails co-mentality without presupposing it. Now suppose there are two simultaneous experiences, E_1 and E_2, which are of exactly the same type, but, failing to be sensibly compresent, belong to different minds. And suppose there is a later experience E_3 which is supposed to be a recollection of E_1. The question is: what makes E_3 a recollection of E_1 rather than of E_2? Clearly, the answer cannot lie in the intrinsic character of the three experiences or in their temporal relations, since, in these respects, the alternative pairings are indistinguishable. The answer must surely be that E_1 stands in some requisite causal relation to E_3 and that E_2 does not. But how is the reductionist to account for this causal relation, given that E_1 and E_2 are simultaneous duplicates? What sort of laws would allow him to select E_1, rather than E_2, as the cause? If the causal relation is either unmediated (action over a temporal distance) or mediated only by other mental events in the person's mind, he would presumably need laws which employed the relation of co-mentality – laws which specified that, in certain conditions, the occurrence of one type of experience was nomologically necessary or sufficient for the occurrence, in a certain temporal relation, of another type of experience *in the same mind*. (It is true that he could sometimes substitute 'in the same stream of experience' for 'in the same mind' here, but this would not help in the crucial cases where we are concerned with the memory-links between different streams.) On the other hand, if, as seems likely, the causal relation between E_1 and E_3 is mediated by a series of physical states in the person's brain, then the reductionist needs laws which causally attach E_1, rather than E_2, to the relevant brain. This brings us back to the original problem of psychophysical causal pairings, whose solution, it seems, requires postulating laws with singular references to minds.

At all events, Ayer's own view is that, in normal circumstances, what assigns two streams to the same mind is their attachment to the same body, though (perhaps not entirely consistently) he allows for cases in which, with a radical divergence between the criteria of bodily identity and memory, 'the criterion of memory could be allowed to prevail' (*CQ*, 116). This, of course, raises the question of how this bodily attachment is to be analysed. And by this stage he has become aware of the problem of causal pairings, in the form in which I expounded it in an unpublished paper.[34]

> . . . if causality is to be analysed, as I believe it should be, in terms
> of uniform spatio-temporal relations, then since it is conceivable
> that two different persons should at the same moment be having
> qualitatively identical experiences, and since in the case of
> experiences and their physical causes it is only temporal relations that
> have to be considered, it will not be possible to pair these
> experiences with their respective causes unless their attachment to
> different bodies has already been established. This is not to deny

that our experiences are causally dependent upon our bodily states, but rather to suggest that the attachment of experiences to bodies is logically not the outcome of this causal dependence, but its precondition. (*OP*, 274)

Of course, the problem of causal pairings would only affect the attachment of *streams* to bodies in cases where either a whole stream, or the whole series of bodily states which successively caused the experiences in a stream, had a simultaneous duplicate. And such duplication is not likely to occur very often, if at all. But its mere possibility is enough to pose a challenge to the bodily criterion. For obviously Ayer has to analyse the co-mentality of streams in a way which is equipped to deal with such cases, irrespective of whether, or how frequently, they occur. And this means that he needs some method of attaching streams to bodies which is not affected by the simultaneous occurrence of duplicate streams or duplicate sequences of bodily states.

Reviewing the situation a decade later, Ayer thinks he may have conceded my point too quickly:

> It seems to me that one might be able to exclude the unwanted pairings by augmenting the causal generalisation that when a brain B is in state S an experience E occurs, in such and such a temporal relation to S, by a set of subjunctive conditionals to the effect that, if B were to be put in such and such other states, then such and such other experiences would occur which would be sensibly compresent or continuous with E. (*Replies*, 317–18)

In other words, in the case of Smith and Jones, what causally pairs the brain event B_1 with the experience E_1 and the brain event B_2 with the experience E_2 is the temporal law L_1 (that any ϕ-event is half a second earlier than some ψ-event), together with a range of subjunctive-conditional facts relating B_1 and E_1, to the effect that if B_1 were accompanied or followed by such and such other events in the same brain, there would be such and such other experiences sensibly compresent or continuous with E_1, and a similar range of subjunctive-conditional facts relating B_2 and E_2.

I find this proposal puzzling in more than one way. To begin with, it is not even clear how these conditional facts account for the causal pairings, since it seems to be logically conceivable that an experience should be caused by an event in one brain, but some other brain be disposed to produce experiences which are compresent or continuous with it. If Ayer is willing to secure the pairings by subjunctive conditionals, it seems that he could have done this more simply and more effectively by appealing to the fact that if B_1 had occurred without B_2, E_1 would have occurred without E_2, and if B_2 had occurred without

B_1, E_2 would have occurred without E_1. Of course, to base the pairings on these singular counterfactuals would not, if it was the terminus of explanation, accord with the reducibility thesis. And if the pairings were to be objective, it would not accord with Ayer's own austere account of what such counterfactual statements assert. But these points equally apply to Ayer's proposal, which also involves, though in a more complex way, attributing singular counterfactual connections to the relevant pairs of events. To be fair to him, Ayer himself confesses a certain dissatisfaction with an 'analysis that terminates in subjunctive conditionals', but thinks that 'in this case there may be some mitigation in the fact that subjunctive conditionals are already implicit in the invocation of causality' (*Replies*, 318). What he seems to have overlooked is that unless he is willing to abandon his Humean conception of causality, the only causal facts he is entitled to invoke are ones which are wholly covered by generalizations of law (i.e. on his view, generalizations of fact to which we have the appropriate nomological attitude), and that, unless he is willing to abandon his analysis of counterfactuals, the only singular counterfactual connections he is entitled to invoke are the truth-functional connections asserted by material conditionals. In short, without a double *volte-face*, the problem of causal pairings remains.

If the attachment of streams to bodies cannot be analysed causally, the only alternative seems to be to analyse it in terms of bodily sensations. This would be, to some extent, to revert to Ayer's account in *LTL*, where a total experience was attached to a body by containing bodily sensations located in it. The main difference now is that what we have to attach to bodies are streams rather than experiences, and this improves things in two respects. First, we no longer have to insist that every total experience which occurs in the sense-history of some person contains a bodily sensation, since a stream can be attached to a body through the bodily sensations contained in just *some* of its constituents. Secondly, we can allow for the possibility of two persons feeling sensations in the same body, since the bodily attachment of a stream will be determined by a 'majority verdict'; that is, stream S will be assigned to body B just in case S contains at least one bodily sensation located in B and contains more bodily sensations located in B than in any other particular body.

In *OP*, where he acknowledges the problem of causal pairings, Ayer regards this approach to bodily attachment as 'the most promising' (*OP*, 274), though he sees problems in getting it to cover every conceivable case. Nor does this view seem to have been affected by his second thoughts on the cogency of my argument. For, as recently as *PTC*, he still feels able to write, concerning the 'question how a given series of experiences is to be allocated to one body rather than another' (*PTC*, 189):

. . . I now tend to think the most important factor of all is the compresence of experiences of all other kinds with bodily sensations. It is seldom that these sensations are explicitly attended to, but it seems that they are usually present as forming a relatively constant background to more prominent items of experience. And even in the cases where our experience lacks this background, it is probable that they have a relation of direct or indirect sensible continuity to experiences which possess it. (*PTC*, 190)

Again, as the probabilistic form of his final sentence indicates, he does not see this factor as covering every conceivable case; for it would be possible for a person's experiential biography to include a stream which contained no bodily sensations at all. If it did, then this stream would either have to be attached to the body in some other way or linked with the other streams by some purely mental relation.

Even if we ignore this difficulty, it is easy to envisage cases where, taken as a necessary or a sufficient condition of co-mentality, this form of bodily attachment yields implausible results. Two obvious cases are the ones we mentioned earlier of the 'disembodied' and the transplanted brains. In both cases, it is plausible to suppose that the experiences which the brain generates in its new situation are co-mental with those it generated when it was lodged in its original body. But any sensations it generates are, in the one case, not located in any body at all (compare the case of the 'phantom limb') and, in the other, located in a different body. It must be remembered, however, that Ayer does not intend the bodily criterion of co-mentality to be decisive in *all* cases: he leaves room for exceptional circumstances in which, with a radical divergence between the criteria of bodily identity and memory, 'the criterion of memory could be allowed to prevail' (*CQ*, 116). The transplanted brain is the very case he has in mind here, and perhaps he would treat the 'disembodied' brain in an analogous way.

The point I want to stress now, however, is that the phenomenological analysis of bodily attachment will not enable Ayer to avoid the problem of causal pairings. For the very notion of a sensation's location in a body has to be analysed partly in causal terms. I am not denying, of course, that, simply in virtue of its intrinsic character, a bodily sensation has a phenomenal location in a somatic field, in the same way that a visual colour-patch has a phenomenal location in a visual field. The point where causality enters is in the role of the somatic field as perceptually representing a particular real body, just as it enters quite generally as part of what makes a perceptual experience a perception of a particular physical object. And it is only by this perceptual link between the somatic field and a certain body that the sensation can be said to have a bodily location. It might be objected that this perceptual link could be achieved by a purely qualitative relation, i.e by the qualitative fit of the somatic field and its constituent sensations with a particular body and what is taking place within it. But this would not take account of simultaneous duplication. At any given time, there could be more than one body which qualitatively fits some total somatic experience and more than one total somatic experience which qualitatively fits a particular body. The only way in which we can account for the unique perceptual pairings is by appealing to the causal dependence of the somatic experience on the body it represents. The exact form which this causal dependence must take is a complicated question, and one which we need not pursue; presumably, it will be analogous to the kind of causal dependence (of perceptual experience on perceived physical object) which is required in other cases of perception, except that in this case (apart from paranormal examples) the causal chain is entirely within the subject's body. The crucial point is that, in appealing to this causal dependence at all, we are back with the problem of psychophysical causal pairings. Or rather *Ayer* is back with it, if he retains the reducibility thesis.

Having made this point, I must now add one important qualification. In claiming that the bodily location of a sensation is partly determined by causal factors, I am assuming a realist account of the physical world. If the physical world were merely a logical construction out of sense-experience, bodily sensations would derive their bodily location from the way in which they contributed to the construction. This indeed, as we have seen, is Ayer's line in *LTL*, where he speaks of organic sense-contents as *elements* of bodies. But it is not in accord with the realist outlook of his later work, with which we are now concerned. Moreover, it is very doubtful whether, in this phenomenalistic framework, the co-mentality of streams could, without circularity, be defined in terms of their bodily attachment. For it seems likely that the phenomenalist would require some way of grouping streams into minds before he could undertake the construction of physical objects, though this is not an issue which I shall investigate.[35]

At any rate, if we assume a realist conception of the physical world, and continue to discount the possibility of appealing to the identity thesis, it seems clear that the attachment of streams to bodies will have to be analysed at least partly in causal terms. And if I am right in thinking that, given the possibility of simultaneous duplication, the reductionist cannot account for the causal relations involved except by postulating laws which refer to particular minds and particular bodies, then Ayer will either have to abandon the reducibility thesis or give up his attempt to analyse the co-mentality of streams predominantly in terms of their bodily attachment. He could, of course, do both. And, in my view, this would be the right course. As we have seen, the reducibility thesis has problems in other areas: it cannot, it seems, account for the directionality of causation, either in respect of the principle that the cause cannot be later than the effect, or in respect of the inherent asymmetry in the causal relation itself; nor does it yield plausible results in the case of the two spheres. And, as I shall now try to show, even if we take the notion of bodily attachment for granted, the suggestion that we should use it to group streams into minds is fundamentally mistaken.

What I have in mind here is not the familiar objection that we can envisage cases of someone surviving in a wholly disembodied form, without even retaining his brain, or of someone moving from one body to another without the transference of any of his bodily organs. For unless we have an independent argument against the bodily criterion, the assumption that such cases are logically possible just begs the question. And, of course, we cannot fall back on cases in which the disembodiment or transference involves the survival of the original brain, since, by selecting the appropriate kind of corporeal continuant (i.e. that bodily organ on whose states experiences directly causally depend) and the right kind of attachment (i.e. causal), these are cases which the bodily criterion can accommodate.

The objection I want to press (and I raised a similar objection against the 'restructured' version of Ayer's earlier causal analysis) is that once we have agreed to analyse the co-mentality of experiences *within* a stream in terms of the mental relations of sensible compresence and sensible continuity, it is most implausible to suggest that the co-mentality of streams is to be analysed in some radically different way. Of course, what unites streams within a single mind cannot be exactly the same as what unites experiences within a single stream – otherwise there could not be a genuine plurality of co-mental streams. But if our conception of a single mind is to have any rationale, we must surely see the unifying relations between streams as in some way analogous to, and a natural extension of, the unifying relations within a stream. The relations of compresence and continuity and the attachment of streams to the same body are just too disparate to count as different species of a single generic unity. Even if our actual concept of co-mentality involved this disparity – and surely it does not – it would need to be revised.

Given this, I think the most plausible response, short of accepting the Cartesian view, would be to define the co-mentality of streams in terms of their potential for forming portions of a single stream. In other words, our definition should be: two streams are co-mental if and only if they are separated by a temporal interval and there is something which ensures that, with the later stream held constant and with the earlier stream hypothetically extended up to the time when the later stream begins, the two streams would join. This seems intuitively right, and clearly it represents the unifying relation between streams as a natural extension of the unifying relations within a stream. The only problem is to think of some plausible way in which the condition specified by the *definiens* could be satisfied. What gives co-mental streams their potential for joining? What ensures that, if the later stream is held constant, the earlier one would, if sufficiently extended, run into it? It is tempting to appeal to their co-mentality, but that, of course, would be circular.

It is here, I think, that bodily attachment, and in particular causal attachment to a brain, may play a role. Once we have rejected the reducibility thesis, it becomes possible to include causation among the properties and relations that there are laws *about*. And given this, we can plausibly suppose that there are three laws of nature to the effect that:

(1) Any experience directly causally depends on (events in) only one brain.
(2) Experiences in the same stream directly causally depend on the same brain.
(3) Experiences which are both simultaneous and directly causally dependent on the same brain are sensibly compresent (i.e. are parts of the same total experience).

Now if they obtain, these laws ensure that each stream is causally attached to a single brain, and that two streams are co-mental, in the sense of the definition, just in case they are causally attached to the same brain. Thus, to focus on the most crucial case, suppose that S_1 and S_2 are two streams separated by a temporal interval, with S_1 earlier than S_2. Laws (1) and (2) ensure that each of these streams is attached to a single brain. If they are attached to the same brain, law (2) ensures that, with S_2 held constant, any hypothetical extension of S_1 to the time when S_2 begins would terminate in an experience which was simultaneous with, and directly causally depended on the same brain as, the first experience in $S_{w-.+2}$; and law (3) then ensures that these two experiences would be sensibly compresent (possibly, though not necessarily, by being identical), thus making S_1 and S_2 portions of a single stream. Conversely, if S_1 and S_2 are attached to different brains, then law (2) ensures that, even with a sufficient extension of S_1, they would never form portions of a single stream. So even though the co-mentality of streams cannot be defined in terms of bodily attachment, it is plausible to take attachment to the same brain to be that on which, in practice, their co-mentality is nomologically grounded.

I argued for this position in my contribution to Ayer's Festschrift,[36] and his comment was that unless I can think of some other way in which streams could be rendered co-mental in accordance with my definition, my best course would be simply to define their co-mentality as their attachment to the same brain.[37] However, it is not this attachment on its own which ensures that the streams are potentially joinable, but this attachment in the framework of certain contingent laws. What Ayer

281

should have said is that if there is no conceivable way in which two streams could satisfy the conditions of my definition except by their attachment to the same brain and the obtaining of the specified laws, then we could reformulate the definition in terms of this attachment and these laws. In fact, of course, there are bound to be other *conceivable* ways, however implausible, if only because we could vary the content of the suggested account without changing its general structure. Indeed, in *my* ontology, we can even envisage ways which do not involve the physical world at all. For example, let us suppose that human experiences are directly controlled by angelic volition. If we now postulate the same three laws, but with 'angel' in place of 'brain', we get the result that each stream is causally linked with a particular angel, and that two streams are co-mental just in case they are linked with the same angel. On the view that each of us has his own guardian angel, the idea is perhaps not even wildly implausible.[38]

Where I think my Festschrift paper went seriously astray was in my attempt to combine this Humean approach to the unity of the mind with a Cartesian conception of the self. It was not that I failed to see the obvious *prima facie* conflict between the two positions, but I thought that the truth was divided between them. It seemed to me correct to analyse the unity of the mind in the way I have just outlined – by defining a stream in terms of the overlapping of successive total experiences and by defining the co-mentality of streams in terms of their potential for joining. And, at the same time, it seemed to me self-evident that any experience must be the state of some genuine, ontologically primitive subject. Consequently, I was led to accept a compromise, in which I construed the self as a non-physical substance with an irreducible exist-ence, but analysed its identity in terms of the unifying relations between its experiential states. I now think that this compromise, as I then formu-lated it, is untenable. We cannot separate the existence and the identity of the self in that way.

Despite this confession of error, I do not want to disown my former position entirely. Indeed, I still believe that the Cartesian conception of the mental subject and the Humean account of his persistence are both correct: the subject is a non-physical substance with an irreducible exist-ence and identity; his persistence through time is to be analysed in terms of the actual and potential sensible continuity of his experience. This sounds like further confusion; for if the subject's existence and identity are irreducible, how can his persistence be amenable to any further analysis beyond the fact that *he*, the very same subject, exists through a period of time? The answer is that, in my view, the time-dimension through which the subject persists is to be logically constructed from the very relations which give the mind its experiential unity. The Cartesian and Humean accounts can be reconciled, because, when properly developed, the Humean account records those pre-temporal facts about the subject's experience from which his contingent temporal existence is derived. How these 'subjective' time-dimensions are to be constructed is something which I have discussed in detail elsewhere[39] and I shall not pursue the matter here. But it should be noted that their construction is part of a much larger construction which terminates in a framework of inter-subjective time – a framework in which the separate subjective dimensions are temporally related. This larger construction depends crucially on the actual and potential causal relations between different minds. And, as I mentioned earlier,[40] I think it is the principles involved in this construction which explain the temporal direction of causation.

9 *Free will*

Even if the Cartesian and Humean accounts *could* be reconciled in this recherché way (and the theory of time it presupposes is bound to be controversial), Ayer would continue to argue that the Cartesian element was both unverifiable and gratuitous. And the fact that we can specify the unity of the mind in terms of the actual and potential sensible continuity of experience has made Ayer's position easier to defend, even if any plausible explanation of the *potential* continuity (e.g. by appealing to the causal dependence of experiences on states of the brain) would involve his abandoning the reducibility thesis. There still remain the questions of whether the self is introspectively discernible and whether it makes sense to suppose that there could be mental events without a genuine mental subject, and on these points I do not find Ayer's arguments entirely convincing. But I shall not pursue these issues any further. Instead, I want, in conclusion, to investigate one quite different area where it is arguable that only a Cartesian conception of the self does justice to the facts – or to the facts as we ordinarily understand them. This new area of investigation is concerned with the subject as *agent* and is bound up with the traditional issue of free will.

Ayer himself has discussed the issue of free will on a number of occasions. Perhaps his most important contribution is his early essay 'Freedom and Necessity'.[41] What makes this essay particularly interesting is that it presents the issue in a new perspective.[42] It is normally assumed that the main challenge to the libertarian position comes from determinism, whether of a physical or a psychological variety. A person has only acted freely if he could have acted otherwise; and determinism, which asserts that all events are causally determined, seems to imply that a person could never have acted in any other way than he did. But, as Ayer sees it, the libertarian is in difficulties irrespective of whether determinism is true. The libertarian wants to credit people with a freedom of choice which renders them morally responsible for the actions they perform. But how could the failure of determinism help to sucure that kind of freedom?

> Either it is an accident that I choose to act as I do or it is not. If it is an accident, then it is merely a matter of chance that I did not choose otherwise; and if it is merely a matter of chance that I did not choose otherwise, it is surely irrational to hold me morally responsible for choosing as I did. But if it is not an accident that I choose to do one thing rather than another, then presumably there is some causal explanation of my choice: and in that case we are led back to determinism. (*PE*, 275)

If this argument is correct, then the main challenge to the libertarian comes not from determinism, but from the fact that there seems to be no way of even conceiving of the freedom which he thinks we possess. If our choices are causally determined by prior conditions, they are unavoidable. If they are not causally determined, then, to that extent, they are the product of chance and no more within our control than if they were forced on us by causal necessity. Either way, we are the helpless victims of the choices which occur within us and cannot be held to be morally responsible for the actions to which they lead.

It might be objected that Ayer has ignored the distinctively rational character of human deliberation and choice. He is assuming that there is no middle ground between the tyranny of causation and the arbitrariness of chance. But the libertarian might claim that choice-for-a-reason is precisely what falls in between. Thus suppose I have an hour to spare before my next tutorial and I am wondering how I should spend it. There are a number of options, but, on reflection, I decide to go to Blackwell's to look over the new philosophy books. The libertarian will say that my decision was not causally determined by my prior physical or psychological condition: I had it in my power to take a different decision, such as to try to finish next week's lecture or to go for a walk in Christ Church Meadows. At the same time, my decision did not just occur by chance, since it was taken for a reason. I was keen to see the new philosophy books and my decision was a rational response to that desire. But if my decision is both causally undetermined and rationally explicable, it seems to avoid both horns of Ayer's dilemma – being neither the product of necessity nor the outcome of chance.

The trouble with this reply is that, unless it is interpreted in causal terms, the rational explanation for my decision does not seem to remove its accidental character – or, indeed, to count as a proper explanation at all. Let us grant the libertarian that, in desiring to see the new philosophy books, I had a reason for taking my decision. And let us also grant him that, independently of causal considerations, there is a sense in which this desire counts as the 'operative' reason for my decision; for in taking my decision, it was this desire which I was intending to fulfil. But the question still remains as to why I yielded to it. Either the desire was causally overriding, in which case we are back with determinism; or it was not, in which case it must have been, to that extent, a matter of chance that I decided to satisfy it. It will not even help to suppose that my desire to see the new philosophy books was, in some non-causal sense, stronger than any rival desire which I also had an opportunity to satisfy. For while this may make my decision more rational than the possible alternatives, it still does not explain it in a way which avoids the dilemma. Either I was causally determined to pursue the most rational course or it was left to chance. Either way, it seems that I as such have no control over, or responsibility for, what happens.

A quite different way of trying to avoid the dilemma would be to point out that, even in terms of causal explanation, complete determination and total randomness are not exhaustive alternatives. Thus we can envisage a situation in which the conditions obtaining at time t are causally sufficient for a certain disjunction of choice-types at $t + 1$, without being causally sufficient for any disjunct. Then the occurrence of a particular disjunct D at $t + 1$, in response to these conditions at t, is neither causally determined (since some other disjunct could have occurred) nor wholly a matter of chance (since there was a limited range of causally possible alternatives). As a further refinement, we could suppose that while the initial conditions do not determine which of the alternatives occurs, they do assign a greater probability to some than to others. For example, perhaps there are just two alternatives, X and Y, such that the initial conditions assign a probability of 9/10 to X and a probability of 1/10 to Y. If X then occurs, its occurrence is even less a matter of chance than if Y occurs.

However, none of this will be of any use in meeting Ayer's argument. For even if the occurrence of a certain decision is neither completely determined nor wholly a matter of chance, its occurrence is, for all we have shown, still exhaustively covered by a combination of these factors. To the extent that the causal pressures towards its occurrence fall short of sufficiency, its occurrence is purely accidental; to the extent that its occurrence is not purely accidental, it is causally explicable. And if causality and chance are the only factors, there seems to be no room for freedom of choice or moral responsibility. The subject is just the passive recipient of the decisions which, in combination, causality and chance impose on him.

The conclusion which Ayer draws from his argument is not that the concept of free choice is incoherent, but that, in the context of the traditional dispute, it has been misunderstood.

Now we began with the assumption that freedom is contrasted with causality: so that a man cannot be said to be acting freely if his action is causally determined. But this assumption has led us into difficulties and I now wish to suggest that it is mistaken. For it is not, I think, causality that freedom is to be contrasted with, but constraint. And while it is true that being constrained to do an action entails being caused to do it, I shall try to show that the converse does not hold. I shall try to show that from the fact that my action is causally determined it does not necessarily follow that I am constrained to do it: and this is equivalent to saying that it does not necessarily follow that I am not free. (*PE*, 278)

He then goes on to distinguish two ways in which an agent may be constrained and thus fail to be acting freely. The first way covers those cases in which the agent is compelled to do something by someone else who is threatening him:

In a case of this sort the compulsion need not be such as to deprive one of the power of choice. . . . It is enough that he [the other person] should induce me to do what he wants by making it clear to me that, if I do not, he will bring about some situation that I regard as even more undesirable than the consequences of the action that he wishes me to do. (*PE*, 279)

The second covers cases in which the agent has, in the relevant situation, been deprived of the power of choice: either he has lost the capacity to go through the deliberative process that leads to a decision or, even if he has retained this capacity, any such deliberation is simply irrelevant, having no influence on the course of action he takes. Ayer gives as examples the case of kleptomania and the case of someone who is conditioned to be wholly subservient to someone else. His conclusion is that to say that someone has acted freely is to say that he would have acted differently if he had so chosen and that, in acting as he did, he was not constrained in either of these two ways. This, of course, allows free action to be causally determined. So freedom and determinism are reconciled, and the problem of finding some middle ground between causation and chance is removed.

Ayer's position is open to a number of objections. I shall begin by raising a relatively minor objection, which challenges the details of his account rather than his general approach.

As we have just seen, Ayer thinks that there are two ways in which an agent may be acting under constraint: in one case, the agent is compelled to do something by someone else who is threatening him; in the other case, the agent has lost his power of choice. Now I do not see why, in the first case, the constraint should be held to remove or diminish the agent's freedom, if it operates in the way Ayer envisages. As Ayer envisages it, the agent is compelled to perform the relevant action because, taking account of the threat, he sees that it would be prudent to do so. But why should this count as removing or diminishing his freedom, unless we are prepared to say (and Ayer is not) that freedom is always removed or diminished whenever someone chooses the course of action which reason dictates? The situation would be different if Ayer had characterized the compulsion as one which deprived the agent of his power of choice – which prevented him from engaging in the normal process of deliberation or made that process irrelevant to the behavioural response. This sort of thing can happen in cases of very immediate and dramatic threats, as in Ayer's own example of the pistol pointed at one's head. The panic which such a threat induces may indeed compel a certain behavioural response in which the normal processes of reasoning are bypassed. But this is not what Ayer has in mind. The subject who is threatened is assumed to retain his capacity to weigh up the situation and choose the course of action which seems, on balance, to have the least undesirable consequences. The threat is simply a factor which he rationally takes into account. If so, I do not see how it differs from ordinary cases in which the agent acts in response to rational considerations.

The reason why Ayer thinks that there is a loss of freedom is that he sees the agent as relieved of moral responsibility.

> . . . if the circumstances are such that no reasonable person would be expected to choose the other alternative, then the action that I am made to do is not one for which I am held to be morally responsible. (*PE*, 279)

But here Ayer is surely confusing responsibility and blameworthiness. A cashier who hands over the money to the gunman, and does so after cool, if quick, consideration of the consequences of the alternatives open to him, is morally responsible for his action – assuming, at least, that people can be morally responsible for their actions in normal circumstances. But he may not be deserving of blame, simply because, all things considered, he may be morally justified in acceding to the gunman's demand. The fact that the demand was immoral does not mean that the cashier was wrong to accede to it.

Consequently, I think Ayer would do better to restrict the cases of constraint to those of the second type, in which the agent is deprived of his power of choice. This, of course, would leave the essentials of his position intact. He could still claim that what eliminates freedom is constraint rather than causality. What we must now consider is whether his position can be challenged in more fundamental respects.

Perhaps the most obvious objection, and one which Ayer himself anticipates, is that there is no basis for the distinction between causes which constrain and causes which do not.

> For why should we distinguish, with regard to a person's freedom, between the operations of one sort of cause and those of another? Do not all causes equally necessitate? And is it not therefore arbitrary to say that a person is free when he is necessitated in one fashion but not when he is necessitated in another? (*PE*, 281)

Part of Ayer's answer is that causation as such does not involve any objective necessitation at all beyond mere constant conjunction:

> . . . there is an invariable concomitance between the two classes of events; but there is no compulsion, in any but a metaphorical sense. (*PE*, 282)

> . . . we tend to form an imaginative picture of an unhappy effect trying vainly to escape from the clutches of an overmastering cause. But . . . the fact is simply that when an event of one type occurs, an event of another type occurs also, in a certain temporal or spatio-temporal relation to the first. The rest is only metaphor. (*PE*, 283)

That Ayer should endorse this Humean view of causality comes as no surprise. What is still unclear is how it helps him to meet the objection. For if causation is not as such constraining, why should it be thought to be so in those special cases which Ayer selects? I think Ayer's point is that once we have accepted the Humean view, we can allow the concept of constraint to be defined in terms of those factors which we ordinarily recognize as removing the agent's freedom. It is not that the kleptomaniac (for example) is subject to a *stronger* kind of causal determination than the ordinary, rationally motivated thief. It is just that, because the causation bypasses the normal processes of rational deliberation, we regard him as the victim of an alien obsession. Because his decision to steal is not sensitive to rational considerations (such as whether the item is one he wants and whether he is likely to be caught), we think of it as outside his control. In this sense we can speak of him as acting under constraint.

But in what sense does Ayer's account allow the agent any real control over his decisions in the normal case, where the processes of rational deliberation are efficacious? It is true that in such a case the agent is unlikely to feel 'alienated' from his decision in the way in which, perhaps, the kleptomaniac does. But this does not mean that he had the power to avoid it. And if the decision was causally determined by prior physical or psychological conditions – conditions which determined the precise form which the rational deliberation would take – it seems that the outcome was unavoidable. It might be objected that we are forgetting the Humean character of the causation, as Ayer interprets it. But leaving aside the objections to the Humean account, how would the removal of obective necessity help to transfer power to the agent? The fact that the causal laws are only factual regularities does not as such put them within the agent's control. And surely Ayer is not supposing that they do fall within his control – that it is left to the discretion of the agent as to whether the regularities which have held hitherto will continue in the future. But then how does Ayer's account leave room for freedom of choice in any morally significant sense? If the agent is not in control of the decision-making process, how can he be morally responsible for the outcome?

Presumably Ayer would reply that the sort of freedom which his account attributes to the agent is the only one which is, in principle, available. We simply cannot conceive of a way in which the agent could have control over his decisions in any stronger sense. And here, of course, he would refer us to the original dilemma. To the extent that our decisions are not causally determined, they are merely the product of chance, and if they are the product of chance, there is no sense at all in which they fall within our control. Either we settle for his account, which reconciles freedom with certain (rational) forms of causal determination, or, he would argue, we condemn the notion of freedom to incoherence.

But has Ayer really shown that this is so? Let us look more closely at the supposed dilemma. The orthodox libertarian denies that, in normal circumstances, our decisions are causally determined by prior conditions, since that would mean that we had no control over them. Ayer's retort is that, to the extent that our decisions are not causally determined by prior conditions, they must occur by chance, which still puts them beyond our control. But what does Ayer mean when he speaks of a decision as occurring by *chance*? If he just means that it is not causally determined by prior conditions, then it becomes a tautology that decisions which are not thus determined occur by chance; but equally, Ayer has yet to show that decisions which in that sense occur by chance lie outside the subject's control. On the other hand, if he means that, as well as not being causally determined by prior conditions, the decision is something which just happens to the subject, something of which he is just a passive recipient, then it is clear that decisions which in that sense occur by chance lie outside the subject's control; but equally, Ayer has yet to show that decisions which are not causally determined by prior conditions occur by chance in that sense. In other words, the apparent cogency of Ayer's argument stems from a concealed equivocation. The self-evidence of the claim that a decision which is not causally determined by prior conditions occurs by chance depends on interpreting *chance* as no more than the failure of such determination. The self-evidence of the claim that a decision which occurs by chance lies outside the subject's control depends on interpreting *chance* as additionally implying the passivity of the subject. This means that Ayer's argument never comes to grips with the (orthodox) libertarian position at all. For the libertarian takes a free decision to be an event which is not only not causally determined by prior conditions, but also something for which the subject himself is, at the time of its occurrence, directly causally responsible.

It does not follow, of course, that the libertarian position is correct or even coherent. And there is no denying that it is philosophically perplexing. For what could it mean to say that the subject *himself* is, at the time of its occurrence, directly causally responsible for his decision? Presumably it implies, amongst other things, that the decision is not causally determined (at least not determined in an objectively necessitating way) by prior conditions; otherwise, the causal initiative would not rest with the subject himself at the time in question. But obviously this negative condition must be a consequence of something positive in the notion of the subject's causal role. And it is here that the libertarian position seems so perplexing. For how can the subject *himself* be the cause of something? It seems that the only way in which an event could be caused by the subject would be by being caused by some event in, or some state of, the subject's mind, and this, of course, is just what is excluded by assigning causal responsibility to the subject *himself*. Admittedly, we could take the notion of causation-by-a-subject as primitive and claim that it is only perplexing when we try to reduce it to something else.[43] But if we can accept a primitive notion of causation by a *subject*, why not also accept a primitive notion of causation by a *table* or causation by a *number*? And surely these latter notions are manifestly absurd. But then why is it not equally absurd to speak of a subject as the cause of something, unless this is just a misleading way of saying that the event is caused by some aspect of the subject's psychological condition?

The libertarian is likely to reply that the causal responsibility of the subject is to be understood in terms of the familiar notion of agency. Quite apart from the philosophical issue over free will, we ordinarily draw a distinction between two types of mental event – between (1) those mental events with respect to which the subject is *passive*, events which just *happen to* the subject, events of which he is merely the *recipient*, and (2) those mental events with respect to which the subject is *active*, events of the subject *doing* something, events in which he is the *agent*. Let us call events of the first type *P-events* and events of the second type *A-events*. Among events which we classify as P-events are sensations and sense-experiences; and among events which we classify as A-events are decisions (i.e. conscious choices of action) and acts of trying. It is important to stress that we apply the distinction solely in virtue of the intrinsic character of the events in question. Someone may deliberately induce in himself a certain sensation – he may even (let us suppose) induce it just by willing it to occur. But we would still classify the sensation itself as a P-event (as something which just happens to the subject), even though the subject is active with respect to the volition which induced it. Conversely, someone may, in taking a certain decision, be yielding to psychological pressure, such as might come from a threat or a strong desire. But we would still classify the decision-taking itself as an A-event (as an event of the subject doing something), even though the subject is passive with respect to the pressure.

Now I think the libertarian is likely to claim that it is the notion of agency, as it features in this ordinary distinction, which explains his notion of the subject's causal responsibility. In cases where the subject *himself* is directly causally responsible for some mental event, such as a decision, it is not that he causes it in the way in which one event may cause another; nor, or course, that the event is caused by some aspect of his psychological condition. Rather (the libertarian will claim), it is that the event is, in itself, an event of subject-agency. The causal initiative rests with the subject because the event is, in virtue of its intrinsic nature, the subject's own mental action, an event of the subject doing something. If the libertarian adopts this position, then, of course, he will not speak of some decisions as free and others as unfree. He will claim that *all* decisions are free, in the relevant sense, since all decisions are events of subject-agency and thus events for which the subject himself is, in the requisite way, causally responsible.

The main problem with this position is that the notion of subject-agency is, philosophically, hardly less perplexing than the notion of causal responsibility it is intended to explain. For what does it mean to say that a mental event is an event of agency? In what sense is decision-taking a case of the subject doing something, in a way which contrasts with the passive reception of sensation? And if sensations and decisions are equally mental and equally events in the biography of the subject, how is there room for any distinction in the manner of the subject's involvement in them? It seems that any answers to these questions would have to fall back on the nature of the subject's causal role: the events of agency are the events of which the subject himself is the causal initiator. But then, of course, we are just going round in circles, explaining the subject's causal role in terms of agency and explaining agency in terms of this causal role.

However, there is another possibility. The libertarian needs to interpret the notion of agency in a way which puts the causal initiative for events of agency (i.e. for A-events) in the hands of the subject, and we know that, for the causal initiative to rest with the subject, it is at least required that the events be not causally determined (i.e. causally

291

necessitated) by prior conditions. We also know that, if there are events
of agency, they qualify as such solely in virtue of their intrinsic character.
Thus if some particular event of decision-taking qualifies as an A-event,
it is not because, on this occasion, the subject happens to play the
appropriate causal role in its production – a role which he may fail to
play on other occasions when events of the same kind occur. Rather, it
qualifies as an A-event because, by its intrinsic nature, it is a mental
action, an event of the subject doing something. Finally, it is clear that
if something is a P-event, it is logically possible for there to be an event
of exactly the same intrinsic type which is causally determined by prior
conditions. A mental event of which the subject is a passive recipient,
such as a pain or a visual experience, may fail to be causally determined
by prior conditions, but there is nothing in the intrinsic nature of the
event to preclude such determination.

Putting these points together, we have three crucial propositions which
the libertarian's account of agency has to accommodate. If we abbreviate
the phrase 'causally determined by prior conditions' to 'PC-determined',
these three propositions can be formulated as follows:

(1) It is logically necessary that if something is an A-event, it is not PC-
determined.
(2) If something is an A-event and if T is its intrinsic type, it is logically
necessary that any event of type T is an A-event.
(3) If something is a P-event and if T is its intrinsic type, it is logically
possible for there to be an event of type T which is PC-determined.

Let us say that an event is *intrinsically autonomous* just in case, if T is
its intrinsic type, it is logically impossible for there to be an event of
type T which is PC-determined. Then from (1) and (2) we can immediately deduce that all A-events are intrinsically autonomous. Moreover,
(3) can be reformulated as the claim that no P-events are intrinsically
autonomous. Since any mental event must be either a P-event or an A-
event,[44] it follows that, between them, the three propositions entail that
a mental event is an A-event if and only if it is intrinsically autonomous.
So the libertarian could define agency in terms of intrinsic autonomy.
He could say that for an event to be an event of subject-agency is just
for it to be mental and intrinsically autonomous. This would avoid any
circularity, since intrinsic autonomy is defined solely in terms of concepts
which can be grasped independently of the notions of agency and the
subject's causal responsibility. In describing an event as intrinsically
autonomous, we are merely saying that its intrinsic nature excludes the
possibility of its being causally determined by prior conditions.

One drawback of this definition, as it stands, is that the notion of
intrinsic autonomy omits the role of the subject altogether. In saying
that the subject is active with respect to a certain mental event, we are

surely saying something about the nature of the subject's involvement in that event, even if this involvement is in some way tied up with the event's intrinsic autonomy. The trouble with defining agency as autonomy is that this makes no reference to the subject's involvement at all: the definition may be extensionally accurate (for it may be logically necessary that a mental event is an event of subject-agency if and only if it is intrinsically autonomous), but, without some explicit mention of the subject's involvement, it does not fully capture what, in speaking of agency, we actually mean.

Now, at first sight, it might seem that this weakness in the definition is irremediable. For how can we specify the subject's involvement without bringing ourselves back into the circle? How can we characterize this involvement except as the subject's role as the agent or causal initiator of the event? But there is an answer. For we can specify the involvement in terms of the intrinsic autonomy which it sustains. We can say that for a subject to be the agent or causal initiator of a certain mental event is for him to be involved in it in whatever way it is which makes events of that type intrinsically autonomous. More precisely, we can offer as the analysis of 'S is the agent of E':

(1) E is mental.
(2) S is the subject of E.
(3) There is some mode M of involvement such that:
    (a) S is M-involved in E;
    (b) if T is E's intrinsic type, then it is logically necessary that, for any event E' of type T, the subject of E' is M-involved in E';
    (c) it is logically impossible for there to be a mental event E' such that the subject of E' is M-involved in E' and E' is PC-determined.[45]

In other words, agency is a special involvement of the subject which qualifies as agency because it sustains intrinsic autonomy. And it sustains intrinsic autonomy because, where it obtains, it is both part of the intrinsic nature of the mental event in question and what puts that event, and others of the same type, beyond the reach of PC-determination.

But now there seems to be a new problem. For if the libertarian defines agency not as intrinsic autonomy, but as that form of subject-involvement which sustains autonomy, surely he owes us an account of what such involvement is in itself. Surely he has to tell us what sort of involvement it is which is part of the intrinsic nature of the relevant class of events and which makes it logically impossible for events of those types to be causally determined by prior conditions. And how can he do this without appealing to the very notions of the subject's agency and causal responsibility which he is trying to define? But the answer is that the libertarian does not need to meet this challenge at all. With any kind of conscious state, there is bound to be an aspect of its intrinsic nature which we cannot specify – an aspect which we can only grasp introspectively, by knowing what it is like, subjectively, to be in that state. This is why we cannot fully communicate to a congenitally blind person what it is like to see or to a congenitally deaf person what it is like to hear. The case of mental agency is no different. There is nothing more to be *said* about the nature of the subject's special involvement in A-events other than that it is what renders them intrinsically autonomous and, thereby, makes them his *actions* rather than merely events which happen to him. What more there is to be known is known introspectively – by the subject's knowing, from the inside, what it is like to be involved in that way, i.e. to be mentally doing something. The availability of this introspective knowledge does not, of course, make the suggested analysis of the concept of agency redundant. The point of the analysis is to reveal the sense in which the involvement, whose intrinsic nature is known introspectively, qualifies for the theoretical description 'agency', with all that this description implies concerning the causal role of the subject.

A much more serious difficulty for the libertarian is that the notion of intrinsic autonomy seems, on the face of it, to be incoherent, not because we have failed to give it a clear meaning, but because it seems inconceivable that an event should be autonomous in that way. For how could any event be of an intrinsic type such that it was logically impossible for an event of that type to be causally determined by prior conditions? Surely, whatever the intrinsic type, it is logically possible for it to be a law of nature that whenever certain conditions obtain an event of that type occurs in the appropriate context, whether spatial or mental, a moment later. And if such a law obtained and the relevant conditions occurred, the resulting event would be causally determined. Of course, if we take 'determined' to mean 'objectively necessitated' and if we also deny the possibility of objective natural necessity, we can conclude that all events are intrinsically autonomous. But this would be of no help to the libertarian; for it would mean that autonomy could no longer serve as the distinctive feature of events of agency.

The libertarian will reply that if intrinsic autonomy seems inconceivable, this is only because we are considering the issue in the abstract, rather than in relation to the particular kinds of events for which, in his account, autonomy is claimed. Considered in the abstract, intrinsic autonomy seems inconceivable because our ordinary conception of an event makes no provision for it. Moreover, for all ordinary kinds of events such autonomy *is* inconceivable: we cannot, for example, envisage a flash of lightning or a gust of wind whose intrinsic character precludes its being PC-determined. However, when we focus on such mental events as decision-takings and tryings, our intuitions pull us in another direction. Our intuition is that these events are, in virtue of their intrinsic nature, events of subject-agency, and the very notion of agency involves the assignment of causal responsibility to the subject himself. But this surely means that our intuitive understanding of these events commits us to the view that they are intrinsically autonomous. For how can we interpret the claim that the subject's causal responsibility is part of the intrinsic nature of these events except as the claim that their intrinsic nature includes some form of subject-involvement which makes it logically impossible for events of those types to be PC-determined?

However, this hardly settles the issue. For the anti-libertarian will say that its very commitment to the intrinsic autonomy of these events shows our intuitive understanding of them to be erroneous. After all, when we consider the notion of intrinsic autonomy in the abstract, our intuition is that there can be no such thing. And the anti-libertarian will say that it is this intuition which is to be trusted and used to correct our intuitions about agency. Admittedly, he will then owe us an account of why the distinction between P-events and A-events should seem intuitively so compelling. But it is not clear that he cannot do this. Presumably part of his answer would be that the events which we think of as events of agency are ones whose types normally fall within the control of the subject's rational deliberations; for where events are controlled by rational deliberation, we are more likely to think of them as controlled by the subject himself.

Clearly, the issue is extremely complicated and, as things stand at present, finely balanced. There are intuitions on either side; and each of the disputants can make some attempt to explain away the intuitions to which the other appeals. How the matter is to be resolved I am not sure, though my sympathies are with the libertarian. I am not even sure that what I have offered as the analysis of the notion of agency is correct, though I cannot at the moment see any alternative.

The point I want to press, however, is that there is a genuine issue here, and one which Ayer has overlooked in posing the original dilemma. If 'occurs by chance' just means 'is not PC-determined', then the libertarian need not be embarrassed by the fact that, on his account, our choices of action occur by chance. For chance in that sense could leave the causal initiative in the hands of the subject himself. On the other hand, if 'chance' additionally implies the passivity of the subject, then Ayer has just begged the question; for the libertarian will simply deny that the subject's choices are events of which he is the passive recipient. In some of his later work, Ayer seems to realize that the libertarian will lay stress on the causal role of the subject – a role which Ayer characterizes as the 'power of self-determination'.[46] But he thinks that, even if we credit the subject with such a power (and, in his view, this would be incoherent), the dilemma stands.

295

Either the exercise of this power would fit into a causal pattern, or it would occur at random, and in neither case would it appear to justify an ascription of responsibility. (*H*, 78)

I do not follow Ayer's reasoning here. If 'random' means 'not PC-determined', then the exercise of the power of self-determination must, if it is to meet the libertarian's requirements, be random in that sense. And obviously randomness in that sense is no bar to moral responsibility (it is *moral* responsibility that Ayer has in mind here): it would be absurd for someone to plead moral innocence on the grounds that his choice of action was *not* causally imposed on him by prior conditions. But if the failure of PC-determination does not obstruct the ascription of responsibility, what does? The passivity of the subject? But such passivity is presumably just what is excluded by the assumption that, in making his choice, the subject is exercising his power of self-determination.

It might be suggested that even though Ayer's dilemma is misconceived, he has already dealt with the issue of libertarianism in his argument against the Cartesian view. For if there is no Cartesian self, then there is no entity which could play the role of agent in the relevant sense, and thus nothing which could possess the kind of freedom of choice and moral responsibility which the libertarian (i.e. orthodox libertarian) is concerned to establish. But Ayer can hardly base his rejection of libertarianism on his rejection of Cartesianism. For his argument against Cartesianism was that it was unverifiable and gratuitous, and the correctness of this argument will depend, in part, on the outcome of the present issue. After all, the libertarian is claiming that we cannot do justice to the nature of such mental events as decisions and tryings unless we construe them as events of genuine agency and thus commit ourselves to the Cartesian view.

Although in his later writings Ayer continues to press the cause–chance dilemma and sees it as decisive against the orthodox libertarian position, there is one respect in which his own position changes. As we have seen, the conclusion which he drew from the dilemma, in his original essay, was not that our ordinary notions of freedom and moral responsibility are incoherent, but that such freedom and responsibility are, not, as the libertarian supposes, incompatible with determinism: in claiming that someone has reached a decision of his own free will and is morally accountable for it, we are not implying that the decision was not causally determined, but only that is was not determined in a special 'constraining' way. In his later writings, however, Ayer comes to doubt this conclusion and, in the end, to reject it. He comes to think that, despite its incoherence, our ordinary notions of freedom and responsibility do embody the libertarian view: 'in a muddled fashion, we credit ourselves and others with . . . a power of self-determination' (*H*, 78).

Since he now regards these notions as incoherent, his correct course, presumably, would be to discard them, or to revise them in a way which eliminated their libertarian character. But, as Ayer sees, taking this course is not quite so easy as it sounds. The problem is that the libertarian view seems to pervade our whole way of looking at ourselves and others in personal and social terms. It seems to be implicit not only in our judgments of moral responsibility and desert, but also in, as Ayer puts it, 'the affective attitudes of pride or shame, gratitude or resentment, reverence or indignation, which the moral judgements sustain' (*PTC*, 17). He continues a little later:

> . . . I doubt if it is in my power to give up such attitudes as I have mentioned in favour of a strictly scientific approach to myself and my fellow men, and I doubt if I should wish to, even if it were in my power. I think, therefore, that there is a case for retaining a muddled concept of free will, just in so far as the myths which it engenders are salutary. (*PTC*, 17)

Even for Ayer, it seems, incoherence has its uses. But this, it must be stressed, is a unique occurrence. In all other respects, as far as one can tell, he is content to adapt — at least to try to adapt — his ordinary modes of thought to the rigours of his empiricist outlook. He sees no reason to retain, for example, the muddled notions of objective necessitation, the substantival ego, absolute morality, or God.[47] No doubt he does not find sufficient that is salutary in the myths which they engender.

Of course, in describing these notions as 'muddled' and the beliefs they engender as 'myths', I am expressing Ayer's viewpoint, not my own. For I believe that, in the end, it is his own empiricist outlook which is at fault; not, admittedly, because it is incoherent, but because it is needlessly austere. As a curb on the conceptual extravagances of speculative metaphysics and as a guard against the uncritical endorsement of our ordinary modes of thought, this austerity has its merits, and the philosophical world should acknowledge a debt of gratitude to Ayer for his consistent pursuit of economy and rigour. But even austerity becomes excess when it is not constrained by reason. And, if I am right, the scope of coherent human thought is seen, on rational reflection, to be wider than Ayer's empiricism allows.

'. . . if I could be thought even to have played Horatio to Russell's Hamlet, I should consider it glory enough.' It is with this aspiration that Ayer, reflecting on the significance of his philosophical career, closes his autobiography.[48] Taking advantage of the analogy and mindful of my reservations about his empiricism, I could aptly retort: 'There are more things in heaven and earth, Horatio, than are dreamt of in your philosophy.' But while this riposte would express my reservations, it should not be seen as casting doubt on the stature of Ayer's work or on the value of his achievements. On these matters, indeed, his own aspirations to glory seem too modest. For, notwithstanding his debt to Russell, it is Ayer himself who, over the past fifty years, has played the leading role in the promotion of the empiricist viewpoint. And, whatever the merits and defects of this viewpoint, I doubt if it could receive a more eloquent and authoritative exposition or a more vigorous defence.

Notes

Part I Meaning and Verification

1 In his *Introduction* to the 2nd edition of *LTL*, p. 5.
2 See *LTL*, pp. 15–16.
3 *LTL*, pp. 15–16
4 *LTL*, pp. 1–16, 68–9.
5 *LTL*, pp. 46–7 However, commenting on his *LTL*-position some forty years later, Ayer felt able to say: 'Meaning was also accorded to sentences expressing propositions like those of logic and pure mathematics, which were true or *false* only in virtue of their form.' (*CQ*, 24; my italics)
6 *LTL*, pp. 5–8.
7 He certainly speaks of statements as being either significant or nonsensical and this is in line with his terminology in the *Introduction*. But it is possible that, in the original text, he was thinking of a statement as something made by someone who utters a sentence rather than as something expressed by a sentence in abstract.
8 L. J. Cohen, 'Is a Criterion of Verifiability Possible?', in *Midwest Studies in Philosophy* V (edited by French, Uehling and Wettstein), University of Minnesota Press, 1980, pp. 347–52.
9 *Ibid.*, p. 348.
10 In both cases, when Cohen says that S, *and its negation*, are observationally verifiable at the relevant level if and only if S satisfies the specified conditions, what he really means, I think, is that S is observationally verifiable at this level if and only if either S or its negation satisfies these conditions.
11 *Ibid.*, p. 349.
12 *Ibid.*, p. 349.
13 *Ibid.*, p. 349.
14 The article first appeared in *Revue Internationale de Philosophie*, vol. 4 (1950) and was subsequently republished in *LP*.
15 There is one slight qualification to this. Unlike the evidence-principle, the content-principle permits a significant sentence to contain a nonsensical component, so long as the component is logically idle. For example, if the content-principle assigns significance to 'P', it will also, for any nonsensical

'N', assign significance to the logically equivalent sentence 'P and (N or not-N)', whereas the evidence-principle, as we have formulated it, classifies the sentence as nonsensical. Strictly speaking, this discrepancy should be eliminated, either by weakening the evidence-principle or by strengthening the content-principle, since it is irrelevant to the genuine difference between the two approaches. But the question of how such sentences should be classified is so unimportant that we can just ignore the discrepancy in our subsequent discussion.

16 The relativity of observationality to the standpoint of the assertor will be discussed more fully in Part I, section 7.

17 See, e.g., Moritz Schlick, *Philosophical Papers*, vol. II (edited by H. L. Mulder and B. van de Velde-Schlick, D. Reidel, 1979), p. 311.

18 Schlick himself sometimes formulates his verification principle in a way which includes this qualification, as we shall see in section 4.

19 The only slight qualification to this is that, in the case of ethics, Ayer does attempt to provide what I take to be an independent argument against 'absolutism'. But the argument is not, in my view, cogent (I shall examine this issue in section 8); and, in any case, it would not provide any real support for the verification principle as such, even if it disposed of an objection to the application of the principle in that particular area.

20 *Mind*, 1934, pp. 335–45.

21 Strictly speaking, the claim is false, since two propositions with different meanings may be analytically equivalent and thus have the same truth-conditions. However, as we shall see in section 6, those aspects of meaning which allow equivalent propositions to differ in meaning fall outside the scope of Ayer's philosophical concern.

22 *Mind*, 1934, p. 337. Ayer also gives, as an allegedly succinct reformulation of the second claim: 'I understand a proposition when I know what facts would verify it.' But, in effect, this formulation hovers, by equivocation, between the other two.

23 *Ibid.*, p. 345.

24 The article first appeared in *Erkenntnis*, vol. III (1932/3).

25 *Treatise of Human Nature* (ed. Selby-Bigge), p. 2.

26 *Ibid.*, p. 5–6.

27 *H*, pp. 32–3.

28 *Enquiry Concerning Human Understanding* (ed. Selby-Bigge), p. 165.

29 See his 'Principle of Verifiability' in *Mind*, 1936, pp. 202–3.

30 I shall discuss this aspect of Ayer's position in section 7.

31 I shall discuss this definition in Part II.

32 E.g. the (explicit) naturalistic definition of an ethical term (say, 'good' defined as 'generally approved of', or 'right' defined as 'maximizing happiness') involves a sufficiently radical change in ideological perspective to count as reductive. For it involves the reduction of something ostensibly evaluative or normative to something purely descriptive and empirical. See section 8.

33 See especially *LTL*, pp. 40–1 and 138–46.

34 See my *The Case for Idealism*, Routledge and Kegan Paul, 1982.

35 There is more than one reason for this. In the first place, even if physical facts are nothing over and above phenomenal facts, the phenomenal truth-

conditions for physical statements could be to some degree indeterminate. Second, and more fundamentally, in *The case for Idealism* (Ch. 14) I drew a distinction between 'prospective' and 'retrospective' sustainment. Where a fact or set of facts F_1 *prospectively* sustains a fact F_2, it is possible to deduce the obtaining of F_2 from the obtaining of F_1 and thus possible to establish the sustainment on the basis of the knowledge of F_1 alone. But where F_1 *retrospectively* sustains F_2, this deductive link is absent and the sustainment cannot be established without independent knowledge of F_2. Now by taking physical facts to be retrospectively sustained by phenomenal facts, we can claim that physical facts are nothing over and above phenomenal facts, while denying that any physical statement can be deduced from even an infinite set of phenomenal statements, and this denial would entail that no physical statement was *equivalent* to a phenomenal statement or infinite complex of phenomenal statements in Ayer's sense. In fact it was a phenomenalism of this sort that I tried to defend in that book.

36 See, for example, *FEK*, pp. 229–43 and *LTL* (*Introduction*), p. 24. We shall discuss this concession in Part II, section 11.

37 See my *The Case for Idealism* (Routledge & Kegan Paul, 1982), Part IV. The reason why my phenomenalism would not meet Ayer's objectives is that I take the sustainment of physical facts by phenomenal facts to be 'retrospective' (see note 35 above).

38 In section 3.

39 *Theoria* 1953, republished in *PE*.

40 There are, of course, *some* disagreements in logic, e.g. over the status of the law of the excluded middle.

41 On this point, see J. L. Mackie *Ethics: Inventing Right and Wrong* (Penguin, 1977), Ch. 1.

Part II Knowledge and Scepticism

1 Even as late as 1960, in his inaugural lecture 'Philosophy and Language' (republished in *CP*), we find Ayer saying: 'For my part I have no wish to disown the verification principle . . .' (*CP*, 20). And he still seems to interpret this principle as content-restricting: 'In very rough terms, the assumption is that the meaning of a sentence is yielded by a description of the observations which would make it true' (*CP*, 20). At the same time, he concedes that the principle 'suffers from a vagueness which it has not yet been found possible to eradicate' (*CP*, 20–1) and that there is room for philosophical dispute (not itself resolved by the principle) as to what counts for these purposes as the description of an observation.

2 *PK*, p. 16.

3 'Is Justified True Belief Knowledge?' in *Analysis* 1963.

4 If we want to weaken Ayer's second condition to '*S* believes that *p*', the emended definition will run as follows: *S* knows that *p* if and only if (1) it is true that *p*, (2) *S* believes that *p*, (3) *S* is justified in believing that *p*, (4) what justifies *S* in believing that *p* gives *S* the right to be sure that *p*, and (5) there is no false proposition, that *q*, such that *S*'s being justified in believing that *p* logically depends on his right to be sure that *q*.

301

5 See Armstrong *Perception and the Physical World* (Routledge & Kegan Paul, 1961) and *A Materialist Theory of the Mind* (Routledge & Kegan Paul, 1968), Ch. 10.

6 See Part I, section 7.

7 First published in *Theoria*, vol. xix, 1953.

8 I am indebted for this point to Howard Robinson.

9 Routledge & Kegan Paul, 1961.

10 Routledge & Kegan Paul, 1968.

11 *A Materialist Theory of the Mind*, pp. 222–3.

12 I discuss this issue briefly in Part III, section 7.

13 *A Materialist Theory of the Mind*, p. 218.

14 *Perception and the Physical World*, p. 130.

15 *A Materialist Theory of the Mind*, pp. 219–20.

16 *Ibid.*, p. 220.

17 *Ibid.*, p. 220.

18 *Ibid.*, pp. 220–1.

19 See my *The Case for Idealism* (Routledge & Kegan Paul, 1982), Ch. 6.

20 E.g. C. J. Ducasse in *Nature, Mind and Death* (Open Court, 1951) and Roderick M. Chisholm in *Perceiving* (Cornell, 1957).

21 See Frank Jackson, *Perception* (Cambridge, 1977), Ch. 3.

22 I owe this point to Howard Robinson.

23 That is, from *The Origins of Pragmatism* onwards.

24 Ayer's use of this term is not quite the same as Goodman's. For Goodman only uses it to signify the *simplest* qualitative elements in the content of sense-experience. Thus, in the case of visual experience, Goodman's only qualia are colours, field-places, and phenomenal moments.

25 The phenomenalist can also allow the physical language a conceptual autonomy of a more radical kind if, as I do, he takes the sustainment of physical facts by phenomenal facts to be 'retrospective' (see Part I, note 35). Ayer never considers this possibility, and I do not pursue it in the present book.

26 This article first appeared in *The Proceedings of the Aristotelian Society*, 1947–8, and was republished in *PE*.

27 *Principles of Human Knowledge*, section LVIII.

28 Ayer uses the term 'percept' to signify particularized qualia, i.e. qualia realizations. It is thus extensionally equivalent to 'sense-datum'. Ayer avoids the latter term because he now prefers the qualia theory (or qualia language) to the sense-datum theory (or sense-datum language) as an account of the nature of sense-experience (see section 10, p. 176).

29 In *The Case for Idealism*, Routledge & Kegan Paul, 1982.

30 Of course, the phenomenalistic route would not be available if we took the sustainment of physical facts by the sensory order to be 'retrospective' (see Part I, note 35, and Part II, note 25). But since Ayer never envisages a phenomenalism of this sort, I ignore this point here, though I have discussed it in *The Case for Idealism* (Ch. 14).

31 This second reply, of course, would not be plausible in the framework of phenomenalism. For the god is unlikely to have the power to induce the beliefs without also having the power to induce the appropriate experiences.

Part III Man and Nature

1 *H*, p. 32. Ayer does not himself speak of the concept featuring in the theory *non-redundantly*, but is is clear that this is what he intends.

2 Hume, *A Treatise of Human Nature* (ed. Selby-Bigge), p. 89.

3 I say 'or nearly always' because I do not dismiss all reports of non-gravitational behaviour (such as levitation), though in most cases I am sceptical.

4 Ayer's discussion of this is in *PAE*, pp. 30–3.

5 See his *The Logic of Scientific Discovery* (Hutchinson, 1959), Part I, his *Conjectures and Refutations* (Routledge & Kegan Paul, 1963), Ch. 1, and his *Objective Knowledge* (Oxford, 1972), Ch. 1.

6 In *Fact, Fiction and Forecast* (Bobbs-Merrill, 2nd edn, 1965), Ch. 3.

7 *A Treatise of Human Nature* (ed. Selby-Bigge), p. 89.

8 In 'Induction, Explanation and Natural Necessity', *The Proceedings of the Aristotelian Society*, 1982–3. Most of this article is reproduced in the present section. Shortly afterwards, though quite independently, D. M. Armstrong proposed a similar solution in his book *What is a Law of Nature?* (Cambridge, 1983).

9 Ayer offers an attitudinal account of laws, and we shall examine this later.

10 This first appeared in *Revue Internationale de Philosophie*, no. 36, 1956, and is republished in *CP*.

11 *H*, p. 32. We noted his endorsement of this principle in section 2.

12 Of course, we also noted that it was only in its content-restricting form that the verification principle had any chance of a rationale.

13 On the question of whether the past regularity calls for explanation, see also my 'Induction, Explanation and Natural Necessity' (*The Proceedings of the Aristotelian Society*, 1982–3), pp. 92–3.

14 I am here, of course, using the term 'metaphysical' in a way which allows empiricism itself to count as a metaphysical position.

15 See: *OP*, I,2,B; and *PAE*, III,A.

16 J. L. Mackie puts forward this view in *The Cement of the Universe* (Oxford, 1974), Ch. 2.

17 *A Treatise of Human Nature* (ed. Selby-Bigge), p. 170.

18 *An Enquiry Concerning Human Understanding* (ed. Selby-Bigge), p. 76.

19 *Treatise* (ed. Selby-Bigge), p. 170.

20 *Enquiry* (ed. Selby-Bigge), p. 77.

21 J. A. Robinson, 'Hume's Two Definitions of "Cause" ', *Philosophical Quarterly*, 1962.

22 *Enquiry* (ed. Selby-Bigge), p. 77.

23 In *The Case for Idealism* (Routledge & Kegan Paul, 1982), Ch. 16.

24 Blackwell, 1980. The relevant argument occurs in lecture III.

25 At least, all *B*'s essential properties will surely be of the same general kind as those of other (non-neural) physical events. In *The Case for Idealism* (Routledge & Kegan Paul, 1982), Ch. 7, I argue that, even from the standpoint of physical realism, these properties might be mental. This does not affect Kripke's point.

26 On this point, see Howard Robinson, *Matter and Sense*, (Cambridge, 1982), Ch. 1, section 2.

27 'Identity and Reference' in *Philosophia*, vol. 5, no. 3, 1975.

28 See *CQ*, pp. 129–32.

29 *PTC*, pp. 187–9.

30 See: *OP*, p. 265; *CQ*, p. 60 and p. 121.

31 Hume's argument is found in his *A Treatise of Human Nature*, Book 1, Part 4, section 6.

32 James, *The Principles of Psychology* (Dover, 1950), vol. 1, pp. 606–7. Quoted in *OP*, pp. 243–4.

33 I have elaborated this conception of a stream in more detail in 'In Self-defence' (in G. F. Macdonald (ed.) *Perception and Identity*, Macmillan, 1979) and in still greater detail in *The Case for Idealism* (Routledge & Kegan Paul, 1982), Ch. 16.

34 A revised version of this paper was published as 'Psychophysical Causal Relations' in *American Philosophical Quarterly*, 1968.

35 In *LTL*, of course, Ayer's position is blatantly circular, since, in constructing material objects, he takes for granted the notion of a *series* of sense-fields (clearly intended to be co-mental), while he later defines the co-mentality of total experiences in terms of their attachment to the same body. But this circularity could be avoided by defining the notion of a series in terms of overlapping total experiences and by confining the role of bodily attachment to that of providing a definition of the co-mentality of streams.

36 'In Self-defence' *Perception and Identity* (ed. G. F. Macdonald), Macmillan, 1979.

37 *Perception and Identity*, p. 318.

38 It might be objected that we are presupposing the unity of the angelic mind. But, even from a Humean standpoint, this will not be problematic. For we can assume that, necessarily, angels are perpetually conscious, so that each angelic mind contains only one stream.

39 In *The Case for Idealism* (Routledge & Kegan Paul, 1982), Part V.

40 At the end of section 6.

41 This first appeared in *Polemic*, 1946, and was later republished in *PE*.

42 Admittedly, this new perspective was *partly* anticipated by Hume in his *Enquiry Concerning Human Understanding*, section 8.

43 This is the view of Roderick Chisholm in 'Freedom and Action', in K. Lehrer (ed.) *Freedom and Determinism*, Random House, 1966.

44 By 'mental event', of course, I here (and in what follows) mean a genuinely *unitary* mental event. Obviously, a complex of an A-event and a P-event would not fall into either category.

45 Strictly speaking, clause (3)(a) is redundant, since it follows from (2) and (3)(b). I have included it only for the sake of clarity.

46 See: *H*, p. 78; 'Free-will and Rationality', in Z. von Straaten (ed.) *Philosophical Subjects* (Oxford, 1980), pp. 12–13; *PTC*, p. 17.

47 But presumably he could be made to see a reason for retaining the notion of a substantival ego, in so far as it is presupposed by the libertarian view.

48 *Part of My Life* (Collins, 1977), p. 312.

Index